KRISHNAMACHARYA ON KUṆḌALINĪ

KRISHNAMACHARYA ON KUṆḌALINĪ

The Origins and Coherence of his Position

Simon Atkinson

equinox

SHEFFIELD UK BRISTOL CT

Published by Equinox Publishing Ltd.

UK: Office 415, The Workstation, 15 Paternoster Row, Sheffield,
South Yorkshire S1 2BX

USA: ISD, 70 Enterprise Drive, Bristol, CT 06010

www.equinoxpub.com

First published 2022

British Library Cataloguing-in-Publication Data
A catalogue record for this book is available from the British Library.

Library of Congress Cataloging-in-Publication Data
Names: Atkinson, Simon, author.
Title: Krishnamacharya on Kundalini : the origins and coherence of his position / Simon Atkinson.
Description: Bristol : Equinox Publishing Ltd, 2022. | Includes bibliographical references and index. | Summary: "Krishnamacharya on Kuṇḍalinī explores a distinctive teaching of 'the father of modern yoga', T. Krishnamacharya"—Provided by publisher.
Identifiers: LCCN 2021052951 (print) | LCCN 2021052952 (ebook) | ISBN 9781800501515 (hardback) | ISBN 9781800501522 (paperback) | ISBN 9781800501539 (epdf) | ISBN 9781800501768 (epub)
Subjects: LCSH: Krishnamacharya, T. (Tirumalai), 1888–1989. | Kuṇḍalinī.
Classification: LCC BL1175.K723 A85 2022 (print) | LCC BL1175.K723 (ebook) | DDC 294.5/436–dc23/eng/20220103
LC record available at https://lccn.loc.gov/2021052951
LC ebook record available at https://lccn.loc.gov/2021052952

ISBN–13 978 1 80050 151 5 (hardback)
978 1 80050 152 2 (paperback)
978 1 80050 153 9 (ePDF)
978 1 80050 176 8 (ePub)

Typeset by JS Typesetting Ltd, Porthcawl, Mid Glamorgan

Dedicated to two remarkable women:
Isabelle Glover (a very patient Sanskrit teacher)
and
Enid Atkinson (a very patient mother)

CONTENTS

Tables, figures and plates viii
Acknowledgements ix
Preface x

1 Introduction 1
2 The *Yogayājñavalkya*: Krishnamacharya's main source on *kuṇḍalinī* 10
3 *Kuṇḍalinī* in other *Vaiṣṇava* texts 31
4 A union of *yoga-s*: Linking *haṭhayoga* and *Patañjali* via *kuṇḍalinī* 58
5 The symbolism of serpents 84
6 *Kuṇḍalinī* in Śrīvaiṣṇavism 129
7 Discussion and conclusion 182

Appendix: Dating the Yogayājñavalkya *and related texts* 199
Glossary 203
Bibliography 214
Index 237

TABLES, FIGURES AND PLATES

TABLES

1 Comparison of the *Yogayājñavalkya*, *Vasiṣṭhasaṁhitā* and *Pādmasaṁhitā* 32
2 Five translations of equivalent verses in the *Yogayājñavalkya*, *Pādmasaṁhitā* and *Vasiṣṭhasaṁhita* 39
3 Vedāntadeśika's works 142
4 Summary of dating estimates for six texts 202

FIGURES

1 The locations of *kuṇḍalinī* and *agni* in upright postures and inversions 68
2 Teachings on subtle anatomy found in the *Upaniṣad-s*, *Vivekacūḍāmaṇi* and *Yogayājñavalkya* 96

PLATES

1 T. Krishnamacharya 3
2 Viṣṇu under a canopy of Śeṣa's hoods – fresco in Thoopal Vedanta Desikar Temple, Kanchipuram 90
3 Snakes adorning the ears of Garuḍa – terracotta figure outside Sri Vedantha Desikar Devasthanam, Chennai 111
4 Srimad Desikan's Avatara Sthanam and Thoopal Vedanta Desikar Temple, Kanchipuram 139
5 Vedāntadeśika idol in Srimad Desikan's Avatara Sthanam, Kanchipuram 140
6 Vedāntadeśika saved from an attacking serpent by Garuḍa – fresco in Thoopal Vedanta Desikar Temple, Kanchipuram 141
7 The Parakāla Math, Mysore, 2018 149
8 The 12th Swāmi of the Srirangam Srimath Andavan Ashramam, Śrīmat Śrī Varāha Mahādeśika Swāmi, with Simon Atkinson 172
9 Vedāntadeśika's parents have dreams foretelling his birth – fresco in Thoopal Vedanta Desikar Temple, Kanchipuram 177

ACKNOWLEDGEMENTS

I thank all those who supplied references, notes, documents and contacts: Sheila Baker, Jason Birch, Stephen Brandon, Paul Harvey, Karin Horowitz, Leslie Kaminoff, Gill Lloyd, James Mallinson, Margaret McGlashan, A.G. Mohan, R.K. Narayan, Chris Priest, Rebecca Somerscales, Marion Rastelli and R. Thirunarayanan. Many thanks to Sylviane Gianina for translating a quotation from French and for all her teaching and guidance over the years. I also thank Karin Horowitz and Emma Furuta for their continual encouragement, and the fellows and scholars of Gonville and Caius College for their interest and advice. Special thanks go to those who provided feedback on drafts of the whole text (Peter Connolly, Karin Horowitz) and single chapters (Laurie Cozad, Paul Harvey, Leslie Kaminoff and R. Manickavelan).

I would also like to thank those who gave permission for me to publish photographs and figures:

Plate 1 Photograph by Paul Harvey and published with his kind permission.

Plate 2 Photograph by Simon Atkinson and published with kind permission from P.V. Satakopa Tatacharya, a trustee of the Sri V.P.T.V. Trust.

Plate 5 Published with kind permission from the photographer, P.V. Satakopa Tatacharya, who is also a trustee of the Sri V.P.T.V. Trust.

Plate 6 Photograph by Simon Atkinson and published with kind permission from P.V. Satakopa Tatacharya, a trustee of the Sri V.P.T.V. Trust.

Plate 8 Published with kind permission from Śrīmat Śrī Varāha Mahādeśika Swāmi and the photographer, R. Thirunarayanan. I extend my thanks to Rajan Rajagopal, Raman Aravamudhan and Geetha Anand for helping me to contact the Andavan Ashramam to obtain permission from the Swāmi.

Plate 9 Photograph by Simon Atkinson and published with kind permission from P.V. Satakopa Tatacharya, a trustee of the Sri V.P.T.V. Trust.

Figures 1 and 2 published with kind permission from John Wilcox, who converted Simon Atkinson's rough sketches into those diagrams.

PREFACE

This book is the result of over twenty years of enquiry. I started practising *yoga* in 1991, taught by a teacher influenced by T.K.V. Desikachar. Since 1998, I have had one-to-one lessons in this tradition, first with Felicity Leigh (trained by Paul Harvey) and then with Sylviane Gianina (trained by Claude Maréchal).

I first read about Krishnamacharya's teachings on *kuṇḍalinī* in T.K.V. Desikachar's *Heart of Yoga* shortly after it was published in 1995. I was struck by how different Desikachar's account was from other descriptions of *kuṇḍalinī.* As Desikachar referenced his account of *kuṇḍalinī* to the *Yogayājñavalkya*, I obtained a copy of the critical edition in 2000. At that time, however, I could not yet read Sanskrit and I gleaned little from its chapter summaries. I then read the translations by T.K.V. Desikachar and A.G. Mohan, which were confusingly different.

I started learning Sanskrit in 2001 and after twelve years began translating verses from the *Yogayājñavalkya* and other texts. I improved my translations in light of feedback from Isabelle Glover, Varun Khanna and Lidia Wojtczak. I am greatly indebted to all three. Many of my improved translations eventually formed the backbone of this book but I take responsibility for any remaining errors.

In parallel, I attended many workshops, courses, lectures and retreats taught by students of Krishnamacharya (Menaka Desikachar, T.K.V. Desikachar, A.G. Mohan, Indra Mohan and Srivatsa Ramaswami); students of T.K.V. Desikachar (Kausthub Desikachar, Colin Dunsmuir, Paul Harvey, Peter Hersnack, Leslie Kaminoff, François Lorin and Mark Whitwell); teachers trained by Paul Harvey (including Sheila Baker, David Charlton, Geoff Farrer, Andrew Curtis Payne, Ranju Roy and Sarah Ryan); and Sylviane Gianina. In 2004, Dr Latha Sathish (another student of T.K.V. Desikachar) taught me the *Haṭhapradīpikā* at the Krishnamacharya Yoga Mandiram, Chennai, in one-to-one lessons over two weeks. Some of these events led to quotations I present in this book, including some specifically about *kuṇḍalinī.* Many other events covered related topics and practices through which I learned much about this broad tradition, which I consider myself to be part of. I do not claim seniority as I know many with greater experience. Nevertheless, my experience is substantial enough for this task.

In 2013, I started to write this book to clarify my thinking and share what I had learned. In my day job, I teach academic skills and academic English in the University of Cambridge. This gave me access to many libraries, all of which I thank. They included the Cambridge University Library, the libraries of the Faculties of Divinity, and Asian and Middle Eastern Studies, and the library of the Centre of South Asian Studies. I also used the libraries of the University of Oxford, and SOAS, University of London.

In December 2018, I revisited South India. I thank all those I met: the 12th Andavan Swāmi Śrīmat Śrī Varāha Mahādeśika Swāmi, Prof. R. Thirunarayanan and Mr Varadharajan (who both translated at my meetings with the Andavan Swāmi), Prof. M.A. Lakshmithathachar (founder of the Academy of Sanskrit Research, Melkote), Dr M.A. Alwar (Mysore Sanskrit College), Dr K.S. Balasubramanian (Kuppuswami Sastri Research Institute, Chennai), Dr K. Dayanidhi (University of Madras), and Dayanidhi's graduate student, Mr R. Manickavelan. I also thank the libraries I used: The Oriental Research Institute (Mysore), The Kuppuswami Sastri Research Institute (Chennai), The Adyar Library (Chennai) and The Academy of Sanskrit Research (Melkote). Special thanks go to R.K. Narayan of The Academy of Sanskrit Research for shedding new light on the *Saṅkalpasūryodaya* and summarizing a Kannada commentary thereon.

This book combines five main sources of information:

1 analysis of quotations from *yoga* workshops, courses and retreats within the broad tradition;
2 quotations from publications from within the tradition;
3 insights from academic studies and other published works;
4 philological study of Sanskrit texts; and
5 quotations from scholars I met in India.

I would argue that only a scholar-practitioner with access to all these sources could have written this book. My objectives are to investigate the origins of Krishnamacharya's position on *kuṇḍalinī* and to evaluate its coherence.

Many of the translations are my own. Whereas I respect scholars who reflect the beauty of the Sanskrit in their translations, I am less concerned with aesthetics than with accuracy, clarity and transparency. My translations represent the Sanskrit as literally as possible while keeping the translation readable. I use [square brackets] to insert words absent in the

Sanskrit that are necessary to make the English intelligible. I use (round brackets) to add interpretive information or words from the Sanskrit.

I use *italics* for Sanskrit and Tamil words and phrases, and for the names of texts (or groups of texts). I do not use *italics* for the names of people or organizations but an exception is *Patañjali*, which I give in *italics* regardless of whether it refers to the text or the person traditionally regarded as its author. I add '-*s*' to the end of Sanskrit words that have been made plural by adding the English suffix 's'. *Tamas*, without a hyphen, is not the plural of '*tama*'. However, I have not used hyphens or *italics* for other Sanskrit words that have changed according to English morphology (such as yogic, tantric or brahminized), instead leaving them in plain text. Scholars are split between those who write the Sanskrit *anusvāra* symbol as ṁ or ṃ. I use the former. There are no capital letters in Sanskrit so I use them following English-language conventions: I use initial capitals for the names of people, places, organizations, texts and groups of texts.

To ensure transparency, I present quotations verbatim without altering their spelling, punctuation, use of italics, capitals and diacritics, even when they are idiosyncratic or erroneous. I hope this does not confuse readers who see diacritics, spellings and capitalization in quotations that differ from main text.

Given my background as a *yoga* practitioner taught within this broad tradition, I do not claim to be completely objective. Nevertheless, this book is neither a defence of Krishnamacharya nor a hagiography. I have tried to put aside personal affiliations and biases to view the tradition from within as fairly and accurately as possible. My agenda is not to promote or discredit any person, organization or teaching. Rather, the book is a sincere attempt to better understand my own tradition's teachings on the concept of *kuṇḍalinī*. I have not shied away from criticizing two teachers whom I greatly respect and admire: T.K.V. Desikachar and A.G. Mohan. Indeed, it is because of my respect that I spent so much time, effort and money investigating their translations, claims and arguments. Wherever I give criticisms, they are of ideas, translations, claims, arguments, interpretations or scholarly practices. No criticism is implied of anyone's personality or character. I exclude B.K.S. Iyengar, Pattabhi Jois and T.K. Sribhashyam (another son of Krishnamacharya) because I have not been taught by them or their students. I do not attempt to rank Krishnamacharya's students or T.K.V. Desikachar's students. The quotations reflect who I have been taught by and which of them happened to teach relevant topics.

I hope this book will be of interest not just to academics but also the growing number of *yoga* students interested in scholarly perspectives on *kuṇḍalinī* and perhaps the most influential *yoga* teacher of modern times, Krishnamacharya. My meetings in India indicate that many *Śrīvaiṣṇava-s* may also welcome a fresh perspective on their tradition and its roots in *Pāñcarātra* and *Vaikhānasa.*

To make the book accessible to this wide audience without compromising the academic content, I have included a glossary, mainly for Sanskrit words not translated or explained in the immediate context or in footnotes. I also did not want the book to be purely theoretical. Chapter 4 therefore gives a sense of how *yoga* is actually practised in this tradition through the lens of teachings on *kuṇḍalinī.* For most of my translations, I give the Sanskrit verses in Roman transliteration in footnotes. I hope this will help the substantial number of *yoga* students who know some Sanskrit words but who cannot read the traditional *devanāgarī* script.

Within the tradition, T.K.V. Desikachar is usually referred to simply as 'Desikachar', whereas his son Kausthub Desikachar is usually referred to simply as 'Kausthub'. To differentiate between the two, I will use T.K.V. Desikachar and K. Desikachar most of the time, contrary to the usual academic convention of only using the surname. I will drop the T.K.V. initials only when the context makes it patently clear that I am referring to the father rather than the son. I will never refer to Kausthub Desikachar as 'Desikachar'. Similarly, I will cite Menaka Desikachar as M. Desikachar. I will also cite two references as V. Krishnamacharya to differentiate that scholar from T. Krishnamacharya, the *yogi.*

Just as I have corrected others' mistakes, I ask readers to correct any errors I have made.

Simon Atkinson
Cambridge, England
March 2021

1 Introduction

1.1 T. KRISHNAMACHARYA

Tirumalai Krishnamacharya (1888–1989) is often referred to as the father of modern *yoga*. His global influence on modern *yoga* has been 'second to none',[1] although this has largely been through his students. These included B.K.S. Iyengar and Pattabhi Jois, who studied with Krishnamacharya from 1934 to 1937,[2] and from 1927 to 1953,[3] respectively. Iyengar and Jois therefore represent Krishnamacharya's early teaching in Mysore.

Krishnamacharya relocated to Madras (Chennai) in 1950.[4] A representative picture of Krishnamacharya's teachings from the latter part of his life can be gained from three of his longest-standing students: Krishnamacharya's son T.K.V. Desikachar, who studied with his father from 1961 to Krishnamacharya's death in 1989;[5] Srivatsa Ramaswami, a student from 1955 to 1988;[6] and A. G. Mohan, a student from 1971 to 1989.[7]

Krishnamacharya displayed two contrasting qualities: he was both an ardent traditionalist and a radically creative innovator.[8] He was traditional as he valued Vedic ritualism and the chanting of the *Veda-s* - see verse 9 of his *Yogāñjalisāram*.[9] Krishnamacharya was also a committed *Śrīvaiṣṇava*.[10]

1. Singleton (2011, p. 786).
2. De Michelis (2004, p. 196).
3. Stern (2010, p. xv).
4. Srivatsan (1997, p. 61).
5. Krishnamacharya Yoga Mandiram (2006, p. 15).
6. Ramaswami (2007, p. 14).
7. Mohan and Mohan (2015, p. 152).
8. Connolly (2007, pp. 206–207).
9. Krishnamacharya (2001, pp. 18–19).
10. Singleton and Fraser (2014).

His *Śrīvaiṣṇava* background was reflected most strongly in his *yoga* teachings in the latter decades of his life,[11] and traces of Śrīvaiṣṇavism are frequently evident in the publications of organizations established in his name. The Krishnamacharya Yoga Mandiram was established in 1976 by T.K.V. Desikachar,[12] with help from A.G. Mohan.[13] The Krishnamacharya Healing and Yoga Foundation, briefly called the Sannidhi of Krishnamacharya Yoga, was founded by T.K.V. Desikachar and his son Kausthub Desikachar in 2006.[14] Krishnamacharya

> is typically described as a 'man with great faith' who nevertheless did not wish to impose his personal beliefs on his students. However, the question does arise as to what extent these 'personal beliefs' de facto influence the views of those inspired by him.[15]

In this book, I will question the extent to which T.K.V. Desikachar accurately communicated his father's *Śrīvaiṣṇava* beliefs when he quoted the *Śrīvaiṣṇava* polymath Vedāntadeśika on *kuṇḍalinī.*

Krishnamacharya's credentials as a radical reformer are also well attested. He revolutionized *āsana* and *prāṇāyāma* practice into sequences called *vinyasa-s.*[16] From the 1980s, he allowed women to practise Vedic chanting.[17]

Krishnamacharya had a critical attitude towards some *yoga* texts and *haṭhayoga* techniques. According to A.G. Mohan, he did not teach the *bīja mantra-s*, associated with the five elements, because they could lead to mental disturbance rather than mental steadiness.[18] In his 1934 *Yogamakaranda*, Krishnamacharya cautioned against 'such *Kriyā-s* and *Mudrā-s* as *Vajroli, Amaroli, Khecarī* etc., because the results of such practices may be entirely different, if not opposite from what the scriptures maintain'.[19] Although there is some such critical evaluation in the *Yogamakaranda*, Krishnamacharya became more critical in his later

11. Nevrin (2005, p. 70).
12. Krishnamacharya Yoga Mandiram (2006, p. 41).
13. Krishnamacharya, foreword to Mohan (1993, p. xv).
14. Krishnamacharya Healing and Yoga Foundation (no date). I have not been taught by Kausthub Desikachar since May 2012.
15. Nevrin (2005, p. 68).
16. Singleton (2010, pp. 175–210).
17. Srivatsan (1997, p. 75).
18. Mohan (2015).
19. Krishnamacharya (2011, p. 111).

Plate 1
T. Krishnamacharya.

Photograph: Paul Harvey

years. Mohan states that 'The Yoga Makaranda is not representative of Krishnamacharya's teachings in several respects as it glosses over the critical thinking and insight that usually characterized his classes on haṭha-yoga.'[20] Although I will quote from the *Yogamakaranda*, I will place more emphasis on the last few decades of Krishnamacharya's teaching.

Krishnamacharya's critical attitude extended to whole texts and their authors. He thought that the *Gheraṇḍasaṁhitā* and *Śivasaṁhitā* 'could mislead insufficiently prepared students' as these texts were 'written written at a time when *āsana* and *prāṇāyāma* were completely dissociated from each other'.[21] He also criticized the *Haṭhapradīpikā* for its contradictions.[22] Hence, Krishnamacharya had a 'dynamic and creative relationship with the textual tradition on which he draws for his teaching'.[23] While one might expect a staunch *Vaiṣṇava* to be critical of *Śaiva* texts such as the *Śivasaṁhitā*, I will show in Chapter 3 that Krishnamacharya was also selective in which concepts he taught from *Vaiṣṇava* texts teaching *yoga*. I will show in Chapter 6 that he even went against established *Śrīvaiṣṇava* doctrine in his conception of *kuṇḍalinī*.

Some of Krishnamacharya's selective rejection of *haṭhayoga* techniques or reinterpretation of concepts stemmed from his adherence to the *Yogasūtra* of *Patañjali* and *Vedānta*. Hence, he sought to justify *yoga* theory and practice with what he considered to be 'Vedic' sources. For example, in an unpublished translation of his *Yogāsanagalu*, Krishnamacharya states:

> It is distasteful that some people propagate through books that *nauli*, *neti*, *basti*, *vajrolī*, *dhauti*, and *khecarī* and other *kriyās* (Cleansing Acts) are part of Yoga ... But the main source for yoga, Patañjali Darśana, does not include them. Nor do they appear in the Upaniṣads or other works on Yoga ... It is gravely disappointing that they defile the name of Yoga.'[24]

Krishnamacharya also blamed such *mudrā-s* for the condemnation of *yoga* by *Vedāntin-s*.[25] I will argue in Chapter 6 that his interpretation of *kuṇḍalinī*

---

20. Mohan and Mohan (2017, p. xiii).
21. Maréchal (1989, p. 40), translation from the French – Sylviane Gianina.
22. Mohan (no date a).
23. Singleton and Fraser (2014, p. 98).
24. Translation by Autumn Jacobsen and R.V.S. Sundaram quoted in Singleton (2012, p. 340).
25. T.K.V. Desikachar (1982, p. 36).

was influenced by his desire to interpret *haṭhayoga* in terms of what he considered Vedic, or at least Vedāntic, sources.

1.2 *KUṆḌALINĪ* (= *KUṆḌALĪ*)

The concept of a central channel (*nāḍī* or *hitā*) can be traced to early *Upaniṣad-s*. The *Chāndogya* (8.6.6) and *Kaṭha* (2.3.16) *Upaniṣad-s* share a verse describing 101 channels emanating from the heart, one of which rises to the crown of the head. The *Maitri Upaniṣad* (6.21) is the oldest text to name that channel the *suṣumnā*. 'Through it, by joining the breath, the syllable *Om*, and the mind, one may go aloft.'[26] According to the *Kaṭha Upaniṣad*, when one attains *Brahman*, 'all desires *[kāma]* clinging to one's heart fall off' (2.3.14) and 'the knots *[granthi-s]* of the heart are destroyed' (2.3.15).[27] I will show in Chapter 5 that the concept of something enveloping the heart was developed in an *Advaitavedānta* text using snake metaphors that resemble Krishnamacharya's presentation of *kuṇḍalinī*.

The term *suṣumnā* became widely used in *tantra* and *haṭhayoga*. Although various traditions shared conceptions of something ascending through the *suṣumnā*, they differed over what rises: the *jīva* (the self), *prāṇa* (breath), *bindu* (semen) or *kuṇḍalinī*.[28]

James Mallinson has been unravelling different strands within *haṭhayoga*. He argues that there was a dichotomy between the original *haṭhayoga* and the tantric traditions which later greatly influenced it. The earliest *haṭha* traditions, exemplified by the *Vaiṣṇava Dattātreyayogaśāstra* (13th century CE), were framed in terms of raising *bindu* to the head and keeping it there. A characteristic feature was their use of *mudrā-s* (bodily seals). This original *haṭhayoga* tradition was then overlaid with techniques from *layayoga*, particularly the raising of *kuṇḍalinī* energy to the head.[29]

There have been very few serious scholarly studies on *kuṇḍalinī*. This is partly because the topic is enormously complicated and partly because the term *kuṇḍalinī* has undergone significant semantic shift: it means different things in different contexts and at different times.[30]

---

26. Translation – Hume (1931, p. 437).
27. Translation – Gambhīrānanda (1989, pp. 228–231), my insertions in brackets.
28. Hatley (forthcoming); Mallinson and Singleton (2017, p. 173).
29. Mallinson (2011, p. 774).
30. Wallis (2018).

Whereas most modern *yoga* traditions teach that *kuṇḍalinī* is a type of energy that rises, Krishnamacharya, defined it differently. When questioned about whether *kuṇḍalinī* rises through the *suṣumnā* to the *sahasrāra* (on the crown of the head), he replied 'No. It is the prāṇa vāyu that moves through the suṣumna.'[31] T.K.V. Desikachar notes that 'To Krishnamacharya, *kundalini* was a blockage – the nucleus of imbalance in the body.'[32] 'It is also called Śakti because its power is so great that it is able to block the flow of prāṇa into the suṣumṇā.'[33] 'Through proper practice, it was released to permit the flow of *prana*.'[34]

1.3 EPISTEMOLOGY

This book explores the origins and coherence of Krishnamacharya's position on *kuṇḍalinī*. It is therefore necessary to consider epistemology: the critical study of how one can know anything. Various systems of South Asian philosophy/theology accept different *pramāṇa-s* – means by which one can reach a valid understanding of a 'state, condition, fact, object, or principle'.[35]

The *Yogasūtra* of *Patañjali* (see Chapter 4), *Sāṁkhya* (which underpins *Patañjali*) and *Viśiṣṭādvaitavedānta* (the philosophical system of Krishnamacharya's religious tradition) all accept three *pramāṇa-s* – direct perception, inference and valid testimony. The terms used vary slightly. *Patañjali* 1.7 uses *pratyakṣa*, *anumāna* and *āgama*, respectively. The *Sāṁkhyakārikā* uses *dṛṣṭa*, *anumāna* and *āptavacana*.[36] According to Vedāntadeśika, whose work I will survey in Chapter 6, the equivalents in *Viśiṣṭādvaitavedānta* are *pratyakṣa*, *anumāna* and *śabda*.[37] Other systems, including *Advaitavedānta*, include additional *pramāṇa-s* such as analogy, but *Sāṁkhya*, *Patañjali* and *Viśiṣṭādvaita* argue that they can be subsumed under direct perception, inference and valid testimony.[38]

---

31. Srivatsan (1997, p. 112).
32. T.K.V. Desikachar and Cravens (1998, p. 108).
33. T.K.V. Desikachar (1980, p. 244).
34. T.K.V. Desikachar and Cravens (1998, p. 108).
35. Whicher (1998, p. 143).
36. *Sāṁkhyakārikā* 4 – Virupakshananda (1995, p. 12).
37. Narayanan (2008, p. 9).
38. Veda Bharati (1986, p. 151). I am not aware of any *haṭhayoga* text that lists accepted *pramāṇa-s*. This could be because *haṭhayoga* is a practice that can be undertaken by those from any philosophical tradition. However, the overall emphasis of *haṭha* texts is on direct

Chapter 3 of *Patañjali* outlines how a special kind of meditative insight can be gained via *saṁyama* (*dhāraṇā*, *dhyāna* and *samādhi*) on an object. For example, 3.29 states that through *saṁyama* on *nābhi cakra*, knowledge of the arrangement of the body can be obtained. Some traditional commentators on *Patañjali* have tried to classify such insight as a type of direct perception in line with verse 1.7.[39] However, Bernard Bouanchaud (a long-term student of T.K.V. Desikachar) states that ordinary direct perception via the senses (*pratyakṣa*) can give knowledge of both objects outside our bodies and 'such sensations as body aches or sentiments'.[40] It should therefore be capable of supplying knowledge about internal experiences perceived to be involving *prāṇa* and *kuṇḍalinī*, even if they are experienced without *saṁyama*.

Bouanchaud also acknowledges that direct experience, inference and testimony 'are interdependent ... It is difficult to conceive of one of these three modes of mental grasp, or understanding, apart from the other two.'[41] It would seem that previous conditioning can colour how a direct experience is interpreted and analysed. Whereas an educated South Asian *yogi* from around 700 years ago may have described an experience in terms of *prāṇa*, *agni* and *kuṇḍalinī*, an educated European Christian in the same era could have described a similar experience in terms of the Holy Spirit or demonic possession. Nevertheless, *Patañjali* and Vyāsa's commentary deal with experience, inference and testimony separately. According to the commentary on *Patañjali* 1.7, inference and valid testimony can only give information on general or generic (*sāmānya*) qualities of an object whereas direct perception is mainly concerned with individual, specific or particular (*viśeṣa*) qualities.[42]

Valid testimony includes information from both sacred texts (*āgama/śruti/śabda*) and a trustworthy personal authority.[43] According to Vyāsa's commentary on *Patañjali* 1.7,

> That testimony may be false, *i.e.* cannot at all be a Pramāṇa, if the person communicating the knowledge is not trustworthy or is deceitful or is one

---

experience through practice, which seems broadly in line with putting direct perception before inference and testimony.

39. Veda Bharati (1986, p. 154).
40. Bouanchaud (1997, pp. 11–12), commentating on *Patañjali* 1.7.
41. Bouanchaud (1997, pp. 11–12), commentating on *Patañjali* 1.7.
42. Hariharānanda Āraṇya (1983, p. 21).
43. T.K.V. Desikachar (1995, p. 151).

> who has neither seen nor experienced what he seeks to communicate. That transferred cognition which has its basis in the direct experience of the first authoritative exponent or in his correct inference is genuine and perfectly valid.[44]

The 'first authoritative exponent' can be interpreted as the founder of a lineage.[45] There is no widely accepted 'lineage' among followers of Krishnamacharya but if we accept Vyāsa's commentary, the speech or writings of any follower of Krishnamacharya could be deemed 'genuine and perfectly valid' if they are based on Krishnamacharya's direct experience or his correct inference.

I will return to the *Pramāṇa-s* in the conclusion, but I ask readers to keep in the back of their minds when reading the following chapters which of the following sources of information the evidence is based on:

1. the *testimony of Krishnamacharya based on his own experience* and communicated in his own writings, transcriptions of interviews with him or in the writings of his students;
2. the *inference of Krishnamacharya* communicated in his own writings, transcriptions of interviews with him or in the writings of his students;
3. the original *testimony of a follower of Krishnamacharya based on his or her own experience*;
4. the original *inference of a follower of Krishnamacharya*; or
5. *testimony* based on traditional *texts*.

The *Yogasūtra*,[46] *Sāṁkhyakārikā*,[47] and Vedāntadeśika[48] all present direct perception via the senses as superior to inference and valid testimony, both of which ultimately depend on direct perception, they claim. This is reflected in the commentaries on *Patañjali* 1.7 by T.K.V. Desikachar and his students Bernard Bouanchaud and Frans Moors.[49] Moors states that 'Yoga gives priority to direct personal experience whenever possible.'[50] I ask readers to consider whether this is actually reflected in practice

---

44. Translation – Hariharānanda Āraṇya (1983, p. 21).
45. Veda Bharati (1986, p. 161).
46. Whicher (1998, p. 145).
47. Virupakshananda (1995, p. 13).
48. Narayanan (2008, p. 156).
49. T.K.V. Desikachar (1995, p. 151); Bouanchaud (1997, p. 11); Moors (2012, p. 32).
50. Moors (2012, p. 32).

in the tradition following Krishnamacharya in discourse on *kuṇḍalinī*. Readers may like to bear in mind that in searching for the textual origins of Krishnamacharya's ideas, I may be biasing my account to item 5 above: testimony from texts. However, I do include other sources of information wherever possible, including the writings of Krishnamacharya's students (and those trained by them) and teachings orally communicated in workshops and retreats.

The remainder of this book explores Krishnamacharya's teaching on *kuṇḍalinī* by searching for its origins and examining how it fits into a wider picture of South Asian thought. Chapter 2 examines the text that Krishnamacharya's students cite to justify his position: the *Yogayājñavalkya*. It shows that whereas the text largely supports Krishnamacharya's teaching, one verse from the critical edition contradicts him. Chapter 3 traces verses from the *Yogayājñavalkya* to texts from two sects of *Vaiṣṇava* temple priests: *Pāñcarātra* and *Vaikhānasa*. It shows, however, that one of those texts also contains sections that do not support Krishnamacharya's position. Chapter 4 shows how Krishnamacharya used *kuṇḍalinī* to bridge between *haṭhayoga* and the *Yogasūtra* of *Patañjali*. Chapter 5 shows how Krishnamacharya's conception of *kuṇḍalinī* fits into a wider stream of thought that uses snake metaphors to represent something to be overcome. Chapter 6 then investigates whether Krishnamacharya's conception of *kuṇḍalinī* originates in his tradition of Śrīvaiṣṇavism. It challenges the accuracy of quotations on *kuṇḍalinī* that T.K.V. Desikachar ascribed to the 13th century polymath Vedāntadeśika.

Chapter 7 then draws together those strands and evaluates Krishnamacharya's position. I argue that Krishnamacharya's teaching on *kuṇḍalinī* has a valid textual basis but the number of supporting texts is quite limited. I challenge a claim that all texts support Krishnamacharya's view and argue that his conception of *kuṇḍalinī* is only one of several textually-valid conceptions. Furthermore, I call for a rebalancing of the weight given to direct experience, inference and textual testimony in understanding *kuṇḍalinī*. Rather than regarding Krishnamacharya's conception of *kuṇḍalinī* as an accurate realist account of something that has objective existence, I argue that it is best regarded as an idealized and simplified model for one's subjective experience. It should be judged primarily by how useful it is in describing experience and guiding practice, not by how well it is supported by texts.

2

The *Yogayājñavalkya*

Krishnamacharya's main source on *kuṇḍalinī*

2.1 THE TEXT

Krishnamacharya listed the *Yogayājñavalkya* as one of twenty-seven authoritative sources in his *Yogamakaranda* although he did not identify any one source text for *kuṇḍalinī*.[1]

Both T.K.V. Desikachar and A.G. Mohan present the *Yogayājñavalkya* as Krishnamacharya's central text on *kuṇḍalinī*. According to Mohan, 'Krishnamacharya valued the Yoga Yājñavalkya for its systematic and detailed description of the kuṇḍalinī and related concepts'.[2] When discussing *kuṇḍalinī*, T.K.V. Desikachar stated that 'my explanations are based on what I think is the best, classic and most straightforward text, the Yoga Yājñavalkya. I think the explanation found in it ... is more coherent than any other I know.'[3] According to Mohan and Mohan, Krishnamacharya had written down verses from the *Yogayājñavalkya*.[4] A printed edition was published in Trivandrum,[5] and a critical edition was issued by the Bombay Branch of the Royal Asiatic Society.[6]

Two English-language translations of the *Yogayājñavalkya* were published by students of Krishnamacharya. The first edition of A.G. Mohan's

1. Krishnamacharya (2011, p. 42).
2. Mohan and Mohan (2013, p. ii).
3. T.K.V. Desikachar (1980, p. 247).
4. Mohan and Mohan (2013, p. i).
5. Śāstri (1938).
6. Divanji (1954).

translation was published in 1999 with extensive introductory material.[7] A year later, T.K.V. Desikachar published his own translation through the Krishnamacharya Yoga Mandiram. In his introduction, Desikachar recalls Krishnamacharya reciting the text to him between 1967 and 1969. Krishnamacharya wrote the whole text in the Telugu script, and 'corrected those manuscripts that were incomplete'.[8] This was challenged in a second edition of Mohan's translation. When Mohan began studying the *Yogayājñavalkya* in 1975, Krishnamacharya relied on notes and had not memorized the text. When shown Divanji's critical edition by Mohan, Krishnamacharya accepted it as 'more complete and accurate' and recommended its use.[9] Mohan and Mohan note that Desikachar's translation is based on the Trivandrum edition, with about 60 missing words inserted,[10] as verified by Wujastyk.[11]

Taking both accounts at face value, it seems that T.K.V. Desikachar's translation is based on the Trivandrum edition, as taught to him in 1967–1969, while Mohan's is based on the Divanji's critical edition, which Krishnamacharya taught to both Mohan and T.K.V. Desikachar in a small study group in the 1970s. It remains unclear why T.K.V. Desikachar reverted to a single published edition despite citing Divanji's critical edition three times.[12] As Birch notes, it is seldom possible to rely on one manuscript; several are needed for a complete and coherent translation.[13] Wujastyk states that Divanji's critical edition is 'the best edition to date in the sense that it gives a critical account of the manuscript tradition and an apparently workmanlike collation of the variant readings from a representative sample of sixteen manuscripts from different parts of India and five earlier printed editions',[14] including the Trivandrum edition.

In 2013, A.G. Mohan released a second edition, with his son Ganesh Mohan, containing a slightly modified translation.[15] When quoting A.G.

7. Mohan (no date b). The publication date of that book is stated in Mohan and Mohan (2015, p. 155).
8. T.K.V. Desikachar (2000, p. XIX).
9. Mohan and Mohan (2013, pp. i–ii).
10. Mohan and Mohan (2013, p. iii).
11. Wujastyk (2017, p. 163).
12. T.K.V. Desikachar (1980, p. 285); T.K.V. Desikachar (1995, p. 231); T.K.V. Desikachar (2000, p. XIX).
13. Birch (2015, p. 12).
14. Wujastyk (2017, p. 167).
15. Mohan and Mohan (2013).

Mohan, I will mainly quote from this second edition. I will revert to the first edition for points from its extensive introduction that are absent in the second edition. As T.K.V. Desikachar's version has fewer verses than Mohan's, the verse numbers do not always correspond. Where the verses are numbered differently, I will state the number given in the edition I am referring to or translating: either the critical edition by Divanji,[16] Mohan and Mohan's translation,[17] which follows the numbering and purports to reproduce the Sanskrit of the critical edition, or T.K.V. Desikachar's edition,[18] which follows the Trivandrum edition by Śāstri.[19] I will give the equivalent verse number in the other edition, often in a footnote. Where no equivalent verse number is given, the numbering in the two versions is identical, although the Sanskrit may differ.

The *Yogayājñavalkya* discusses *kuṇḍalinī* in chapters 4, 6 and 12. I will examine it thematically in terms of first, the location of *agni* (fire), the *kanda* and *nābhi cakra*; second, the location of *kuṇḍalinī*; third, the role of *kuṇḍalinī* in blocking the movement of *prāṇa*; and fourth how *kuṇḍalinī* can be burned and 'awakened'.

2.2 THE LOCATION OF *AGNI, KANDA* AND *NĀBHI*

Whereas the digestive fire, *agni*, is often located at the solar plexus, close to *nābhi cakra*, in the *Yogayājñavalkya* it is located in the perineum:

> In the *dehamadhya* (the centre of the body) is a place of flame, splendid [like] molten gold (4.11b). In men, the *dehamadhya* is two *aṅgula-s* [finger widths] above the anus and two *aṅgula-s* below the penis, in the middle of these two (4.14).[20]

Other features of the subtle body are located with reference to the *dehamadhya*. In 4.16 the *kandasthāna* ('bulb place') is located nine *aṅgula-s* above

16. Divanji (1954).
17. Mohan and Mohan (2013).
18. T.K.V. Desikachar (2000).
19. Śāstri (1938).
20. *Yogayājñavalkya* 4.11b and 4.14, my translation of Divanji (1954, pp. 24–25):

> dehamadhye śikhisthānaṁ taptajāmbūnadaprabham || 4.11b ||
> gudāttu dvayaṅgulādūrdhvamadho meḍhrācca dvyaṅgulāt |
> dehamadhyaṁ tayormadhyaṁ manuṣyāṇāmitīritam || 4.14 ||
> = 4.15 in T.K.V. Desikachar (2000, p. 45)

the *dehamadhya* and is four *aṅgula-s* in height and width. In the middle of the *kandasthāna* is *nābhi* (the navel) and in *nābhi* is a *cakra.* Twelve spokes are joined to it and the body is held up by it.[21]

2.3 *KUṆḌALINĪ'S* LOCATION AT THE LOWEST *CAKRA* OF THE *SUṢUMNĀ*

In many texts, *kuṇḍalinī* is located at the base of the spine in *mūlādhāra cakra.*[22] See, for example, *Ṣaṭcakranirūpaṇa* 10–11,[23] *Śivasaṁhitā* 2.22–2.23,[24] and *Gheraṇḍasaṁhitā* 3.40.[25] In contrast, verses across three chapters of the *Yogayājñavalkya* locate it at (or close to) *nābhi* (the navel). Verses 12.8 and 12.10 state that *kuṇḍalinī* 'is always seated/encamped at *nābhi*' and 'is always situated at *nābhi*', respectively.[26] According to 12.11a, *kuṇḍalinī* is 'dwelling in the *nāḍī-s* in the middle of the *kanda*'.[27] Similarly, 6.69 locates *kuṇḍalinī* in the middle of *nābhi.* Two slight variations are 4.21a, which states that 'obliquely above *nābhi* is the place of *kuṇḍalinī*',[28] and 4.22, which states that *kuṇḍalinī* 'is always constantly present around [and] on the sides of the *kanda*, completely blocking the pathways of air, water, food etc'.[29]

---

21. My translation of Divanji (1954, pp. 25–26):

    kandasthānāṁ manuṣyāṇāṁ dehamadhyānnavāṅgulam |
    caturaṅgulamutsedhamayāmaśca tathāvidhaḥ || 4.16 ||
    tanmadhyaṁ nābhirityuktaṁ nābhau cakrasamudbhavaḥ |
    dvādaśārayutaṁ tacca tena dehaḥ pratiṣṭitaḥ || 4.18 ||

22. Mallinson and Singleton (2017, p. 178).
23. Avalon (1974, pp. 346–347).
24. Mallinson (2007b, p. 31).
25. Mallinson (2004, p. 73).
26. My translation of Divanji (1954, pp. 104–105):

    nābhau sadā kuṇḍalinīniviṣṭam | 12.8b |
    nābhau sadā tiṣṭati kuṇḍalī | 12.10b |

27. My translation of Divanji (1954, p. 105): kandamadhyagatanāḍiṣu* [= ... īṣu] saṁsthām
    *I accept Mohan and Mohan's (2013, pp. 115, 168) correction of *nāḍiṣu* to *nāḍīṣu*, making a locative-plural feminine noun.
28. My translation of Divanji (1954, p. 26): tasyordhvaṁ kuṇḍalīsthānaṁ nābhestiryagathordhvataḥ | 4.21a |
29. My translation of Divanji (1954, p. 27):

    yathāvadvāyusaṁcāraṁ jalānnādīni nityaśaḥ |
    paritaḥ kandapārśveṣu niruddhyaiva sadā sthitā || 4.22 ||

The *Yogayājñavalkya* does not include all six of the usual *cakra-s*.[30] The *cakra-s* often described below *nābhi* (*svādhiṣṭhāna* and *mulādhāra*) are absent so *nābhi* forms the lower terminus of the *suṣumnā*. It is therefore not surprising to find *kuṇḍalinī* there. As Hatley notes, texts that describe *nābhi* or *nābhi-kanda* as the lower terminus of the *suṣumnā* also locate *kuṇḍalinī* there.[31] The *Yogayājñavalkya* calls that place *mūlacakra* - 'the base-*cakra* of the *jīva*'.[32] The term *mūlacakra*, which refers to *nābhi*, should not be confused with *mūlādhāra cakra*, which the *Yogayājñavalkya* does not mention.

T.K.V. Desikachar's translation of the *Yogayājñavalkya* is misleading in the inconsistent locations it gives for *kuṇḍalinī*. In verse 4.22, T.K.V. Desikachar correctly locates *kuṇḍalinī* 'just above' *nābhi*.[33] He also presents a diagram that shows *kuṇḍalinī* behind and slightly above *nābhi*.[34] In contradiction, however, in T.K.V. Desikachar's translation of one verse and in a separate note, he locates *kuṇḍalinī* at *mūlādhāra* contrary to the Sanskrit text. He also gives five further incorrect mentions of *mulādhāra*, four in mistranslations of the text and one in another note. I will now examine each of T.K.V. Desikachar's mentions of *mūlādhāra* in turn.

First, T.K.V. Desikachar translates verses from Chapter 6 inaccurately. He incorrectly locates *kuṇḍalinī* at *mūlādhāra* while the Sanskrit text does not:

> Whoever remains in this practice and focuses on the location of *śakti* (*kuṇḍalini*) at *Mūlādhāra*, will have a sense lightness (sic) of body and good digestion. *Gārgi* ! With the mind focused on *kuṇḍalini*, reciting the *mantra*, the *prāṇa* must be brought to *nābhi*. As long as the mind is fixed around the *nābhi*, as if the mind and *nābhi* have merged like firewood and the fire, so long this practice must be pursued.[35]

30. Divanji (1954, p. 122).
31. Hatley (2013, p. 284).
32. Balasubramanian (2017, p. 108), translating *jīvasya mūlacakra* from *Yogayājñavalkya* 4.20 in Divanji (1954, p. 26).
33. T.K.V. Desikachar (2000, p. 47).
34. T.K.V. Desikachar (2000, p. 48).
35. *Yogayājñavalkya* 6.65–66, translation – T.K.V. Desikachar (2000, pp. 91–92):

dṛṣṭacihnastatasthānānmanasāropya mārūtam |
mantramuccārayet gārgi nābhimadhye nirodhayet || 6.65 ||
yāvanmano layatyasminnābhau savitṛmaṇḍale |
tāvatsamabhyasedvidvānindhanedindhanāśanam || 6.66 ||
= 6.67–68 in Divanji (1954, pp. 56–57).

I would translate the Sanskrit T.K.V. Desikachar presents as follows:

> Having seen those signs [and] on account of being established for a long time [and] having raised *prāṇa* with the mind, [one] should recite the *mantra*, O Gārgī, [and] contain *prāṇa* in the middle of *nābhi* (6.65). As long as the mind merges in this divine solar power in *nābhi* [as] one kindles fire [and] firewood, that long the learned one should practise (6.66).

Mūlādhāra is not in the Sanskrit T.K.V. Desikachar presents.[36]

The second of T.K.V. Desikachar's incorrect mentions of *mūlādhāra* is in his translation of verses 9.19–24, which describe a *saguṇa* meditation/visualization:

> The eight petal lotus whose centre is yellow (*kesari*) is the place of highest learning. **Rising from *Mūlādhāra*, the *nāḍi* reaches the *nābhi*.** It should be brightened through *prāṇāyāma*. This place, known as *Maṇipūrāka* must be warmed up through *prāṇāyāma*. This fire called *Vaiṣvānara* is pointing in all directions. It is the highest fire. It warms the body from the feet to the top of the head. This fire must be visualised, as a steady flame not disturbed by the wind. At the tip of this flame, God must be visualised. His form is as follows: His brightness is like the lightning of a dark cloud. It is as small as the tip of the paddy grain. It is yellow in colour like the fresh paddy. It is the protector of all. Knowing this form from the teacher and visualising him to be with the self (I am his servant). This is *saguṇa dhyānaṁ* according to the experts of Yoga. Mastering *Vaiṣvānara*, the *dhyāta* becomes one with the *Īśvara*.[37]

---

36. Although presented by T.K.V. Desikachar (2000, p. 92) as part of his translation of verses 6.65 and 6.66, the words 'will have a sense of lightness of body and good digestion' actually translate the second half of 6.64 = 6.66 in Divanji (1954, p. 56).

37. *Yogayājñavalkya* 9.19–24, translation – T.K.V. Desikachar (2000, pp. 123–124), my emphasis added in bold:

> aṣṭaiśvaryadalopete vidyākesarasaṁyute |
> jñānanāle bṛhatkande prāṇāyāmaprabodhite || 9.19 ||
> viśvārciṣaṁ mahāvahniṁ jvalantaṁ viśvatomukham |
> vaiśvānaraṁ jagadyoni śikhātanvinamīśvaram || 9.20 ||
> tāpayantaṁ svakaṁ dehamāpādatalamastakam |
> nivātadīpavattasmindīpitaṁ havyavāhanam || 9.21 ||
> dṛṣṭvā tasya śikhāmadhye paramātmānamakṣaram |
> nīlatoyadamadhyasthavidyullekheva bhāsvaram || 9.22 ||
> nīvāraśūkavadrūpaṁ pītābhaṁ sarvakāraṇam |
> jñātvā vaiśvānaraṁ devaṁ so 'hameveti yā matiḥ || 9.23 ||
> saguṇeṣūttamaṁ hyotra dhyānaṁ yogavido viduḥ |
> vaiśvānaratvaṁ samprāpya mūrti tenaiva gacchati || 9.24 ||

The 'eight petal lotus' T.K.V. Desikachar mentions must refer to the heart because a few verses earlier, verse 9.12 states that 'twelve *aṅgula-s* above *nābhi* is the heart lotus with eight petals, which is four *aṅgula-s* in size'.[38] I interpret 'it' in the third sentence of T.K.V. Desikachar's translation as *nābhi*. There is, however, no mention in the Sanskrit of a *nāḍī* rising from *mūlādhāra* to *nābhi*.

This passage (9.19–9.24) is not easy to translate. My best attempt is as follows:

> [The heart lotus] has eight *siddhi-s* (powers) as its petals, united with true perception (*vidyā*) as its filament, knowledge (*jñāna*) as its stalk and *Paramātman* as its base. [The heart lotus] awakens (*svabodha*) [due to] *prāṇāyāma* (9.19). The whole of the radiant great fire [called] *Vaiṣvānara*, the divine cause of the universe, blazing in all directions, [in the form of] a thin flame (9.20), causes the body to shine from head to foot, illuminated like a flame undisturbed by wind in this [body?] (9.21). Having seen the imperishable *Paramātman* in the centre of the flame, its brilliance [like a] streak of lightning established in the centre of a dark cloud (9.22), which has a form [like] a tip of rice (i.e. thin or small), yellow/gold in colour, the cause of all, [and] having known the divine *Vaiṣvānara* [and] understood [that] 'that [divine *Vaiṣvānara*] surely [is] I' (9.23), [this is] excellent *saguṇa dhyāna* [according to] a wise knower of *yoga*. Having reached [the realization that] 'you [are] *Vaiṣvānara*', [one] 'goes with it' (i.e. one is liberated) (9.24).[39]

In the third erroneous inclusion of *mūlādhāra* in his translation, T.K.V. Desikachar translates verses 6.74–77a as follows:

> If the person decides to leave the body (*śarīra tyāga*), practising thus, praying to the Divine while reciting *Praṇava*, with the power of *prāṇa* **bringing it from *Mūlādhāra* to *Brahmarandhra*** (after exhale during retention and after exhale [sic]). Then piercing the *Brahmarandhra*, *prāṇa* along with *ātma*, merges with the Divine. This is mastery of one's self by the brave. *Gārgī*, those who die thus are free from rebirth. Therefore you too follow the daily discipline.[40]

---

38. Translation – T.K.V. Desikachar (2000, p. 123).

39. My translation of *Yogayājñavalkya* 9.19–9.24 from the Sanskrit in T.K.V. Desikachar (2000, pp. 123–124).

40. Translation – T.K.V. Desikachar (2000, p. 94), my emphasis added in bold:

> ekākṣaraṁ paraṁ brahma dhyāyanpraṇavamīśvaram |
> saṁbhidya manasā mūrghni [=mūrdhni?] brahmarandhraṁ savāyunā || 6.74 ||

T.K.V. Desikachar's use of 'it' is unclear but the pronoun must refer to *prāṇa*. However, the Sanskrit does not mention bringing *prāṇa*, or anything else, from *mūlādhāra* to *brahmarandhra*. My translation of the Sanskrit T.K.V. Desikachar presents is:

> Meditating on *Īśvara*/pure *Brahman* [by reciting] the *praṇava*, having pierced the *brahmarandhra* at the top of the head with the mind along with *vāyu* (*prāṇa*) (6.74), **[the yogi] should pull up the *prāṇa* by the root**. Subsequently, when the body is gone, when the *prāṇa* [is merged] in the great *prāṇa* in the centre of the sun (the divine), when the ocean is merged in the void, when the pole star/sky is in step (i.e. unmoving?), (6.75) [and] when in the highest bliss by mental effort [the *yogi's*] own *ātman* joins [the *paramātman*, then he] will become *Brahman*, O Gārgī, [and] will not be reborn (6.76). And therefore, may you regularly practise ritual action towards elevation (6.77a).[41]

I translate *prāṇam-ud-mūlayet* in 6.75 above as 'should pull up the *prāṇa* by the root', i.e. should uproot the *prāṇa*. This does not mean that it must be raised from *mūlādhāra*, which is absent. The term *ud-mūlayet* could also be translated as 'must be eradicated', and it gives the sense of *prāṇa* being completely lifted.[42] The equivalent verse of the critical edition instead uses *ud-mocayet*,[43] combining the prefix *ud* (up) with the root *muc* (must loosen/let loose/free/let go/release).[44] *Mūlādhāra* is neither in the original Sanskrit nor a valid inference from it.

T.K.V. Desikachar's fourth incorrect mention of *mūlādhāra* relates to *nāda*, the unstruck internal sound, in his translation of *Yogayājñavalkya* 6.54–55a:

---

prāṇamunmūlayetpaścānmahāpraṇe khamadhyame |
dehātīte jagatprāṇe śūnye nitye dhruve pade || 6.75 ||
ākāśe paramānande svātmānaṁ yojayeddhiyā |
brahmaivāsau bhavedgārgi na punarjanmabhāgbhavet || 6.76 ||
tasmāttvaṁ ca varārohe nityaṁ karma samācara | 6.77a |
= 6.76–79a in Divanji (1954, p. 59).

41. My translation of 6.74–77a in T.K.V. Desikachar (2000, p. 94).
42. The same verb appears as *ut-mūlya* in *Yogatārāvalī* 19, where Desikachar and Desikachar (2003, pp. 50–51) translate it as 'rooting out' – see Chapter 5.
43. *Yogayājñavalkya* 6.77 in Divanji (1954, p. 59).
44. Monier-Williams (1899, p. 820).

> Remaining in this position one must listen to the sound like a vina string produced in the *suṣūmna* which is pure white in color like a crystal, **this sound will be felt from *Mūlādhāra* to *Sahasrāra*.**[45]

I would translate that passage as follows:

> Inside the *brahmarandhra* in the *suṣumnā* [is] a thread like a fibrous lotus root. And [when] *nāda* reaches (ascends to) the top of the head, the *nāda* verily appears like (sounds like?) pure crystal, [like the sound] arising [from a] *vīṇā* string.

The *sahasrāra* is located on the crown of the head (*ā-mūrdhno* in 6.55a) so T.K.V. Desikachar's introduction of *sahasrāra* is a valid inference. *Nāda* reaching the top of the head implies that it rises from some undisclosed lower location, but the text does not mention *mūlādhāra*. T.K.V. Desikachar adds in a footnote to his translation of this verse that 'If there are any impurities along the spine in the *cakra*-s or if the *Mūlādhāra* is not tightly lifted up, this sound will not be there.'[46] The mention of tightly lifting *mūlādhāra* clearly refers to *mūla bandha* – see Chapter 4. Mohan also adds a footnote making the same point:

> The human spine is comparable to the vīṇā, an ancient Indian string instrument, the vertebrae of the spine being likened to the nodes of the vīṇā. The practice of mūlabandha tightens the base of the spine, similar to the tightening of the vīṇā at its base. Only when the strings are properly tightened and in proper tension, is the sound (nāda) from the vīṇā proper. Similarly, the practice of the bandhas are (sic) useful for proper nādānusandhāna.[47]

T.K.V. Desikachar's fifth incorrect mention of *mūlādhāra* in his translation is less serious. His translation of 12.1 ends with 'visualise the flame of the fire located near *Mūlādhāra*'.[48] Again, there is no mention of *mūlādhāra* in

---

45. Translation – T.K.V. Desikachar (2000, p. 89), my emphasis added in bold:

> brahmarandhre suṣumnāyāṁ mṛṇālāntarasūtravat |
> nālotpattistvanenaiva śuddhasphaṭikasannibhā || 6.54 ||
> āmūrdho vartate nādo vīṇādaṇḍavadutthitaḥ | 6.55a |

46. T.K.V. Desikachar (2000, p. 89).

47. Mohan and Mohan (2013, p. 65 n.60). Unlike T.K.V. Desikachar, Mohan and Mohan do not mention *mūlādhāra* in their actual translation.

48. T.K.V. Desikachar (2000, p. 149):

> savyena gulphena gudaṁ nirudhya savyetareṇaiva nipīḍya sandhim |
> savyetaraṁ nyasya karetarasminśikhāṁ samālokaya pāvakasya ||

the text. As shown above, verses 4.11b and 4.14 locate 'the place of fire' at the *dehamadhya*, the centre of the body, which is in the perineum between the anus and the penis. This is near the usual location for *mūlādhāra* so perhaps Desikachar was trying to provide a convenient reference point, albeit one beyond the terms of reference of the text he translated.

In addition to the above five incorrect mentions of *mūlādhāra* in Desikachar's translations of verses, he uses the term twice more in notes. In the first note, he states that '*Kuṇḍalini* is located between *Mūlādhāra* and *nābhi*.'[49] This statement is sandwiched between contradictory translations on the same page of 12.10 and 12.12, which state that *kuṇḍalinī* is 'located at the *Nābhi*' and 'located in *nābhi.* area', respectively. Less seriously, a note under his translation of 12.28 states that *prāṇa* moves 'up from *Mūlādhāra* to *Sahasrāra*', which is not in the Sanskrit he translates.[50]

In total, T.K.V. Desikachar's five mistranslations and two misleading footnotes significantly misrepresent the *Yogayājñavalkya*. He effectively extends *suṣumnā* from its lower terminus at *nābhi* down to *mūlādhāra*, which the *Yogayājñavalkya* does not mention. He also erroneously relocates *kuṇḍalinī* from *nābhi* to *mūlādhāra*. His other mistranslations stipulate the raising of *prāṇa* from *mūlādhāra* to *sahasrāra*, leading one to feel the internal sound *nāda* all the way between those *cakra-s*.

It is unclear why T.K.V. Desikachar changed the content in this way. First, he could have been reflecting his own personal experience of *kuṇḍalinī*. He stated that 'these concepts [*kuṇḍalinī* etc.] and techniques must be explained by someone who has not only a great wealth of practical experience and well-founded knowledge, but also considerable proficiency in Sanskrit, the language in which the texts are written. Very often there is a lack of both.'[51] However, T.K.V. Desikachar told K.S. Balasubramanian of the Kuppuswami Sastri Research Institute, Chennai, that he relied upon texts for his understanding of *kuṇḍalinī* because he was not sure about the topic, not having experienced it himself.[52] Alternatively, T.K.V. Desikachar could have been attempting to reflect his father's teachings. However, notes from an essay by Krishnamacharya on *kuṇḍalinī* explicitly state that

---

49. T.K.V. Desikachar (2000, p. 152).
50. T.K.V. Desikachar (2000, p. 158):

> samīraṇe viṣṇupade niviṣṭe jīve ca tasminnamṛte ca saṁsthe |
> tasmintadā yāti mano layaṁ cenmukteḥ samīpaṁ taditi bruvanti || 12.28 ||.

51. T.K.V. Desikachar (1995, p. 139).
52. Balasubramanian (2018).

'Kuṇḍalinī is found above and below Nābhicakra.'[53] This is consistent with the *Yogayājñavalkya* but inconsistent with Desikachar's mistranslation thereof. A complication is that Krishnamacharya wrote in the same essay that 'Brahmanāḍī (Suṣumnā) begins from Mūlādhāra and goes till the crown of the head.'[54] It would seem, therefore, that Krishnamacharya located *kuṇḍalinī* part way along the *suṣumnā*. This is unusual. It is incompatible with the system of the *Yogayājñavalkya*, in which *nābhi* is the lower terminus of the *suṣumnā*. I have found no quotations in which Krishnamacharya locates *kuṇḍalinī* at *mūlādhāra*. In the *Yogamakaranda*, he states that *kuṇḍalinī* 'is lying dormant in the *Kanda-sthāna*'.[55] I will show in Chapter 4 that there was some conceptual drift in where Krishnamacharya located the *kanda* when he tried to accommodate and harmonize divergent teachings from incompatible texts. Perhaps T.K.V. Desikachar may have done something very similar in his translation of the *Yogayājñavalkya*.

Both T.K.V. Desikachar and A.G. Mohan comment that *nāda* (the unstruck internal sound) is felt from *mūlādhāra*, suggesting that they are both reflecting Krishnamacharya's teachings. In contrast to T.K.V. Desikachar, however, Mohan restricts such comments to footnotes or introductory comments and does not include *mūlādhāra* in his translation of the *Yogayājñavalkya*. For the passages related to *kuṇḍalinī*, Mohan's translation is much more accurate and literal, being closer to the original Sanskrit that Mohan presents than T.K.V. Desikachar's translation is to his version of the text. Even though the quotations about *nāda* from Mohan and T.K.V. Desikachar mention *mūlādhāra*, neither state that *kuṇḍalinī* is located there. We will see in Chapter 3 that another of Krishnamacharya's source texts, the *Ahirbudhnyasaṁhitā*, locates *kuṇḍalinī* at *mūlādhāra* only in relation to *nāda*, otherwise locating it at *nābhi*.

There are further hints of why T.K.V. Desikachar relocated *kuṇḍalinī* to *mūlādhāra*. Writing with K. Desikachar, he described how *kuṇḍalinī* represents a collection of 'obstacles' including poor health, habits, ignorance and ego:

> Since these obstacles were the causes of ill health, the ancient masters positioned the *Kunḍalini* at the base of the spine, which is the lower most point of reference. Also, the ancient masters visualized the *Kunḍalini* as something

53. Jayaraman (2015, p. 217).
54. Jayaraman (2015, p. 217).
55. Krishnamacharya (2011, p. 109).

> that needs to be eliminated and the *cakra* coinciding with the function of elimination of waste was the *Mūlādhāra*, hence the positioning of the *Kuṅḍalini* at the base of the spine. ... The ancient masters knew that two of the major obstacles to the equilibrium of the human mind were sexual and gastronomic urges. Hence, the *Kuṅḍalini* which also symbolized these obstacles, was located at the *Mūlādhāra*, which is the lower most *cakra*. The logic behind this positioning is not just because the digestive and reproductive organs are located below the navel, but more importantly because these urges make us succumb by the sheer force of their pull.[56]

Seven years later at a workshop on *nāḍī-s*, *cakra-s* and related concepts, K. Desikachar gave a different explanation: the location of *kuṇḍalinī* at *mūlādhāra* is symbolic as that place corresponds to the elements of attachment: earth and water.[57] Support for this would seem to come from a *Saiddhāntika* (*Śaiva Siddhānta*) text. The *Kaulajñānanirṇaya* locates *kuṇḍalī* between *jyeṣṭha* (earth) and *vāmā* (water), elements which are commonly mapped onto the lowest two *cakra-s*.[58] However, in *tantra*, such elements can be 'installed' in different *cakra-s*. For example, in the *Saiddhāntika* tradition, earth is frequently 'installed' in the heart *cakra*,[59] which in many early *Saiddhāntika* texts is the base of the *nāḍī-s*.[60] It is unsurprising therefore that another *Saiddhāntika* text, the *Sārdhatriśatikālottaravṛtti*, locates *kuṇḍalinī* at the base of the *nāḍī-s* at the heart *cakra*.[61] Other texts stipulating *nābhi* as the base of the *nāḍī-s* also locate *kuṇḍalinī* there,[62] including some *Vaiṣṇava* texts I examine in the next chapter. There is nothing to stop earth being 'installed' at *nābhi* in such systems. An association with the earth element does not, therefore, necessitate the location of *kuṇḍalinī* at

---

56. Desikachar and Desikachar (2003, pp. 81–82).

57. K. Desikachar (2010). K. Desikachar made this comment as part of a substantial description of *kuṇḍalinī*. It came just after the claim that I explore in Chapter 5, in which K. Desikachar linked *kuṇḍalinī* to *avidyā* via the symbolism of serpents. After this comment, he stated that most *avidyā* comes from attachment and the elements of attachment are earth and water, located at *mūlādhāra*.

58. White (2003, p. 152). *Kuṇḍalinī* and *kuṇḍalī* are often synonymous in tantric texts and texts describing *haṭhayoga* (Goodall 2004, p. 110; Mallinson and Singleton 2017, p. 178).

59. Wallis (2016).

60. Hatley (2013, p. 284).

61. *Sārdhatriśatikālottaravṛtti* 12.1 from Goodall (2004, p. 110):

> candrāgnir iva saṁyuktā ādyā kuṇḍalinī tu yā |
> hṛtpradeśe tu sā jñeyā aṅkurākāravat sthitā ||

62. Hatley (2013, p. 284).

mūlādhāra, as K. Desikachar argued. In Chapter 4, I will show how locating *kuṇḍalinī* at either *nābhi* or *mūlādhāra* led students of Krishnamacharya to give to diverging explanations of how *kuṇḍalinī* is affected in inverted postures.

Whatever the reasons for modifying his father's teaching, T.K.V. Desikachar's inaccurate presentation of the *Yogayājñavalkya* is incompatible with his claim that the text is 'more coherent than any other I know' about *kuṇḍalinī*.[63] Indeed, Desikachar's misrepresentation of the *Yogayājñavalkya* greatly reduces its coherence. Readers may be confused when trying to reconcile places where he correctly locates *kuṇḍalinī* at or close to *nābhi* with places where he incorrectly locates it at *mūlādhāra*. Balasubramanian states that T.K.V. Desikachar's translation of the *Yogayājñavalkya* 'does not give a comprehensive, literal and authentic picture of the original text'.[64] For the passages I have examined related to *kuṇḍalinī*, Balasubramanian is correct.

Perhaps motivated by the shortcomings of T.K.V. Desikachar's translation, the Krishnamacharya Yoga Mandiram published a revised translation of the *Yogayājñavalkya*. It removes T.K.V. Desikachar's mentions of *mūlādhāra* from all its verse translations. It does, however, retain all T.K.V. Desikachar's 'insightful notes',[65] including the two misleading references to *mūlādhāra*, which is not mentioned in the Sanskrit text (see above).[66] Moreover, the new edition introduces a new error in its translation of *Yogayājñavalkya* 6.69, describing when *kuṇḍalinī* 'has woken up and has started to move about in the the (sic) Mūlādhāra'.[67] The mistake probably originates from *mūle*, meaning 'at the root' (not *mūlādhāra cakra*). Mohan and Mohan's translation of the corresponding verse of the critical edition

63. T.K.V. Desikachar (1980, p. 247).

64. Balasubramanian (2017, p. 147). I only scrutinized the parts of chapters 4, 6 and 10 related to *kuṇḍalinī*. I have not examined in detail T.K.V. Desikachar's translation of the rest of the *Yogayājñavalkya* so I cannot verify Balasubramanian's assessment of Desikachar's translation as a whole.

65. Jayaraman (2015, Publisher's Note).

66. Jayaraman (2015, pp. 196, 205).

67. Translation – Jayaraman (2015, p. 122):

> prabuddhe saṁsmaratyasminnādimūle tu cakriṇi |
> brahmarandhre suṣumnāyāṁ prayāti prāṇasaṁjñakaḥ || 6.69 ||
> = 6.71 in Divanji (1954, p. 58), which differs slightly

correctly states 'this cakra at the base of the navel (nābhi)'.[68] See my translation below.

2.4 *KUṆḌALINĪ* IS A BLOCKAGE

The *Yogayājñavalkya* clearly describes *kuṇḍalinī* as a blockage, not only to *prāṇa* and not only to the *suṣumnā:*

> She *[kuṇḍalinī]* has the form of eight *prakṛti-s* and is coiled eight times in a spiral (4.21b). [She] always completely blocks the pathways of air, water, food etc. around [and] on the sides of the *kanda* (4.22) [and] completely covers the opening of the *brahmarandhra* (entrance to the *suṣumnā*) with [her] mouth.[69]

Kuṇḍalinī blocks *prāṇa* from entering the *suṣumnā:*

> Having entered into (i.e. blocked/covered) the *suṣumnā* with [her] mouth and other *nāḍī-s* with [her] hood, holding [her] own tail in [her] mouth, *[kuṇḍalinī]* restrains/constrains the path of the gathered *prāṇa* (*marut gaṇānām*).[70]

Many texts describe *kuṇḍalinī* as coiled three and a half times, e.g. *Gheraṇḍasaṁhitā* 3.40, *Śivasaṁhitā* 2.23 and *Ṣaṭcakranirūpaṇa* 10–11.[71] The three and a half coils are interpreted variously.[72] However, in

---

68. Mohan and Mohan (2013, p. 67).

69. *Yogayājñavalkya* 4.21b–23a, my translation of Divanji (1954, pp. 26–27):

> aṣṭaprakṛtirūpā sā aṣṭadhā kuṇḍalīkṛtā || 4.21b ||
> yathāvadvāyusaṁcāraṁ jalānnādīni nityaśaḥ |
> paritaḥ kandapārśveṣu niruddhyaiva sadā sthitā || 4.22 ||
> mukhenaiva samāveṣṭya brahmarandhramukhaṁ tathā | 4.23a |

70. *Yogayājñavalkya* 12.9, my translation of Divanji (1954, p. 104):

> śirāṁ samāveṣya mukhena madhyāmanyāśca bhogena śirāstathaiva |
> svapucchamāsyena nigṛhya samyakpathaśca saṁyamya marudgaṇānām || 12.9 ||

71. Mallinson (2004, p. 73); Mallinson (2007b, p. 31); and Avalon (1974, pp. 346–347) respectively.

72. Sivananda (1994, p. 53) and Adishakti.org (no date) agree that the three coils represent the three *guṇa-s* (*sattva, rajas* and *tamas*) with the half coil representing *vikṛti-s*, i.e. changes, alterations, perturbations or agitations (Monier-Williams 1899, p. 954). The Kundalini Research Project (no date) widens that explanation: 'The 3 coils represent the 3 mantras of Om, which relate to past, present and future; to the gunas: tamas, rajas and sattva; to the 3 states of consciousness: waking, sleeping and dreaming; and to the types of experience:

Yogayājñavalkya 4.21, *kuṇḍalinī* is coiled eight times, representing eight aspects of *prakṛti*. The same metaphor is used in other *Vaiṣṇava* texts: see Chapter 3. Note that in *Yogayājñavalkya* 12.9, *kuṇḍalinī* blocks not just the *suṣumnā* but also other *nāḍī-s*.

2.5 *KUṆḌALINĪ* IS 'AWOKEN' BY BURNING IT WITH *AGNI* (FIRE) AND *PRĀṆA*

> He who mindfully burns *kuṇḍalinī*, [which is] in the form of a snake dwelling in the *nāḍī-s* in the centre of the *kanda*, severing/removing it with flames of fire [distributed/fanned] by *prāṇa*, is an excellent man (12.11).[73]

Chapter 6 paints a similar picture:

> By this *dhāraṇā*, established on the centre of *nābhi*, the *prāṇa* (*māruta*) goes to the *kuṇḍalinī* and fire (*vahni*) burns [it] there, without a doubt (6.69). There [in *nābhi*], heated by fire [and] caused to move by *vāyu*, she *[kuṇḍalinī]* by herself then awakens (*prabodhaṁ-yāti*); [her] hood [and] the body bearing it are spread (i.e. her hood spreads and her body straightens) (6.70).

Prāṇa and *agni* then rise:

> When *[kuṇḍalinī]* has been awoken, that which is called *prāṇa* (*prāṇa-saṁjñaka*) moves in this *cakra* at the root (bottom) of *nābhi* and goes along the *suṣumnā* [towards] the *brahmarandhra* (6.71).[74]

---

subjective experience, sensual experience and absence of experience. The ½ coil represents the state of transcendence, where there is neither waking, sleeping nor dreaming.' In contrast, Khecaranatha (2017) claims that 'The three coils represent the three levels of kuṇḍalinī energy: prāṇa kuṇḍalinī, the energy that gives life to our breath and to our physical body; cit kuṇḍalinī, which gives life to our mental and emotional capacity; and para kuṇḍalinī, the energy of our spiritual self, the core and essence of our being. The final half coil is the serpent's head turned back on itself, fast asleep.'

73. *Yogayājñavalkya* 12.11, my translation of Divanji (1954, p. 105):

> vāyunā vihṛtavahniśikhābhiḥ kandamadhyagatanāḍiṣu* [= ... īṣu] saṁsthām |
> kuṇḍalīṁ dahati yastvahirūpāṁ saṁsmarannaravarastu sa eva || 12.11 ||

*I accept Mohan and Mohan's (2013, pp. 115, 168) correction of *nāḍiṣu* to *nāḍīṣu*, making a locative-plural feminine noun.

74. *Yogayājñavalkya* 6.69–6.71, my translations of Divanji (1954, pp. 57–58):

> etena nābhimadhyasthadhāraṇenaiva mārutaḥ |
> kuṇḍalīṁ yāti vahniśca dahatyatra na saṁśayaḥ || 6.69 ||

This 'awakening' process is similarly described in chapter twelve:

> There [in the *kanda*] heated by fire [and] caused to tremble by *prāṇa*, she [*kuṇḍalinī*] then awakes and [her] hood and body are spread (12.12). Upon this awakening [of *kuṇḍalinī*] in the centre of *nābhi cakra*, *prāṇa-s* in this body, after coming together, all move with the fire, like the motion of thread[s] in a garment (12.13).[75]

Chapter 4 also describes *prāṇa* and *agni* rising together:

> *Vāyu*, with the help of the friend of *vāyu* (fire), goes [up] along the *suṣumnā*.[76]

2.6 A CONTRADICTORY VERSE

In an interview, Krishnamacharya was asked a question: 'Some people describe that the kuṇḍalini goes through the suṣumna to the sahasrāra. Is it correct?' He replied: 'No. It is the prāṇa vāyū that moves through the suṣumṇa.'[77] However, the critical edition of *Yogayājñavalkya* 12.17 contradicts Krishnamacharya's reply:

> When by this (meditating on flames in the heart), *vāyu* together with the friend of *vāyu* (fire) is restricted in the centre of the heart (*hṛdi*), **the snake (*dvijihvaḥ*)**, having entered the mouth of the thousand-petalled [lotus] (*sahasra-patrasya*), should make the face [of that lotus] rise (face upwards) again.[78]

---

santaptā vahninā tatra vāyunā cālitā svayam |
prasāryaṁ phaṅabhṛdbhogaṁ prabodhaṁ yāti sā tadā || 6.70 ||
prabuddhe saṁsaratyasminnābhimūle tu cakriṇi |
brahmarandhre suṣumṇāyāṁ prayāti prāṇasaṁjñakaḥ || 6.71 ||
= 6.67–69 in T.K.V. Desikachar (2000, p. 92).

75. *Yogayājñavalkya* 12.12–13, my translation of Divanji (1954, p. 105):

santaptā vahninā tatra vāyunā ca pracālitā |
prasārya phaṇabhṛdbhogaṁ prabodhaṁ yāti sā tadā || 12.12 ||
bodhaṁ gate cakriṇi nābhimadhye prāṇāḥ susambhūya kalevare 'smin |
caranti sarve saha vahninaiva yathā paṭe tantugatistathaiva || 12.13 ||

76. *Yogayājñavalkya* 4.24b, my translation of Divanji (1954, p. 27):

vāyurvāyusakhenaiva tato yāti suṣumṇayā || 4.24b ||

77. Srivatsan (1997, p. 112).

78. *Yogayājñavalkya* 12.17, my translation of Divanji (1954, p. 106):

nirodhitaḥ syādhṛdi tena vāyuḥ madhye yadā vāyusakhena sārdham |
sahasrapatrasya mukhaṁ praviśya kuryātpunastūrdhvamukhaṁ dvijihvaḥ || 12.17 ||

The final word of this verse in the critical edition is *dvijihvaḥ*, literally 'two tongued', i.e. a snake.[79] The English equivalent is 'fork tongued'. In the context, the only plausible meaning is *kuṇḍalinī*. After entering the thousand-petalled lotus, *kuṇḍalinī* causes it to face upwards again. Jayaraman broadly agrees: 'the serpent will attain the opening of the thousand petals (Sahasrāra) and will make it face upwards'.[80] In an online course on the *Yogayājñavalkya* in 2020, Srivatsa Ramaswami commented that after intense practice, *kuṇḍalinī* ultimately reaches the *brahmarandhra*. His specific mention of *kuṇḍalinī* seems to have been based on *dvijihvaḥ* in verse 12.17 as Ramaswami was speaking about verses 12.14–12.20 at the time.[81]

Verse 12.17 opens up a gaping crack in the coherence of the *Yogayājñavalkya* and therefore of Krishnamacharya's position (as communicated by T.K.V. Desikachar and A.G. Mohan). *Kuṇḍalinī* may initially be a blockage but it is not destroyed. It rises all the way along the *suṣumnā* to the thousand-petalled lotus at the crown. T.K.V. Desikachar's translation of the equivalent verse does not mention a snake because the text he presents comes from the Trivandrum edition, which does not include

79. Monier-Williams (1899, p. 504). Both *kuṇḍalinī* and *jihvā* are feminine but *dvijihvaḥ* is a nominative-singular masculine noun. *Dvijihvaḥ* is therefore the subject. Monier-Williams confirms that *dvijihva* can be masculine, feminine or neuter. It is unusual for *kuṇḍalinī* to be represented with a masculine term but that is the case here.

80. Jayaraman (2015, p. 199). The brackets and their contents are in the original from Jayaraman.

81. Ramaswami (2020). I did not attend the online course myself. This account is based upon detailed notes taken by Dr Karin Horowitz, who did attend, supplemented by Hotowitz's explanation and clarification of those notes and their context. Horowitz was unsure which version of the *Yogayājñavalkya* text Ramaswami based his comments on. Participants on the course were given diagrams from Jayaraman's (2015) edition, which includes *dvijihvaḥ* (=*kuṇḍalinī*) in the Sanskrit text of 12.17. Ramaswami could have based his comments on that edition. Alternatively, Ramaswami may have been using Divanji's (1954) critical edition, which also includes *dvijihvaḥ* in 12.17. It seems unlikely that Ramaswami's comments were based on the Trivandrum edition (Śāstri 1938) or the Sanskrit text in T.K.V. Desikachar's (2000) translation, which is based on the Trivandrum edition, because those two publications do not include *dvijihvaḥ* in the text of 12.17. Ramaswami was also taught the *Yogayājñavalkya* 'in detail' by Krishnamacharya (Ramaswami 2007, p. 21) and I would expect that Ramaswami's comments on the *Yogayājñavalkya* were also informed by what Krishnamacharya taught him. However, the teaching that *kuṇḍalinī* rises all the way to the *Brahmarandhra* differs from the presentation of Krishnamacharya's teachings given by T.K.V. Desikachar and A.G. Mohan.

dvijihvaḥ.[82] Curiously, Mohan and Mohan's translation of *Yogayājñavalkya* 12.17 contains no mention of a snake or *kuṇḍalinī* either, even though they claim to be translating the critical edition:

> By this, when the vāyu along with the agni is stopped in the center of the heart, it enters the opening of the thousand-petalled heart-lotus and must be made to face (move) upwards again.[83]

There are two curious features of Mohan and Mohan's translation. First is the mention of a 'thousand-petalled heart-lotus'. Verse 9.12 clearly describes the heart lotus as having eight petals, as Mohan and Mohan reflect in their own translation.[84] The only possible 'thousand-petalled' lotus is at the crown of the head at *sahasrāra*, whose very name indicates a thousand. Jayaraman acknowledges this in his translation of 12.17.[85]

The second curious feature of Mohan and Mohan's above translation is that the Sanskrit they present is not identical to Divanji's critical edition. They have substituted *dvijendre* for *dvijihvaḥ*, thereby critically editing the critical edition without informing their readers.[86] *Dvijendre* is a locative noun that could be translated as 'in the moon'.[87] It could potentially be a synonym of *candra* - a widely used term in texts. For example, the *Kaṅkālamālinītantra* states that 'In the pericarp of the thousand petalled lotus there is the orb of the full moon.'[88] The *Śārṅgadharapaddhati* describes Śiva as having 'the radiance of the moon, a shining faultless light, in the thousand-petalled lotus'.[89] The *Amṛtasiddhi* states that 'The moon is on the peak of Meru and has sixteen digits.'[90] This 'peak of Meru' could correspond to the thousand-petalled lotus. Substituting *dvijendre* for *dvijihvaḥ*

82. T.K.V. Desikachar (2000, p. 154).
83. *Yogayājñavalkya* 12.17, translation – Mohan and Mohan (2013, p. 116). The brackets and their contents are in Mohan and Mohan's translation.
84. Mohan and Mohan (2013, p. 95).
85. Jayaraman (2015, p. 199).
86. The Sanskrit in the first edition of A.G. Mohan's translation (Mohan no date b, pp. 129–130) is identically worded and translated (apart from minor differences in spelling, capitalization and diacritics).
87. Apte (1957, p. 848).
88. Translation – Kuvalayānanda and Shukla (2006, p. 81). Here, 'moon' = *candra*, not *dvijendra*.
89. Mallinson (2007a, pp. 28–29).
90. Translation – Mallinson (2020, p. 413). Here, 'moon' = *candra*, not *dvijendra*.

to produce the amended Sanskrit of *Yogayājñavalkya* 12.17 that Mohan and Mohan present would change my translation to the following:

> When by this (meditating on flames in the heart), *vāyu* together with the friend of *vāyu* (fire) is restricted in the centre of the heart (*hṛdi*). Having entered the mouth of the thousand-petalled [lotus, the *yogi*] should make the face [of that lotus] **in the moon** rise (face upwards) again.

However, texts do not always locate the moon in the thousand-petalled lotus. The *Khecarīvidyā* locates the moon 'in the middle of the forehead', 'between the eyebrows' and 'at the top of the skull'.[91] According to *Gorakṣapaddhati* 2.32, 'the moon, of the essence of nectar, is always situated at the root of the palate'.[92] Furthermore, Brahmānanda's *Jyotsnā* commentary on the *Haṭhapradīpikā* states that the nectarine secretion from the *candra* is 'located internally to the left side between the eyebrows'.[93] An interpretation of *dvijendre* as 'in the moon' is therefore far from certain.

An alternative translation of *dvijendre* would combine *dvija*, meaning 'twice born', with *indra*, here meaning 'the best',[94] producing the locative form 'in the best among the twice born'. Indeed, the nominative form, *dvijendraḥ*, is translated a few verses later in 12.42 by Mohan and Mohan as 'greatest among brahmins' and by Jayaraman as 'the twice born (Yājñavalkya)'.[95] Adopting that meaning would change my translation of the text Mohan presents of 12.17 to the following:

> When by this (meditating on flames in the heart), *vāyu* together with the friend of *vāyu* (fire) is restricted in the centre of the heart (*hṛdi*) **in [one who is] best among the twice born**, having entered the mouth of the thousand-petalled [lotus, the *yogi*] should make the face [of the thousand-petalled lotus] rise (face upwards) again.[96]

Whatever the best translation of *dvijendre*, Mohan and Mohan's translation of his amended version of *Yogayājñavalkya* 12.17 above does not mention *dvijendre* and does not attempt to translate it.

---

91. Mallinson (2007a, pp. 127, 221).
92. Feuerstein (1998, p. 549).
93. Maheshananda and Sharma (2012, p. 242).
94. Monier-Williams (1899, p. 506); Apte (1957, p. 384) respectively.
95. Mohan and Mohan (2013, p. 121); Jayaraman (2015, p. 211) respectively.
96. I have related *dvijendre* to the other locative words, *hṛdi* and *madhye*, which together mean 'in the centre of the heart'.

It could be argued that *dvijendre* should be preferred to *dvijihvaḥ*. Divanji chose to use *dvijihvaḥ* in his critical edition despite it occurring in only two of the sixteen manuscripts he analysed. In contrast, ten manuscripts and all five previously published editions used *dvijendre*.[97] Nevertheless, even if Mohan felt he had good justification for this substitution, he should have openly declared it.

A.G. Mohan claims that his translation of the *Yogayājñavalkya* is 'based on' Divanji's critical edition.[98] He stresses that Divanji's edition 'is easily more complete and error free' than other versions,[99] yet he still edited the Sanskrit of 12.17. In effect, Mohan critically edited the critical edition, for one word at least, thereby avoiding a contradiction of Krishnamacharya's position. Making such a change without declaring and justifying it is poor scholarly practice.[100]

In summary, the model of *kuṇḍalinī* presented in most verses of the *Yogayājñavalkya* is relatively clear. *Kuṇḍalinī* is located in (or around) *nābhi*

---

97. Divanji (1954, pp. 106–107).

98. Mohan (no date b, p. 1); Mohan and Mohan (2013, p. ii).

99. Mohan and Mohan (2013, p. iii).

100. It could be argued that it has been common practice in the history of South Asian thought for commentators and redactors to change words in a text to suit their purposes. That is one way in which manuscripts of a text are caused to diverge. My criticism of 'poor scholarly practice' comes from a different cultural norm. However, A.G. Mohan studied engineering to degree level (Mohan and Mohan 2010, p. 12) and is highly likely to be aware of what is considered acceptable and unacceptable in international modern scholarship in the English language, even in the very different field of religious studies. Speaking in Glasgow, A.G. Mohan (2015) asked 'Why is it that the only area of our lives where we do not use critical analysis is *yoga*?' I would argue that my critique of his translation is consistent with the sort of critical analysis that he called for. Mohan and Mohan (2013, p. iv) state that theirs is 'a translation from the view of a yoga practitioner and teacher, not an academic scholar'. Nevertheless, it is a scholarly work. A.G. Mohan also stresses his scholarly credentials in workshops, including the study that he has done since Krishnamacharya's death with a scholar from the Sanskrit College, Madras (Mohan, Mohan and Mohan 2006; Mohan 2015, 2018a). However, in his own critical analysis, K.S. Balasubramanian (2017, p. 147), Professor of Sanskrit from the Kuppuswami Sastri Research Institute (part of the Sanskrit College, Madras), claims that A.G. Mohan's English translation of the *Yogayājñavalkya* has 'numerous mistakes'. Although I have not checked all of Mohan's translation, the passages I surveyed in chapters 4, 6 and 12 contained only minor clerical errors in the original Sanskrit of the second edition. These are inconsequential accidental slips. There is also one correction, which I accept, of a clear spelling mistake in the Sanskrit of the critical edition: see note 73 above. I found no serious errors and no changes comparable to A.G. Mohan's undeclared editing of the Sanskrit in 12.17.

cakra in the middle of the *kanda*. It blocks the flow of *prāṇa*, water and food in the *suṣumnā* and other *nāḍī-s*. When burned by *agni* (fire) and fanned with *prāṇa*, it awakens, allowing *prāṇa* and *agni* to enter the *suṣumnā* and ascend along it. This account is not very different from that presented in other *haṭha* texts, the main difference being the alleged absence of statements that *kuṇḍalinī* rises up the *suṣumnā*. We have, however, already seen one verse open up a crack in Krishnamacharya's position – one that has only been smoothed over by A.G. Mohan being very selective over which manuscripts he used to source a particular word. We have also seen how T.K.V. Desikachar significantly altered the content of the *Yogayājñavalkya* in his translation, introducing ambiguity about the location of *kuṇḍalinī*. I will return to the location of *kuṇḍalinī* when I examine inversions and *bandha-s* in Chapter 4.

Meanwhile, the next chapter explores another grey area on *kuṇḍalinī* in a section of the *Yogayājñavalkya* common to two other *Vaiṣṇava* texts. I will also trace similar teachings, differently phrased but written with similar vocabulary and style, to related texts belonging to *Vaiṣṇava* traditions closely linked to Krishnamacharya's own. I will show how these texts are not always consistent in their presentation of *kuṇḍalinī*, usually affirming Krishnamacharya's position but sometimes contradicting it.

3
Kuṇḍalinī in other *Vaiṣṇava* texts

Although students of Krishnamacharya cite the *Yogayājñavalkya* to support his position on *kuṇḍalinī*, similar teachings appear in other *Vaiṣṇava* texts. This chapter will first trace some verses from the *Yogayājñavalkya* to the *Vasiṣṭhasaṁhitā*. It will then trace some of those verses to the *Pādmasaṁhitā*, from the *Vaiṣṇava* tradition of *Pāñcarātra*, and will examine another text from the same tradition, the *Ahirbudhnyasaṁhitā*. It will finally present some similar verses from the *Vimānārcanākalpasaṁhitā*, a text of the rival *Vaiṣṇava* sect of *Vaikhānasa*.

3.1 *VASIṢṬHASAṀHITĀ*

The critical edition of the *Yogayājñavalkya* contains 428 verses.[1] Out of these, some 269 also occur in the *Yogakāṇḍa* of the *Vasiṣṭhasaṁhitā*.[2] Many verses related to *kuṇḍalinī* in *Yogayājñavalkya* chapter 4 occur in the *Vasiṣṭhasaṁhitā*, either with identical wording or with minor differences – see the first two columns of Table 1.

Like the *Yogayājñavalkya*, the *Vasiṣṭhasaṁhitā* is clearly *Vaiṣṇava*. It also places *haṭhayoga* within the context of Vedic orthodoxy, prescribing

1. Divanji (1954).
2. Digambaji et al. (2005, p. 28). Hence, Mallinson identifies no verses in the *Haṭhapradīpikā* (see Chapter 4) as coming from the *Yogayājñavalkya*. Instead, he identifies fifteen and a half verses originating in the *Vasiṣṭhasaṁhitā*, about two thirds of which also appear in the *Yogayājñavalkya* (Mallinson 2014, pp. 239–244). The *Vasiṣṭhasaṁhitā* should not be confused with the *Yogavāsiṣṭha*, which is a different text.

Table 1
Comparison of the *Yogayājñavalkya, Vasiṣṭhasaṁhitā* and *Pādmasaṁhitā*.

***Yogayājñavalkya* (YY)**	***Vasiṣṭhasaṁhitā – Yogakāṇḍa* (VS)**	***Pādmasaṁhitā – Yogapāda* (PS)**
4.11b	2.8a identical to YY	2.4a identical to YY and VS
4.12a	2.8b identical to YY	2.4b minor difference cf. YY and VS
4.12b	2.8c almost identical to YY	–
4.13a	2.9a identical to YY	–
4.13b	2.9b almost identical to YY	–
4.14a	2.10a almost identical to YY	–
4.14b	–	cf. 2.7b
4.15a	–	–
4.15b	–	–
4.16a	2.11a similar to YY	2.8b almost identical to YY
4.16b	2.11b almost identical to YY	cf. 2.9a
4.17a	c.f. 2.12a	cf. 2.9b
4.17b	–	–
4.18a	2.12b almost identical to YY	–
4.18b	2.13a almost identical to YY	–
4.19a	2.13b almost identical to YY	–
4.19b	2.14a almost identical to YY	2.12b almost identical to YY
4.20a	2.14b identical to YY	–
4.20b	2.15a minor difference to YY	c.f. 2.13a
4.21a	2.15b almost identical to YY	2.13b identical to YY, almost identical to VS
4.21b	2.16a almost identical to YY	2.14a almost identical to YY and VS
–	2.16b	–
4.22a	c.f. 2.16c	2.14b very similar to YY
4.22b	c.f. 2.16c	2.15a almost identical to YY
4.23a	2.17a almost identical to YY	2.15b identical to YY, almost identical to VS
4.23b	2.17b minor difference to YY	2.16a similar to YY and VS (YY closer to VS than PS)
4.24a	2.18a almost identical to YY	2.16b almost identical to YY and VS
–	2.18b	–
4.24b	2.18c identical to YY	2.17a almost identical to YY and VS

performance of duties according to *varṇa* (caste) and *āśrama* (stage of life).[3] This emphasis would have appealed to Krishnamacharya's traditional tendencies.

Most scholars believe that the *Yogayājñavalkya* was written around the end of the period between the 10th and 14th centuries CE and that it borrowed more than half its verses from the *Vasiṣṭhasaṁhitā*, which was

3. Digambaji et al. (2005, pp. 1–2).

written around the 13th century CE. Balasubramanian disagrees, dating the *Yogayājñavalkya* earlier and arguing that the *Vasiṣṭhasaṁhitā* borrowed from it.[4] See the Appendix.

3.2 PĀDMASAṀHITĀ

For our purposes, the direction of borrowing between the *Yogayājñavalkya* and the *Vasiṣṭhasaṁhitā* is unimportant. More important is that some *Vasiṣṭhasaṁhitā* verses relating to *kuṇḍalinī* closely resemble equivalent verses in the earlier *Pādmasaṁhitā*, which is from a *Vaiṣṇava* tradition of temple priests: *Pāñcarātra.* It is not surprising that Krishnamacharya's teachings on *kuṇḍalinī* originate in *Pāñcarātra*, which profoundly influenced Krishnamacharya's own *Śrīvaiṣṇava* tradition – see Chapter 6.

Traditionally, there are 108 *Pāñcarātra* texts but Schrader lists 210, many of which are lost.[5] The ideal *Pāñcarātra Saṁhitā* contains four topics: *jñāna* (spiritual knowledge), *yoga*, *kriyā* (building temples and installing idols) and *carya* (rituals for worship and festivals). The *Pādmasaṁhitā* is divided in this way although the *kriyā* and *carya* chapters dominate, establishing a textual basis for temple building and worship.[6]

Pāñcarātra theology combines *Sāṁkhya*, *Bhāgavata* and *Vedānta.* It is replete with *Sāṁkhya* ideas and vocabulary,[7] reshaped with extra *tattva-s* to make it compatible with theistic *Bhāgavata*, forming '*Sāṃkhya* plus god'.[8] *Tantra* is also prominent. *Pāñcarātra* uses tantric and Vedic *mantra-s*, whose efficacy is increased using *nyāsa*, the placement of the hands at bodily locations where *mantra-s* are installed.[9] Some *Pāñcarātra* texts also discuss *kuṇḍalinī/kuṇḍalī. Pādmasaṁhitā yogapāda* 2.14–17 closely resembles *Yogayājñavalkya* 4.21–24, corresponding to *Vasiṣṭhasaṁhitā* 2.16–18. See all three columns of Table 1. The scholarly consensus is that the *Pādmasaṁhitā* predates both the *Yogayājñavalkya* and *Vasiṣṭhasaṁhitā* so it is the origin of the verses common to those texts.[10]

---

4. Balasubramanian (2017, pp. 28–36, 120).
5. Schrader (1916, pp. 6–12).
6. Sanderson (2009, p. 61 n.64). See Smith (1963) for detail on the *kriyā pāda* (chapter).
7. Kumar (2005, p. 136).
8. Connolly (1992, pp. 169–172). The direct quotation is from p.170.
9. Gonda (1977, p. 89). See Flood (2006, pp. 188–193) for an account of *mantra* and *nyāsa* in the *Jayākhyasaṁhitā* - another *Pāñcarātra* text.
10. See the Appendix. My investigation of the verses in common between the three texts in Table 1 confirms that the greatest similarity is between the *Yogayājñavalkya* and the

Mallinson and Singleton translate 2.13c–2.17b of the *Pādmasaṁhitā* as follows:

> Above and to the side of [the navel *cakra* in the middle of the bulb] is the place of Kuṇḍalī. (14–15) Taking the form of the eight constituents of matter (*prakṛti*), she is eightfold and coiled. Located all around the edge of the bulb, she constantly blocks the correct movement of the breath and the regular [functioning of] fire and so forth, and thus covers the opening of the aperture of Brahmā with her mouth. (16) And when, during yoga, she has risen because of the breath together with fire, she bursts forth into the void of the heart in the form of a snake, blazing brightly. (17) Then the breath travels through the breath aperture along the Suṣumnā.[11]

Here, *kuṇḍalinī* is described as 'a coiled obstruction that must be straightened out with heat in order to allow breath to rise up the central channel'. This 'seems to have been how the renowned twentieth-century yogi T. Krishnamacharya ... understood the nature and function of Kuṇḍalinī'.[12] I will first show how the *Pādmasaṁhitā's* teachings on *kuṇḍalinī* broadly support Krishnamacharya's position. I will then further examine the above verse, common to the *Pādmasaṁhitā*, *Vasiṣṭhasaṁhitā* and *Yogayājñavalkya*, highlighting a complication.

The *Pādmasaṁhitā* presents *kuṇḍalinī* within an elaborate philosophical and theological framework. Like the *Yogayājñavalkya*, *Pādmasaṁhitā yogapāda* 2.14 describes *kuṇḍalinī* as *aṣṭaprakṛti*, eight forms of *prakṛti*, which Schwarz-Linder lists as *mūlaprakṛti*, *buddhi*, *ahaṁkāra* and the five *tanmātra-s*.[13] T.K.V. Desikachar gives a different list: 'the five senses,

---

Vasiṣṭhasaṁhitā. Curiously though, five half-verses from the *Pādmasaṁhitā* (2.8b, 2.12b, 2.14b, 2.15a and 2.15b) seem closer to the *Yogayājñavalkya* than to the *Vasiṣṭhasaṁhitā*. This hints that the *Yogayājñavalkya* could predate the *Vasiṣṭhasaṁhitā*, contrary to most scholarly opinion. However, caution is merited. I have only inspected a fraction of the 269 verses that the *Yogayājñavalkya* and *Vasiṣṭhasaṁhitā* share. One would have to inspect all those verses in the various different manuscripts of each text to come to a firmer conclusion about the direction of borrowing.

11. Mallinson and Singleton (2017, p. 213). The brackets and their contents are in the original translation by Mallinson and Singleton. 'The bulb' refers to the *kanda*. *Kuṇḍalinī* and *kuṇḍalī* are often synonymous in tantric texts and those describing *haṭhayoga* (Goodall 2004, p. 110; Mallinson and Singleton 2017, p. 178).

12. Mallinson and Singleton (2017, pp. 179, 180, 490 n.21).

13. Schwarz-Linder (2014, p. 220).

mind, *ahamkāra* and *buddhi*'.[14] Mohan and Mohan substitute the five elements for the five senses, citing *Bhagavadgītā* 7.4,[15] which uses the phrase *bhinnā-prakṛtir-aṣṭadhā* (literally *prakṛti* divided eightfold). Mohan and Mohan's list agrees with what Krishnamacharya wrote in an essay.[16]

This equation of *kuṇḍalinī* with *prakṛti* enables the further equation of *kuṇḍalinī* with *māyā*. *Śvetāśvatara Upaniṣad* 4.10 states that 'one should know that Nature (Prakṛiti) is illusion (*māyā*), And that the Mighty Lord (*maheśvara*) is the illusion maker (*māyin*)'.[17] In the *Pādmasaṁhitā*, *kuṇḍalinī* is linked to *māyā* using *haṭhayoga* terms. The *kuṇḍalinī* lies sleeping, coiled like a snake and closing the entrance to the *suṣumnā*, which leads up to the *sahasrāra* and therefore to *Brahman*. As Schwarz-Linder explains,

> The author(s) of the *Pādmasaṃhitā* make use of this image in order to express their own idea about the character of hindrance on the way towards liberation pertaining to *prakṛti*: the latter, confining the soul within a psycho-physical material abode, hinders the union of *jīva* and *brahman*.[18]

Furthermore, by 'symbolizing *prakṛti*, *kuṇḍalinī* represents the material, psycho-physical support of the *jīva*', which can be manipulated by 'yogic practices aimed at overcoming her obstructive nature'.[19] When the *kuṇḍalinī* obstruction is removed, 'it is the *jīva* – not *kuṇḍalinī* – who, urged by the wind, ascends the *suṣumnā* and, by going back to his source – the Supreme Soul – eventually achieves union with the *brahman* beyond *brahmarandhra*'.[20]

This conception of *kuṇḍalinī* sits within a theology without *Śakti*. Instead, the *Pādmasaṁhitā* 'adjusts the notion of *kuṇḍalinī* to its creation theory'.[21] The Supreme Person (*Puruṣottama* = *Brahman*) emanates in three forms: the God Vāsudeva, individual *puruṣa-s* (selves) and *prakṛti*.[22] *Brahman* has the 'contradictory yet complementary divine functions of veiling and unveiling, bewildering the *jīva-s* by means of the illusory power of the divine

---

14. T.K.V. Desikachar (2000, p. 47).
15. Mohan and Mohan (2013, p. 34).
16. Jayaraman (2015, p. 217).
17. Translation – Hume (1931, p. 404). The brackets and their contents are part of Hume's translation.
18. Schwarz-Linder (2014, p. 221).
19. Schwarz-Linder (2014, pp. 220–221).
20. Schwarz-Linder (2014, p. 222).
21. Schwarz-Linder (2014, p. 220).
22. Schwarz-Linder (2014, p. 38).

māyā and revealing the salvific teaching which shows the path towards liberation'.[23] We will see below that such functions are delegated to *śakti-s* in another *Pāñcarātra* text, the *Ahirbudhnyasaṁhitā*.

The *Pādmasaṁhitā jñānapāda* elaborates on the connection between *māyā* and the *guṇa-s*:

> [Brahmā:] Which is the reason of the connection of man with *prakṛti?*
> O Bhagavān, disclose this mystery, [which is] difficult to be grasped for me. (5.1)
> [Śrī Bhagavān:] O Brahmā, this *māyā*, existing from eternity, imperishable, is the cause which connects man with the *prakṛti* formed by the *guṇa-s*. (5.2)
> [Brahmā:] Now, how might there be connection with or disjunction from these *guṇa-s?* (5.34ab)
> [Śrī Bhagavān:] ... these three *guṇa-s* occur and do not occur for man due to [his] connection with and disjunction from *māyā*. *Māyā*, never ceasing, eternal, constant, is based upon myself. (5.34c–5.35)[24]

The integration of *kuṇḍalinī* into the *Pādmasaṁhitā's* theology is incomplete. Schwarz-Linder argues that its descriptions of *kuṇḍalinī* and related concepts 'are inconsistent both in terms of their contents and of their position in the text of the *yogapāda*'. They 'appear as breaks within the main argumentation ... introduced by weak, or even absent, logical connection with the context in which they are inserted'.[25]

Schwarz-Linder further argues that there are *yoga*-related rituals in the *caryapāda* that involve the ascent of *jīva* from *nābhi* up the *suṣumnā* without mentioning *kuṇḍalinī*. This 'indicates that the notion of *kuṇḍalinī* - borrowed by the author(s) of the *Pādmasaṃhitā* from foreign sources and included in their vision of the subtle physiology by adapting it to their general views – has never been integrated into the yogic-ritual system of the *Pādmasaṃhitā*'.[26]

This leads to the question of what these 'foreign sources' are. On the one hand, the original *Pādmasaṁhitā* has been modified by interpolations and additions from outside of *Pāñcarātra*.[27] On the other hand, parts of the *yogapāda* contain ideas introduced from two earlier *Pāñcarātra*

23. Schwarz-Linder (2014, pp. 146–147).
24. Schwarz-Linder (2014, pp. 135–136).
25. Schwarz-Linder (2014, pp. 186–187).
26. Schwarz-Linder (2014, p. 223).
27. Schwarz-Linder (2014, p. 40).

texts: the *Ahirbudhnyasaṁhitā* and *Paramasaṁhitā*.[28] I will examine the *Ahirbudhnyasaṁhitā* later in this chapter before suggesting a possible origin of its ideas about *kuṇḍalinī*. First, though, I will examine a verse common to the *Yogayājñavalkya*, *Vasiṣṭhasaṁhitā* and *Pādmasaṁhitā* that complicates the picture of *kuṇḍalinī* as a stationary blockage.

We have seen that a passage of the *Yogayājñavalkya* can be traced to the *Pādmasaṁhitā*, which presents *kuṇḍalinī* as a blockage at *nābhi*. However, in the *Pādmasaṁhitā* extract translated by Mallinson and Singleton above, *kuṇḍalinī* rises to the heart. This does not sit easily with the teaching that *kuṇḍalinī* is a blockage only, but it does indeed seem to be Krishnamacharya's position. Krishnamacharya wrote that

> The practitioners of the limbs of Yoga by the strength of their practice of Prāṇayama and three Bandhas and mudrā make their Prāṇa pure. It moves along with the yogic fire. Unable to withstand the heat, Kuṇḍalinī which lies as if asleep becomes luminous. It starts hissing like a snake. Being hit by the hot Prāṇa Vāyu (heated by Yogic fire) it leaves it (sic) position and travels till the space of the heart (Hrdayaakasha).[29]

Kuṇḍalinī ascends to the *hṛdayākāśa* in *Yogayājñavalkya* 4.23–24, *Vasiṣṭhasaṁhitā* 2.18 and *Pādmasaṁhitā* 2.16. These verses are very similar and the versions of the *Yogayājñavalkya* that T.K.V. Desikachar and Mohan present are virtually identical. We can therefore directly compare their translations of the *Yogayājñavalkya* with the translations of the *Pādmasaṁhitā* by Schwarz-Linder, and by Mallinson and Singleton, and the translation of the *Vasiṣṭhasaṁhitā* by Digambaji et al..

Firstly, T.K.V. Desikachar translates *Yogayājñavalkya* 4.23 and 4.24 as follows:

> *Kuṇḍalini* blocks the opening of *brahmarandhra*. *Yogi-s*, through the power of *apānavāyu* and *jāṭharāgni*, **reduce** the *kuṇḍalini* (4.23).
> Then **the fire that resides twelve *aṅgula-s* above the navel in *hṛdaya***, with the help of *prāṇavāyu*, moves in the *suṣūmna* (4.24).[30]

---

28. Schwarz-Linder (2014, p. 194).
29. Krishnamacharya in Jayaraman (2015, p. 217).
30. T.K.V. Desikachar (2000, p. 49):

> mukhenaiva samāveṣṭya brahmarandhramukhaṁ tathā |
> yogakāle tvapānena prabodhaṁ yāti sāgninā || 4.23 ||
> sphurantī hṛdyākāśe nāgarūpā mahojjvalā |
> vāyurvāyusakhenaiva tato yāti suṣumnayā || 4.24 ||

I will challenge the parts I highlighted in bold. Most of T.K.V. Desikachar's translation of 4.23 gives a reasonably clear representation of the Sanskrit. However, his translation of *prabodhaṁ* as 'reduce', rather than awaken,[31] is incorrect.[32] Desikachar's translation of 4.24 is also problematic. There is nothing in the Sanskrit to indicate that the fire 'resides twelve *aṅgula-s* above the navel in *hṛdaya'*. Indeed, verse 4.14 states that in humans, fire exists in the *dehamadhya* (centre of the body) in the perineum. Verse 4.15 adds that it is in the centre of the belly only in birds.[33]

T.K.V. Desikachar also ignores some important words in the Sanskrit of 4.24. Firstly, *sphurantī* can be translated variously: darting/bounding/springing; 2. trembling/throbbing/quivering/palpitating/twitching/flashing/glittering/gleaming/twinkling/sparkling/shining/being brilliant/breaking forth/bursting out/becoming displayed or expanded/stretching.[34] T.K.V. Desikachar also ignores *nāga-rūpā*, literally 'snake-form', and *mahā-ujjvalā*, meaning 'of great splendour' or 'of great brightness'.[35] Taken together, Desikachar's omissions and mistranslations divert attention from a picture of *kuṇḍalinī* that is highly dynamic and luminous. *Kuṇḍalinī* rises from *nābhi* to the heart space. This is incompatible with T.K.V. Desikachar's note immediately below his mistranslation of the same verse: 'It is *prāṇa* with *jāṭharāgni* that moves in *suṣūmna*, not *kuṇḍalini*.'[36]

Mohan and Mohan's translation (see Table 2) slightly glosses over the issue of *kuṇḍalinī* rising to the heart by translating *hṛdaya-ākāśa* as 'internal space'. Whereas it could be argued that *hṛdaya* might mean the centre or core of the human body, this is imprecise. Schwarz-Linder,[37] like Mallinson and Singleton, translates *kuṇḍalinī* as rising to the 'cavity of the heart' – see Table 2.

T.K.V. Desikachar's mistranslation and Mohan's glossing over of this grey area both divert attention from aspects of this verse that could

31. A more literal translation of *prabodhaṁ yāti* would be 'goes [into] awakening' – Monier-Williams (1899, p. 683); Apte (1957, p. 1097); Macdonell (2001, p. 179).

32. Alwar (2018).

33. A partial explanation could be that after *kuṇḍalinī* awakens, *agni* rises, along with *prāṇa*, all the way to the crown of the head (*Yogayājñavalkya* 12.16), passing through the heart *en route* (*Yogayājñavalkya* 12.17). However, *agni* passing through the heart is not the same as *agni* residing there.

34. Monier-Williams (1899, p. 1270).

35. Monier-Williams (1899, p. 174).

36. T.K.V. Desikachar (2000, p. 49).

37. Schwarz-Linder (2014, p. 221).

Table 2

Five translations of equivalent verses in the *Yogayājñavalkya*, *Pādmasaṁhitā* and *Vasiṣṭhasaṁhita*.

T.K.V. Desikachar (2000, p. 49) – *Yogayājñavalkya* 4.23–24

mukhenaiva samāveṣṭya brahmarandhramukhaṁ tathā |
yogakāle tvapānena prabhodhaṁ yāti sāgninā | | 23 | | sphurantī hṛdyākaśe
nāgarūpā mahojjvalā | vāyurvāyusakhenaiva tato yāti suṣumnayā | | 24 | |

Kuṇḍalini blocks the opening of *brahmarandhra*. *Yogi-s*, through the power of *apānavāyu* and *jāṭharāgni*, reduce the *kuṇḍalini* (4.23). Then the fire that resides twelve *aṅgula-s* above the navel in *hṛdaya*, with the help of *prāṇavāyu*, moves in the *suṣūmna* (4.24).

Mohan and Mohan (2013, p. 35) – *Yogayājñavalkya* 4.23b–24

yogakāle tvapānena prabhodhaṁ yāti sāgninā | | 23b | | sphurantī hṛdyākaśe
nāgarūpā mahojjvalā | vāyurvāyusakhenaiva tato yāti suṣumṇayā | | 24 | |

It (the kuṇḍalinī) is awakened during the practice of yoga by the apāna [vāyu] along with the fire, throbbing, shining brightly in the form of a snake in the internal space (hṛdayākāśa). Then the prāṇa with (by the help of) agni goes [up] by the suṣumnā.

Mallinson and Singleton (2017, p. 213) – *Pādmasaṁhitā* 2.16

yoga kāle ca marutā sāgnin ā codita sāti |
sphuritā hṛdayākaśe nāgarūpā mahojvalā | |

And when, during yoga, she* has risen because of the breath together with fire, she bursts forth into the void of the heart in the form of a snake, blazing brightly.

Schwarz-Linder (2014, p. 221) – *Pādmasaṁhitā* 2.16

yoga kāle ca marutā sāgnin ā codita sāti |
sphuritā hṛdayākaśe nāgarūpā mahojvalā | |

At the time of *yoga*, being incited by the wind together with the fire, [she i.e. *kuṇḍalinī*]† is flashing in the cavity of the heart, having the form of a serpent of great brightness.

Digambaji et al. (2005, p. 31) – *Vasiṣṭhasaṁhitā* 2.18

sphurantī hṛdyākāśānnāgarūpā mahojjvalā |
yogināṁ hṛdyākaśe nṛtyantī nityamadhyamā |
vāyurvāyusakhenaiva tato yāti suṣumṇayā | | 2.18 | |

It‡ flashes forth from the space of heart, in the form of a cobra, starts dancing being very bright always in the space of heart of yogis, the vāyu (prāṇa) with the help of the heat of apana the it (sic) enters Suṣumṇā.

---

*'She' refers to kuṇḍalī in 2.13c and 2.14.

†The brackets and their contents are in Schwarz-Linder's original translation.

‡The first 'it' in this translation clearly refers to *kuṇḍalī* in 2.16. The *Vasiṣṭhasaṁhitā* contains an extra line, 2.18b, compared to the *Yogayājñavalkya* and the *Pādmasaṁhitā*. The extra words merely re-emphasize the mobile nature of *kuṇḍalī-kuṇḍalinī* and its movement in the heart.

undermine their description of *kuṇḍalinī* as a blockage only. It seems then that *kuṇḍalinī* is not only a static blockage. If *kuṇḍalinī* rises as far as the heart, can it not rise further up the *suṣumnā*, as in *Yogayājñavalkya* 12.17 (see Chapter 2)? Kausthub Desikachar tried to square this circle by applying some creative exegesis. In a footnote to his father's translation of Krishnamacharya's *Yogamakaranda*, he argued that

> Many *Haṭhayoga* texts ... make a mention of the awakening of the *Kuṇḍalinī*. However, what is of significance is actually, what happens after this. The *Haṭhayoga* texts mention clearly, that the coiled serpent called *Kuṇḍalinī*, blocks the flow of *Prāṇa*, into the central *Nāḍī*, the *Suṣumnā*. Once awake, the *Kuṇḍalinī*, enters the middle passage, only to be consumed by the *Jāṭharāgni*. When this happens, the *Prāṇa*, smoothly flows into this canal, all the way up to the last *Cakra*, and the *Yogin* is in harmony. So, it is quite clear that it is not the *Kuṇḍalinī* that rises all the way to the crown of the head, but *Prāṇa*.[38]

This argument stretches exegesis to the limits of plausibility. Nevertheless, it is consistent with Krishnamacharya's statement that *kuṇḍalinī* rises as far as the heart (see above). It could even help explain why T.K.V. Desikachar relocated *agni* from the perineum to the heart in his translation of *Yogayājñavalkya* 4.24: if *kuṇḍalinī* rises to the heart, the presence of fire there would enable *kuṇḍalinī* to be burned and destroyed. This does not explain, however, the appearance of *kuṇḍalinī* at the crown of the head in *Yogayājñavalkya* 12.17 (see the previous chapter), which is inconsistent with K. Desikachar's above argument.

---

38. K. Desikachar in Krishnamacharya (2011, p. 106 n.60). The passage quoted occurs as a footnote to a statement from Krishnamacharya about the 'benefits' of *jālandhara bandha mudrā* – 'The *Nāḍī-s* and *Cakra-s* are cleaned thoroughly, and it facilitates the awakening of the *Kuṇḍalinī*.' The title page of the English-language edition of Krishnamacharya's *Yogamakaranda* (Krishnamacharya 2011) states 'English Translation by *Śrī* TKV Desikachar with the assistance of *Śrī* ER Ramaswamy Iyengar' and 'Editing and additional notes by Dr. Kausthub Desikachar'. The quote I present is entirely in a footnote to the translation so it must have been written by K. Desikachar. Nevertheless, it does not seem to have been K. Desikachar's original idea. Paul Harvey also teaches that when *kuṇḍalinī* is awoken, the 'snake is moved and moves part way up the *suṣumnā*', where it is destroyed by *agni*. This 'leaves the royal highway open for *prāṇa* to move upwards' (Harvey 2011). Harvey was a long-term student of T.K.V. Desikachar but neither taught, nor was taught by, K. Desikachar. Hence, it seems that T.K.V. Desikachar taught this explanation to both Paul Harvey and K. Desikachar.

Instead of bending over backwards with such elaborate exegesis, it is more realistic to acknowledge that the *Yogayājñavalkya*, *Vasiṣṭhasaṁhitā* and *Pādmasaṁhitā* are inconsistent on *kuṇḍalinī*. Whereas most verses of these texts describe *kuṇḍalinī* as a blockage at (or near) *nābhi*, the above verses describe *kuṇḍalinī* as rising, at least to the 'heart space'. If Schwarz-Linder is correct that the author(s) of the *Pādmasaṁhitā* took teachings on *kuṇḍalinī* from earlier sources and recast them to fit with their theological framework, then perhaps these verses of the *Pādmasaṁhitā* contain a remnant, incompletely recast or edited, from a source text in which *kuṇḍalinī* was more mobile and not only a blockage.

3.3 AHIRBUDHNYASAṀHITĀ

Krishnamacharya cited another *Pāñcarātra* text, the *Ahirbudhnyasaṁhitā*.[39] It contains detailed *Pāñcarātra* theology but is even more inconsistent regarding *kuṇḍalinī*. I will first examine chapter 32, which supports Krishnamacharya's position and resembles parts of the *Pādmasaṁhitā*, *Yogayājñavalkya* and *Vasiṣṭhasaṁhitā*, presenting similar ideas with similar vocabulary and style but different phrasing. I will then survey the theology of the *Ahirbudhnyasaṁhitā* to examine how it may be compatible with Krishnamacharya's conception of *kuṇḍalinī*, before examining other sections presenting *kuṇḍalinī* in a way that contradicts Krishnamacharya. I will use Matsubara's translation of chapters 1 to 7 and my own translation of Rāmānujācārya's edition for the remainder.[40]

Chapter 32 states:

> The *kanda* (bulb) of *nāḍī-s* is said [to be] nine *aṅgula-s* above the penis. [It is] four *aṅgula-s* high and four *aṅgula-s* wide, egg-shaped [and] covered by fat, flesh, bone and blood (32.7–8a).[41] There (in the *kanda*) is *nābhi cakra*, [which has] twelve spokes. By it, the body is held. In it, *kuṇḍalī* dwells (32.8b–9a).[42]
>
> *Kuṇḍalī-vaiṣṇavī* is around the *cakra* (*nābhi*), which has eight openings, having wrapped around [it] with eight forms of *prakṛti*, [representing] enjoyment (*bhoga*). *[Kuṇḍalī-vaiṣṇavī]* covers up/closes the *brahmarandhra*

39. Krishnamacharya (2011, p. 42); Srivatsan (1997, p. 109).

40. Matsubara (1994); Rāmānujācārya (1916).

41. This resembles *Yogayājñavalkya* 4.16, *Vasiṣṭhasaṁhitā* 2.11–12a and *Pādmasaṁhitā* 2.8b–2.9a.

42. This resembles *Yogayājñavalkya* 4.18 and *Vasiṣṭhasaṁhitā* 2.12b–13a.

> in the *suṣumnā* with [her] mouth (32.11b–12).[43] Mounted on *prāṇa*, the *jīva* always moves within this *cakra* (*nābhi*), like a spider stays inside [its] web (32.22).[44]
>
> Of the five openings of *suṣumnā*, four are filled with blood; the central and excellent *Brahmarandhra* is shut/covered/closed (*pihitaṁ*) by *kuṇḍalī* (32.23). Having pierced the mouth of *kuṇḍalī* by means of *prāṇāyāma* (lit. 'with risen *prāṇāyāma*') and by *agni*, rest in the centre of *suṣumnā* (32.62).[45]

These verses are *prima facie* in agreement with the position that *kuṇḍalinī-kuṇḍalī* is a blockage only. Before further exploring the extent to which Krishnamacharya's position is supported by the *Ahirbudhnyasaṁhitā*, I will review the place of *śakti* within that text's theology, which differs from that of the *Pādmasaṁhitā*.

Firstly, *māyā* is equated on a cosmic level with *prakṛti*:

> First he, the all-pervading God, in a playful act made the names and forms of all. Then, having created (*sṛṣṭvā*) *prakṛti*, who has the nature of the three *guṇa-s*, who is known as illusion (*māyā*), and who assists in the divine play (*līlā*), Janārdana (Viṣṇu) delighted in her. And she, possessing 'this and that' *śakti*, pleases all living beings (*sarvāṇi bhutāni*), stretching in

43. This resembles *Yogayājñavalkya* 4.21–23, *Vasiṣṭhasaṁhitā* 2.15b–17 and *Pādmasaṁhitā* 2.13–15. In *Ahirbudhnyasaṁhitā* 32.11b–12, *kuṇḍalī* is synonymous with *vaiṣṇavī*. However, in *Yogayājñavalkya* 4.31, *vaiṣṇavī* is synonymous with the *suṣumnā*. *Bogha* could also mean the coil or hood of a snake (Apte 1957, p. 1212), i.e. the coil of *kuṇḍalī*, perhaps in an intentional double meaning.

44. This resembles *Yogayājñavalkya* 4.19, *Vasiṣṭhasaṁhitā* 2.14 and *Pādmasaṁhitā* 2.12b.

45.

> meḍhrānnavāṅgulādūrdhvaṁ nāḍīnāṁ kanda ucyate |
> caturaṅgulamutsedhaṁ caturaṅgulamāyatam || 32.7 ||
> aṇḍākāraṁ parivṛtaṁ medomāṁsāsthiśoṇitaiḥ |
> tatraiva nābhicakraṁ tu dvādaśāraṁ pratiṣṭitam || 32.8 ||
> śarīraṁ dhriyate yena tasminvasati kuṇḍalī | 32.9a |
> vartate paritaścakramaṣṭavakrā 'tha kuṇḍalī | 32.11b |
> aṣṭaprakṛtirūpeṇa bhogenāveṣṭya vaiṣṇavī |
> brahmarandhraṁ suṣumnāyāḥ pidadhāti mukhena vai || 32.12 ||
> prāṇārūḍho bhavejjīvaścakre 'sminbhramate sadā |
> ūrṇanābhiryathā tantupañjarāntarvyavasthitaḥ || 32.22 ||
> pañcarandhryāḥ suṣumnāyāścatvāro raktapūritāḥ |
> kuṇḍalyā pihitaṁ śaśvadbrahmarandhraṁ tu madhyamam || 33.23 ||
> prāṇāyāmotthitenaiva vāyunā sāgninā mukham |
> kuṇḍalyāstu vinirbhidya suṣumnāmadhyavartinā || 32.62 ||

her own mind (*dhiyām*), which is to be enjoyed. In that way, she exists for covering (*chādanāya*) the true nature (*svarūpa*) of the *jīva* (*jīvātman*) and *parā* (*paramātman*) (38.11–13).[46]

Chādanāya comes from the root *chad*, 'to cover', which recurs in other texts we will examine in later chapters. The *Ahirbudhnyasaṁhitā* uses *chad* to define *avidyā:*

> This great secret I tell you, so listen. By *avidyā*, *tattva*-knowledge of the true nature (*paraṁ rūpaṁ*) of these two, the *jīvātman* and *paramātman*, is covered (*saṁchādyate*, from *saṁ+chad*). But [the covering process] is reversed by mastery of *yoga* of the self [whereby] the highest knowledge arises (45.3–4).[47]

The individual-level *avidyā* described here correlates with the cosmic-level *prakṛti-māyā-śakti* described above in 38.11–13 as both accounts involve covering or obscuring. In other chapters of the *Ahirbudhnyasaṁhitā*, a specific part of *śakti* has this obscuring effect.

According to *Ahirbudhnyasaṁhitā* 3.4–5, 'the transcendent Brahman, ... Bhagavat, possesses the Śakti, which pervades Its whole being, just as the moon possesses moonlight'.[48] *Śakti* has two divisions: *kriyāśakti* and *bhūtiśakti*. *Bhūtiśakti*, just 'one [small] portion of this Goddess',[49] is the

---

46.

sa pūrvaṁ nāmarūpāṇi cakre sarvasya sarvagaḥ |
līlopakaraṇāṁ devaḥ prakṛtiṁ triguṇātmikām || 38.11 ||
māyāsaṁjñāṁ punaḥ sṛṣṭvā tayā reme janārdanaḥ |
sā tu sarvāṇi bhūtāni tattacchaktisamanvitā || 38.12 ||
modayantī ca tanvānā svasyāṁ bhogyadhiyaṁ [=dhiyām?] tathā |
vartate jīvaparayoḥ svarūpācchādanāya sā || 38.13 ||

Following Lidia Wojtczak's suggestion, in 38.13a, I propose to change *dhiyaṁ* (Rāmānujācārya 1916, p. 378) to *dhiyām*. This change makes grammatical sense as *dhiyām* is a feminine locative singular noun meaning 'mind' so it agrees with *svasyāṁ*, meaning 'in her own'. The change also makes conceptual sense as the mind is the agent of enjoyment in *Sāṁkhya-Yoga*.

47.

paramaṁ guhyametatte kathayāmi yathā śṛṇu |
avidyayā paraṁ rūpaṁ jīvātmaparamātmanoḥ || 45.3 ||
saṁchādyate tayostattvavedanaṁ tu nivartyate |
adhyātmayogādhigamātparaṁ jñānaṁ prajāyate || 45.4 ||

48. Translation – Matsubara (1994, pp. 183–184).
49. Matsubara (1994, p. 187).

material cause of the world.[50] *Bhūtiśakti* further subdivides threefold into *avyakta, kāla* and *puruṣa.*[51] At the start of evolution, *avyakta* is *mūlaprakṛti,* an undifferentiated phase of *prakṛti.*[52] *Kāla* is time, and *puruṣa* is 'the aggregate of all selves'.[53]

Śakti's active component is *kriyāśakti,* the instrumental cause of the world.[54] *Kriyāśakti* is '*śakti's* vibration in the form of will'.[55] It is Viṣṇu's discus weapon and is also called *sudarśana cakra,* literally 'wheel-beauteous-to-behold'.[56] Due to 'a spontaneous independent resolve' when *śakti* awakens, *bhūtiśakti* is set in motion by *sudarśana/kriyāśakti.*[57] The *guṇa-s* of *sattva, rajas* and *tamas* then evolve, producing a chain of *Sāṁkhya*-based *tattva-s,* including *buddhi, ahaṅkṛiti* (=*ahaṁkāra*), five *tanmātra-s,* eleven sense organs and five gross elements.[58]

This emanation process is only one of the five functions of *kriyāśakti.* One of the others can be compared to Krishnamacharya's notion of *kuṇḍalinī* as a blockage.

> That which is called the will [of God] is known as *sudarśana.* Despite being of infinite form, it appears fivefold (14.14) as the essence of creation (*sṛṣṭi*), steadying/preservation (*sthiti*), destruction (*antakāreṇa*), binding/suppression (*nigraha*) and favouring (*anugraha*). That *śakti* concealing/covering (*tirodhāna-karī*) is called *nigraha* (14.15).[59]

Nigraha can mean holding down, holding back, seizing, stopping, restraining, suppressing, contracting or closing.[60] These meanings are close

50. Schrader (1916, p. 31).
51. Matsubara (1994, p. 186).
52. Matsubara (1994, pp. 191–192).
53. Matsubara (1994, p. 220).
54. Schrader (1916, p. 31).
55. Matsubara (1994, pp. 218, 204).
56. Begley (1973, p. 2).
57. Matsubara (1994, p. 204).
58. Matsubara (1994, pp. 218–219).
59. *Ahirbudhnyasaṁhitā* 14.14–15 – my translation of Rāmānujācārya (1916, p. 124):

    saṁkalpo nāma yastasya sudarśanasamāhvyaḥ |
    satyapyanantarūpatve pañcadhā sa vijṛmbhate || 14.14 ||
    sṛṣṭisthityantakāreṇa nigrahānugrahātmanā |
    tirodhānakarī śaktiḥ sā nigrahasamāhvayā || 14.15 ||

60. Monier-Williams (1899, p. 546).

to blocking. Indeed, Kumar translates *nigraha* as 'obstruction'.[61] The *Ahirbudhnyasaṁhitā* elaborates on what is obscured:

> By herself, she (*nigrahaśakti*) causes a man['s] embodied consciousness (*jīva-saṁjña*) to be obscured (*tirobhāvayati*) with *karma*, covering form (*ākāra*), lordship (*aiśvarya*) and wisdom (*vijñāna*) (14.16). Synonyms [of *nigrahaśakti*] are said to be illusion (*māyā*), nescience (*avidyā*), great delusion (*mahā moha*), great gloom (*mahā tāmistra*), darkness (*tamas*), binding/bondage (*bandha*) and the 'knot of the heart' (*hṛd granthi*) (14.17).

Note the presence of *māyā*, *avidyā*, *moha* and binding, which are all sometimes represented by snakes – see Chapter 5. These verses show *nigrahaśakti* to be comparable to *kuṇḍalinī* in its role of blocking the entry of *prāṇa* into the *suṣumnā*, thereby obscuring the *ātman* by preventing it from ascending towards *Brahman*. The *Ahirbudhnyasaṁhitā* strengthens this link by mentioning *kleśa-s* (a theme I develop in Chapter 4):

> From the covering/obscuring (*tirodhāna*) of form (*ākāra*) [comes] atomicity (*aṇutva*) of the self (*puṁs*), it is proclaimed. From the concealment (*tirobhāva*) of lordship (*aiśvarya*), [comes that which] is known as impotence (*akiṁcit-karatā*) (14.18). From the complete shrinking of man's wisdom (*vijñāna*) [comes] nescience (*ajñatva*), it is said. The self (*pumān*) is covered/obscured/concealed (*tirohita*) by *śakti*, which is Viṣṇu's will taken form (14.19). They (*aṇutva*, *akiṁcit-karatā* and *ajñatva*) are also called *aṇu* (atomicity), *kiṁcit-kāra* (impotence – lit. 'doing little') and *kiṁcit jña* (lit. 'knowing little') [respectively]. [They] are called the three impurities (*mala-s*) or the three binds (*bandha-s*) by the wise (14.20). When one has thus reached a position of bondage (*bandha*) caused by *vaiṣṇavī*, the obscuring *śakti*, impurity (*mala*) accumulates (*samupacinvate*) due to nescience (*avidyā*), egotism (*asmitva*), desire (*rāga*) etc. (14.21). Afflicted (*kleśita*) by tormenting *kleśa-s* such as *avidyā*, one hastening towards (*anusaṁpatan*) the *āgama-s*, driven by the desire for obtaining (*prepsā*) and the desire[s] for discarding/abandoning (*jihāsa*) (14.22), for achieving the desired goal and for the destruction of undesirable [outcomes? desires?], the ardently desirous one (*lālasaḥ/kāmī*) performs action, giving rise to agreeable and disagreeable fruits (*phala*) (14.23). Therefore, one dwelling on the fruition of action experiences the bondage of mixed agreeable [and] disagreeable [results, such as] birth (in a caste) [and] long life, impelled (*coditaḥ*) by the law [of *karma*] (14.24). Pleasant and other (unpleasant) subtle impressions (*vāsana-s*) very slowly accumulate,

61. Kumar (1997, p. 24 n.8).

and this [is] the covering/veiling sequence (*tirodhāna-paraṁparā*) of *nigrahaśakti* (14.25).[62]

Nigrahaśakti's role of obscuring/covering the *ātman* is comparable to Krishnamacharya's conception of *kuṇḍalinī* blocking the flow of *prāṇa* and preventing the *jīvātman* from ascending to *Brahman*. This similarity prompts the question of whether *nigrahaśakti* can be equated with *kuṇḍalī*.

I present in a footnote an argument that *kuṇḍalī* can indeed be regarded as a manifestation of *nigrahaśakti*.[63] A weakness of the argument is that

---

62. *Ahirbudhnyasaṁhitā* 14.16–25 – my translation of Rāmānujācārya (1916, pp. 124–125):

pumāṁsaṁ jīvasaṁjñaṁ sā tirobhāvayati svayam |
ākāraiśvaryavijñānatirobhāvanakarmaṇā || 14.16 ||
māyā 'vidyā mahāmoho mahātāmistramityapi |
tamo bandho 'tha hṛdgranthiriti paryāyavācakāḥ || 14.17 ||
ākārasya tirodhānādaṇutvaṁ puṁsa iṣyate |
aiśvaryasya tirobhāvādakiṁcitkaratā smṛtā || 14.18 ||
puṁso vijñānasaṁkocādajñatvaṁ samudāhṛtam |
tirohitaḥ pumāñchaktyā viṣṇusaṁkalparūpayā || 14.19 ||
aṇuḥ kiṁcitkaraśceti kiṁcijjñaśceti kathyate |
malatrayamidaṁ proktaṁ bandhatrayamidaṁ budhaiḥ || 14.20 ||
tirobhāvanaśaktyaivaṁ vaiṣṇavyā bandhameyuṣaḥ |
avidyā 'smitvarāgādyā malaṁ samupacinvate || 14.21 ||
kliśyadbhiḥ kleśitaḥ kleśairavidyādibhirīdṛśaiḥ |
nunnaḥ prepsājihāsābhyāmāgamānanusaṁpatan || 14.22 ||
iṣṭārthaprāptaye 'niṣṭavidyātāya ca lālasaḥ |
karmatatkurute kāmī śubhāśubhaphalodayam || 14.23 ||
tataḥ karmavipākasthaḥ śubhāśubhavimiśritān |
jātyāyuranubandhānsa prāpnoti vidhicoditaḥ || 14.24 ||
sukhādivāsanāstāstāḥ saṁcinoti śanaiḥ śanaiḥ |
eṣā nigrahaśaktestu tirodhānaparaṁparā || 14.25 ||

Note that shortly after Śaṅkara's death, *Advaitavedānta* also began referring to *avidyā* as a *śakti* (Bartley 2002, p. 14). This resembles *nigrahaśakti* in the *Ahirbudhnyasaṁhitā*.

63. First, *Ahirbudhnyasaṁhitā* 16.55 (see below in the main text) refers to *kuṇḍalī* as *kuṇḍalī-śakti*, so it is a *śakti*. Second, *kuṇḍalī* is clearly not part of *bhūtiśakti* so it must be part of *kriyāśakti*. Third, the role of *kuṇḍalī* in blocking the rise of *prāṇa* in *Ahirbudhnyasaṁhitā* 32.7–12, 32.22–23 and 32.62 (see above in the main text) is inconsistent with *kriyāśakti's* other four manifestations: creation, steadying/preservation, destruction and favouring of the *ātman*. Fourth, in 32.11, *vaiṣṇavī* is synonymous with *kuṇḍalī* while in 14.20, *vaiṣṇavī* is synonymous with *nigraha*, 'the obscuring *śakti*'. Hence, it would seem that *kuṇḍalī* is synonymous with *nigrahaśakti*. Furthermore, *Ahirbudhnyasaṁhitā* 14.17 clearly equates *nigrahaśakti* with *avidyā* and 14.21 connects *nigrahaśakti* with three of the five *kleśa-s* listed in *Patañjali* 2.3: *avidyā*, *asmitva* (similar to *asmitā*) and *rāga*. I will also show later this chapter that *kriyāśakti* is equated to *kuṇḍalī* in *Ahirbudhnyasaṁhitā* chapter 16. These pieces of

it links terms from various sections of the text which may define them differently. It could be argued that because the *Ahirbudhnyasaṁhitā* does not explicitly equate *kuṇḍalī* and *nigrahaśakti*, linking these two concepts is an unsound inference. However, the writers of the text incompletely explain how *kuṇḍalī* fits within their theology. The connection exists, or seems to exist, but is implicit rather than explicit. Like the *Pādmasaṁhitā*, the *Ahirbudhnyasaṁhitā* reads like a draft in need of editing for coherence. I will now examine a contrasting section of the *Ahirbudhnyasaṁhitā* that is inconsistent with Krishnamacharya's conception of *kuṇḍalinī*.

Ahirbudhnyasaṁhitā chapter 16 is a mystical account of how *kriyāśakti/kuṇḍalī* is involved in the creation of sounds in the body. Sounds originate in *mūlādhāra* (16.57) and rise to *nābhi* (16.59), *hṛdabja* ('water-heart', 16.61) and to *kaṇṭha* (the throat, 16.64). 16.55 describes how *kuṇḍalī-śakti* expands/springs forth (*vi-jṛmbhate*) from *Viṣṇu* like a dancer (*naṭīva*). In 16.57–58a, she is mobile and not confined to *nābhi*:

> By such things as creation/pronunciation (*sṛṣṭi*), exhaling/voiding/relinquishing (*sarga*), aspiration/sending forth/letting go (*visarga*) and discharging (*visarjana*), she, the pure and tranquil one [*kuṇḍalī śakti*], rises from *mūlādhāra* (*mūlādhārāt samudyantī*) [and] meanders (*aṅkṣyantī*) via each of these *saṁskāra-s*, which are impure/inky (*nirañjanā*), with the *anuttara* sound 'a' (*samanuttaram*).[64]

Since the *saṁskāra-s* are impure or inky (*nirañjanā*), they are not purificatory rituals. They are more likely subliminal tendencies (as in *Patañjali* 2.15) or may represent impure *nāḍī-s* along which *kuṇḍalī* can move. *Sṛṣṭi*, *sarga*, *visarga* and *anusvāra/bindu* all refer to the pronunciation of sounds, although Schrader links *visarga* and *anusvāra/bindu* (in 16.66) to

---

evidence together suggest that the *kuṇḍalī* blockage in *Ahirbudhnyasaṁhitā* chapter 32 can be interpreted as equivalent to (or perhaps a manifestation of) *nigrahaśakti*, even though the link is not directly stated.

64. My translation of Rāmānujācārya (1916, p. 151)

> sṛṣṭiḥ sargo visargaśca visarjanamitīdṛśaiḥ |
> mūlādhārātsamudyantī sā śāntā sā nirañjanā || 16.57 ||
> aṅkṣyantī sā 'ñjanaistaistaiḥ saṁskāraiḥ samanuttaram |
> dṛṣṭidṛśyātmatāṁ prāpya śabdārthatvavivartinī || 16.58 ||
> paśyantī nāma nābhau sā yogadṛśyodayaṁ gatā |
> śaktiḥ sā vaiṣṇavī sattā mantramātā samañjanā || 16.59 ||

Dṛṣṭi in 16.58 means 'seeing' or 'the faculty of seeing' (Apte 1957, p. 832), i.e. 'sight' (Monier-Williams 1899, p. 492).

soma (moon) and *sūrya* (sun) respectively, and therefore to *iḍā* and *piṅgalā nāḍī-s.*[65]

Kuṇḍalī's initial location at *mūlādhāra* is inconsistent with other chapters of the *Ahirbudhnyasaṁhitā*, which locate it at or around *nābhi*. *Mūlādhāra's* association with sound could, however, explain why, according to both A.G. Mohan and T.K.V. Desikachar, Krishnamacharya taught that *nāda*, the internal unstruck sound, rises from there, even though their accounts do not link *nāda* to *kuṇḍalinī*. See Chapter 2.

In contrast, the following verses, 16.58b–16.59a, locate *kuṇḍalī* at *nābhi* in the next stage in the creation of sounds:

> Having reached (*prāpya*) the essence (*ātman*) of [the distinction between] seeing (*dṛṣṭi*) and the seen (*dṛśya*), she [who is] called *Paśyantī* [and] develops (*vi-vartinī*) the meaning of words in the navel 'goes into rising' due to yogic vision (*yoga-dṛśya-udayaṁ gatā*).

In *Patañjali* 2.17–2.24, *avidyā* causes the false identification of the seer (*draṣṭṛ*) and the seen (*dṛśya*). The distinction between those is the quintessential 'yogic vision'. There appears to be a similar distinction here between sight/seeing (*dṛṣṭi*) and the seen (*dṛśya*). *Paśyantī* is one of the 'four states of sound': *parā, paśyantī, madhyamā* and *vaikharī*.[66] In *Śaiva tantra-s*, these four stages are located at *mūlādhāra, nābhi, hṛdaya* and *kaṇṭha* respectively.[67] *Ahirbudhnyasaṁhitā* chapter 16 closely resembles *Śaiva* accounts of *kuṇḍalinī's* involvement in the production of sounds.[68]

Kuṇḍalī rises higher still. In *Ahirbudhnyasaṁhitā* 16.61, *kuṇḍalī*, humming (*ninadantī*) like a large black female bee (*bhṛṅgī*) in the water-heart (*hṛdabja*), goes into a state of widening/spreading/extending (*yāti vistṛtim*) related to a state of creation (*vivartana*) called 'powerful' (*samarthāhkyāṁ*). Then *kuṇḍalī/kriyāśakti* rises again. When she reaches the throat (*kaṇṭha*), there is first an exhalation/aspiration (*visargiṇī*) and, *kriyāśakti-kuṇḍalī* evolves into fourteen vowels, starting with the vowel 'a' (16.64).

Ahirbudhnyasaṁhitā 16.55 uses the term *kuṇḍalīśakti* and then 16.56 and 16.63 use *kriyāśakti* as a synonym for it. Furthermore, 16.59 equates *kriyāśakti* with 'that *śakti vaiṣṇavī*' (*śaktiḥ-sā-vaiṣṇavī*). Recall that 14.21–25 equates *vaiṣṇavī* with *nigrahaśakti*, while 32.11b–12 equate *vaiṣṇavī* with

65. Schrader (1916, p. 119).
66. Schrader (1916, p. 119); cf. Padoux (1990, pp. 83–84).
67. Padoux (1990, p. 146).
68. See Padoux (1990, pp. 86–165); Wallis (2013, pp. 163–174).

kuṇḍalī in its role as a blockage. Recall also that 14.14–15 lists five manifestations of *kriyāśakti*. In chapter 32, *kuṇḍalī* would seem to be *kriyāśakti* in the form of obscuration (*nigraha*). In chapter 16, the dynamic *kuṇḍalīśakti* is involved in the creation/pronunciation (*sṛṣṭi*) of sounds, so it could be regarded as *kriyāśakti* in the form of creation (*sṛṣṭi*) although that equation is not stated in the text.

Schrader correctly summarizes that the actively mobile *kuṇḍalinīśakti* in chapter 16 proceeds from *mūlādhāra* to the navel, heart and throat.[69] Recall K. Desikachar's argument that *kuṇḍalinī* 'enters the middle passage, only to be consumed by the *Jāṭharāgni*'.[70] K. Desikachar's exegesis could theoretically be extended to explain how *kuṇḍalī/kuṇḍalinī* can rise to the level of the throat as *jāṭharāgni* ascends along with *prāṇa* all the way along the *suṣumnā*.[71] *Agni* could therefore burn and destroy *kuṇḍalinī* at any point. Such an argument, however, would stretch exegesis beyond the limits of credibility. Moreover, Krishnamacharya himself was vague about what ultimately happens to *kuṇḍalinī* after it is 'awakened'. When asked the question 'What happens to the kuṇḍalini when the highest of Haṭhayoga is mastered?', Krishnamacharya replied 'It is not explained in our śāstras. It's (sic) position itself is disputed, i.e. where and what happens to the kuṇḍalini is not clearly mentioned in the śāstras.'[72] Rather than deploying K. Desikachar's far-fetched exegesis, it is more convincing to concede that the different chapters of the *Ahirbudhnyasaṁhitā* mentioning *kuṇḍalī* are inconsistent. This could be because the different chapters describe *kuṇḍalī* as different manifestations of *kriyāśakti*. It could also be because parts of the text have been borrowed from incompatible sources (see below).

Krishnamacharya argued against *kuṇḍalinī* being a form of *prāṇa*. He taught A.G. Mohan that 'There is only one śakti or energy in us and that is prāṇa. How can there be another śakti called kuṇḍalinī?'[73] Similarly, T.K.V. Desikachar states that 'If we say kuṇḍalinī is an energy that gives us truth, then we have to accept the fact that we have two energies in life, prāṇa

69. Schrader (1916, p. 119).
70. K. Desikachar in Krishnamacharya (2011, p. 106 n.60). See note 43 above.
71. *Yogayājñavalkya* 12.16.
72. Srivatsan (1997, p. 112).
73. Mohan and Mohan (2017, p. 91).

and kuṇḍalinī. ... What is meant by this? Many of these ideas, I'm sorry to say, are based on incorrect translations.'[74]

Contrary to Krishnamacharya's position, the third chapter of the *Ahirbudhnyasaṁhitā* indicates that *kuṇḍalinī* can indeed be regarded as a form of *prāṇa*. 3.29–30 defines *kriyāśakti* as 'Viṣṇu's will in the form of *prāṇa*'.[75] It is not surprising, therefore, that one of the names of *śakti* given in 3.15 is *prāṇa*. The inclusion of *kuṇḍalinī* as another name for *śakti* in the same list (3.12)[76] suggests that *kuṇḍalinī* is not just a blockage but can also be a form of *prāṇa*. A possible counter argument would be that *kuṇḍalinī* and *prāṇa* are two different manifestations of *kriyāśakti* and therefore *kuṇḍalinī* is not necessarily *prāṇa*. A more convincing explanation, however, is to acknowledge that ideas across different sections of the *Ahirbudhnyasaṁhitā* are inconsistent. This could be because *kuṇḍalī* takes different forms as two of the five manifestations of *kriyāśakti: sṛṣṭi* (creation) and *nigraha* (binding/covering). Alternatively, it could be because the text assimilated diverse accounts of *kuṇḍalinī* from sources external to *Pāñcarātra* and incompletely harmonized them.

Any such external sources probably included Kashmir Śaivism. According to *tantra* expert Alexis Sanderson, there are 'numerous indications' that Kashmir Śaivism contributed both linguistically and conceptually to the *Ahirbudhnyasaṁhitā*.[77] For example, the five manifestations of *sudarśana* (*sṛṣṭi, sthiti, antakāreṇa, nigraha* and *anugraha*) are virtually identical to Śiva's five functions (*kṛtya-s*) in Kashmir Śaivism, which also uses the term *kriyāśakti*.[78] The ritual system of *Pāñcarātra* is also 'remarkably close' to that of the *Śaiva Mantramārga* in, for example, the use of *maṇḍala* and *nyāsa* in worship, leading Sanderson to regard it as 'highly probable'

74. T.K.V. Desikachar (1980, p. 248). This argument notwithstanding, T.K.V. Desikachar's wife, Menaka Desikachar, emphasized to a *yoga* workshop that *prāṇa*, *apāna*, *vyāna*, *udāna* and *samāna* are merely five different forms of *prāṇa*, not separate categories (M. Desikachar 2011). I can see no reason why *kuṇḍalinī* cannot be regarded as an additional form of *prāṇa* - perhaps one produced when other *prāṇa-s* merge. Furthermore, it is ironic that T.K.V. Desikachar criticized 'incorrect translations' given that his translation of the *Yogayājñavalkya* is so inaccurate regarding *kuṇḍalinī*.

75. My translation of *prāṇarupo viṣṇoḥ saṁkalpaḥ* (from *Ahirbudhnyasaṁhitā* 3.30). See also Matsubara (1994, p. 186).

76. Matsubara (1994, pp. 184–186). In different sections, the *Ahirbudhnyasaṁhitā* uses both *kuṇḍalinī* and *kuṇḍalī*. These terms are frequently synonymous in tantric texts (Goodall 2004, p. 110) and those discussing *haṭhayoga* (Mallinson and Singleton 2017, p. 178).

77. Sanderson (2001, p. 36).

78. Sharma (2013, pp. 23–27); Wallis (2013, pp. 111–123).

that *Pāñcarātra* ritual borrowed from and reformed *Śaiva* sources.[79] Where *Śaiva* rituals are recycled in *Vaiṣṇava* texts, 'in some cases we find a degree of awkwardness that is consistent only with a clumsy attempt to adapt Śaiva materials to their new context'.[80] Similar awkwardness can be seen in *Pāñcarātra's* attempt to assimilate external ideas about *kuṇḍalī*. Sanderson further warns that incoherence and inconsistencies are

> a predictable consequence of the method of redaction itself, in which materials are taken over and edited to fit the context of a new revelation. It would have been only too easy to overlook the details in one part of the text that had become incongruous as the result of revision in another ... While there are some scriptures that are just as coherent as works of good scholarship claimed by authors as their own, there are others that are little better than careless bricolage.[81]

A possible *Śaiva* precursor of the *Pāñcarātra* teaching of *kuṇḍalī* as a blockage is the *Netratantra*. The text 'mentions a blockage called Kuṇḍalā',[82] where *kuṇḍalā* is the name of '*nirodhikā* ("the obstructing one")'.[83] Caution is merited, however. It is sometimes not easy to determine the origins of teachings common to *Pāñcarātra* and *Śaiva* traditions because ideas were transmitted both ways.[84]

Whatever the ultimate sources of the passages in the *Ahirbudhnyasaṁhitā*, they locate *kuṇḍalī* in different places, including *mūlādhāra* and *nābhi*. One passage describes *kuṇḍalī* rising to the heart and throat. Other passages indicate that *kuṇḍalinī* is a form of *prāṇa*. If Krishnamacharya had looked to the *Ahirbudhnyasaṁhitā* for evidence that *kuṇḍalī-kuṇḍalinī* is a blockage only and is located at *nābhi*, he would have had to be very selective and/or very critical.

We have seen that the *Ahirbudhnyasaṁhitā*, despite its inconsistencies, is a significant source of teachings describing *kuṇḍalī-kuṇḍalinī* as a blockage. However, not all *Pāñcarātra* texts contain that teaching. For example,

79. Sanderson (2009, pp. 61–62).
80. Sanderson (2009, p. 67).
81. Sanderson (2001, p. 41).
82. *Netratantra* 7.21 – Mallinson and Singleton (2017, p. 179).
83. Bäumer (2018, p. 21).
84. Padoux (1990, p. 67–68); Rastelli (forthcoming).

the *Īśvarasaṁhitā* does not.[85] In his *Yogamakaranda*, Krishnamacharya also cited the *Nāradapāñcarātrasaṁhitā*.[86] However, I agree with Bhandarkar that despite the text's name, it is not a *Pāñcarātra* work and seems closer to the tradition of Vallabha.[87] Its passages referring to *kuṇḍalinī* bear no relation to the *Pādmasaṁhitā* and *Ahirbudhnyasaṁhitā* and shed no light on Krishnamacharya's position. However, the teaching that *kuṇḍalinī* is only a blockage is indeed found in a rival sect of *Vaiṣṇava* temple priests: *Vaikhānasa*.

3.4 *VIMĀNĀRCANĀKALPASAṀHITĀ*

Wujastyk thought it likely that parts of the *Yogayājñavalkya* could be traced to a text of the *Vaikhānasa* sect: the *Vimānārcanākalpasaṁhitā*.[88] I will now examine the *Vimānārcanākalpasaṁhitā* for teachings on *kuṇḍalinī* that could have influenced both the author(s) of the *Yogayājñavalkya* and Krishnamacharya.

---

85. The *Īśvarasaṁhitā* emphasizes *dharma*, *artha* and *kāma* over *mokṣa* (Lakshmithathachar and Varadachari 2009, vol. 2 p.19 n.64) and contains only tangential references to *yoga*. For example, the incense holder used in worship is described as bearing the marks of a lotus and a wheel, which are symbolic of subtle anatomy. Terms which are frequently synonyms of *kuṇḍalinī* are used are used in its description but they do not mean a blockage to the *suṣumnā*:

> The wheel (of the vessel) is the heart of that wheel and the lotus is the cavity of the heart. Those spokes of the wheel are held to be the twelve veins. O brahmins! the small bells (there) are to be understood as the subtle veins the central power of which is comparable to the curved serpent with grey colour like that of smoke and has rent the cosmic egg and gone beyond it.
>
> (*Īśvarasaṁhitā* 3.43–45, translation – Lakshmithathachar and Varadachari 2009, vol. 2 p.89)

The phrase translated as 'central power ... curved serpent' is *madhyamā-śaktiḥ-bhujaṅga-kuṭilā*, the last three words of which are all sometimes synonyms of *kuṇḍalinī*. However, Lakshmithathachar and Varadachari (2009, vol. 2 p.89) note that the snake metaphor represents 'smoke rising from the vessel. The smoke moves across the sky in a zigzag manner presenting the appearance of a moving snake.' It does not describe *kuṇḍalinī* as a blockage. The same verses appear in *Pārameśvarasaṁhitā* 6.57b–60a – see Govindācārya (1953, p. 28).

86. Krishnamacharya (2011, p. 42). See Das (2005) and Vijnananand (2011).

87. Bhandarkar (1965, p. 41).

88. Wujastyk (2017, p. 164). This connection is not surprising as the *Vimānārcanākalpasaṁhitā* is the origin of teachings on *mayūrāsana* found in the *Vasiṣṭhasaṁhitā* (Mallinson 2014, pp. 227–228).

In the *Taittirīya Brāhmaṇa* and *Taittirīya Āraṇyaka*, the term *Vaikhānasa* described seers or sages. Later, it came to mean a tradition of South Indian temple priests. By the early 21st century, around 40 of the 108 *Vaiṣṇava* sacred sites were run by *Vaikhānasa-s.*[89]

Like *Pāñcarātra* texts, *Vaikhānasa Saṁhitā-s* focus on ritual, architecture and iconography. However, *Vaikhānasa-s* claim Vedic orthodoxy and, according to Rao, '*tāntrik* involvements ... are conspicuous by their absence'.[90] *Kuṇḍalinī*, however, is conspicuous by its presence:

> The penis is two *aṅgula-s* higher than the anus. Between them, one *aṅgula* [from both] is the centre of the body (*dehamadhya*).
>
> Nine *aṅgula-s* above that is the *kanda* place. It is four *aṅgula-s* high, is egg-shaped [and] is surrounded/covered (*bhūṣita*) with the seven *dhātu-s* (the 'tissues' of *Āyurveda*), such as skin etc. In the middle of the *kanda* is the navel (*nābhi*). In the navel is *nābhi cakra* [, which has] twelve spokes. There in the *cakra*, set in motion (*pracodita*) by merit (*puṇya*) and sin (*pāpa*), the *jīva*, mounted on *prāṇa*, moves around, just like a spider (*lūtika*) [moves around] the central place [of] a cobweb-cage.
>
> Meandering (*tiryaggatā*) to the side of *nābhi* [and] then going up, in the form of a snake coiled eight times, the eight-fold *prakṛti*, having obstructed the door with her lightning mouth (*vidyut mukha*), is coiled up (*kuṇḍalī-bhūtā*) [and] located at the side of the *kanda*. Having covered (*upagūhya*) with [her] hood the opening (*randhra*) of the *ātman's suṣumnā nāḍī*, known as the *Brahmarudra*, *kuṇḍalinī-śakti* abides, possessing the lustre of a circular jewel in her hood.[91]

---

89. Colas (2011, p. 603).
90. Rao (2005a, p. 59).
91. *Vimānārcanākalpasaṁhitā paṭala* 90 – my translation of Bhaṭṭācārya and Mādhavācārya (1998, pp. 313–314). The translation is grouped into three paragraphs, as below:

> (gudādārabhya dvyaṁgulādūrdhvaṁ meḍhraṁ meḍhrāttadvyaṁgulādhastānmadhyekāṁgulaṁ dehaḥ)
>
> (p.313, last paragraph).

The above text is given in brackets in both Bhaṭṭācārya and Mādhavācārya (1998, pp. 313) and Bhaṭṭācārya and Mādhavācārya (1926, p. 500). This indicates that the passage has been inserted by the editors but it is needed to understand what follows:

> tadūrdhve navāṁgulaṁkandasthānaṁ | caturaṁgulotsedhāyāmāṁ, tvagādi saptadhātubhirbhūṣitaṁ, (ma) aṇḍākṛtikaṁ, kandamadhye nābhiḥ nābhau (nābheḥ) dvādaśārayutaṁ cakraṁ, tatra cakre puṇyapāpapracoditastantupañcaramadhyastho lūtika iva prāṇārūḍhaḥ pravarttate (bhramati) jīvaḥ |
>
> (p.314, first paragraph)

This closely resembles the *Yogayājñavalkya* and *Vasiṣṭhasaṁhitā* in style, vocabulary and content. *Kuṇḍalinī* is also equated with the eight forms of *prakṛti* in *Yogayājñavalkya* 4.21, *Vasiṣṭhasaṁhitā* 2.16, *Pādmasaṁhitā* 2.14 and *Ahirbudhnyasaṁhitā* 32.12.

The central channel is 'the *ātman's suṣumnā nāḍī*' because the embodied *ātman* ascends along this channel before becoming disembodied at the crown. *Brahmarudra* is a synonym for *suṣumnā*. There is a South Asian folk belief that snakes keep precious jewels in their hoods – see Chapter 5. The *Vimānārcanākalpasaṁhitā* reflects this by likening the opening (*randhra*) of the *suṣumnā* to a shining jewel in a snake's hood.

The presence of *kuṇḍalinī* here undermines Rao's above claim that *Vaikhānasa* is purely Vedic. Indeed, the *Vaikhānasa-s* incorporated into their texts 'a considerable number of non-Vedic rites and practices'.[92] Although they did that 'only reluctantly and sparingly' compared to *Pāñcarātrin-s*, the resultant mix is 'so characteristic' of *Vaikhānasa*.[93] Other tantric elements adopted include *bīja mantra-s*, *nyāsa* and *maṇḍala-s*.[94]

The *Vimānārcanākalpasaṁhitā* built upon earlier teachings about raising *prāṇa*. As early as c.4th century CE, the *Vaikhānasasmārtasūtra* described a group of *yogi-s* called *Bhrūmadhyaga-s* who 'lead (the vital air) between the eyebrows, draw it through vital points, and effectuate its egress (*niṣkramaṇa*) to the point of dissolution or union of consciousness with the supreme being'.[95] Centuries later, the *Vimānārcanākalpasaṁhitā* may have re-described such practices using the term *kuṇḍalinī*, redefined as a blockage.

There are four reasons why Krishnamacharya would have respected *Vaikhānasa*. First, the tradition emphasizes Vedic orthodoxy and austerity,[96] which would have appealed to him. Second, the sect belongs to the

---

tasyordhve nābhau (bheḥ) tiryaggatā adha ūrdhve gatā aṣṭaprakṛtiraṣṭadhākuṭilā nāgarūpā vidyutmukhena* mūtra (ūrdhva) dvāraṁ saṁrudhya, kandapārśve sthitā kuṇḍalībhūtā sarpaphaṇāmaṇimaṁḍalaśriyamupeyuṣī kuṇḍalinīśaktiḥ ātmanaḥ phaṇena brahmarudrākhyaṁ suṣumnānāḍīrandhramupagūhya tiṣṭati |

(p.314, second paragraph)

*I accept Bhaṭṭācārya and Mādhavācārya's correction of *vidyut-mukhena* instead of *vidyā-mukhena*.

92. Gonda (1977, p. 141).
93. Gonda (1977, pp. 142, 147).
94. Gonda (1977, p. 143).
95. Colas (2011, p. 592).
96. Rao (2005a, p. 16).

Taittirīya branch of the Black *Yajurveda*,[97] as did Krishnamacharya.[98] Third, Krishnamacharya's parents 'were great devotees' at the temple at Tirupati,[99] which is run by *Vaikhānasa* priests.[100] Fourth, although Krishnamacharya's own *Śrīvaiṣṇava* tradition officially endorses *Pāñcarātra*, it also respects *Vaikhānasa*. For example, Vedāntadeśika, a *Śrīvaiṣṇava* theologian I will discuss in Chapter 6, regarded the validity of *Vaikhānasa* as equal to that of *Pāñcarātra*.[101]

Krishnamacharya would have had every opportunity to become familiar with *Vaikhānasa-s* and their texts. In the 1920s, modern *Vaikhānasa* associations were founded and numerous works were published.[102] Indeed, a *devanāgarī* edition of the *Vimānārcanākalpasaṁhitā* was published in 1926 in Madras.[103] The text remained an important reference for 20th century temple architects.[104] In the mid-1950s, two *Vaikhānasa* organizations were established in Madras and there were twelve *Vaikhānasa* temples there.[105]

Hence, Krishnamacharya would almost certainly have respected *Vaikhānasa* as a valid tradition closely related to his own. He would also have had every opportunity to read the *Vimānārcanākalpasaṁhitā*, which could have influenced his ideas on *kuṇḍalinī*.

97. Rao (2005a, pp. 1, 17); Varadachari (1982, p. 82).
98. Harvey (2017). This explains why the *Taittirīya Upaniṣad* is the most commonly taught *Upaniṣad* in this tradition - Harvey (2016); Roy (2013); Hersnack (2018, pp. 106–112). It also explains why the vast majority of the Vedic texts chanted by followers of T.K.V. Desikachar are from the *Taittirīya Saṁhitā*, *Brāhmaṇa*, *Āraṇyaka* and *Upaniṣad* (see Krishnamacharya Yoga Mandiram 2007).
99. Srivatsan (1997, p. 12).
100. Aiyangar (1940, pp. 265, 290).
101. Colas (2011, p. 595); Sridhar (2018, p. 52).
102. Colas (2011, p. 598).
103. Bhaṭṭācārya and Mādhavācārya (1926). The 1926 and 1998 texts had the same editors, V. Raghunāthacakravarti Bhaṭṭācārya and Setu Mādhavācārya, so the latter publication seems to be a reissue of the former. In the 1926 edition, Bhaṭṭācārya and Mādhavācārya are both described as grammar experts (*vyākaraṇa paṇḍita-s*) who purified (*śodhayitvā*) the text - i.e. edited it. Two other people are mentioned, Śrīsvāmīhāthīrāmajī and Śrī Prayāgadāsajī, which has led scholars to cite the 1926 version differently. Compare Mallinson and Singleton (2017, p. 452) with Wujastyk (2017, p. 184).
104. Colas (2011, p. 595).
105. Colas (2011, pp. 601, 597).

3.5 DIRECTIONS OF INFLUENCE

The transmission of ideas through the *Pāñcarātra* and *Vaikhānasa* texts is unclear. Colas tentatively dates the *Vimānārcanākalpasaṁhitā* to as early as the 9th century CE, while Mallinson dates it to *c.*9th–10th centuries CE.[106] Similarly, Mallinson and Singleton date the *Pādmasaṁhitā* to *c.*10th century CE, but Schwarz-Linder believes it is early 12th to late 13th century CE.[107] Schrader dated the *Ahirbudhnyasaṁhitā* to 300–800 CE.[108] However, Sanderson and Schwarz-Linder date it after *c.*1050 CE.[109] These three texts are therefore of a similar age. See the Appendix.

According to Colas, the *Vimānārcanākalpasaṁhitā* 'contains passages more or less comparable' to parts of the *Ahirbudhnyasaṁhitā* and *Vasiṣṭhasaṁhitā*.[110] Mallinson, traces an account of *mayūrāsana* back to the *Vimānārcanākalpasaṁhitā*, from which it was 'reworked' into the *Pādmasaṁhitā* and the *Ahirbudhnyasaṁhitā* before appearing in the *Vasiṣṭhasaṃhitā*.[111] However, it is not easy to date *Saṁhitā-s*, which 'often consist of various passages from different dates'.[112] In *Vaiṣṇava* circles, borrowing may have happened in more than one direction. It remains uncertain, therefore, where the description of *kuṇḍalinī* as a blockage first appeared.

Whatever the directions of copying on *kuṇḍalinī*, this chapter has traced Krishnamacharya's teachings on *kuṇḍalinī* to the *Pādmasaṁhitā*. It has also highlighted how that text, and subsequently the *Vasiṣṭhasaṁhitā* and *Yogayājñavalkya*, contain a verse in which *kuṇḍalinī* rises to the heart. This teaching, which Krishnamacharya accepted, can only be made to conform with the argument that *kuṇḍalinī* is only a blockage if some far-fetched exegesis is employed. We have also seen how the *Ahirbudhnyasaṁhitā* contains inconsistent accounts of *kuṇḍalinī* - some that portray it as a blockage, one that describes it rising as far as the throat, and another that seems to describe it as a form of *prāṇa*. If Krishnamacharya looked to the *Ahirbudhnyasaṁhitā* to support his position, he would have needed more than far-fetched exegesis: he would also have needed to be very

106. Colas (2010, p. 158); Mallinson (2014, p. 227); Mallinson (2011, p. 772).
107. Mallinson and Singleton (2017, p. 179); Schwarz-Linder (2014, p. 31).
108. Schrader (1916, pp. 97–99).
109. Sanderson (2001, p. 35); Schwarz-Linder (2014, p. 30).
110. Colas (2011, p. 594).
111. Mallinson (2014, pp. 227–228).
112. Rastelli (2011, p. 448).

selective about which parts of that text he accepted, rejected or radically reinterpreted.

This chapter has also shown how certain texts link *kuṇḍalinī* with *māyā* and *avidyā* via *aṣṭaprakṛti*. The next chapter examines a further connection between *kuṇḍalinī* and *avidyā* in the *Haṭhapradīpikā* and shows how Krishnamacharya used this connection to link *haṭhayoga* and the *Patañjali Yogadarśana*.

4

A union of *yoga*-s

Linking *haṭhayoga* and *Patañjali* via *kuṇḍalinī*

4.1 *HAṬHAPRADĪPIKĀ*

According to T.K.V. Desikachar, the *Haṭhapradīpikā* (=*Haṭhayogapradīpikā*) by Svātmārāma 'contains contradictory descriptions' of *kuṇḍalinī*.[1] There are indeed both internal inconsistencies within the text and inconsistencies with its *Jyotsnā* commentary by *Brahmānanda*.[2] The first inconsistency is the lack of clarity about what ascends the *suṣumnā*. In some verses, *prāṇa* and *apāna* rise:

> *Uḍḍīyāna bandha* is so named by *yogi-s* because when restrained by it in the *suṣumnā*, *prāṇa* flies up (3.55).
> Downward moving *apāna* is made to go upwards by forceful contraction. That [technique] is called *mūla bandha* by *yogi-s* (3.62).[3]

In other verses, however, *kuṇḍalinī* enters the *brahmanāḍī* (*suṣumnā*):

1. T.K.V. Desikachar (1995, p. 138).
2. Maheshananda and Sharma (2012).
3. My translation of the Sanskrit in Maheshananda and Sharma (2012, pp. 249, 254):

baddho yena suṣumnāyāṁ prāṇastūḍḍīyate yataḥ |
tasmāduḍḍīyanākhyo 'yaṁ yogibhiḥ samudāhṛtaḥ || 3.55 ||
adhogatimapānaṁ vai ūrdhvagaṁ kurute balāt |
ākuñcanena taṁ prāhurmūlabandhaṁ hi yoginaḥ || 3.62 ||

> Thus heated [by *prāṇa*, *apāna* and fire], the sleeping *kuṇḍalinī* is awoken. Like a snake hit with a stick, [it] hisses and straightens (3.68). Like [a snake] entering its burrow, [it] enters the *brahmanāḍī* (*suṣumnā*) (3.69a).[4]

Furthermore, *kuṇḍalinī śakti* ascends with great force:

> Having grasped hold of the tail [of the] sleeping snake, wake her up. Leaving sleep behind, that *śakti [kuṇḍalinī]* rises forcefully (*haṭhāt*) (3.111).[5]

Haṭhapradīpikā 3.69a and 3.111 would seem to contradict Krishnamacharya's position. Mohan acknowledges this. In notes taken in a lesson with Krishnamacharya, under verse 3.69 he wrote 'My guru differs with Svatmarama. Prāṇa moves up, not kuṇḍalinī.'[6] However, across the *Haṭhapradīpikā* as a whole, the contradiction is not so strong. In the context of techniques for moving *kuṇḍalinī* (*śakticālana*), verse 3.177 states that

> From being caused to move for two *muhūrta-s* (=96 minutes), that [*kuṇḍalī*] enters the *suṣumnā* [and] is drawn upwards somewhat (*kiñcit*).[7]

There is no statement in the *Haṭhapradīpikā* that *kuṇḍalinī* rises as far as the *sahasrāra*. Overall the text gives more support to Krishnamacharya's position that *kuṇḍalinī* is a blockage. *Haṭhapradīpikā* 3.177 above could have

---

4. My translation of the Sanskrit in Maheshananda and Sharma (2012, p. 258):

   tena kuṇḍalinī suptā santaptā samprabudhyate |
   daṇḍāhatā bhujaṅgīva niḥśvasya ṛjutāṁ vrajet || 3.68 ||
   bilaṁ praviṣṭeva tato brahmanāḍyantaraṁ vrajet | 3.69a |

5. My translation of the Sanskrit in Maheshananda and Sharma (2012, p. 291):

   pucche pragṛhya bhujagīṁ suptāmudbodhayecca tām |
   nidrāṁ vihāya sā śaktirūrdhvamuttiṣṭhate haṭhāt || 3.111 ||

   Haṭhāt could mean either 'due to great force' (indicating the use of forceful *haṭhayoga* techniques), or 'with great force'/'forcefully' (indicating a powerful energetic discharge). Mohan and Mohan (2017, p. 93) choose the latter: 'rises upwards with great force'. That choice is well justified. Birch (2011, p. 548) argues that 'the "force" of Haṭhayoga qualifies the effects of its techniques, rather than the effort required to perform them'. Birch translates *haṭhāt* in the second line of that verse accordingly: 'Free from sleep, [*Kuṇḍalinī*] *Śakti* rises up forcefully' (Birch 2011, p. 537).

6. Mohan and Mohan (2017, p. 81).
7. My translation of Maheshananda and Sharma (2012, p. 296):

   muhūrtadvayaparyantaṁ nirbhayaṁ cālanādasau |
   ūrdhvamākṛṣyate kiñcitsuṣumnāyāṁ samudgatā || 3.177 ||

informed the argument that the *kuṇḍalinī* rises part way along the *suṣumnā* only to be destroyed by *agni* (see previous chapter), although this is inconsistent with Krishnamacharya's above statement to Mohan that *kuṇḍalinī* does not 'move up'.

There is a more pronounced inconsistency between the *Haṭhapradīpikā* and Brahmānanda's *Jyotsnā* commentary on the location of *kuṇḍalinī*. *Haṭhapradīpikā* 3.106 describes *kuṇḍalinī* as blocking the entrance to the *suṣumnā* with her mouth, but it does not specify where that entrance is:[8]

> The great goddess (*kuṇḍalinī*) sleeps, having blocked with her mouth that door [to] the path which should be followed to the place of *Brahman* [, which is] without affliction.[9]

3.107a describes *kuṇḍalinī śakti* as 'sleeping above the *kanda*'.[10] Verse 3.113 locates the *kanda* one *vitasti* (=12 *aṅgula-s*) 'above' (*ūrdhvaṁ*), without specifying what it is above. Brahmānanda's commentary to that verse adds that the *kanda* is 12 *aṅgula-s* above the *mūlasthāna* 'root place' (probably either the anus or *mūlādhāra*) and is in the middle of the *mūlasthāna* and *nābhi*. This seems to give an intermediate position for the *kanda*, somewhere between *nābhi* and *mūlādhāra*. Given that the *kuṇḍalinī* sleeps 'above the *kanda*' (3.107 – see above), it sleeps closer to *nābhi* (roughly its position in the *Yogayājñavalkya*) than to *mūlādhāra*. However, Brahmānanda's commentary to 3.108 states that

> He who causes that *kuṇḍalī-śakti* to move, leading [it] upwards from *mūlādhāra*, is liberated due to turning away from the bondage of nescience.[11]

---

8. The *Yogayājñavalkya* locates the entrance at *nābhi*; many texts locate it at *mūlādhāra*.
9. My translation of the Sanskrit in Maheshananda and Sharma (2012, p. 288):

> yena margeṇa gantavyaṁ brahmasthānaṁ nirāmayam |
> mukhenācchādya taddvāraṁ prasuptā parameśvarī || 3.106 ||

10. My translation of the Sanskrit in Maheshananda and Sharma (2012, p. 288): kandordhve kuṇḍalīśaktiḥ suptā.
11. *Jyotsnā* 3.108 – My translation of the Sanskrit in Maheshananda and Sharma (2012, p. 289):

> sā kuṇḍalī śaktiryena puṁsa cālitā mūladhārādūrdhvaṁ nītā sa mukto jñānabandhānnivṛttaḥ |

The Sanskrit here could be missing an *avagraha* (a symbol of elision/ellipsis). *Jñānabandhānnivṛttaḥ* could be *'jñānabandhānnivṛttaḥ* (= *ajñānabandhānnivṛttaḥ*) as one is bound by nescience, not by knowledge. However, in *Śaiva tantra*, one is indeed bound by *incomplete* knowledge: *vidyā*, rather than *avidyā*, is one of the five veils (*kañcuka-s*) that

This quotation from Brahmānanda relocates *kuṇḍalinī* from above the *kanda* (as in *Haṭhapradīpikā* 3.107) to *mūlādhāra* and describes it as rising from there.

K. Desikachar addresses such inconsistencies by repeating the sort of elaborate exegesis he used previously.[12] K. Desikachar first acknowledges an apparent contradiction as there seem to be two 'entirely different location'[s] for *kuṇḍalinī*. *Haṭhapradīpikā* 3.107 describes *kuṇḍalinī* as 'sleeping above the *kanda*' but verse 3.106 locates it at the lower terminus of the *suṣumnā*, which K. Desikachar assumes to be 'exactly at the *Mūlādhāra*', perhaps following *Jyotsnā* 3.108. K. Desikachar attempts to explain the inconsistency:

> This may seem initially to be an error of contradiction. However, on closer analysis, it can be understood that the first part of *Śakti-cālana* is to move the *Kuṇḍalinī* from the *Mūlādhāra* region towards the *Kanda*. The next stage is when it is moved up towards *Jāṭharāgni*, where it is consumed by the fire and the path for *Prāṇa* in the central channel becomes free. So the idea is that *Kuṇḍalinī* is eventually destroyed, not that it goes all the way up to *Sahasrāra*.[13]

There are reasons to question this account. Firstly, notes from an essay by Krishnamacharya explicitly state that '*kuṇḍalinī* is found above and below *Nābhicakra*',[14] not at *mūlādhāra*, as K. Desikachar states. Krishnamacharya's statement follows the *Yogayājñavalkya* and is close to the location of above the *kanda* given in *Haṭhapradīpikā* 3.107.[15] Misleadingly, *Jyotsnā* 3.108, upon which K. Desikachar may be relying, locates *kuṇḍalinī* at *mūlādhāra*.

Speaking at a *yoga* workshop in 2012, K. Desikachar stressed how important the 19th century *Jyotsnā* is for understanding the *Haṭhapradīpikā*. He

unfold from *māyā* (Wallis 2013, pp. 135–136). Perhaps the translation could be 'turning away from the bondage of [incomplete] knowledge'.

12. K. Desikachar in Krishnamacharya (2011, p. 106 n.60) – see Chapter 3.

13. K. Desikachar (2016, p. 297 n.243), written as a footnote commentary on *Haṭhapradīpikā* 3.113. That verse describes the location of the *kanda*. The verse sits within the wider context of a collection of verses on *śakticālana* - techniques for awakening *kuṇḍalī*. The footnote actually mentions verses 4.107 and 4.106, but that is probably a minor accidental slip. K. Desikachar seems to have intended verses 3.107 and 3.106.

14. Jayaraman (2015, p. 217).

15. Krishnamacharya also states in the *Yogamakaranda* that *kuṇḍalinī* 'is lying dormant in the *Kanda-sthāna*' (Krishnamacharya 2011, p. 109). This seems to locate *kuṇḍalinī* at (or at least close to) *nābhi*, where it is located in the *Yogayājñavalkya* - see Chapter 2.

argued that its author, Brahmānanda, wrote at a time that was closer to that of the author of the *Haṭhapradīpikā*, Svātmārāma, and could therefore more fully understand and explain that text than we can in the 21st century.[16] Commentaries do frequently shed light on how a text is interpreted within a tradition but they can also be misleading. It is possible that Brahmānanda was biased by later *haṭha* texts, produced closer to his lifetime, which more frequently located *kuṇḍalinī* at *mūlādhāra*.[17] Indeed, Maheshananda and Sharma argue that Brahmānanda 'has given importance to the contemporary tradition while explaining the terms used'.[18] If we rely excessively on Brahmānanda's *Jyotsnā* without critically analysing it, we risk replacing our prejudices from the 21st century with Brahmānanda's prejudices from the 19th. This may hinder rather than help us understand a text compiled four or five centuries before the commentary.

There are also clear reasons why the *Haṭhapradīpikā* is internally inconsistent. *Haṭhapradīpikā* 1.3 states that

> The extremely compassionate Svātmārāma places the *Haṭhapradīpikā* [before those who], not knowing *rājayoga*, [are] confused in the darkness [of] many different opinions.[19]

The *Haṭhapradīpikā* aims to be a guide for the perplexed, reconciling different opinions and standardizing *haṭhayoga*. The result, however, is often incoherent, containing verses borrowed from various incompatible sources with insufficient editing to iron out the differences. Mallinson has shown that the *Haṭhapradīpikā* is a composite work that borrows verses from fifteen *Śaiva* and *Vaiṣṇava* texts. These include the *Vasiṣṭhasaṁhitā*, which

---

16. K. Desikachar (2012) said this in a direct response to a question that I asked in front of all participants in the workshop. I was listening intently and he spoke loudly and clearly. I am completely confident that I understood him perfectly and that I remember what he said accurately.
17. Mallinson and Singleton (2017, p. 178).
18. Maheshananda and Sharma (2012, p. 29).
19. My translation of the Sanskrit in Maheshananda and Sharma (2012, p. 51)

> bhrāntyā bahumatadhvānte rājayogamajānatām |
> haṭhapradīpikāṁ dhatte svātmārāmaḥ kṛpākaraḥ || 1.3 ||

Krishnamacharya equated *Rājayoga* and the *Yoga Sūtra* (*Patañjaliyogadarśan*). The *Jyotsnā* calls the text the *Haṭhapradīpikā* - not the *Haṭhayogapradīpikā*, as it is commonly called.

locates *kuṇḍalinī* at *nābhi*, and other texts which locate it at *mūlādhāra*.[20] Given the hybrid nature of the *Haṭhapradīpikā*, it is not surprising that it should contain what T.K.V. Desikachar calls 'contradictory descriptions' of *kuṇḍalinī*.[21]

There is mixed evidence about Krishnamacharya's approach to such contradictions. Regarding the position of the *kanda*, he tried to bridge the gap between inconsistent descriptions. Commenting on *Haṭhapradīpikā* 3.62 (see above), Krishnamacharya taught Mohan that 'All the nāḍī-s start from mūlādhāra (root of the pelvis). The mūlādhāra mentioned here may also be referred to as kanda.'[22] Krishnamacharya's statement appears to be a fudge between those texts that locate the base of the *nāḍī-s* at *mūlādhāra* and others, including the *Yogayājñavalkya*, that locate it some distance above at the *kanda/nābhi*.

There is, however, also evidence that Krishnamacharya not only identified inconsistent and incompatible statements in the *Haṭhapradīpikā*, but he also selectively rejected some of them. Indeed, he condemned Svātmārāma, the author of the *Haṭhapradīpikā*, as a donkey (*gadhā* in Hindi), partly because of 'the mix-up of some of the practices as well as the contradictions in this text'.[23] In notes taken during lessons with Krishnamacharya on the *Haṭhapradīpikā*, A.G. Mohan wrote 'My guru differs with Svatmarama. Prāṇa moves up, not kuṇḍalinī.'[24] Krishnamacharya added that 'The goal in haṭha-yoga is to burn the kuṇḍalinī; in śākta traditions, it is to awaken the kuṇḍalinī.'[25] 'We use prāṇa to move kuṇḍalinī. In the śākta tradition, kuṇḍalinī is considered the deity of prāṇa. The approach there is different.'[26]

Krishnamacharya's recognition that different conceptions of *kuṇḍalinī* are presented alongside each other in the *Haṭhapradīpikā* is consistent with Mallinson's finding that it is a composite text.[27] It is also a more convincing explanation than the elaborate exegesis given by K. Desikachar.[28]

---

20. Mallinson (2014)
21. T.K.V. Desikachar (1995, p. 138).
22. Mohan and Mohan (2017, p. 78).
23. Mohan (no date).
24. Mohan and Mohan (2017, p. 81).
25. Mohan and Mohan (2017, p. 58).
26. Mohan and Mohan (2017, p. 91). The tradition following Krishnamacharya also stresses the role of *agni* (fire) in moving *kuṇḍalinī*. See below in the main text.
27. Mallinson (2014).
28. K. Desikachar in Krishnamacharya (2011, p. 106 n.60); K. Desikachar (2016, p. 297 n.243).

4.2 KUṆḌALINĪ = AVIDYĀ

Despite their inconsistencies, the *Haṭhapradīpikā* and *Jyotsnā* provide an important clue for understanding Krishnamacharya's thinking on *kuṇḍalinī*. T.K.V. Desikachar stated that 'kuṇḍalinī is nothing but what has been called avidyā'.[29] A key justification for that is *Haṭhapradīpikā* 3.14:

> The great *kleśa-s* (afflictions), *doṣa-s* (imbalances of bodily humours), death etc. are reduced/destroyed by that [practice] and the best sages call [it] *mahāmudrā*.[30]

Brahmānanda specifies that the 'great *kleśa-s*' are *avidyā*, *asmitā*, *rāga*, *dveṣa* and *abhiniveśa* - nescience, 'am-ness', desire, aversion and fear of death, respectively. Brahmānanda thereby exactly reproduces the list of *kleśa-s* from *Patañjali* 2.3.[31]

The *Haṭhapradīpikā* is the only *haṭha* text I know of that connects *kuṇḍalinī* with *kleśa-s*. Brahmānanda's link with *Patañjali* is not universally accepted. Maheshananda and Sharma from the Kaivalyadhama Swami Kuvalayananda Marg, Lonavla, reject the link as 'inappropriate', arguing that Brahmānanda excessively explained technical vocabulary in the *Haṭhapradīpikā* in terms of *Patañjali*. Instead, Maheshananda and Sharma interpret the *mahākleśa-s* as the five diseases listed three verses later in *Haṭhapradīpikā* 3.17: 'tuberculosis, leprosy, constipation, tumor, indigestion etc.'.[32] Paul Harvey, a long-term student of T.K.V. Desikachar, is unconvinced by their argument, countering that the term *kleśa* is never used elsewhere to indicate a disease.[33]

The link between *kuṇḍalinī* and the *kleśa-s* is important for Krishnamacharya's followers. Some students of T.K.V. Desikachar even generalize the connection to all *mudrā-s*. K. Desikachar claimed that *mudrā* is by definition 'that which removes the *kleśa-s*' while according to Colin

---

29. T.K.V. Desikachar (1980, p. 244).

30. My translation of the Sanskrit in Maheshananda and Sharma (2012, p. 216):

    mahākleśādayo doṣāḥ kṣīyante maraṇādayaḥ |
    mahāmudrām ca tenaiva vadanti vibudhottamāḥ || 3.14 ||

31. Krishnamacharya commented on this verse that 'Mudrā-s are the indirect cause of these results. When the mind becomes clear and steady through these practices, the kleśa-s will diminish. The text presents indirect causes as direct causes in many verses' (Mohan and Mohan 2017, p. 63).

32. Maheshananda and Sharma (2012, pp. 31–32).

33. Harvey (2020).

Dunsmuir, Krishnamacharya defined *mudrā* as 'that which burns *kleśa*'.[34] Harvey, however, points out that these statements only apply to *haṭha mudrā-s* (which influence *prāṇa* and *agni*), not *rāja mudrā-s* (which influence *saṁskāra* and *vāsana*).[35] *Haṭhayoga mudrā-s* include *uḍḍīyāna-*, *mūla-* and *jālandhara-bandha-s* and *mahāmudrā*, which is mainly practised after *āsana-s* and before *prāṇāyāma*. *Rājayoga mudrā-s* include *cinmudrā*, *nyāsa* and *jihvā bandha*, which is used for 'sustaining sensitivity of attention and subtle awareness'. These *rājayoga mudrā-s* are mainly used in *prāṇāyāma*, chanting and *dhāraṇā*.[36] *Haṭhapradīpikā* 3.22–23 mentions *jihvā bandha* as an alternative to *jālandhara bandha*. *Jihvā bandha* 'stops the upward movement [of the prāṇa] through all the nāḍī-s [except suṣumnā]'.[37] Harvey's classification of *nyāsa* and *jihvā bandha* as *rājayoga* effectively redeploys these originally *haṭha* or tantric techniques into a *Patañjali*-based framework. Harvey explained that *jihvā bandha* can be either a *haṭhayoga* or *rājayoga mudrā*. *Tantra* is itself a meditational process, he added, so it cannot easily be separated from *rājayoga*,[38] which for Krishnamacharya was *Patañjali* – see below.

According to T.K.V. Desikachar, the three main *haṭhayoga bandha-s* 'are an attempt to direct the fire or heat of the body in order to remove the kuṇḍalinī bit by bit'.[39] More specifically, 'Uḍḍīyana bandha brings the apāna up towards the fire ... we use mūla bandha to keep it near the fire' and we use *jālandhara bandha* to 'make the pipeline straight' (keep the spine erect), thereby 'keeping the draft in line with the fire'.[40] These *bandha-s*, which Krishnamacharya taught in *prāṇāyāma*, *āsana* and *mahāmudrā*, while not mentioned in the *Yogayājñavalkya*, are in line with that text's definition of *Prāṇāyāma* as 'the joining of *prāṇa* with *apāna*'.[41] This verse was

34. K. Desikachar (2012); Dunsmuir (2015).

35. Harvey (2020).

36. Harvey (2011).

37. Translation – Mohan and Mohan (2017, p. 65).

38. Harvey (2020).

39. T.K.V. Desikachar (1980, p. 244).

40. T.K.V. Desikachar (1980, p. 195). Note the very realist language.

41. My translation of *prāṇāpānasamāyogaḥ prāṇāyāma from Yogayājñavalkya* 6.2. The indeclinable *samā* means 'with' or 'together with' (Apte 1957, p. 1632). Mohan and Mohan's (2013, p. 54) translation 'balancing prāṇa and apāna' and Kaminoff's (2017) 'the balanced joining of the in-breath and the out-breath' both seem to misread *samā* as *sama*, which can mean 'identical', 'equal' or 'even' (Apte 1957, p. 1628), i.e. balanced. T.K.V. Desikachar (2000, p. 75) avoids this problem but his translation, '*Prāṇāyāma* is the meeting of *Prāṇa* and *Apāna*', does not indicate joining. Teachers in the broad tradition frequently link this

'key to Krishnamacharya's teachings' not just for *prāṇāyāma*, but also for *bandha-s* and for correct breathing pattern in *āsana-s*.[42] Claude Maréchal, a long-term student of T.K.V. Desikachar, elaborates:

> As the text [*Yogayājñavalkya* 6.2] indicates, the inhaled breath must be brought to meet with the exhaled breath. Krishnamacharya stipulates how to correctly use the thoracic, dorsal and diaphragm musculature in the work of inhalation in order to feel it as a movement descending towards the epigastric region. Likewise for exhalation, the Professor [Krishnamacharya] explains how to employ the abdominals with a view to instigating the sensation of an ascending movement towards the epigastric region. Beginning from these principles, all of the technology of *pranayama* is designed, ordered, justified, and acquires its coherence. In this perfect edifice, the *bandhas* naturally find their place in serving the union of *prana* and *apana* vayus.[43]

According to Kaminoff, by equating *kuṇḍalinī* with *avidyā* and by emphasizing the role of *bandha-s* and *prāṇāyāma* in reducing *kuṇḍalinī/avidyā*, Krishnamacharya produced a 'wonderful integration' of *haṭhayoga* practices and the psychological framework of *Patañjali's yogadarśan*.[44] Krishnamacharya also gave a *Patañjali*-based explanation of how one of the *kleśa-s* is reduced by *bandha-s*. Commentating on *Haṭhapradīpikā* 3.3, he explained that

> 'Kālasya vañcanam' is translated as 'death is deceived.' It means that the fear of death recedes. How does this happen? The practice of prāṇāyāma with the bandha-s leads to the realization that 'I am not the body.' The instinctive survival fear – abhiniveśa kleśa as described in Yoga Sūtra II.9 – is diminished.[45]

Hence, Krishnamacharya interpreted *haṭhayoga* in terms of *Patañjali*.

Yogayājñavalkya verse to *Bhagavadgītā* 4.29: 'Some offer inhalation into exhalation, And others exhalation into inhalation, Restraining the path of inhalation and exhalation, Intent on control of the vital breath', translation – Sargeant (1994, p. 229).

42. Kaminoff (2016).

43. Maréchal (no date), with my additions in brackets.

44. Kaminoff (2016). Leslie Kaminoff was taught by T.K.V. Desikachar from 1988 (Kaminoff 2016).

45. Mohan and Mohan (2017, p. 59).

Kaminoff teaches the 'directional breathing' pattern outlined above by Maréchal using a *tantra*-based process that maps textual concepts onto the body. Kaminoff achieves this mapping via a self-devised *nyāsa* sequence to accompany a chant he was taught by T.K.V. Desikachar:

Om namo pranayá
Pranaya nama om
Pranaya swahä
Om namo apanayá
Apanaya nama om
Apanaya swahä
Om swahä
Haríḥ om[46]

During the chanting, hand *mudrā-s* are used to touch the front of the body and show how *prāṇa* moves down and *apāna* moves up, converging in the abdominal area. Kaminoff's process of visualization, chanting *mantra-s* and placing the hands in *nyāsa* is an innovative contemporary development of the tantric tendency that Flood calls 'an entextualisation of the body'. This is 'part of the practitioner's aligning of himself with tradition and part of the construction of his body in tradition-specific ways to attain the tradition-specific goal'.[47] The text here being 'embodied' is *Yogayājñavalkya* 6.2, and the 'tradition-specific goal' is the meeting of *prāṇa* and *apāna* in the abdomen.

Although Kaminoff did not mention *kuṇḍalinī* in connection with this practice, the abdominal location for the meeting of *prāṇa* and *apāna* corresponds with Krishnamacharya's location of *kuṇḍalinī* at *nābhi*. It is taught in the tradition that when *kuṇḍalinī* is awakened, *prāṇa* and *apāna* merge, enter the *suṣumnā* and ascend.[48] In the *Yogayājñavalkya*, *kuṇḍalinī* covers the lower entrance of the *suṣumnā* at *nābhi*, so if we follow that text, there is some logic to converging *prāṇa* and *apāna* there. However, *agni* (fire/heat) is required to cause *prāṇa* and *apāna* to merge.[49] If *agni* is located in the perineum, as in the *Yogayājñavalkya*, *Vasiṣṭhasaṁhitā*, *Pādmasaṁhitā*,

46. Kaminoff (2016), verbatim from the class handout.
47. Flood (2006, p. 162).
48. Sathish (2004).
49. Harvey (2020).

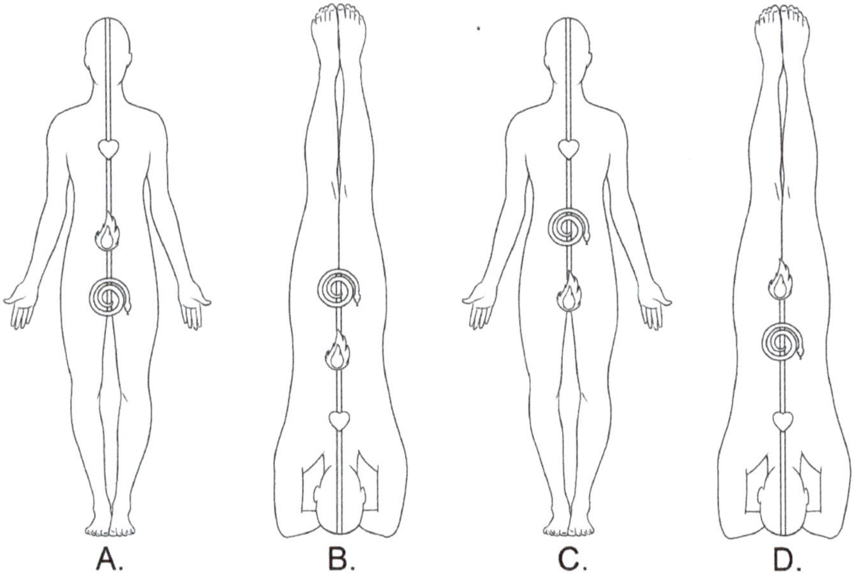

Figure 1
The locations of *kuṇḍalinī* and *agni* in upright postures and inversions.

Ahirbudhnyasaṁhitā, *Gorakṣaśataka* and *Gorakṣapaddhati*,[50] it is hard to see how it could provide the heat necessary for the merging of *prāṇa* and *apāna* in the abdomen. See Figure 1C. Hence, followers of Krishnamacharya

50. *Yogayājñavalkya* 4.11b and 4.14. The *Yogayājñavalkya* and *Vasiṣṭhasaṁhitā* share several verses on the *dehamadhya* - see Table 1 in Chapter 3. The *Pādmasaṁhitā* shares a minority of these verses and its overall description is similar to those in the *Yogayājñavalkya* and *Vasiṣṭhasaṁhitā:*

> In the *dehamadhya* (the centre of the body) is a place of flame, splendid [like] molten gold. [It is] triangular in two-footed animals (including humans), rectangular in quadrupeds, round in creatures moving in the air, hexagonal in water-born creatures, octagonal in sweat-producing creatures (insects and vermin), and in it [is] a bright flame (2.4–2.5). In humans, [the *dehamadhya* is] two *aṅgula-s* above the anus, below the penis, on the left. [It is] in the middle of the penis in quadrupeds (2.7).

Pādmasaṁhitā 2.4, 2.5 and 2.7 – my translation of Padmanabhan and Sampath (1974, p. 40):

> dehamadhye śikhisthānaṁ taptajāmbūnadaprabham |
> trikoṇaṁ dvipadāmanyaccaturaśraṁ catuṣpadām || 2.4 ||
> vṛttaṁ vihaṅgamānāṁ tu ṣaḍaśraṁ jalajanmanāṁ |
> aṣṭāśraṁ svedajānāṁ tu tasmin dīpavadujjvalaḥ || 2.5 ||
> apānāt dvayaṅgulādūrdhvaṁ adho meḍhrasya vāmataḥ |
> dehamadhyaṁ manuṣyāṇāṁ meḍhramadhyaṁ catuṣpadāṁ || 2.7 ||

advocate inverted postures, combined with *mudrā-s* and *bandha-s*, to provide the necessary heat.

4.3 INVERSION AND *KUṆḌALINĪ*

T.K.V. Desikachar, Srivatsa Ramaswami and A.G. Mohan all describe how inverted postures, *mudrā-s* and *bandha-s* can be practised. However, the three students of Krishnamacharya give different explanations of how these practices work.

Srivatsa Ramaswami gave his explanation in an online course on the *Yogayājñavalkya*. His account of inversions located *kuṇḍalinī* at *nābhi* and *agni* in the perineum, as in the *Yogayājñavalkya*, although that text includes no inversions, *bandha-s* or *mudrā-s*. According to Ramaswami, when the body is inverted in a headstand, gravity takes the *agnisthāna*, located two inches below the penis, downwards towards the *apāna*, which is thereby heated. *Mūla bandha* and *uḍḍīyāna bandha* are then applied to move the heated *apānasthāna* towards *kuṇḍalinī* at *nābhi*:

> Because you are able to bring *agni* and *apāna* closer together by getting into headstand, the position of the fire goes further down (i.e. towards the navel), moves closer and closer to the *apāna* and *apāna vāyu* gets more warm, heated. And then you pull the pelvic muscles upwards (i.e. towards the navel), then it is able to reach the position of *kuṇḍalinī*, and *kuṇḍalinī* immediately feels the heat of the hot *apāna vāyu* and is supposed to be aroused ... [51]

Ahirbudhnyasaṁhitā 32.5–6 contains a very similar account: see Schwarz-Linder (2014, pp. 211–212). Despite not using the term *dehamadhya*, the *Gorakṣaśataka* and *Gorakṣapaddhati* share a very similar verse:

> Situated below the penis is the triangular city of fire, flashing forth like lightning bolts and resembling molten gold.
>
> (*Gorakṣapaddhati* 1.20, translation – Feuerstein 1998, pp. 535, 587 n.24)

The equivalent in the *Gorakṣaśataka* is verse 1.20 – See Brzezinski (2015, p. 175).

51. Ramaswami (2020). Ramaswami made these comments in an online course on the *Yogayājñavalkya*, which I did not attend myself. This account relies on information supplied by Dr Karin Horowitz, who did attend and who re-listened to the relevant sections online several times after the course, taking detailed notes which she showed me. The words inserted in brackets are my own interpretations to clarify possible confusion between up and down directions in Ramaswami's description of what happens in an inverted body.

For Ramaswami, therefore, inversions are used to take *agni* from the perineum towards *apāna* in the abdomen and towards *kuṇḍalinī* at the navel: see Figure 1D. Conversely, in the accounts by T.K.V. Desikachar and his students, inversions are used to take *agni* from the belly towards *kuṇḍalinī* at *mūlādhāra.* In T.K.V. Desikachar's teaching, the positions of *kuṇḍalinī* and *agni* are reversed compared to those given in the *Yogayājñavalkya. Kuṇḍalinī* is relocated to *mūlādhāra* and *agni* is relocated to the abdomen as *jāṭharāgni* – 'the digestive fire of the stomach'.[52] See Figure 1A,B.

T.K.V. Desikachar's dual relocation of *kuṇḍalinī* and *agni* could have been inspired by the *Jyotsnā.* Commenting on *Haṭhapradīpikā* 3.66, the *Jyotsnā* quotes verses 4.11b–13a from the *Yogayājñavalkya,* which describe the *dehamadhya.* It thereby effectively equates the triangular *dehamadhya* of the *Yogayājñavalkya* with the triangular *vahnimaṇḍala* of the *Haṭhapradīpikā,* which the *Jyotsnā* locates 'below the navel'. By not quoting *Yogayājñavalkya* 4.14, which locates the *dehamadhya* in the perineum, the *Jyotsnā* blurs the differences between the two texts. We have already seen that *Jyotsnā* 3.108 locates *kuṇḍalinī* at *mūlādhāra* so Brahmānanda effectively swaps the positions of *agni* and *kuṇḍalinī* found in the *Yogayājñavalkya.*

Positioning *agni* in the abdomen as *jāṭharāgni* could be said to facilitate the hot merging of *prāṇa* and *apāna* there by the directional breathing that the tradition teaches. However, the merged *prāṇa-apāna* along with *agni* would then have to descend to *mūlādhāra* and dislodge *kuṇḍalinī* from covering the mouth of the *suṣumnā* there before they could enter the *suṣumnā* and ascend it. T.K.V. Desikachar and his students teach that this process is facilitated by using inversions.

Diagrams used by Kaminoff in his workshops show how in an upright posture, with the head above the body, the flame of *agni* in the abdomen

---

52. Apte (1957, p. 733). An alternative spelling is *jaṭharāgni* (Apte 1957, p. 724). As far as I am aware, no students of T.K.V. Desikachar teach in line with the texts that locate fire in the perineum. They all locate *agni* in the belly. This location for *agni* seems to have first arisen in a Buddhist text that I have never heard quoted by followers of T.K.V. Desikachar: the *Amṛtasiddhi.* Verses 5.1 and 5.2 use the term *vahni* rather than *jāṭharāgni* but locate fire in the belly: 'Endowed with ten digits, in the middle of the sphere of the sun in the region of the stomach dwells fire, which digests food. Fire is the sun; the sun is fire. The two look the same [but] differ subtly.' Translation – Mallinson (2020, p. 414). According to Mallinson (2020, p. 413), 'The *Amṛtasiddhi* is the first text to relocate to the body the old tantric triad of sun, moon and fire. The idea of a moon in the skull dripping *amṛta* is found in many earlier tantric works, but that of the sun in the stomach consuming it is new, as is the conflation of the sun and fire.' The *Amṛtasiddhi* seems to predate at least two 13th century CE *haṭhayoga* texts that borrow from it (Mallinson 2020, p. 412).

points up from the belly away from the *kuṇḍalinī* at *mūlādhāra*. See Figure 1A. When, the body is inverted in *śīrṣāsana* (headstand), *sarvāṅgāsana* (shoulderstand) or *viparītakaraṇī mudrā* (a *mudrā* version of these *āsana-s*), the flame points upwards towards the *kuṇḍalinī* at *mūlādhāra*, which it burns.[53] T.K.V. Desikachar presents a similar diagram.[54] See Figure 1B, which is based on those diagrams by Kaminoff and T.K.V. Desikachar.

According to T.K.V. Desikachar and K. Desikachar,

> in such inverted postures *[viparītakaraṇī mudrā, sarvāṅgāsana* and *śīrṣāsana]*, the direction of the flame changed. The flame was always directed upwards. When the human body was inverted, the fire continued to rise upwards, and was now directed towards the *Kuṅḍalini*, which was located at the *Mūlādhāra*. Consequently, the blockage at the *Mūlādhāra* was eliminated, facilitating a balanced flow of *prāṇa*.[55]

If, in contrast, the *kuṇḍalinī* were located at *nābhi cakra*, as Krishnamacharya wrote,[56] and if *agni* were located in the perineum (as in the *Yogayājñavalkya*, *Vasiṣṭhasaṁhitā*, *Pādmasaṁhitā*, *Ahirbudhnyasaṁhitā*, *Gorakṣaśataka* and

53. Kaminoff (2017).

54. T.K.V. Desikachar (1994a, p. 10).

55. Desikachar and Desikachar (2003, p. 83). My addition is in brackets. Note that this a very realist description of a flame in the belly. It does not describe something to be visualized. It describes how something is.

56. Jayaraman (2015, p. 217). This reference is to English-language 'notes' of 'select points' from an essay written by Krishnamacharya in Kannada and held in the archives of the Krishnamacharya Yoga Mandiram (Jayaraman 2015, Publisher's Note). The 'notes' give a very clear location for *kuṇḍalinī*: '*Kuṇḍalinī* is found above and below Nābhicakra.' This is consistent with the *Yogayājñavalkya*, upon which it seems to be based. However, the location given for *agni* is less clear: 'Agnisthāna is in Dehamadhya in the Golden coloured lump of flesh. If the blood is pure then that colour is attained. The shape of Agnisthāna is triangular.' This is consistent with the *Yogayājñavalkya*, upon which it could be based. The 'lump of flesh' could refer to the perineum but that location is not explicitly stated. In contrast, the notes also state that 'By the practice of the limbs of Yoga the fire in the abdomen can be increased ...'. If the phrase 'in the abdomen' is indeed present in Krishnamacharya's essay, then it would seem that Krishnamacharya, like the *Jyotsnā*, blurred the position of *agni*, presenting an account of the *dehamadhya*, located in the perineum in texts such as the *Yogayājñavalkya*, alongside a statement locating *agni* in the abdomen. If, on the other hand, the phrase 'in the abdomen' was not present in Krishnamacharya's essay and was added by the translator and summarizer, then perhaps T.K.V. Desikachar, rather than his father, introduced the teaching that *agni* is located in the abdomen. In contrast, it seems that Ramaswami follows the teaching that *agni* is in the *dehamadhya*, in the perineum, as the *Yogayājñavalkya* states.

Gorakṣapaddhati), then inverting the body would take the flame away from *kuṇḍalinī* rather than towards it. See Figure 1D. This problem does not occur within the *Yogayājñavalkya.* That text contains no inversions and there is no indication of the fire in the perineum burning the *kuṇḍalinī* in the navel when the *yogi* is standing or sitting upright, as in Figure 1C. Note that Ramaswami's account of inversions does not mention a flame that is always pointing upwards.

T.K.V. Desikachar gave a more detailed explanation of inversions in a 1994 article. He regarded *śīrṣāsana* as not just an *āsana* but a form of *viparītakaraṇī mudrā.* As well as changing the direction of the flame, it facilitates the deployment of a range of *haṭha* techniques to encourage *prāṇa* to enter the *suṣumnā.* First, *śīrṣāsana* enables good exhalation 'through which alone it is possible for the *prāṇa* to move from the *mūlādhāra* to the *sahasrāra cakra*'. Second, *bāhya kumbhaka* (pausing the breath after exhalation) is used, 'which further helps the movement of *prāṇa* from the *mūlādhāra* to the *sahasrāra cakra* and also helps to correctly position the *mūlādhāra cakra* making it easy for the *prāṇa* to enter'. Third, *uḍḍīyāna bandha* and *mūla bandha* are applied, 'which further help the *mūlādhāra cakra* be in the correct position'. Fourth, inhalation and *antaḥ kumbhaka* (pausing after inhalation) are used, 'which draw the fire towards the *apāna* and help eliminate both the impurities and the *kuṇḍalini.*' Fifth, '*tamoguṇa* is used to draw the *mūlādhāra cakra* towards the *sahasrāra*' while inverted (apparently using gravity). Sixth, 'the nature of fire [is] to always burn upward and so in an inverted posture it burns the *apāna* which is now right above it. ... When the body is inverted, the fire which originally had the *apāna* below it will now be burning the *apāna.* What was sought to be achieved (the elimination of the *apāna*) through breathing, is now achieved through posture.'[57] See Figure 1B. One of T.K.V. Desikachar's students extended his teachings on the flame always pointing up.[58]

---

57. T.K.V. Desikachar (1994a, p. 9). Again, this a very realist description of a flame in the belly. It does not describe something to be visualized. It describes how something is.

58. Peter Hersnack extended the argument that the flame always points upwards. If the orientation of the body is changed so that one lies on one's front, as in *bhujaṅgāsana* (the cobra), the flame moves towards the back of the body. Conversely, when one lies on one's back in *dvipādapīṭham* (two-foot support/the bridge), the flame rises towards the front of the body and 'cooks' there (Hersnack 2018, p. 47). Even though Hersnack uses the phrase 'fire metaphor', the rest of his account of a flame in the belly is very realist. It does not describe something to be visualized. It describes how something is.

T.K.V. Desikachar's account not only locates *kuṇḍalinī* at *mūlādhāra*, it also describes *apāna, kuṇḍalinī* and 'impurities' as being eliminated. Note the contrast between *apāna* being 'eliminated' in the above Desikachar quote, and the 'union of prana and apana vayus' in the above Maréchal quote. The 'impurities' Desikachar mentions resemble the 'dirt' (*mala*) which *nigrahaśakti* accumulates according to the *Ahirbudhnyasaṁhitā*.[59] He could be referring to the Āyurvedic term *āma*, which to Krishnamacharya was synonymous with *kuṇḍalinī*.[60] *Āma* is a 'toxin', which is said to be 'neutralized' by *agni*.[61]

Mohan gives a similar account of inversions using the terms 'dirt' and 'impurities' but not *kuṇḍalinī* or *apāna:*

> In a normal upright position gravity pulls impurities and the abdomen itself downward. For this reason this area is considered the seat of sickness. When the feet are elevated above the head, this process is reversed and gravity automatically moves the dirt towards the fire. Correct breathing is instrumental in this reversal process, because it can burn the impurities and remove them from the body more effectively.[62]

Mohan adds that breath 'affects the quality of the flame' and 'regulates the flow of impurities toward the fire for burning'. He locates the fire in the abdomen,[63] (like T.K.V. Desikachar) rather than in the perineum (like Ramaswami).

---

59. See *Ahirbudhnyasaṁhitā* 14.21 in Chapter 3.
60. Harvey (2011).
61. Lad (2002, pp. 84, 191).
62. Mohan (1993, p. 111).
63. Mohan (1993, p. 161). Mohan (1993, p. 160) also notes that 'the *Yoga Sutras* does (sic) not differentiate between physical and mental impurities', calling them all *'asuddhi'*, meaning 'that which is not clean, which should not be in the system, or which is in a place where it does not belong'. Mohan also emphasizes links between *agni* in *haṭhayoga* and similar ideas in *Vedānta.* First, he connects the *Yogayājñavalkya's agni* to *Vedānta's jñānāgni*, which he defines as 'that which reduces everything to its final form', citing the *Bhagavadgītā* (apparently 4.37). He adds that 'This passage is a reference to burning the dross of ignorance in the fire of knowledge, the Divine fire which burns down our ego' (Mohan no date, p. 12). Furthermore, 'In Vedic thought, Agni symbolizes the Divine (Paramatma). Just as Agni burns impurities, the Divine can burn the impurities within us, the Klesas or impurities of ignorance and ego, which leads us to our ultimate, true form as the Seer. Hence the Agni ... should not be understood as mere physical fire' (Mohan no date b, p. 57 n.2). Mohan also connects *agni* to *Bhagavadgītā* 15.14, in which Kṛṣṇa says: 'I am inside all human beings, holding the body together. Holding the prana and apana in balance, I digest

The same *haṭha* ideas can also be used to inform the practice of non-inverted *āsana-s*. For example, Krishnamacharya 'would lay great emphasis on postures like *pascimatānāsana*, *mahāmudrā* and *upaviṣṭakoṇāsana*, which aid exhalation ... It is on exhalation that the *prāṇa* is taken up the *suṣumnā* towards the *sahasrāra cakra*. ... This is why we are instructed, right from the beginning, both in *āsana* and *prāṇāyāma*, to master the exhalation. Without this our practice is meaningless.'[64] Krishnamacharya's principles can also determine the order of *āsana* practice. According to Harvey, a long-term student of T.K.V. Desikachar, a twist such as *jaṭharaparivṛtti* can be performed to increase *agni* before practising *paścimatānāsana*, a forward bend, to bring *apāna* and *mala* up to the fire in the belly.[65] If *agni* were located in the perineum, as the *Yogayājñavalkya* and some other texts state, Harvey's rationale would be illogical.

4.4 FURTHER LINKS BETWEEN *HAṬHAYOGA* AND *PATAÑJALI*

The connection between *haṭhayoga* and the *Yogasūtra* of *Patañjali* is very important to followers of Krishnamacharya. A fundamental connection is described in *Haṭhapradīpikā* 1.1:

> Salutations to Śrī Ādinātha, by whom knowledge of *haṭhayoga* was taught, [which] gleams like a ladder for one wishing to ascend to the highest *rājayoga*.[66]

The term *rājayoga* was not used until the 12th–14th centuries, when it was often in a list of four *yoga-s*: *mantrayoga*, *layayoga*, *haṭhayoga* and *rājayoga*.[67] Krishnamacharya, however, equated *rājayoga* with the *Yogasūtra* of *Patañjali*. White argues that Krishnamacharya's early writings did not emphasize the *Yogasūtra*.[68] However, in at least the last few decades of his teaching, Krishnamacharya certainly regarded *Patañjali* as 'the most fundamental

---

the food': translation - Mohan (no date, p. 12). In total, Mohan's account of *agni* seems more symbolic and less plainly realist than accounts by T.K.V. Desikachar and his students.

64. T.K.V. Desikachar (1994a, p. 8).
65. Harvey (2011).
66. My translation of the Sanskrit in Maheshananda and Sharma (2012, p. 47):

    śrī ādināthāya namo'stu tasmai yenopadiṣṭā haṭhayogavidyā |
    vibhrājatepronnatarājayogamāroḍhumiccho radhirohiṇīva || 1.1 ||

67. Schreiner (2011, p. 760); see also Birch (2014).
68. White (2014, pp. 197–224).

text on yoga'.[69] He rejected any *yoga* inconsistent with *Patañjali*,[70] as an interview with Krishnamacharya illustrates:

> Q. There are many approaches to the word 'yoga'. Which of these have to be refuted?
> A. Adharmika yoga has to be refuted.
> Q. What is Adharmika yoga?
> A. Adharmika yoga is the yoga that has not been mentioned in the Yoga Sūtra.[71]

While *kuṇḍalinī* is not mentioned in the *Yogasūtra*, *avidyā* is. The equation of *kuṇḍalinī* with *avidyā* therefore enabled students of Krishnamacharya to forge connections between *haṭhayoga* and *Patañjali*, allowing them to use the terminology of the two traditions interchangeably. For example, T.K.V. Desikachar explains that

> In the same way that avidyā has become so powerful that it stops puruṣa from seeing, kuṇḍalinī blocks prāṇa from entering the suṣumṇā. The moment avidyā is not there is the same moment that kuṇḍalinī is removed. Then prāṇa enters the suṣumṇā. As it enters it rises slowly to the top. That is why this is also part of rāja yoga. Rāja yoga is the process in which the prāṇa, which is the friend of puruṣa, little by little ascends to the top and then the man is like a king, a master.[72]

T.K.V. Desikachar equates *rājayoga* with the *Yogasūtra*, to which 'stops *puruṣa* from seeing' is a reference. He continues:

> Whatever happens to the state of mind happens to the whole person. That is the basis in the Yoga Sūtra. In various yogas, the same thing is stated in different ways, that is all. The results are the same because these are merely interpretations of the same thing.[73]

69. T.K.V. Desikachar (1995, p. 230).
70. Ramaswami (2007, p. 19).
71. Srivatsan (1997, p. 110). In the same interview, Krishnamacharya said that in the context of *Haṭhayoga* preparing a person to practise *Rājayoga*, 'Rāja yoga here means the bringing together of the jīvātma and Paramātma through Asaṁprajnāta Samādhi' (Srivatsan 1997, p. 108). This Vedāntic explanation seems less in line with *Patañjali* than with the *rājayoga* taught by the Brahma Kumaris organization, in which *yoga* is 'communion with the supreme soul' (Schreiner 2011, p. 767).
72. T.K.V. Desikachar (1980, pp. 244–245).
73. T.K.V. Desikachar (1980, p. 247).

A.G. Mohan makes a similar point, again mixing terminology from *haṭha-yoga* and *Patañjali:*

> The kuṇḍalinī blocking or covering the opening to the brahmarandhra (the door to freedom) at the bottom of the suṣumnā nāḍī, refers to the Seen (prakṛti), binding the Seer and blocking its way to freedom. Bound to the Seen, the Seer is unable to ascend to its true abode at the brahmarandra (sic).[74]

Commenting on *Haṭhapradīpikā* 3.1–3.3, Krishnamacharya deepens the connections with *Patañjali:* 'When kuṇḍalinī is burnt, prāṇa goes into suṣumnā. What this means is that the mind turns inwards and focuses on the self (ātman).'[75] Furthermore, 'Kuṇḍalinī is the power of our saṁskāra-s. In the presentation of the Yoga Sūtra, it is our saṁskarā-s (sic) that need to be burnt. Burning the kuṇḍalinī philosophically refers to the "burnt seed" (dagdha-bīja) state in Vyāsa's commentary on Yoga Sūtra II.4.'[76] This link is highly innovative.

Mohan also equates the *nābhicakra* of *Patañjali* with the *nābhi* of *haṭha* texts. Because 'The cakra at the navel is the center for the origins of all the nāḍīs', *saṁyama* (*dhāraṇā*, *dhyāna* and *samādhi*) on this place can give the *yogi* understanding of 'the arrangement of the structures of the body'.[77] This reflects *Patañjali* 3.29. However, when commenting on *Haṭhapradīpikā* 3.62, Krishnamacharya told Mohan that 'All the nāḍī-s start from mūlādhāra (root of the pelvis).'[78] That is inconsistent with *Patañjali* and the *Yogayājñavalkya.* Krishnamacharya immediately adds, however, that 'The mūlādhāra mentioned here may also be referred to as kanda.'[79] Hence, there was some conceptual drift in Krishnamacharya's ideas when he tried to accommodate and harmonize incompatible teachings from inconsistent texts.[80]

---

74. Mohan and Mohan (2013, p. 34 n.25).
75. Mohan and Mohan (2017, p. 59).
76. Mohan and Mohan (2017, p. 58).
77. Mohan and Mohan (2013, p. 33 n.21).
78. Mohan and Mohan (2017, p. 78).
79. Mohan and Mohan (2017, p. 78).
80. *Haṭha* texts give different locations for the *kanda*. *Dhyānabindu Upaniṣad* verse 50b states that 'above the penis and below nābhi [is] the *kanda*, which is [like] a bird's egg'. Nevertheless, verse 73a states that 'the *yogi* [who knows that] *kuṇḍalī-śakti* [is] above the *kanda* is a fit person [for] accomplishment [in *yoga*]'. – my translations from Sastri (1920, pp. 198, 202). This still positions the *kuṇḍalī* closer to *nābhi* than to *mūlādhāra*.

Another connection between *haṭhayoga* and *Patañjali* is *Haṭhapradīpikā* 2.2, which was a favourite quote of Krishnamacharya:[81]

> When the breath is unsteady, the mind is unsteady. When the breath is steady, the mind is steady [and] the *yogi* obtains steadiness. Therefore, [one] should restrain the breath.[82]

Krishnamacharya taught three types of *nirodha: kāya-nirodha* (restraining bodily movement), *prāṇa-nirodha* (restraining the breath), and *cittavṛtti-nirodha* (restraining the psyche). Whereas *rājayoga* is the main practice for *cittavṛtti-nirodha, haṭhayoga* involves both *kāya-* and *prāṇa-nirodha.*[83] According to Krishnamacharya, *sthāṇutva* (steadiness) in *Haṭhapradīpikā* 2.2 above means that 'the body becomes rooted like the trunk of a tree'.[84]

Harvey also describes how *āsana-s* can be practised in *haṭha* and *rāja* (*Patañjali*-based) ways for different purposes. A *haṭha* approach could involve dynamic movement between *āsana-s* such as *adhomukha śvānāsana* (dog head down) and *ūrdhvamukha śvānāsana* (dog head up) with a breath-length consistent over a number of repetitions, but not lengthened. Such a practice would build stamina towards a primary aim of practising *mahāmudrā*; other *āsana-s* would play a supporting and preparatory role. In contrast, a *rāja* (*Patañjali*-based) approach to *jānuśīrṣāsana* (head to knee posture) could involve lengthening the four components of the breath in turn, first by extending the exhale, then by adding a pause after the exhale (*bāhyakumbhaka*), and then by adding a pause after the inhale (*antarkumbhaka*). This could develop the ability to stay comfortably in a cross-legged seated *āsana* for *prāṇāyāma, pratyāhāra, dhāraṇā* and *dhyāna.*[85]

Mohan also radically reinterprets *Patañjali* 4.3 in *haṭhayoga* terms. This *sūtra* occurs in a *Sāṁkhya*-based section of *Patañjali* discussing *pariṇāma:* the process of change. Feuerstein translates it as follows:

ūrdhvaṁ meḍrādadho nābheḥ kando yo 'sti khagāṇḍvat || 50b ||
kandordhvakuṇḍalīśaktiḥ sa yogī siddhibhājanam || 73a ||

81. Harvey (2015b).

82. My translation of the Sanskrit in Maheshananda and Sharma (2012, p. 122):

cale vāte calaṁ cittaṁ niścale niścalaṁ bhavet |
yogī sthāṇutvamāpnoti tato vāyuṁ nirodhayet || 2.2 ||

83. Harvey (2011).

84. Mohan and Mohan (2017, p. 29).

85. Harvey (2011).

> The incidental-cause does not initiate the processes-of-evolution, but [merely is responsible for] the singling-out of possibilities – like a farmer [who irrigates a field by selecting appropriate pathways for the water].[86]

Feuerstein's translation depends on Vyāsa's commentary, which describes how a farmer breaks down obstacles between irrigation channels to allow water to flow into other fields.[87] Mohan references this *sūtra* in connection with the use of *nāḍīśuddhi* (*nāḍīśodhana*) as 'a kind of internal cleansing ... which allows prana to resume its normal flow throughout the body ... This cleansing process involves the removal of increasingly subtle impurities, which continue to affect us due to our mistaken identification of our true self with our body, mind, senses, and external world.'[88] As the *sūtra* is about flow, Mohan's interpretation is plausible. It is, however, unorthodox in three ways: 1. the equation of the flow of *prakṛti* in *pariṇāma* with the flow of *prāṇa*; 2. the identification of the obstacles between the farmer's fields as 'impurities', which are implicitly *avidyā* and other *kleśa-s*; and 3. the interpretation of the removal of those impurities as the *haṭha* practice of *nāḍīśodhana*. *Prāṇa* is not mentioned in the original *sūtra*, in Vyāsa's commentary, or in the glosses attributed to Śaṅkara, Vācaspati Miśra or Vijñānabhikṣu, which all discuss it in terms of *pariṇāma*.[89]

We have seen so far how the followers of Krishnamacharya not only forged theoretical links between *haṭha* texts and *Patañjali*; they also developed different approaches to practice in which either *haṭha* or *rāja* (i.e. *Patañjali*-based) *yoga* are emphasized. However, the techniques of *haṭha-yoga* are not usually used for the traditional *haṭha* aims of awakening *kuṇḍalinī* and raising *prāṇa*. Instead, *haṭha* techniques (particularly *āsana* and *prāṇāyāma*) are usually redeployed to meet the *Patañjali*-inspired goal of calming the mind.

For example, Harvey outlines why his approach to *prāṇāyāma* tends to be based primarily on *Patañjali* rather than *haṭha* texts. Practising *prāṇāyāma* within a *haṭhayoga* framework results in 'an intensification of the personal field of Prāṇa in anticipation of using the tools of Mudrā in order to direct this build up of Prāṇa towards breaking through the blockage in the Suṣumṇā Nāḍī caused by Kuṇḍalinī'. Such a practice is 'much more active

86. Feuerstein (1989, pp. 126–127).
87. Hariharānanda Āraṇya (1983, pp. 348–349).
88. Mohan (no date, p. 11).
89. Rukmani (2001, pp. 129–131); Haughton-Woods (1914, pp. 301–303); and Rukmani (1999, pp. 5–10) respectively.

and potentially destabilising' than practising *prāṇāyāma* within a *rājayoga* framework, which leads to 'a reduction in confusion' (*Patañjali* 2.52), 'fitness for the first steps in the meditative process' (*Patañjali* 2.53) and helps 'towards cultivating an experience of being filled with a subtle sense of stillness' (*Patañjali* 1.3).[90] Harvey further argues that

> our primary need today for most going to Yoga classes is Rāja or psychic stability, rather than even the more popularly perceived version of Haṭha, to allow us to be more skilful within our daily interactions. Given that the ancient practices of Haṭha Yoga had a different priority to this and perhaps one that is questionable within todays society, the only realistic starting point is the Prāṇāyāma as outlined through Chapter Two of the Yoga Sūtra.[91]

Students nowadays turn to *yoga* to find stability, Harvey notes. After practising for some time, those with the 'time, energy and psychic space to explore and skilfully accommodate the outcome of disturbing blockages within the demands and relationships of daily life' can then practise *prāṇāyāma* with more emphasis on *haṭha*.[92]

Roy and Charlton, who both trained with Harvey, are also very cautious about teaching *prāṇāyāma* as taught in *haṭha* texts. They outline a range of different 'rhythms' of *prāṇāyāma* by adjusting the ratio between four components of the breath: inhalation, *antaḥ kumbhaka* (the pause after inhalation), exhalation and *bāhya kumbhaka* (the pause after exhalation). As part of their account, they list four progressively intense 'stimulating' practices. These increasingly lengthen the *antaḥ kumbhaka*, culminating in a ratio of the four components of 1:4:2:0, about which they add a cautionary note:

> Although this last rhythm is presented in the HYP (*Haṭhapradīpikā*), we would be cautious with its application. Such a long AK (*antaḥ kumbhaka*) requires considerable training, and can lead to disturbance and irritability.[93]

---

90. Harvey (no date).
91. Harvey (no date).
92. Harvey (no date).
93. Roy and Charlton (2019, p. 201) with my insertion in brackets. Mohan and Mohan (2017, p. xii) note that Krishnamacharya's *Yogamakaranda* contains some *prāṇāyāma* practices that he did not recommend: 'some practices based on holding the breath after inhalation'.

The 1:4:2:0 ratio is common in *haṭha* texts. For example, the *Gheraṇḍasaṁhitā* teaches it in the immediate context of purifying the *nāḍī-s* (5.33–45) and in the wider context of awakening *kuṇḍalinī* (5.45–63). *Nāḍīśodhana* is widely practised by followers of Krishnamacharya to purify the *nāḍī-s* but seldom with a ratio emphasizing the *antaḥ kumbhaka* and seldom, if ever, with the agenda of awakening *kuṇḍalinī*. In my experience of group classes, workshops and retreats, it is much more common to be taught *laṅghana* (relaxing) *prāṇāyāma* ratios. These instead lengthen first the exhalation and then the pause after the exhalation.[94] That sort of ratio is consistent with both Harvey's above approach and the teaching in *Patañjali* 1.34 to practise exhalation and *bāhya kumbhaka* (the pause after exhalation).[95]

Roy and Charlton extend the use of *Patañjali/Sāṁkhya* terminology in describing the human body and how it moves. They present a model of the body containing a vertical 'axis' running from the head to the coccyx, around which is built the 'form' of the rest of the body. They then relate 'axis' and 'form' to *puruṣa* and *prakṛti*, respectively:

> It is wrong to equate the axis with *puruṣa*, but in construing an imaginary line around which our form dances, we can say that something of *puruṣa* is reflected in the axis. Similarly, although the form is not pure *prakṛti*, it *is* what we can directly observe (the way we are in the world, how we hold ourselves and how we manifest), so it can be seen as a reflection of *prakṛti*.[96]

94. I have also been taught *prāṇāyāma* with *laṅghana* ratios in one-to-one lessons for my personal practice. However, that is based on my personal needs and is not necessarily representative of the personal practice given to others.
95. *Vidhāraṇa* in *Patañjali* 1.34 is sometimes translated as 'retention' of breath (Feuerstein 1989, p. 48; Chapple and Kelly 1990, p. 48). I have been taught that T.K.V. Desikachar interpreted *vidhāraṇa* as *bāhya kumbhaka* (the pause after exhalation) (Ryan 2004). The Sanskrit supports that interpretation. *Vidhāraṇa* is a combination of the root *dhṛ* meaning to hold, with the prefix *vi*, which often means 'asunder, away' (Chapple and Kelly 1990, p. 48), giving a sense of opposition or reciprocal action against holding something (Goldman and Sutherland-Goldman 2011, p. 151). *Vidhāraṇa* therefore means holding the breath out. *Vidhāraṇa* works together with *pracchardana* (exhalation) in the same *sūtra* as a dual instrumental masculine noun: *pracchardana-vidhāraṇabhyāṁ*.
96. Roy and Charlton (2019, p. 158).

When interpreting *Patañjali*, the *tattva* usually regarded as reflecting *puruṣa* is *buddhi*, not the 'axis'.[97] However, in Roy and Charlton's model, *buddhi* is synonymous with *candra* (the moon).[98]

Furthermore, Roy and Charlton note that *saṁyoga* 'at its most global and profound' is 'the confusion between' *puruṣa* and *prakṛti*, which is 'the fundamental *avidyā*'.[99] This straightforwardly reflects *Patañjali* 2.17–25. Extending this concept to fit with their model, Roy and Charlton define the '*saṁyoga* of movement' as 'the unconscious and inefficient use of the body where true support for the movement is eclipsed, resulting in excess and unnecessary effort'.[100]

Roy and Charlton's model should not be seen as representative of the whole broad tradition. It is based on the innovative teaching of Peter Hersnack, who developed his own system based on the teaching he had received from T.K.V. Desikachar.[101] Roy and Charlton are, however, typical of the broad tradition when they state that 'far from being an esoteric and academic text, the Yoga Sūtra is the key to transforming the way we *do* yoga'.[102]

The overall agenda described in their book is not to awaken *kuṇḍalinī*, which is not mentioned. Instead, Roy and Charlton illustrate principles from seventeen *sūtra-s* from *Patañjali.* They use *āsana* and *prāṇāyāma* practices largely taken from or inspired by *haṭha* texts but redeployed, often in a gentle modified form, for *Patañjali*-inspired purposes. Roy has described the *āsana* and *prāṇāyāma* practices he teaches as '*haṭha* light'.[103]

A.G. Mohan's teaching also foregrounds *Patañjali*-based concentration over a *prāṇa*-centred *haṭha* practice. To Mohan, 'Pranayama is not the awakening of the coiled serpent ... Rather, pranayama is the conscious regulation of the breath ... This reduces mental disturbance, and minimizes the impurities in your system. As a result, you become clearer and your understanding is enhanced. The ultimate aim of pranayama, then, is to

97. I have been taught by teachers in the tradition that *buddhi* reflects *puruṣa*, but I cannot find a reference in my notes. Virupakshananda (1995, p. 66) makes a similar point when he states that *buddhi* seems acquires sentience 'owing to its proximity to the sentient faculty', i.e. *puruṣa*.
98. Roy and Charlton (2019, p. 157).
99. Roy and Charlton (2019, p. 156).
100. Roy and Charlton (2019, p. 156).
101. See Hersnack (2018).
102. Roy and Charlton (2019, p. 7).
103. Roy (2016).

focus the mind.'[104] This contrasts with many other modern approaches. For example, for Swāmi Niranjanananda Saraswati from the Bihar School of Yoga, awakening the sleeping *kuṇḍalinī śakti* is 'the fundamental purpose' of *prāṇāyāma*.[105] A.G. Mohan teaches the use of *āsana*, *prāṇāyāma*, *dhāraṇā* and *dhyāna* in the context of mindfulness i.e. 'minding the body and breath', 'minding the senses' and 'minding the mind'.[106] He frequently redeploys techniques taken from *haṭhayoga* for *Patañjali*-inspired purposes.

In summary, the equation of *kuṇḍalinī* (from *haṭha* texts) with *avidyā* (from *Patañjali*) has helped followers of Krishnamacharya not just to prioritize *Patañjali* over *haṭha* texts; it has also helped them justify the use of *haṭha* or tantric techniques to achieve different goals, subsuming them within the overarching framework provided by *Patañjali*. The resultant practices are theoretically as numerous as the number of students practising but there is great emphasis on focusing the mind and developing spiritual discernment. Krishnamacharya's commentary on *Patañjali* 1.13 is that '*Abhyāsa* is the practice of reflecting on the difference between the nature of spirit and matter.'[107] Here, 'spirit and matter' designate *puruṣa* and *prakṛti* respectively.[108]

There is also an emphasis on using *haṭha* techniques for therapeutic purposes or maintaining health. As Krishnamacharya states in his commentary on *Bhagavadgītā* 6.6,

> What good is the sword of wisdom (*Jñāna Asinā*) to cut away the chains of illusion (*Avidyā*) if the holder is too weak to bear it?[109]

This is counterbalanced by Krishnamacharya's commentary on *Patañjali* 2.2:

> If *śarīra* (the body) leads *ātman* (the self), there is *kleśa*. The cause of this is *karma vāsana* and wrong *indriya*.[110]

---

104. Mohan (1993, p. 160).
105. Niranjanananda Saraswati (1994, p. 1).
106. Mohan and Mohan (2015).
107. Harvey (2018). Harvey was taught this by T.K.V. Desikachar.
108. Harvey (2018).
109. Harvey (2013). Harvey was taught this by T.K.V. Desikachar.
110. Harvey (2018), with my additions in brackets. Harvey was taught this by T.K.V. Desikachar. The quote would not be out of place in *Advaitavedānta* but in fact it is deeply rooted in *Viśiṣṭādvaitavedānta*. I will introduce Rāmānuja's system in Chapter 6. It contains a model called the *śarīra-śarīrin*, or body-ensouler model, which operates on both

Hence, Harvey stresses that '*haṭha* needs to be considered correctly in the context of *rāja*',[111] i.e. *Patañjali.*

Whereas some of the connections presented above between the *Yoga Sūtra* and *haṭhayoga* may seem somewhat tenuous, in my experience the practice of *āsana-s* and *prāṇāyāma* using *haṭhayoga* techniques according to a *Patañjali*-based agenda works remarkably well. It could be argued, however, that practitioners give so much attention to *āsana-s* and *prāṇāyāma* that they spend little time going beyond those techniques. In other words, practitioners spend so much time preparing for meditation that they seldom spend much time actually doing it.

Krishnamacharya was not the only 20th century teacher to combine the *Yogasūtra* of *Patañjali* with *haṭhayoga*,[112] but the way he did it notably included teachings on *kuṇḍalinī*. Krishnamacharya's conception of *kuṇḍalinī* not only helped link *haṭhayoga* to *Patañjali*. It also resonated with a stream of thought passing through many South Asian schools of thought, to which we now turn.

---

macroscopic and microscopic levels. The following account is based on Lipner (1986, pp. 37–39, 120–142). On the micro level, the *śarīra* is the human body and the *śarīrin* ('ensouler') is the *jīvātman* (the individual self). On the macro level, the *śarīra* (body) is the whole world and the *Śarīrin* ('ensouler') is the Lord or Supreme Self (Lipner 1986, pp. 37–39).

Concentrating henceforth on the micro level, there are three aspects to the *śarīra-śarīrin* relationship. First, there is a polarity between the support (*ādhāra*) and that which is supported (*adheya*). The support is the *jīvātman* and that which is supported is the material body. Second, there is a polarity between the controller (*niyantṛ*) and that which is controlled (*niyāmya*) - the *jīvātman* controls the material body. Lipner (1986, p. 130) points out that *niyantṛ* can also mean 'charioteer', as in *Maitri Upaniṣad* 2.6: 'The charioteer can either keep his horses "under control" by guiding and restraining them along the recommended path, or he can come to grief by allowing his horses to have their own way. Similarly, ... the finite *ātman*, the controller, can either keep its bodily chariot (the thing-controlled) on course by guiding its potentially wayward senses and other prakṛtic faculties along the dharmic path, or it can "give rein" to these faculties and lose the way to salvation.'

The third aspect of the relationship is the polarity between the principal (*śeṣin*) and the accessory (*śeṣa*) - the *jīvātman* and the material body, respectively. According to Rāmānuja's *Vedārthasaṁgraha*, translated by Lipner (1986, pp. 131, 174), 'the accessory is that whose nature ... is to be given over to the tendency to render due glory to another', that 'other' being the *jīvātman*. 'In other words', Lipner (1986, p. 132) summarizes, 'the body, by acting out its "natural" function, voluntarily or involuntarily, i.e. by being what *it* is, "glorifies" or expresses in some way the due superiority of its self', i.e. the *jīvātman*.

111. Harvey (2018).

112. See Birch (2014, p. 402).

5

The symbolism of serpents

5.1 INTRODUCTION

Speaking in 2010, Kausthub Desikachar attempted to validate Krishnamacharya's position on *kuṇḍalinī* by providing a wider context into which it could fit. He claimed that in India, black snakes are considered 'very evil', representing *avidyā* (nescience) and *asmitā* (am-ness). The metaphor of a black snake needing to be killed 'is constantly repeated' in Indian mythology and art, especially in artistic representations of gods, he said, giving three examples. First, Viṣṇu's eagle, Garuḍa, crushes a black snake; second, Kṛṣṇa dances on a black snake; and third, Gaṇeśa has a belt of a serpent. K. Desikachar made these comments in just a few minutes of a three-day workshop on *nāḍī-s*, *cakra-s* and related concepts. He did not elaborate or cite any supporting evidence.[1]

At first glance, K. Desikachar's statement seems incompatible with the worship of *nāga-s*, divine serpents. Therefore, before analysing his claim, sections 5.2 and 5.3 will outline contemporary snake worship and trace its history in texts. It will show that snakes are represented at different times as either benevolent divinities to be worshipped or malign demons representing something to be overcome. I will then focus largely on the latter

1. K. Desikachar (2010). Just before making that claim, K. Desikachar drew a diagram of 6+1 *cakra-s* with *iḍā* and *piṅgalā* shown criss-crossing a central and straight *suṣumnā nāḍī*. He showed *kuṇḍalinī* at a junction between the three *nāḍī-s* at *mūlādhāra*. He equated *kuṇḍalinī* with *mala*, a 'black snake coiled three and a half times', which should be 'eliminated through *agni*'. I took detailed, comprehensive notes of what K. Desikachar said and I am completely confident that I am quoting him accurately. I interpret *asmitā* as a *kleśa*, in line with *Patañjali* 2.6, rather than in line with *Patañjali* 1.17, where it has another meaning.

stream of thought to show a wider context into which Krishnamacharya's conception of *kuṇḍalinī* as a blockage might fit. Section 5.4 will examine Śeṣa – a brahminized *nāga*. Section 5.5 will show how snakes are depicted as guarding pearls in the hood of cobras or other precious things. Section 5.6 will examine texts where snakes represent *māyā*, *avidyā*, *ajñāna* and related concepts. This will include how *Advaitavedānta* uses the snake-rope metaphor to represent *māyā-avidyā* and how other texts use snakes to represent the ego, pride in the body and *saṁsāra* (rebirth). Section 5.7 will examine how astrology uses snakes to represent eclipses and meteors as omens. Sections 5.8 to 5.11 will examine how snakes are represented in the mythology and iconography of Viṣṇu, Gaṇeśa, Garuḍa and Śiva, respectively. Section 5.12 will then survey extracts from the *Ṛgveda*, *Garuḍapurāṇa*, *Matsyapurāṇa*, *Yajurveda*, *Mahābhārata* and *Rāmāyaṇa* to analyse a claim by A.G. Mohan that snakes represent binding. That section ends by examining the *nāgapāśa* weapon, which uses binding serpents. Next, section 5.13 inspects the *Yogatārāvalī* in light of the preceding evidence. Section 5.14 then inspects the *Śivasaṁhitā* to investigate whether use of serpents to represent something to be overcome necessarily leads to *kuṇḍalinī* being used in a similar way. Section 5.15 discusses whether serpents should be called 'very evil'. The chapter ends in section 5.16 by evaluating K. Desikachar's and Mohan's claims.

5.2 CONTEMPORARY SNAKE WORSHIP

Nāga-s are divine serpentine beings that both bless and curse. They bestow fertility, prosperity and protection when worshipped but cause infertility when mistreated.[2] Harming snakes causes *nāgadoṣa* ('snake blemish'). This astrological problem leads to inauspicious planetary alignments in one's horoscope (see below), causing late marriage and infertility.[3]

Jagannathan and Krishna claim that *nāga-s* are 'a deity on the fringes of society worshipped in groves and open fields outside cities in the form of Naga stones'.[4] While it is true that common worship sites for *nāga-s* include *tīrtha-s* (where water is crossed) and *caitya-s* (near a tree, pool or

2. Allocco (2013, pp. 230–238).
3. Allocco (2013, pp. 238–239).
4. Jagannathan and Krishna (1992, p. 42).

stream),[5] *nāga* stones (*nāgakkal-s*), are 'exceptionally common in contemporary Tamil Nadu',[6] in both rural areas and urban temples.

Consider the *nāga* stones in two *Vaiṣṇava* temples in Kanchipuram: an ancient Tamil Nadu pilgrimage town. First, Śrī Kacchapesvarar Temple occupies approximately five acres and was built by Vijayanagara rulers[7] (*c.*14th–15th centuries CE). In a corner of the courtyard is a large tree surrounded by hundreds of *nāga* stones. They vary from depicting a snake with an odd number of heads (3, 5 or 7), to a pair of intertwining snakes, to a snake with an extended hood. This mixture is typical.[8] The stones are colourfully painted with turmeric powder and vermillion paste and actively worshipped, mainly by women. Second, Ulagalanda Perumāl Temple was built in 846–869 CE and renovated in *c.*10th–13th centuries.[9] In an indoor alcove immediately to the left of the main shrine to Ulagalanda (Viṣṇu) is a huge *nāga* stone. The 5-headed *nāga* is Urakathan ('one who crawls'), who represents Śeṣa (see below) and is worshipped by childless couples.[10] Beyond Kanchipuram, Ferguson discusses temples where *nāga* images are even more central. First, 'In the great temple at Madura', between depictions of Hanūmān and Garuḍa (see below) is 'an image of the seven-headed Naga, richly jewelled, and under a splendid canopy'. Second, 'In the great temple at Seringham, likewise, the principal images are two golden statues of the seven-headed Naga'.[11] Hence, *nāga* worship is not just 'on the fringes of society': it is mainstream.

5.3 A TEXTUAL HISTORY OF SNAKE WORSHIP

Rituals to propitiate *nāga-s* have been practised across South Asia for over two millennia,[12] although only the 'hooded serpent' (cobra) is sacred.[13]

The dual capacity of *nāga-s* to favour and curse is reflected in the complex historical relationship between orthodox traditions and snake worship. Laurie Cozad surveyed orthodox texts from different eras in her book

5. Cozad (2004, p. 4).
6. Allocco (2013, p. 237).
7. Rao (2008, p. 110).
8. Allocco (2013, p. 237).
9. Rao (2008, p. 109).
10. Dasa (no date).
11. Ferguson (1868, p. 73).
12. Cozad (2004, p. 2).
13. Oldham (1905, pp. 7, 30); Alwar (2018).

Sacred Snakes. She shows that attitudes vary across time periods, between texts and even within them. On the one hand, some writers found snake worship threatening. They therefore undermined it by divesting the snake of the elements that prompted its worship and by transferring its powers to gods or *brahmin-s.* On the other hand, other writers reported how indigenous peoples worshipped snakes as powerful deities, and some writers preserved and used snake worship for their own ends.[14] I will first summarize Cozad's findings for texts from three periods: the *Ṛgveda*, the late *Veda-s* and the *Ādiparvan* of the *Mahābhārata.* I will then build on her conceptual framework by adding more evidence from a range of texts and relating it to *kuṇḍalinī.*

Snake worship is first mentioned in the *Ṛgveda*, the earliest Hindu text, which promotes the authority of *brahmin-s* as priestly intermediaries. Snake worship was more directly accessible and viewed as dangerous. The *Ṛgveda* therefore undermined it by portraying snakes as 'threatening, demonic creatures that deserve to die'.[15]

The *Ṛgveda* shows the power of Indra over the natural world when he defeats the supernatural snake Vṛtra, 'the obstructor of heaven and earth'.[16] The battle between Indra and Vṛtra is interpreted variously but a common theme is the obstruction of waters.[17] Vṛtra's name derives from *vṛ*, meaning to enclose or cover something, particularly water; he is also called Apovṛtvī ('encloser of the waters') and Nadīvṛt ('encloser of the rivers').[18] *Nadī* (river) resembles *nāḍī* (artery, vein or nerve) phonologically and conceptually: both terms represent conduits through which something fluid can flow. Nadīvṛt enclosing or covering rivers is therefore loosely comparable with *kuṇḍalinī* enclosing, covering or blocking entry to the *suṣumnā nāḍī.*

Cozad describes how the agenda of the *Ṛgveda* was to kill Vṛtra and transfer his powers to Indra. The text gives a pretext: Vṛtra 'had barricaded those waters with his earthly powers', withholding them from the

14. Cozad (2004, especially p.7). In addition to Hindu sources, Cozad surveyed Buddhist texts, especially the *Mahāvastu* and texts in Pāli. I have not referred to Buddhist texts because they are less related to Krishnamacharya. Cozad used the term 'redactors' rather than 'writers' because they were often interpreting and altering long-existing narratives rather than creating something new and original.
15. Cozad (2004, pp. 4, 8, 9).
16. Oldham (1905, p. 32).
17. Lahiri (1984, pp. 1–80).
18. Cozad (2004, p. 14).

Āryans.[19] The *Ṛgveda* similarly demonizes Arbuda Kādraveya as 'a supernatural snake representative of the demonic forces of darkness and chaos'.[20]

The next period Cozad surveyed was that of the late *Veda-s*. Late Vedic texts include the *Atharvaveda*, the *Śatapathabrāhmaṇa* of the *Yajurveda*, the *Pāñcaviṁśa* and *Sāmavidhāna Brāhmaṇa-s* of the *Sāmaveda* (all *c.*900–600 BCE) and the *Gṛhyasūtra-s* (manuals of domestic rituals, *c.*600–400 BCE). The *brahmin-s* of this period were concerned less with dominance and more with compiling a repertoire of rituals to control nature.[21] Thus, instead of continuing the campaign against snake worship, they promoted it as complementary to Vedic rites.[22]

Late Vedic texts therefore contain 'an amalgam of snake-centered myths and rituals from both priestly and grass-roots sources, all of which share a common objective: to position the snake as a powerful nature deity accessible to all'.[23] Snakes are venerated to obtain sons, abundant harvests and good building foundations, and to prevent snakebite.[24] The *Śatapathabrāhmaṇa* introduced the term *nāga* and even stipulates that one should 'meditate on the divine person as a snake'.[25] The *Gṛhyasūtra-s* then anthropomorphized *nāga-s*, who became less threatening. The *nāga* Arbuda Kādraveya, Indra's foe in the *Ṛgveda*, was rebranded as 'a wise and powerful earth deity' whose sons befriended Indra.[26] In the *Artharvaveda*, four snakes also act helpfully as guardians of the four directions. One of them is called Asita, meaning 'black'.[27] This is inconsistent with K. Desikachar's claim that a black snake signifies something 'very evil'.

By the time of the *Ādiparvan* of the *Mahābhārata* (*c.*300 BCE–300 CE), that text's writers opposed snake worship because the 'prosperity, posterity and longevity' that it offered duplicated what the *brahmin-s* provided. However, the writers also saw an opportunity to co-opt the snake's powers.[28] The *Ādiparvan* depicted *nāga-s* as menacing and untrustworthy, relocated them to the subterranean realm of *Nāgaloka*, made them dependent

19. *Ṛgveda* 1.32.8 – Cozad (2004, p. 16).
20. Cozad (2004, p. 16).
21. Cozad (2004, pp. 10, 11, 24, 48).
22. Cozad (2004, pp. 23–24).
23. Cozad (2004, p. 25).
24. Cozad (2004, p. 49).
25. Cozad (2004, pp. 32, 30).
26. Cozad (2004, pp. 33–34).
27. Cozad (2004, p. 29).
28. Cozad (2004, p. 51).

on mainstream gods, reduced their powers over nature, and provided them with a powerful enemy: Garuḍa.[29] See section 5.10 below. The characteristic power of *nāga-s*, control over water, was transferred to Indra, removing the main reason for worshipping snakes.[30]

5.4 ŚEṢA – THE BRAHMINIZED *NĀGA*

To displace the snake kings, the *brahmin-s* around the time of the *Ādiparvan* created a new brahminized *nāga* called Śeṣa/Ananta/Saṅkarṣaṇa. He is called Ananta (infinite) as he has a thousand heads.[31]

According to the *Ādiparvan*, Śeṣa practised austerities to become powerful. When Brahmā asked him his heart's desire, Śeṣa replied: 'All of my maternal brothers are dull-witted. I cannot bear to live with them. Sir, grant me this wish. Like enemies they are always angry. So I practice austerities so that I do not have to see them ...'. Brahmā asked him to choose a boon and Śeṣa replied: 'The boon that I desire ... is this: Let my mind delight in dharma, in tranquillity, and in austerities, my lord.'[32]

By denigrating his own species, Śeṣa became so brahminized that he became 'god of *dharma*'. Nevertheless, he was still subordinate to Brahmā[33] and Viṣṇu, who reclines upon a bed of Śeṣa's coils or sits under an umbrella made of Śeṣa's hoods – see Plate 2.

In the *Harivaṁśa*, Kṛṣṇa and Saṅkarṣaṇa/Śeṣa

> are really one, but have taken separate forms for the sake of the world ... Together they make up the totality of the universe, since Śeṣa ('remainder') ... is the formless chaos which remains when Viṣṇu/Nārāyaṇa has absorbed all forms into himself.[34]

The idea that Kṛṣṇa and Saṅkarṣaṇa 'are really one' may have originated in *Pāñcarātra* (see Chapter 3). Since *c.*100 CE, *Pāñcarātra* has taught a theory of emanation.[35] The original and most complete form of God is Vāsudeva. From Vāsudeva emanated a chain of three *vyūha-s* (manifestations), start-

29. Cozad (2004, p. 52).
30. Cozad (2004, pp. 57–58).
31. *Sahasraśirasaṁ* - *Śrīmadbhāgavatam* 3.27.27 in Pandurangi (1998, p. 337).
32. *Mahābhārata* 1.32.5–17, translation - Cozad (2004, pp. 66–67).
33. Cozad (2004, p. 68).
34. Matchett (1986, p. 119).
35. Matsubara (1994, p. 139).

Plate 2
Viṣṇu under a canopy of Śeṣa's hoods – fresco in Thoopal Vedanta Desikar Temple, Kanchipuram.

Photograph: Simon Atkinson

ing with Saṅkarṣaṇa (Kṛṣṇa's elder brother, Balarāma or Baladeva). From Saṅkarṣaṇa emanated Pradyumna (Kṛṣṇa's son). From Pradyumna emanated Aniruddha (Kṛṣṇa's grandson).[36]

In Śaṅkara's presentation of *Pāñcarātra* in his *Brahmasūtra* commentary, he links Saṅkarṣaṇa to the *jīva* and Aniruddha to *ahaṁkāra.*[37] There is evidence for this in *Pāñcarātra* texts. According to the *Visvaksenasaṁhitā*, Saṅkarṣaṇa acts as superintendent (*adhiṣṭhātṛ*) 'of all the souls', whereas Aniruddha is the superintendent of *ahaṁkāra.*[38] Similarly, in the *Lakṣmītantra*, Saṅkarṣaṇa represents the *jīva* while *Aniruddha* represents *ahaṁkāra.*[39]

The *vyūha* system was adopted by Krishnamacharya's own tradition, Śrīvaiṣṇavism (see Chapter 6), which seems to have preserved this teaching from the *Lakṣmītantra*. The *paramātman* is *Śeṣin* (the controller) while the *jīva* is Śeṣa ('one who is being controlled').[40] The *paramātman* is 'the residuary' while the individual *ātman-s* are 'remainders' (Śeṣa).[41] *Śrīvaiṣṇava* scholar M.A. Lakshmithathachar confirmed to me that in his tradition, Śeṣa represents the individual self. Śeṣa spits venom to protect the Supreme Being at any cost. The individual self should have similar affection for the Supreme Being and aim to protect him.[42] This reverses the usual attitude, in which people look to God to protect them, but it does not depict Śeṣa as 'very evil'.

Whereas the *Lakṣmītantra* and Śrīvaiṣṇavism interpret Saṅkarṣaṇa as the *jīva*, the *Śrīmadbhāgavatam* interprets it as egotism:

> Thirty thousand *yojana-s* from the bottom of it *[Nāgaloka]* sits indeed that which [is] a small tāmasic form/part (*kalā*) of the Lord called Ananta, thus worshippers of Kṛṣṇa [say. They] declare Saṅkarṣaṇa [to be] the erroneous

---

36. Schrader (1916, p. 35).
37. Śaṅkara's *Brahmasūtra* commentary 2.2.42 – Oberhammer (1977–1978, pp. 222, 224). Śaṅkara links Pradyumna to *manas.*
38. Schrader (1916, p. 40).
39. *Lakṣmītantra* 6.12, 13 – Gupta (2000, p. 36).
40. Sharvani and Sattar (2016, p. 5).
41. Aiyangar (1933, p. 18).
42. Lakshmithathachar (2018). Rāmānuja equated *Śeṣa* with the *jīvātman* - see Chapter 6 and Lester (1976, pp. 112, 141). Whereas the *Lakṣmītantra's* account of the *vyūha-s* seems to have influenced Śrīvaiṣṇavism's position, other *Pāñcarātra* texts give different accounts – see Varadachari V. and Tripathi, G.C. in Lakshmithathachar and Varadachari (2009, vol. 1 pp.96–108).

> self-conception (*abhimāna*) of 'I', [which is] a characteristic sign of the bringing together (*sannikarṣaṇa*) of that which [sees] and *dṛśya* (the seen).[43]

This verse's use of *abhimāna* resembles the definition in *Patañjali* of *asmitā kleśa:* 'I-am-ness is when the two powers of seer and seen [appear] as a single self.'[44] *Asmitā kleśa* leads to 'false identity'.[45] Hence, this verse indirectly supports K. Desikachar's claim that snakes represent *asmitā* (*kleśa*). However, the passage still presents Saṅkarṣaṇa as a form or part (*kalā*) of God, so it is inconsistent with K. Desikachar's claim that (black) snakes are 'very evil'. Moreover, the above *Pāñcarātra/Śrīvaiṣṇava* interpretation of Saṅkarṣaṇa/Śeṣa as representing the *jīva* does not support K. Desikachar's position. Overall, therefore, the evidence for Śeṣa is mixed. I will return to Śeṣa when I consider Śiva and Garuḍa below, but next I present examples of ways in which snakes are depicted as guarding something precious or representing something to be overcome.

5.5 SNAKES GUARDING SOMETHING PRECIOUS: PEARLS, TREASURE AND SACRED SITES

Chapter 3 showed how the *Vimānārcanākalpasaṁhitā* likens the lower opening of the *suṣumnā* to a shining jewel in the hood of a snake. This reflects a belief that pearls originate in cobras' hoods. According to the *Bṛhatsaṁhitā*, a *c.*6th century CE astronomy text,[46]

> Pearls (*muktāphala-s*) are produced in the elephant, snake (*bhujaga*), oyster shell, conch shell [and] pig. Of these, the oyster pearl is abundant and beautiful (81.1).

---

43. *Śrīmadbhāgavatam* 5.23.32 – my translation of Pandurangi (2000, p. 179):

> tasya mūladeśe triṁśadyojanasahasrāntare āste yā vai kalā bhagavatastāmasī samākhyātānanta iti sātvatā yaddṛśyayoḥ sannikarṣaṇamahamityabhimānalakṣaṇaṁ saṁkarṣaṇamityācakṣate ||

I interpret *yad* as 'that which [sees]' because in Prabhupāda's (1982b, pp. 409–410) version of the text, *yad* is replaced by *draṣṭṛ* (the seer). The coming together of *draṣṭṛ* and *dṛśya* (the seer and the seen) is the definition of *saṁyoga* in *Patañjali* 2.17, which describes it as something to be overcome.

44. *Patañjali* 2.6, translation – Chapple and Kelly (1990, p. 59).

45. T.K.V. Desikachar (1995, p. 167).

46. Iyer (1987, p. xiii).

> Inside the hoods of snakes (*pannaga-s*) of the high family of the deities Takṣaka and Vāsuki are glistening lustrous dark-blue pearls (*mukta-s*) (81.25).[47]

The *c.*6th–10th centuries CE *Garuḍapurāṇa*[48] adds that

> A pearl found in the hood of a cobra is round in shape ... and emits a dazzling effulgence from its own natural seat. After copious washing such a pearl assumes the lustre of a well-polished sword. The possessor of a cobra or serpent-pearl, meets with a rare good fortune, and becomes a pious and illustrious king in time, with a treasury full of other species of precious gems. ... Neither the serpents, nor the Rakshas, nor diseases, nor disturbances of any kind would assail the man amidst whose treasure such a snake-pearl would lie.[49]

The ferocity of the snake guarding this treasure is also emphasized: 'Is not the serpent that bears a gem on its hood doubly dangerous for the stone?'[50]

In the *Pañcatantra*, snakes guard treasure buried under an anthill,[51] with which snakes have been associated since *Ṛgveda* 4.20.9. In the *Garuḍapurāṇa*, fierce snakes guard a sacred pool:

> ... serpents of dreadful appearance, guard its shores with their protruding tongues, inspiring terror into the hearts of the wicked and the unrighteous.[52]

---

47. *Bṛhatsaṁhitā* 81.1, 81.25 – my translation of Kern (1865, pp. 409, 413):

    dvipabhujagaśuktiśaṅkhābhraveṇutimisūkaraprasūtāni |
    muktāphalāni teṣāṁ bahumādhu ca śuktijaṁ bhavati || 81.1 ||
    takṣakavāsukikulajāḥ kāmagamā ye ca pannagāsteṣāṁ |
    snigdhā nīladyutayo bhavanti muktāḥ phaṇasyānte || 81.25 ||

48. Gangadharan (1972, p. 147).
49. Translation – Shastrī (1968, pp. 187–188).
50. Translation – Shastrī (1968, p. 332).
51. Vogel (1926, pp. 20–21). The *Pañcatantra* is a collection of fables, not a tantric text.
52. *Garuḍapurāṇa* chapter 84, translation – Shastrī (1968, pp. 225–226).

5.6 SERPENTS REPRESENTING *MĀYĀ*, *AVIDYĀ* AND RELATED CONCEPTS

5.6.1 *Atharvaveda* (serpents representing *māyā*)

The *Atharvaveda* provides an early link between snakes and *māyā* in a colourful verse describing the effects of consuming *arka*, a tree product:

> As the black snake spreads himself at pleasure, making wondrous forms (*vapus*), by the Asura's magic (*māyā*), so let this *arka* suddenly make thy member altogether correspondent (*? saṁsamaka*), limb with limb.[53]

The movement of the *asita* (black snake) is likened to the enlargement of a *śepa* (penis). However, this black snake is not 'very evil', so it is inconsistent with K. Desikachar's claim. Note the snake's association with *māyā*, here meaning magic, i.e. a 'trick, artifice, deceit, jugglery, sorcery, or work of witchcraft'; in other contexts, *māyā* means 'an illusory image or apparition, phantasm, deception of the sight'.[54] In some of the texts examined below, this is extended theologically to mean 'the supreme power that generates and animates the display: the dynamic aspect of the universal Substance', and is often known as *śakti*.[55] Zimmer elaborates:

> Māyā then immediately muffles consciousness within the wrappings of her perishable production. The ego is entrapped in a web, a queer cocoon ... The aim of Indian thought has always been to learn the secret of the entanglement, and, if possible, to cut through into a reality outside and beneath the emotional and intellectual convolutions that enwrap our conscious being.[56]

Note the enwrapping or covering. Let us now turn to other texts that use snakes to represent this aspect of *māyā* or related concepts including *avidyā* and *ajñāna*.

---

53. *Atharvaveda* 6.72.1, translation – Whitney and Lanman (1905, p. 335). The brackets and their contents are part of Whitney and Lanman's translation.
54. Zimmer (1962, p. 24).
55. Zimmer (1962, p. 25).
56. Zimmer (1962, p. 26).

5.6.2 *Vivekacūḍāmaṇi* (serpents representing *ajñāna/ahaṁkāra*)

In the *Vivekacūḍāmaṇi*, an *Advaita* text attributed to Ādiśaṅkara, the treasure guarded or covered by a snake is the *ātman:*

> For [one who has been] bitten by the snake of nescience (*ajñāna*), the only medicine [is] knowledge of *Brahman.*[57]

In *Advaita*, *ajñāna* is synonymous with *avidyā*.[58] The snake metaphor is extended from biting to covering:

> The treasure of the bliss of *Brahman* is guarded by the terrible snake of ego (*ahaṁkāra-ghorāhinā*), which possesses great strength, consists of three fierce heads [representing] the *guṇa-s*, and envelops/surrounds/covers (*saṁveṣṭya*) the *ātman*. Having completely destroyed the illusory snake with three heads with the splendid great-sword known as wisdom (knowledge of the self), the wise one is able to enjoy this treasure, which gives happiness.[59]

Krishnamacharya was familiar with the idea of something enveloping or surrounding the *ātman*, which is usually located in the heart. His commentary to *Patañjali* 2.3 states that 'These five kleśa surround the heart of every individual. They are related to the three Guṇa known as Sattva, Rajas and Tamas.'[60] Similarly, in *Bhagavadgītā* 7.14, Kṛṣṇa's *māyā* is composed of the three *guṇa-s*. These *guṇa-s* are also constituents of *prakṛti*, which itself is equated with *māyā* in *Śvetāśvatara Upaniṣad* 4.10.

Commenting on the *Vivekacūḍāmaṇi* verse above, neo-*Advaitin* Swāmi Chinmayānanda states that

> The treasure of the 'Infinite Bliss-of-*Brahman*' is kept secret in the undisturbed cave of the physical body. This treasure is being guarded by a serpent, the ego-sense, the individuality. Individuality is represented by a

---

57. *Vivekacūḍāmaṇi* 63a – my translation of the Sanskrit in Grimes (2004, p. 90):

    ajñāna sarpa daṣṭasya brahma jñānauṣadhaṁ vinā |

58. Ram-Prasad (2010, p. 708).
59. *Vivekacūḍāmaṇi* 303 – my translation of the Sanskrit in Grimes (2004, p. 187):

    brahmānanda nidhir mahā balavatā 'haṁkāra ghorāhinā
    saṁveṣṭyātmani rakṣyate guṇa mayais caṇḍais tribhir mastakaiḥ |
    vijñānākhya mahāsinā dyutimatā vicchidya śīrṣa trayaṁ
    nirmūlyāhim imaṁ nidhiṁ sukhakaraṁ dhīro 'nubhoktuṁ kṣamaḥ || 303 ||

60. Harvey (2015a).

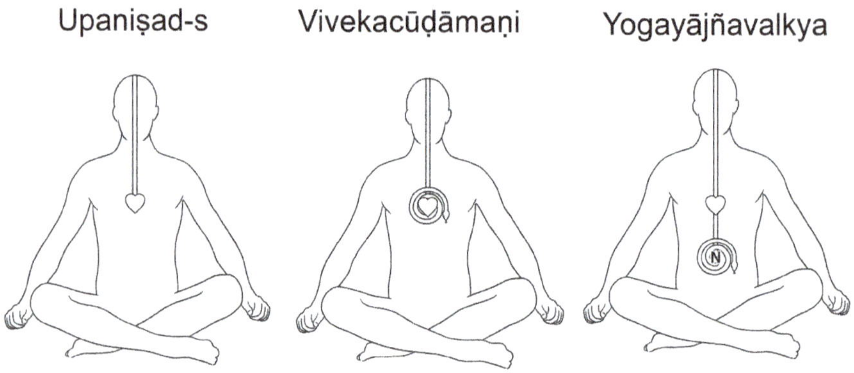

Figure 2
Teachings on subtle anatomy found in the *Upaniṣad-s, Vivekacūḍāmaṇi* and *Yogayājñavalkya*.

> serpent upon which Shri Krishna danced and destroyed--the serpent in the holds of the peacock, the vehicle of Lord Subramanya--the serpent that is worn as an ornament by Lord Siva--all these represent the ego-sense ... This powerful, terrible, serpent, the ego, protects the treasure-trove of Blissful *Brahman* (*Brahma-ananda*). For its own selfish ends, this ego coils round the treasure and protects it. This ego (*Ahamkar*) in us will not allow us to realise the State of *Brahmananda*.[61]

The *Vivekacūḍāmaṇi* account is comparable to the account of *kuṇḍalinī* in the *Yogayājñavalkya*. The Central diagram in Figure 2 shows a coiled snake enveloping *ātman* in the heart, as in the *Vivekacūḍāmaṇi*. The right-hand diagram shows the coiled *kuṇḍalinī* blocking entry into the *suṣumnā* at *nābhi*, as in the *Yogayājñavalkya*. Both those texts build upon teachings in certain early *Upaniṣad-s*, as shown in the left-hand diagram.

5.6.3 *Aṣṭāvakragītā* (serpents representing *ahaṁmāna/ajñāna*)

Another *Advaita* text uses similar imagery. In spiritual instruction to King Janaka, the sage Aṣṭāvakra declares:

61. Chinmayananda (1970, p. 362). 'The undisturbed cave of the physical body' refers to the heart, where the *jīvātman* resides; see *Bṛhadāraṇyaka Upaniṣad* 2.1.17 and *Chāndogya Upaniṣad* 3.14.3. Subramanya's peacock is Garuḍa's son (Atmashraddhananda 2016, p. 67); see Parthasarathy (1983, p. 150).

[You have been] bitten by the great black serpent (*mahā-kṛṣṇa-ahi*) of egotism (*ahaṁmāna*) [by thinking] 'I am the doer'.[62]

The colour black probably signifies *tamas.*[63] *Tamas* in turn signifies 'enveloping', 'covering', or 'obscuring our perception',[64] a theme that will recur below. The next verse, 1.9, uses the term *ajñāna* (nescience), indicating a link with *ahaṁmāna* (egotism). The *Aṣṭāvakragītā* also uses the metaphor of seeing a snake instead of a rope:

From nescience of *ātman*, the world appears; from knowledge of *ātman*, [it] does not appear. [Similarly], from nescience of the rope, the snake appears; from that knowledge [of the rope, the snake] indeed disappears.[65]

In the *Aṣṭāvakragītā*, the snake represents both *ajñāna* (nescience, in 2.7) and *ahaṁmāna* (egotism, in 1.8a).

The snake-rope metaphor originated in *Yogācāra* Buddhism.[66] Gaudapāda, an early *Advaitin*, then employed it in his *Māṇḍūkyakārikā*,[67] before Śaṅkara used it in his commentary on *Brahmasūtra* 1.1.4. Śaṅkara's *Vivekacūḍāmaṇi* deploys the snake-rope metaphor in nine verses.[68] The snake (*sarpa, ahi, bhujaga*) is described as *bhrānti* (false/delusory)[69] and associated with *bhrama* (error/delusion).[70] It is also *kalpitatvān* (imagined) and *na-satya* (not real).[71] Its perception is due to confusion arising from *tamas* (*vimūḍhasya-tamasā*).[72] All these descriptions conform with the *Advaita* use of snakes to represent *avidyā*, although the *Vivekacūḍāmaṇi* does not use that term in the context of the snake-rope metaphor.

62. *Aṣṭāvakragītā* 1.8a – my translation of the Sanskrit in Chinmayānanda (2001, p. 21):

ahaṁ kartetyahaṁmānamahākṛṣṇāhidaṁśitaḥ | 1.8a |

63. Frazier (2013, p. 9).
64. Charlton (2016).
65. *Aṣṭāvakragītā* 2.7 – my translation of the Sanskrit in Chinmayānanda (2001, p. 50):

ātmā 'jñānājjagadbhāti ātmajñānātna bhāsate |
rajjvajñānādahirbhāti tajjñānādbhāsate na hi || 2.7 ||

66. Sharma (1997, pp. 13–20).
67. Verse 17 – see Gambhīrānanda (1958, p. 242). The *Māṇḍūkyakārikā* is a commentary on the *Māṇḍūkya Upaniṣad.*
68. Verses 12, 112, 140, 199, 237, 248, 388, 405 and 407.
69. Verses 12, 199 and 407.
70. Verses 112 and 237.
71. Verse 248.
72. Verse 140.

In the *Vivekacūḍāmaṇi* and *Aṣṭāvakragītā*, the snake of egotism or nescience is not to be awoken, activated or raised: it is to be destroyed. Similarly, Krishnamacharya taught that the snake of *kuṇḍalinī* is not to be raised through the *cakra-s:* it is to be destroyed.

It is possible that Krishnamacharya could have been influenced by the *Aṣṭāvakragītā* and *Vivekacūḍāmaṇi* as he was highly familiar with *Advaitavedānta*. First, he was taught by an *Advaitin*. Krishnamacharya, 'during his boyish days' studied *āsana-s* with Narasimha Bharati Swamigalavaroo at the Śṛṅgeri Muṭṭ, an *Advaita* centre where he may have attended the Sanskrit school.[73] Later, Krishnamacharya studied *Vedānta* at Patna University.[74] He also earned the title *Vedakesari* at Mysore University and he is said to have earned the equivalent of seven PhDs in various subjects.[75] It is virtually inconceivable that such a comprehensive education would have excluded a serious study of *Advaitavedānta*, not least because the *Viśiṣṭādvaita* commentators critiqued it at length (see Chapter 6). Furthermore, Krishnamacharya greatly respected Śaṅkara's *Gītābhāṣya* and the *Yogatārāvalī*,[76] a *yoga* text that T.K.V. Desikachar attributed to Śaṅkara.[77] See section 5.13 below. Krishnamacharya also greatly respected H. H. Chandraśekarabhāratī, the Śaṅkarācārya of the Śṛṅgeri Muṭṭ, and the Paramācārya of the Kānchi Kāmakoṭi Piṭha.[78] Furthermore, Krishnamacharya offered to teach Srivatsa Ramaswami 'the whole Vedānta from an advaitic point of view', respecting Ramaswami's *Smārta* background, which stresses *Advaita*.[79] With such a working knowledge of *Advaita*, Krishnamacharya would probably have been familiar with the *Vivekacūḍāmaṇi* and *Aṣṭāvakragītā*.

5.6.4 *Śrīmadbhāgavatam* (serpents representing *māna*)

A text closer to Krishnamacharya's *Vaiṣṇava* tradition is the *Śrīmadbhāgavatam*, a major *Purāṇa* centred on Kṛṣṇa. In verse 5.12.2, the sage Bhārata has given lengthy spiritual instruction to King Rahūgaṇa, who declares:

73. Sjoman (1999, p. 51).
74. T.K.V. Desikachar and Cravens (1998, p. 40).
75. K. Desikachar (2005, p. 53); T.K.V. Desikachar and Cravens (1998, p. 16).
76. Srivatsan (1997, p. 82).
77. Desikachar and Desikachar (2003, p. 5).
78. Srivatsan (1997, p. 82).
79. Ramaswami (2007, p. 19); Jackson (2011, p. 549–551).

> Just as medicine is to [one with] boundless suffering [and] just as ice is to [one] scorched by the heat of summer, O *brahmin*, your speech is nectarine medicine to me [as I am] blinded, bitten (*vinaṣṭa*) by the serpent of pride (*māna-ahi*) in my miserable body.[80]

Māna can mean 'haughtiness, pride, conceit, self-confidence, vanity'.[81] It is part of both *ahaṁmāna* (egotism) in *Aṣṭāvakragītā* 1.8a and *abhimāna* (erroneous self-conception) in *Śrīmadbhāgavatam* 5.23.32, both discussed above. Pride in one's miserable body is close to identification of one's self with the body - a type of *avidyā* under *Patañjali's* definition.

The *Śrīmadbhāgavatam* uses another snake metaphor to represent the result of *avidyā* - rebirth:

> Salutations to Śuka, lord of *yogi-s*, who [is] *Brahman* in an embodied form [and] liberated King Parikṣit, who [in turn] had been bitten by the snake of rebirth (*saṁsāra sarpa daṣṭaṁ*).[82]

5.7 INAUSPICIOUS ASTROLOGICAL SERPENTS

Serpentine imagery is also used for two astrological demons: Rāhu and Ketu. Rāhu was originally described as a 'disembodied demonic head' that swallows the sun or moon during eclipses.[83] As he has no body, the sun or moon can escape.[84] Rāhu's synonyms include *tamas*.[85] Since *c*.1000 CE, Rāhu has also been described as the head of a huge celestial serpent. The *Bṛhatsaṁhitā* describes Rāhu as a serpent with a head and tail only.[86] Ketu is associated with comets and meteors[87] and is represented in the *Viṣṇudharmottarapurāṇa* as a black snake.[88]

---

80. My translation of Pandurangi (2000, p. 86):

> jvarāmayārtasya yathāgadaṁ sannidāghadagdhasya yathā himāmbhaḥ |
> kudehamānāhivinaṣṭadṛṣṭerbrahmanvacaste 'mṛtamauṣadhaṁ me || 5.12.2 ||

81. Apte (1957, p. 1261).
82. *Śrīmadbhāgavatam* 12.13.21 - my translation of Brahmānandatripāṭhī (1993, p. 3096):

> yogīṁdrāya namastasmai śukāya brahmarūpiṇe |
> saṁsārasarpadaṣṭaṁ yo viṣṇurātamamūmucat || 12.13.21 ||

83. Markel (1990, p. 9).
84. Kochhar (2010, p. 291).
85. Kochhar (2010, p. 288).
86. Kochhar (2010, p. 291).
87. Kochhar (2010, p. 295).
88. Markel (1990, p. 21).

In contemporary Tamil Nadu, inauspicious positions of Rāhu and Ketu in an individual's horoscope are believed to cause *nāgadoṣa* ('snake blemish').[89] To alleviate *nāgadoṣa*, Ketu and especially Rāhu are worshipped.[90] A priest interviewed by Allocco perceives Rāhu as 'the chief *doṣam*-causing entity'.[91]

Artistic depiction of Rāhu and Ketu varies markedly. Rāhu's portrayal as a disembodied head dominated until the late middle ages.[92] Ketu is more often depicted with serpentine features. Sometimes Rāhu and Ketu are both shown with coiled serpentine tails.[93]

In literature, eclipses, comets and meteors are omens of calamity,[94] as are Rāhu and Ketu. The *Chāndogya Upaniṣad* also likens escaping from Rāhu's jaws to the liberation of the *ātman* from the body:

> From the dark I go to the varicolored. From the varicolored I go to the dark. Shaking off evil, as a horse his hairs; shaking off the body (*śarīra*), as the moon releases itself from the mouth of Rāhu; I, a perfected soul (*kṛtātman*), pass into the uncreated Brahma-world – yea, into it I pass![95]

See later in this chapter for a passage by Vedāntadeśika that likens the sun emerging from an eclipse to Kṛṣṇa escaping from the clutches of a snake. Although Rāhu is not always represented as a snake, these examples add to the evidence of snakes being used to represent something to be avoided or overcome. Moreover, the above account of a liberated 'soul' escaping the body could be compared to *prāṇa* entering the *suṣumnā* after being liberated from the blockage of *kuṇḍalinī*. We now turn to snake imagery in the mythology and iconography of some important gods.

---

89. Allocco (2014, p. 3).
90. Allocco (2013, p. 240).
91. Allocco (2014, p. 17).
92. Markel (1990, pp. 9–10).
93. Markel (1990, p. 12 fig.3).
94. Kochhar (2010, pp. 287, 292).
95. *Chāndogya Upaniṣad* 8.13, translation – Hume (1931, p. 273). The term translated as 'evil' is *pāpa*, which also means sin (Apte 1957, p. 1009). See also *Vivekacūḍāmaṇi* 141 (139 in some versions), which compares the veiling power of *tamas* covering the *ātman* to Rāhu covering the sun (Grimes 2004, p. 126).

5.8 *AVATĀR-S* OF VIṢṆU FIGHTING SERPENTS

Stories of Viṣṇu fighting serpents occur for two of his *avatār-s:* Kṛṣṇa and Varāha.

5.8.1 Kṛṣṇa dancing on a serpent

Kṛṣṇa is said to have fought with Kāliya, a *nāga* who resembled 'a pile of black antimony' and who had defiled and polluted a pool of the river Yamunā. When they clashed,

> Kṛishṇa stretched forth both his arms and burst asunder the snake's coils which fettered him. With both his feet he jumped on the huge body of the serpent that issued from the pool, and, suddenly mounting on the large central head of the monster, he danced. Then, being crushed by Kṛishṇa, the serpent dropped his heads, and while a flood of blood poured from each mouth, he spake: 'In my folly, O Kṛishṇa, I have shown this anger. Tamed by thee and deprived of my poison, I have come into thy power, O fair-faced One. Therefore command me; what shall I, together with my wives, off-spring, and kinsmen, do, or to whom shall I submit? I pray thee; grant me my life.' On seeing the serpent with his five-fold head bent down, Kṛishṇa made answer: 'An abode in the waters of Yamunā I allow thee not. Go thou to the ocean with thy wives and kinsmen. If anyone of thy sons or servants shall be seen here again either in the water or on the land, I will surely kill him. May this water henceforth be blessed. Go thou to the ocean.'[96]

This passage from the *Harivaṁśa* depicts a snake covering and restricting something precious: Kṛṣṇa. This resembles the snake of ego covering the *ātman* in the *Vivekacūḍāmaṇi.* It could be viewed as analogous to the *kuṇḍalinī* blockage obstructing the entry of *prāṇa* into the *suṣumnā*, in line with K. Desikachar's claim.

However, *Śrīvaiṣṇava* scholar M.A. Alwar finds K. Desikachar's claim that the story supports Krishnamacharya's position on *kuṇḍalinī* 'totally incorrect' and 'totally untenable'. Instead of representing a blockage to be destroyed, Kṛṣṇa dancing on a snake represents his complete control of *kuṇḍalinī* energy, Alwar argues. The snake signifies that *kuṇḍalinī* energy can create adverse effects and mislead the *yogi* when he tries to attain *siddhi-s.* Alwar was taught this by his guru, K.S. Varadacharya.[97]

96. *Harivaṁśa* 3592–3702, translation – Vogel (1926, p. 89).
97. Alwar (2018).

Varadacharya was in turn a student of Abhinava Ranganātha Parakāla Swāmi, the 33rd pontiff of the Parakāla Math (Mysore) and a contemporary of Krishnamacharya.[98] The *Harivaṁśa* passage seems compatible with Alwar's position. Although Kṛṣṇa threatened to kill Kāliya if he returned, the *nāga* was subdued and controlled, not killed. Another version of the same story in the *Viṣṇupurāṇa* gives more details. When beaten to submission, Kāliya pleaded to Kṛṣṇa:

> I have only acted according to my nature. As you created me with strength and endowed me with poison, so have I behaved. Had I comported myself otherwise, I should have violated the laws laid down by you for every creature according to its kind; I should have challenged the order of the universe and been liable therefore to punishment. But now, even in striking me, you have blessed me with the highest boon, the touch of your hand. My force is broken, my poison spent; I implore you to spare my life to me and declare what I must do.[99]

Matchett elaborates:

> In Kāliya's attack upon Kṛṣṇa the tāmasic elements of the world are seen rebelling against the sāttvic. If the true equilibrium which is Viṣṇu's responsibility is to be restored, the tāmasic element must be put in its appropriate place, in submission to the sāttvic.[100]

Note that *tamas* is subdued, not eliminated. Zimmer continues:

---

98. Ramanuja.org (no date); Parakāla Math (no date a). Krishnamacharya was taught by the 31st and 32nd pontiffs: Kṛṣṇa Brahmatantra Swatantra Parakāla Swāmi (Krishnamacharya's great grandfather) and Vāgīśa Brahmatantra Swatantra Parakāla Swāmi, respectively (T.K.V. Desikachar 1995, pp. 216–217; Srivatsan 1997, pp. 13–18). When the latter died in 1925 (Parakāla Math, no date a), Krishnamacharya was offered the post of pontiff but refused it to continue his studies (Mohan and Mohan 2010, p. 6; Srivatsan 1997, pp. 30–31). Abhinava Ranganātha Parakāla Swāmi then took up the post from 1925 to 1967 (Parakāla Math, no date a). He is still greatly respected. In 2014, the Parakāla Math celebrated the 130th anniversary of his birth (Parakāla Math, no date b). Krishnamacharya is said to have to have completed his studies 'before 1926' (Mohan and Mohan 2010, p. 8) and returned to Mysore in 1924 (T.K.V. Desikachar 1995, p. 220), where he taught at the Sanskrit College from 1932 (Srivatsan 1997, p. 49) and at the Mysore Palace until 1950 (Srivatsan 1997, p. 58). Krishnamacharya would therefore have known Abhinava Ranganātha.
99. *Viṣṇupurāṇa* 5.7, translation – Zimmer (1962, p. 85).
100. Matchett (1986, p. 120).

> Krishna played the role rather of moderator than of annihilator. He liberated mankind from a threat ... and yet recognized the rights of the destructive power; for the venomous serpent was as much a manifestation of the Supreme Being as were the pious cowherds. ... There could be no elimination, once and for all, of this presence which to man seemed wholly negative. Krishna effected only a kind of boundary settlement, a balanced judgement as between demons and men. ... Kāliya was assigned to a remoter sphere, but he was allowed to remain unchanged both in nature and in power. Had he been transformed, redeemed, or altogether eliminated, the counter-play between human and demonic, productive and destructive energies would have been disrupted.[101]

These interpretations do not support K. Desikachar's claim that the metaphor of snakes needing to be killed 'is constantly repeated' in Indian philosophy. However, Vedāntadeśika's later reworking of the tale in his *Yādavābhyudaya* is closer to supporting K. Desikachar's case:

> Then the fierce *nāga* Kāliya rose to [the surface of] the water. With his mouth open like [the jaws of] death, [he] bound Kṛṣṇa with his coils. Having repelled [Kāliya, Kṛṣṇa] bent his hood down and stood on it (4.116). Immediately, Kṛṣṇa trod on Kāliya's hood, which was like a footstool made of a great sapphire with rubies. [Emerging from Kāliya's coils,] Kṛṣṇa shone like the sun emerging from an eclipse (4.117). [Kṛṣṇa] sported with a discus in hand on the snake, [which was] coloured by the splendour of snake jewels (4.118a).[102]

These verses use the imagery of both snake jewels and eclipses. Thathachariar ends his own translation of 4.117 with 'the eclipse of being seized by Rahu'.[103] Rāhu is not mentioned in the Sanskrit but is implied: Vedāntadeśika likens two events involving being seized by a snake and escaping from its clutches. A few verses later is an interesting simile:

---

101. Zimmer (1962, p. 87).

102. *Yādavābhyudaya* - my translation of the Sanskrit in Thathachariar (1976, pp. 119–120):

> athāmbhasaḥ kāliyanāgamugraṁ vyāttānanaṁ mṛtyumivojjihānam |
> bhogena badhnantamapohya śauriḥ prahvīkṛtaṁ tatphaṇamāruroha || 4.116 ||
> madyo mahānīlamayīṁ mukundaḥ sapadmarāgāmiva pādapīṭhīm |
> krāman phaṇāṁ kāliyapannagasya grastodito bhānurivāvabhāse || 4.117 ||
> phaṇāmaṇīnāṁ prabhayoparakte khelan babhau cakriṇi cakrapāṇiḥ | 4.118a |

103. Thathachariar (1976, p. 120). See also *Vivekacūḍāmaṇi* 141 (139 in some versions), which compares the effect of *tamas* covering the *ātman* to Rāhu covering the sun (Grimes 2004, p. 126).

> Having pressed the tail with one hand and the mighty hood with one foot, Hari then wished to destroy (*hantum*) the *nāga*, just like he [wishes to terminate] *saṁsāra* for those dependent on him (*āśritānām*).[104]

Thus, Vedāntadeśika compares a malevolent snake with the result of *avidyā*, rebirth in *saṁsāra*, which Kṛṣṇa wants to terminate. This seems closer to K. Desikachar's position than M.A. Alwar's. However, in three older versions of the tale in the *Harivaṁśa*, *Viṣṇupurāṇa* and *Śrīmadbhāgavatam*, Kāliya is subdued and not killed.[105]

Kāliya is also not completely 'evil':

> Kṛṣṇa may quench the poison fire of Kāliya, but the serpent's power is nevertheless not alien to him. The presence of Balarāma/Saṃkarṣaṇa at his side is a sign that he draws at least a part of his strength from that underworld to which his opponent belongs.[106]

Although Kāliya may seem 'very evil', he merely represents something to be controlled or overcome.

5.8.2 Viṣṇu as Varāha (the boar)

As Varāha (the boar), Viṣṇu subjugates another snake without killing it. *Viṣṇupurāṇa* 1.4 sets the story at the start of the present age.[107] The earth had just been created but an opposing force represented by 'the giant serpent power of the world abyss' caused the earth to be 'ravished from the surface of the cosmic sea to the lowest deep'. Viṣṇu overcame the serpent king and treaded him down until he begged for mercy before raising the earth to the surface of the sea.[108] Zimmer explains:

> Vishnu, as the embodied absolute, is intrinsically not at variance with the serpent principle of the water; nevertheless, in symbolic episodes such as this, the god has to interfere with the serpent's action. The serpent must

---

104. *Yādavābhyudaya* 4.122 – my translation of the Sanskrit in Thathachariar (1976, p. 121):

> ekena hastena nipīḍya bālaṁ pādena caikena phaṇāmudagrām |
> haristadā hantumiyeṣa nāgaṁ sa eva saṁsāramivāśritānām || 4.122 ||

105. Matchett (1986).
106. Matchett (1986, p. 130).
107. Zimmer (1962, p. 77).
108. Zimmer (1962, p. 78).

> be checked, because it endangers the further evolution of the universe ... Operating beyond its bounds at a later stage in the cosmic cycle, it threatens to throw the world back to the shapeless, unconscious condition of the beginnings ... Vishnu counteracts that retrogressive tendency of his own substance by taking form and playing the role of the World Creator and Maintainer.[109]

In contrast, the *Śrīmadbhāgavatam* tells a similar tale of Viṣṇu as Varāha lifting the earth from the waters while confronting the demon Hiraṇyākṣa. Brahmā urges Viṣṇu to kill the demon:

> O God, do not play with this arrogant, uncontrolled and wicked sorcerer (*māyāvinaṁ*), who [is] a snake aroused (*āśīviṣam-utthitam*).[110]

Viṣṇu, himself described as the Lord of *māyā* (*yoga-māyā-Īśvara*, 3.20.17), used his *sudarśana* discus against the demon, whose own *māyā* became dissipated or spent (*vyudastāsu* - 3.20.24). Viṣṇu then kicked the demon, who 'cast off his body' (*tanum-utsasarja* - 3.20.28).

Overall, the evidence from Viṣṇu's *avatār-s* is mixed. The metaphor of a black snake needing to be killed is not 'constantly repeated', as K. Desikachar claimed. It occurs sometimes, but in other accounts the snake is chastized and subdued rather than killed.

5.9 GAṆEŚA AND SERPENTS

Gaṇeśa, the elephant-headed god, appeared from *c.*5th century CE.[111] He was first mentioned in early *Purāṇa-s* (*c.*300–500 CE) and his mythology was detailed in later *Purāṇa-s* (*c.*500–1300 CE).[112] Although his epithet, Gaṇapati, appeared in the *Ṛgveda*, it referred to other gods and was equated with Gaṇeśa later.[113]

---

109. Zimmer (1962, pp. 78–79).

110. *Śrīmadbhāgavatam* 3.19.24 – my translation of Pandurangi (1998, p. 250):

> mainaṁ māyāvinaṁ dṛptaṁ niraṅkuśamasattamam |
> ākrīḍa bālavad deva yadāśīviṣamutthitam ||

111. Courtright (1985, p. 8).

112. Courtright (1985, p. 18).

113. Courtright (1985, pp. 8–9).

Scholars have proposed non-Vedic origins for Gaṇeśa as the totem of a tribe.[114] Courtright maintains, though, that there is no supporting evidence and Gaṇeśa may not have existed before the extant sources.[115] Nevertheless, insight can be gained from the origins of some of his other epithets: Vināyaka (great leader) and Vighneśa (lord of obstacles).

The *Mānavagṛhyasūtra* is a manual of rituals from the 7th–5th centuries BCE. It describes four *Vināyaka-s:* spirits who possess people, prevent the performance of religious rites, and obstruct the achievement of goals.[116] In the *Yājñavalkyasmṛti*, a 1st–3rd centuries CE legal text, the four *Vināyaka-s* coalesce into 'one principal evil force' called Vināyaka. Vināyaka can mean an obstacle or impediment but the name came to mean 'a single source of evil, obstacles, impediments', and rituals were prescribed to nullify his 'evil influences'.[117] Vināyaka was also associated with *nāga-s*, who symbolize malign forces associated with the earth, *pṛthivī*.[118] Vināyaka was described with a twisted trunk and one tusk: features of the classical Gaṇeśa.[119] This completed Gaṇeśa's transition from 'a folk deity, who caused evil',[120] to a mainstream god.

Courtright elaborates on Gaṇeśa's role in obstruction:

> The Sanskrit word for obstacle is *vighna*; Gaṇeśa is sometimes called Vighneśa or lord [*īśa*] of obstacles [*vighna*] ... A *vighna* can be anything that prevents, interrupts, diverts, or impedes anything else. It is any kind of resistance. Every action or undertaking is like the flow of a river or inhaling and exhaling a breath. It has its 'natural' course of action according to the *karma* of the one performing it. But, just like a river can be diverted or a breath can be held, its flow thereby redirected, the undertaking can veer away from the course intended by its author. The diversion or impediment is the action's *vighna*.[121]

Gaṇeśa both causes obstacles and removes them:

114. Courtright (1985, pp. 9–11).
115. Courtright (1985, pp. 11, 12).
116. Krishnan (1999, pp. 25, 26).
117. Krishnan (1999, pp. 26, 27).
118. Krishnan (1999, p. 53).
119. Krishnan (1999, p. 27).
120. Datta (2012, p. 8).
121. Courtright (1985, p. 156).

> he regulates the flow of divine and human power in the context of time and *karma* by putting down or picking up obstacles in the interest of maintaining an intimately harmonious cosmological balance.[122]

The role of such obstacles in impeding the flow of a river or the breath resembles the role of *kuṇḍalinī* in impeding the entry of *prāṇa* into the *suṣumnā* in Krishnamacharya's teaching. But before we jump to any conclusions, we need to examine snakes in Gaṇeśa's iconography and their interpretation.

Yadav reviewed numerous icons of Gaṇeśa. Most show a *nāga yajñopavīta* (serpentine sacred-thread), but some show him wearing a *nāga udarabandha* (snake belt).[123] Note the aspect of binding. Gaṇeśa sometimes holds a snake,[124] has snake bracelets,[125] snake armlets,[126] snake anklets,[127] or a *nāgapāśa* weapon (see below).[128]

Gaṇeśa's snakes are interpreted variously. Krishnan offers three theories.[129] First, Gaṇeśa could have inherited snakes from his father, Śiva, who also has a *nāga yajñopavīta* (see below). Second, the serpents could represent Gaṇeśa's victory over the *nāga-s* Śeṣa and Vāsuki. Indeed, in the *Gaṇeśapurāṇa*, Gaṇeśa made Vāsuki into his scarf.[130] Krishnan, however, argues that such texts attempt to explain iconographical features that precede them.[131] Krishnan's third theory is that a 'Serpent is an omen of evil. So its association with Vināyaka was natural.' His snakes are 'more likely to signify Gaṇeśa subduing the serpent, the embodiment of evil'.[132] These theories are not mutually exclusive. The second and third support K. Desikachar's claim that snakes are 'very evil'.

Others, however, interpret Gaṇeśa's snakes differently. To Mehta, Gaṇeśa's serpent represents *kuṇḍalinī* - 'the coiled and latent psychic energy within each individual'.[133] Keshavadas agrees that the snake around

122. Courtright (1985, p. 157).
123. Yadav (1997, pp. 44, 53, 63, 68–70, 90, 94).
124. Yadav (1997, pp. 42, 55, 59, 82, 87, 98, 101, 110, 118).
125. Yadav (1997, pp. 35, 38, 68, 71).
126. Yadav (1997, p. 51).
127. Yadav (1997, p. 108).
128. Yadav (1997, p. 37).
129. Krishnan (1999, pp. 52–53).
130. Martin-Dubost (1997, p. 202).
131. Krishnan (1999, p. 53).
132. Krishnan (1999, p. 52, 53).
133. Mehta (2006, p. 85).

Gaṇeśa's belly symbolizes 'the cosmic energy *kundalini*'.[134] These popular writers interpret *kuṇḍalinī* as energy, not a blockage. Jagannathan and Krishna apparently agree, describing Gaṇeśa's serpentine belt or sacred thread as 'symbolic of cosmic energy'.[135]

These claims raise the question of whether early iconography is being interpreted in terms of later tantric/haṭhayogic concepts. However, it was mainly *tāntrika-s* who adopted Gaṇeśa as their primary deity[136] and many *Purāṇa-s* are influenced by *tantra*. Furthermore, Gaṇeśa is the presiding deity of *mūlādhāra cakra*.[137] In the description of *mūlādhāra* in the *Śaṭcakranirūpaṇa*, Brahmā sits mounted on Gajendra, 'the king of elephants', and *mūlādhāra* is sometimes drawn containing an elephant.[138] This seems consistent with an association between Gaṇeśa and *kuṇḍalinī* at *mūlādhāra*. The *Gaṇeśapurāṇa* states that Gaṇeśa dwells at 'the base of the sixteen *cakras*', apparently *mūlādhāra*. However, the text continues: 'he has for his dwelling the top of the skull, the *ṣoḍaśānta* ... He dwells in the thousand-petalled lotus'.[139] The picture is therefore unclear.

Gaṇeśa is heavily associated with snakes, but they can be interpreted variously. Whereas Gaṇeśa is associated with obstructions, his snakes are sometimes interpreted as representing *kuṇḍalinī* energy, which does not support K. Desikachar's case.

5.10 GARUḌA AND SERPENTS

Part of K. Desikachar's claim was that Garuḍa 'crushes a black snake'. Garuḍa is a celestial bird of prey who became Viṣṇu's vehicle and the enemy of *nāga-s*. He is often equated with Garutmān (the winged) and Suparṇa (beautiful wing) of the *Ṛgveda*, but his origins may be pre-Vedic or tribal.[140]

The *Atharvaveda* states that Suparṇa was born to counteract poison but it says nothing about hostility to *nāga-s*.[141] The *Ādiparvan* of the

134. Keshavadas (1988, pp. 50–51).
135. Jagannathan and Krishna (1992, p. 97).
136. Datta (2012, p. 7).
137. Rao (2005b, p. 92); Alwar (2018).
138. Avalon (1974, pp. 334, 354) and Mookerjee (1986, p. 41) respectively.
139. Chapter 46 of the *upāsanākhaṇḍa* of the *Gaṇeśapurāṇa* - Martin-Dubost (1997, pp. 107, 111).
140. Parthasarathy (2014, pp. 4, 6, 7, 11).
141. *Atharvaveda* 1.24.1 – Nagar (1992, p. 3).

Mahābhārata develops Garuḍa's legend. Kadrū and Vinatā were both wives of Kaśyapa, who offered each a boon. Kadrū chose a thousand snakes for sons while Vinatā chose two sons who would be more powerful than the snakes. Garuḍa eventually hatched from one of Vinatā's two eggs.[142] Kadrū then tricked Vinatā into becoming her slave, assisted by her snake sons, continuing the *Ādiparvan*'s negative portrayal of snakes. The *nāga-s* then told Garuḍa that his mother would be freed if he stole *amṛta* (nectar) from heaven for them. The *amṛta* was guarded by two poisonous snakes, which Garuḍa blinded with dust before stealing the *amṛta*.[143] This is another example of snakes guarding something precious. Garuḍa then fought with Indra, who feared that the *amṛta* could be used to destroy the *deva-s*.[144] Garuḍa and Indra ceased hostilities and agreed that Indra would retake the *amṛta* after Garuḍa presented it to the *nāga-s*, freeing Vinatā. Indra also granted Garuḍa the boon of eating *nāga-s* in vengeance for them enslaving Vinatā.[145] Garuḍa's continual attacks on *nāga-s* are widely described. For example, in the *Mahābhārata*, he carried away the huge serpent Ṛddhimant.[146]

Garuḍa's association with removing poison is developed in the *Purāṇa-s*. In the *Garuḍapurāṇa* and *Agnipurāṇa*, meditating on Garuḍa, uttering Garuḍa *mantra-s* and displaying magic charms are said to remove poison, especially of *nāga-s*.[147] The *Liṅgapurāṇa* presents an exhortation to eleven epithets of Garuḍa as part of a wider purificatory prayer:

> May the following Garuḍas the vehicles of Viṣṇu, all golden in colour and adorned with various ornaments, dispel my impurity, Garutmān, Khagati, Pakṣirāṭ, Nāgamardana, Nāgaśatru, Hiraṇyāṅga, Vainateya, Prabhañjana, Nāgāśīḥ, Viṣanāśa and Viṣṇuvāhana.[148]

Nāgamardana means '*nāga* crushing', Nāgaśatru means 'destroyer of *nāga-s*' or 'foe of *nāga-s*', and Nāgāśīḥ probably means '*nāga* fang' or '*nāga* venom'.[149]

142. Parthasarathy (2014, p. 41).
143. Parthasarathy (2014, pp. 44–47).
144. Parthasarathy (2014, pp. 50–51).
145. Parthasarathy (2014, p. 51); Chandramohan (2008, p. 5).
146. *Mahābhārata* 3.157.14–15 – Parthasarathy (2014, p. 55).
147. Parthasarathy (2014, p. 93).
148. *Liṅgapurāṇa* 82.62b–64, translation – Motilal Banarsidass (1951, p. 406).
149. Apte (1957, pp. 1242, 1531, 367).

Images of Garuḍa abound in *Vaiṣṇava* temples.[150] Garuḍa is frequently shown with snakes, sometimes in his talons.[151] The Tamil *Paripāṭal* describes Garuḍa decorated with five snakes acting as his waistband, bracelet, garland, head ornament and necklace.[152] Other texts stipulate eight snakes. The *Īśvarasaṁhitā* (a *Pāñcarātra* text) lists serpents located on both ears (see Plate 3), on Garuḍa's head, on his chest, and acting as his bracelet, sacred thread, waist band and necklace.[153] The *Gāruḍa Upaniṣad* gives a similar list of eight.[154] According to tradition, these eight *nāga-s* were given the boon of adorning Garuḍa's body.[155]

Śrīvaiṣṇava tradition (see Chapter 6) also gave both Śeṣa and Garuḍa the status of *nityasūri* – a permanent resident of heaven.[156] *Vaiṣṇava* scholars attributed the cessation of hostilities between them to Viṣṇu's grace, generosity and power.[157] Zimmer gives a different explanation:

> This is a paradox with reason; for Vishnu is the Absolute, the all-containing Divine Essence. He comprises all dichotomies. The Absolute becomes differentiated in polarized manifestations, and through these the vital tensions of the world-process are brought into existence and maintained.[158]
> ... the serpent and the savior [Garuḍa] are two basic manifestations of the one, all-containing, divine substance. And this substance cannot be at variance with either of its polarized, mutually antagonistic aspects. Within it the two are reconciled and subsumed.[159]

Atmashraddhananda concurs: 'This bringing together of contraries symbolizes the balance and harmony for which Vishnu is famous.'[160] Hence, even though some writers have described the snakes Garuḍa kills as 'evil', apparently supporting K. Desikachar's position, their descriptions need to be interpreted with caution. A complementary explanation seems implicit in Cozad's conceptual framework, in which *nāga-s* are depicted as either

150. Chandramohan (2008, pp. 13, 64, 85); Nagar (1992, plates 19–21).
151. Parthasarathy (2014, plate VI fig.4).
152. Parthasarathy (2014, pp. 112–113).
153. Lakshmithathachar and Varadachari (2009, vol. 2 pp.523–527).
154. Parthasarathy (2014, p. 219).
155. Parthasarathy (2014, p. 529).
156. Parthasarathy (2014, pp. 48, 123, 124).
157. Parthasarathy (2014, p. 415).
158. Zimmer (1962, p. 76).
159. Zimmer (1962, pp. 89–90), my insertion in brackets.
160. Atmashraddhananda (2016, p. 67).

Plate 3
Snakes adorning the ears of Garuḍa – terracotta figure outside Sri Vedantha Desikar Devasthanam, Chennai.

Photograph: Simon Atkinson

benevolent deities or malevolent demons. Perhaps a truce could be called because the originally threatening Śeṣa had been tamed and brahminized to such an extent that he no longer needed to be controlled by Garuḍa. Śeṣa and his serpentine powers had been safely subsumed within the Vedic pantheon, perpetuating its dominance.

Nevertheless, Garuḍa is overwhelmingly depicted as an enemy of snakes, which often represent poison and impurity. The evidence therefore broadly supports at least part of K. Desikachar's claim. I have, however, found no mention of Garuḍa crushing a *black* snake. Indeed, Śeṣa is depicted as the black snake upon which Viṣṇu reclines in the inner sanctum of the Sri Ranganatha Swamy Temple, Srirangam.

5.11 ŚIVA AND SERPENTS

In his statement, K. Desikachar did not mention Śiva but snakes form 'an inseparable part' of this major god's decorations.[161] According to the *Purāṇa-s*, Śiva acquired his snakes from forest sages. The sages did not recognize Śiva, became angry and hurled snakes at him, which became his emblems.[162]

In art, snakes form a *mālā* (garland) around Śiva's neck, or a *yajñopavīta* (sacred thread).[163] Śiva often holds snakes in a left hand or sometimes in a right hand.[164] Snake ornaments are found on Śiva's thigh or head,[165] around his forehead,[166] and holding his hair in a bun as a *sarpa jaṭābandha*.[167] Note the element of binding. Other snake ornaments include a girdle,[168] earrings (*kuṇḍala-s*),[169] anklets,[170] armlets,[171] and bracelets.[172]

Śiva's snakes are interpreted variously. Pattanaik claims that 'The hooded cobra around Shiva's neck ... represents stillness' and his 'absolute renunciation, his refusal to react or respond to any threat or temptation'.[173] In contrast, M.A. Alwar told me that the snake around Śiva represents *kuṇḍalinī śakti* in the *Śaiva* system.[174] This suggests *kuṇḍalinī* is a form of *prāṇa* rather than a blockage to *prāṇa*. Atmashraddhananda states that Śiva's snakes 'signify conquest of death through association with the Divine'.[175] None of these interpretations support K. Desikachar's case. However, neo-*Advaitin* Chinmayānanda states that Śiva's ornamental snake represents 'the ego-sense'.[176] Prabhupāda, a *Gauḍīya Vaiṣṇava*, effectively expands upon Chinmayānanda's statement:

---

161. Nagar (1994, pp. xvii, 68).
162. Doniger-O'Flaherty (1976, p. 308).
163. Handa (1992, pp. 98, 44); Nagar (1994, p. 148).
164. Nagar (1994, p. 89); Choudary (2014, pp. 43, 53, 127, 145).
165. Nagar (1994, pp. 181, 171).
166. Choudary (2014, p. 88).
167. Handa (1992, p. 61).
168. Nagar (1994, p. 170); Choudary (2014, p. 165).
169. Choudary (2014, p. 146, 147).
170. Choudary (2014, p. 146).
171. Choudary (2014, p. 88).
172. Handa (1992, p. 20).
173. Pattanaik (2011, p. 43); Pattanaik (1997, p. 98).
174. Alwar (2018).
175. Atmashraddhananda (2016, pp. 122, 123).
176. Chinmayananda (1970, p. 362).

> In order to get release from the false ego, one has to worship Saṅkarṣaṇa. Saṅkarṣaṇa is also worshiped through Lord Śiva; the snakes which cover the body of Lord Śiva are representations of Saṅkarṣaṇa, and Lord Śiva is always absorbed in meditation upon Saṅkarṣaṇa. One who is actually a worshiper of Lord Śiva as a devotee of Saṅkarṣaṇa can be released from false, material ego.[177]

One dictionary definition of Saṅkarṣaṇa is 'egotism' (*ahaṁkāra*).[178] In Prabhupāda's argument, however, Śiva's snakes not only represent 'the ego sense' (as Chinmayānanda claims), they also represent that which releases us from it. Hence, Prabhupāda's statement could, at a stretch, also be regarded as compatible with Pattanaik's claim that 'the serpent around Shiva's neck is Patanjali, who wrote the *Yoga Sutra*'.[179] *Patañjali* is traditionally considered an incarnation of Śeṣa/Saṅkarṣaṇa,[180] and his *Yogasūtra* could be said to release one from egotism. Krishnamacharya equated *Patañjali* and Śeṣa in verse 6 of his short composition in praise of Śeṣa, the *Ādiśeṣāṣṭakam*:

> Salutations to Śeṣa! who revived the aṣṭāṅgayoga to cleanse the body and mind and make it stronger to serve the Lord.

The opening prayer to the *Ādiśeṣāṣṭakam* ends with

> Let this resplendent king of the serpents reveal himself to me in my heart.[181]

In his *Yogamakaranda*, Krishnamacharya presented a different prayer to recite to Śeṣa before *yoga* practice. Among the claimed benefits of the prayer are that it 'forces entry of *Prāṇa* into the *Suṣumnā-nāḍī*'.[182] Krishnamacharya did not mention the *kuṇḍalinī* blockage to *prāṇa* entering the *suṣumnā*.

There is no evidence that Krishnamacharya regarded Śeṣa as representing 'the ego sense', as Chinmayānanda states, or the means to overcome

177. Prabhupāda (1982a, p. 97).
178. Apte (1957, p. 1602).
179. Pattanaik (2011, p. 43).
180. Bühnemann (2018); Jacobsen (2011, p. 746). See White (2014, pp. 18–52) for an account of how a single *Patañjali* became identified with Śeṣa and became considered the author of works on *yoga*, *Āyurveda* and grammar.
181. Translation – Balasubramanian et al. (2001, pp. 12–13).
182. Krishnamacharya (2011, p. 75).

it, as Prabhupāda states. Instead, Krishnamacharya's position seems to be based on the *Śrīvaiṣṇava* interpretation of Śeṣa as representing the *jīva* (see section 5.4 above). In a drawing in a Krishnamacharya Yoga Mandiram publication, *Patañjali* is shown with four arms, three of which hold emblems of Viṣṇu: the *sudarśana* discus, the conch shell and the sword.[183] Krishnamacharya certainly did not regard Śeṣa/Saṅkarṣaṇa as 'very evil' or something to be destroyed.

In summary, the evidence from Śiva is mixed. If his snakes represented 'the ego sense', it would be comparable to K. Desikachar's claim that snakes represent *asmitā* (*kleśa*). However, other interpretations state that Śiva's snakes represent a means of overcoming 'the ego sense', the conquest of death, stillness, the *jīva* or *kuṇḍalinī śakti* as energy. These all conflict with K. Desikachar's statement.

5.12 BINDING SERPENTS

Speaking at a *yoga* workshop in Glasgow, A.G. Mohan said that in Vedic texts, the snake is something that binds. The cosmos moves in the form of a snake and the binding force responsible for the attraction between planets is represented in the *Veda-s* as a snake, he said. 'Just as the cosmos is held together by *nāgaśakti*, the individual is held together by his *saṁskāra-s*, which are represented by *avidyā*'. *Avidyā* is 'nothing but the sum total of our *saṁskāra-s*'. It binds us and is represented as the snake *kuṇḍalinī*.[184] This section will look for evidence of Mohan's claim.

5.12.1 Binding in the *Ṛgveda* and a celestial serpent in the *Garuḍapurāṇa*

The concept of binding has been used to describe the embodiment of the self ever since the *Ṛgveda:*

183. T.K.V. Desikachar (1982, between p.37 and p.41); reproduced in Bühnemann (2018, p. 614). This drawing, 'conceived by Krishnamacharya', represents his teaching that each of the four chapters of the *Yoga Sūtra* was written for a different student. It is similar to a 20th-century print reproduced in Colas (2011, p. 594) of Vaikhanas (founder of the *Vaikhānasa* sect) and his four supposed students.

184. Mohan (2018a). Mohan said this as a direct answer to a question that I asked. I took detailed notes.

> As men bind the yoke with cords for its support, so has (AGNI) placed thy spirit (in the body) for life, not for death, but for security.[185]

Other than the above account of Rāhu and Ketu, the only textual reference I have found to celestial serpents is in the *Garuḍapurāṇa:*

> Vasuki, the lord of the serpents, carried away the bile of that chief of the demons (Vala) and rent in twain the vast expanse of heaven with the sweep of his mighty tail. The body of that primordial Hydra, illumined with the effulgence of gems glowing on his thousand hoods, lay like a bridge of shining silver across the infinite deep of dark blue ether.[186]

Sahi claims that Śeṣa represents the Milky Way, based on his interpretation of a 6th century CE calving.[187] I have found no other references to celestial serpents and no evidence of a snakes representing a binding force between planets, as Mohan claims. I did, though, find texts using serpents to represent other types of binding.

5.12.2 Binding serpents in the *Matsyapurāṇa*

A snake is used to represent binding in a story set in an early period of Hindu mythology. In the *Matsyapurāṇa*, Viṣṇu in the form of a fish with a horn warned King Manu of an impending flood. To rescue those to be saved, Manu was told to commandeer a boat made by the gods and to tether it to Viṣṇu's horn with a rope. Later, during the flood,

> A snake in the form of a rope (*bhujaṅga-rajju-rupeṇa*) approached the vicinity of Manu. Having drawn all living beings to himself by his *yoga* (yogic power), Manu raised the virtuous [onto the boat]. With the snake-rope, [he] fastened the boat onto the horn of the fish.[188]

---

185. *Ṛgveda* 10.60.8, translation – Wilson (1888, p. 155). The word for 'bind' is *nahyanti* from the root *nah. Manas* is usually translated as mind, but Griffith (1897, p. 464) and Prakash-Sarasvati and Vidyalankar (1984, p. 4255) also translate it as 'spirit', in line with the less-common dictionary definitions of 'spirit' and 'living soul' (Apte 1957, p. 1233). Those translators seem to regard *manas* as a synonym for *jīvātman.*

186. *Garuḍapurāṇa* chapter 71, translation – Shastrī (1968, p. 195).

187. Sahi (1980, pp. 161–163). Sahi gives no supporting textual reference.

188. *Matsyapurāṇa* 2.18–19a – my translation of the Sanskrit in Joshi (2007, p. 5):

> bhujaṅgo rajjurūpeṇa manoḥ pārśvamupāgamat |
> bhūtānsarvānsamākṛṣya yogenāropya dharmavit || 2.18 ||
> bhujaṅgarajjvā matsyasya śṛṅge nāvamayojayat | 2.19a |

We have seen above how *Advaita* represents *māyā* using the metaphor of a rope appearing to be a snake. Here, conversely, a snake takes the form of a rope. The word I translated as 'fastened' is *ayojayat*, from the root *yuj*, meaning 'caused to join' – i.e. 'caused to bind'.

5.12.3 Binding serpents in the *Ṛgveda* and *Yajurveda*

The *Ṛgveda* also uses snakes to represent binding. A hymn on weapons eulogizes the bracer (*hastaghna*), an archer's armguard. The bracer 'wraps around (*paryeti*) the arm like a snake (*ahir-iva*) with its coils (*bhogaiḥ*), preventing injury from the bow string'.[189] Bows represent concentration, focus, balance,[190] and power,[191] but this simile seems purely physical. Note the elements of covering and binding. In the *Yajurveda*, snakes also represent binding when they form magical arrows:

> Homage be to the snakes whichsoever move along the earth. Which are in the sky and in heaven, homage be to those snakes. Which are the arrows of sorcerers and of tree-spirits, and which lie in holes, homage be to those snakes.[192]

The theme of snakes forming magical arrows is developed in the two epics: the *Mahābhārata* and the *Rāmāyaṇa*.

5.12.4 Binding serpents in the *Mahābhārata*

In the *Ādiparvan* of the *Mahābhārata*, Agni had tried to burn down a forest but was thwarted by rain. Agni was then assisted by Kṛṣṇa and Arjuna. Arjuna warned that an inexhaustible quiver of arrows was needed to kill the forest's *rākṣasa-s* (monsters) and *nāga-s*. These included the *nāga* prince Aśvasena, who was prevented from leaving the forest by Arjuna's arrows. Later, during the battle of Kurukṣetra, Aśvasena remembered that encounter. By the power of *yoga* (*yoga balena*) he 'assumed the shape of an arrow and entered the quiver of Karṇa', who was fighting Arjuna. Karṇa

189. *Ṛgveda* 6.75.14a, my translation of Tilak Mahārāshtra University (1941, p. 260): ahiriva bhogaiḥ paryeti bāhuṁ jyāyā hetiṁ paribādhamānaḥ | 6.75.14a |

190. Pattanaik (2011, p. 43).

191. Atmashraddhananda (2016, p. 26).

192. *Maitrāyaṇīsaṁhitā* 2.7, 15 of the Black *Yajurveda*, translation – von Schröder (no date), quoted in Vogel (1926, p. 7).

'laid on his bow that terrible, foe-slaying, flaming arrow, snake-mouthed and polished'. When shot, the arrow 'blazed like fire' but was badly aimed by Karṇa, who refused to fire it again. Kṛṣṇa instructed Arjuna to 'Slay the great Serpent with whom thou art in feud.' Arjuna then pierced the *nāga's* body with arrows and the *nāga* fell.[193] This tale demonizes the *nāga* by associating him with *rākṣasa-s* and placing him in opposition to Arjuna. Note that Kṛṣṇa requests the *nāga's* destruction, which is consistent with K. Desikachar's claim that snakes represent something to be killed.

A later section of the *Mahābhārata* gives further evidence of snakes representing binding. King Dhṛtarāṣṭra is told of the fight between Arjuna, of the Pāṇḍava army, and Suśarman's forces, fighting for the opposing Kaurava-s:

> Then the Pāṇḍava killer of hostile heroes, [Arjuna], made foot-bind[s] (*pādabandha*) by repeatedly discharging snake arrow[s] (*nāgam astra*), O great king (21). Those at whom Arjuna aimed on the battlefield and [for whom he] made foot-bind[s] were bound (*badhāḥ*) with those foot-bind[s] by the great-souled Pāṇḍava and did not move, as if made of iron, O king (22). ... Then the great warrior [and] royal lord, Suśarman, seeing [his] army seized (*gṛhītāṁ*), quickly revealed the *sauparṇa* weapon (25). Then birds of prey (*suparṇa-s*) flew down, eating the snakes (*bhujaṅga-s*). Having seen them coming, the *nāga-s* verily fled (26). O lord of the people, that [military] force freed from the foot-bind[s] seemed just like the sun illuminating and heating creatures [when] freed from dense cloud (27).[194]

This extract associates snake arrows (*nāgam astra-s*) with binding. In a verse interpolated in all northern manuscripts,[195] the feet of Suśarman's

193. All the paragraph to this point is from Vogel (1926, pp. 77–80).

194. *Mahābhārata* 8.37.21–27 – my translation of Tokunaga and Smith (2013, pp. 236–237):

> padabandhaṁ tataścakre pāṇḍavaḥ paravīrahā |
> nāgamastraṁ mahārāja saṁprodīrya muhurmuhuḥ || 8.37.21 ||
> yānuddiśya raṇe pārthaḥ padabandhaṁ cakāra ha |
> te baddhāḥ padabandhena pāṇḍavena mahātmanā |
> niśceṣṭā abhavanrājannaśmasāramayā iva || 8.37.22 ||
> tataḥ suśarmā rājendra gṛhītāṁ vīkṣya vāhinīm
> sauparṇamastraṁ tvaritaḥ prāduścakre mahārathaḥ || 8.37.25 ||
> tataḥ suparṇāḥ saṁpeturbhakṣayanto bhujaṅgamān |
> te vai vidudruvurnāgā dṛṣṭvā tānkhacarānnṛpa || 8.37.26 ||
> babhau balaṁ tadvimuktaṁ padabandhādviśāṁ pate |
> meghavṛndādyathā mukto bhāskarastāpayanprajāḥ || 8.37.27 ||

195. Emeneau (1960, p. 293).

soldiers were 'enveloped by snakes'.[196] The word for 'enveloped' is *veṣṭitā*, from the root *viṣṭ/veṣṭ*, to cover or wrap. The metaphor of serpentine foot binds in the *Mahābhārata* is clear: 'the Kauravas have tried to "ensnare" or "entangle" the Pāṇḍavas in "evil," as Vṛtra entangled Indra'.[197] Indeed, Rodrigues translates Vṛtra as 'The Binder'.[198] *Suparṇa-s* are birds of prey like Garuḍa. Garuḍa himself drives away binding snakes in a similar passage in the *Rāmāyaṇa*, which also links snakes to *māyā*.

5.12.5 Binding serpents in the *Rāmāyaṇa*

Vālmīki's *Rāmāyaṇa* describes how Rāma, his brother Lakṣmaṇa and an army of monkeys defeated an army of monsters (*rākṣasa-s*) to rescue Rāma's wife from the monsters' king. When they fought Indrajit, the king's son,

> That monster (Indrajit), angry in battle, pierced all the limbs [of] Rāma and Lakṣmaṇa with arrows consisting of frightful *nāga-s* (*ghorair nāga mayaiḥ*).[199]

The *nāga-s* wrapped themselves around the brothers and immobilized them. Rāma and Lakṣmaṇa appeared dead, but then Garuḍa arrived:

> Having seen he who had come (Garuḍa), those *nāga-s*, by whom the two good men had been bound (*baddhau*) with greatly-powerful arrows, fled.[200]

When Rāma and Lakṣmaṇa revived, Garuḍa addressed them:

> Neither the gods, nor the demons, nor the very brave, nor the very strong together with the celestial musicians with Indra put before [them] would have been able to release (*mokṣayituṁ śaktāḥ*) this terribly frightful arrow-bind (*śara bandha*) made by the wicked action of Indrajit from the power of *māyā* (*māyā balāt*). These *nāga-s*, sons of Kādru [with] sharp fangs

196. My translation of *bhujagair veṣṭitā* from Emeneau (1960, p. 293).
197. Coomaraswamy (1942, p. 342).
198. Rodrigues (2009, p. 475).
199. *Rāmāyaṇa* 6.34.30 – my translation of Vyas (1992, p. 679):

> sa rāmaṁ lakṣmaṇaṁ caiva ghorairnāgamayaiḥ śaraiḥ |
> bibheda samare kruddhaḥ sarvagātreṣu rākṣasaḥ || 6.34.30 ||

200. *Rāmāyaṇa* 6.40.37 – my translation of Vyas (1992, p. 689):

> tamāgatamabhiprekṣya nāgāste vipradudruvuḥ |
> yaistau satpuruṣau baddhau śarabhūtairmahābalau || 6.40.37 ||

and powerful poison, having become arrows by means of the *māyā* of the *rākṣasa*, became attached to you.[201]

Chandramohan comments that 'it is very strange to find that Lakṣmaṇa who was an incarnation of Ādiśeṣa, the King of Snakes, was affected by the *nāgāstra* and Garuḍa, the enemy of snakes, had to restore him back to life'.[202] However, as Zimmer argues above, Garuḍa and Śeṣa are two manifestations of *Brahman* that are reconciled by Viṣṇu, who is present here in the *avatār* of Rāma.

The *Rāmāyaṇa* goes beyond the *Mahābhārata* by associating *nāga*-s with both binding and *māyā*. The *nāga*-s originated not from the illusory *māyā* of Viṣṇu or Lakṣmī, but from the *māyā* of Indrajit's malevolent sorcery.

5.12.6 The *nāgapāśa* weapon in the *Sātvatasaṁhitā*

The *pāśa* is a weapon of many deities, including Gaṇeśa, Kālī, Varuṇa, Yama,[203] and Viṣṇu. The literal meaning of *pāśa* is a noose, 'a weapon to bind enemies'.[204] It frequently has 'dreadful associations'; for example, Yama's noose is called *kālapāśa*, the noose of time.[205] The *pāśa* can symbolize 'desire and attachment'.[206] It can, however, also counter such qualities. To Courtright, it represents 'the restraint of passions and desires'.[207] Martin-Dubost agrees that the *pāśa* 'helps to control the human passions (*rāga*). It also serves to bind and stop the actions of the evil.'[208] Lal concurs that the *pāśa* 'snares *moha* (delusion)'.[209]

---

201. *Rāmāyaṇa* 6.40.47–49 – my translation of Vyas (1992, p. 689):

> asurā vā mahāvīryā dānavā vā mahābalāḥ |
> surāścāpi sagandharvāḥ puraskṛtya śatakratum || 6.40.47 ||
> nemaṁ mokṣayituṁ śaktāḥ śarabandhaṁ sudāruṇam |
> māyābalādindrajitā nirmitaṁ krūrakarmaṇā || 6.40.48 ||
> ete nāgāḥ kādraveyāstīkṣṇadaṁṣṭrā viṣolbaṇāḥ |
> rakṣomāyāprabhāvena śarā bhūtvā tvadāśritāḥ || 6.40.49 ||

202. Chandramohan (2008, p. 13).
203. Wessels-Mevissen (2013, p. 29).
204. Bühnemann (2008, p. 20).
205. Wessels-Mevissen (2013, p. 29). The *kālapāśa* is mentioned in *Haṭhapradīpikā* 3.24.
206. Rao (2005b, pp. 92–93).
207. Courtright (1985, p. 4).
208. Martin-Dubost (1997, p. 187).
209. Lal (1991, p. 56).

Hemacandra's *Triṣaṣṭiśalākāpuruṣacarita*, a Jain reworking of the *Rāmāyaṇa*, likens *nāgapāśa* to *karmapāśa*, the noose of *karma*. The text also uses the term *nāgapāśa* to describe missiles fired at Hanūmān that bound him 'from head to foot'.[210] In that context, *nāgapāśa* is used very much like *nāgabandha*, which may be close synonyms.[211] I have not, however, found a text using the term *nāgabandha* in that sense.[212]

Wessels-Mevissen only identifies Varuṇa's noose as being represented as a serpent,[213] but this is also true for other deities. For example, Devī uses a *nāgapāśa* to bind the demon Mahiṣa.[214] In 13th–16th century CE bronzes in the Government Museum, Chennai, Kālī is shown with a *nāgapāśa* in her uppermost right hand.

Viṣṇu also wields a *nāgapāśa*. The *Sātvatasaṁhitā* (*c*.300–500 CE) is said to be 'the first and foremost' *Pāñcarātra* text.[215] It describes Viṣṇu's characteristic features and weapons for *saguṇa* meditation, including the *nāgapāśa*:

> The *pāśa* (noose) [is] completely covered [by] a number of hooded serpents (*phaṇi*) [with] frightful lightning-tongue[s], the lustre of gold, pale white and black, and horrific face[s] with blood-red eye[s].[216]

Verse 13.34 adds that the noose represents illusion (*pāśa* = *māyā*),[217] so terrifying snakes represent *māyā*. This teaching was repeated in the *Īśvarasaṁhitā*.[218] It may have influenced how the writers of other later *Pāñcarātra* texts, including the *Ahirbudhnyasaṁhitā* and *Pādmasaṁhitā*, conceived of *kuṇḍalī* (see Chapter 3), which is absent in the *Sātvatasaṁhitā*.

---

210. Emeneau (1960, pp. 296, 294).
211. Emeneau (1960, p. 297).
212. *Nāgabandha* is a hand gesture in South Asian dance (Mohanty et al. 2016, p. 530), an architectural term and a design with intertwined serpents (Coomaraswamy 1942, p. 341). In poetry, it is verses whose letters can be arranged into serpentine geometrical patterns (Lakshmithathachar 2018).
213. Wessels-Mevissen (2013, p. 29).
214. Rodrigues (2009, p. 475).
215. Apte (2005, p. vii).
216. *Sātvatasaṁhitā* 13.21b–13.22a – my translation of Dwivedī (2001, p. 264):

> pāśaṁ phaṇigaṇākīrṇaṁ vidyujjihvaṁ bhayānakam || 13.21b ||
> hemālipāṇḍarābhaṁ ca ghorāsyaṁ raktalocanam | 3.22a |

217. Dwivedī (2001, p. 266).
218. *Īśvarasaṁhitā* 7.205–7.217 – Lakshmithathachar and Varadachari (2009, vol. 2 pp.340–343).

Krishnamacharya referenced the *Sātvatasaṁhitā* in his *Yogamakaranda*,[219] so he would have been familiar with these verses.

5.13 *YOGATĀRĀVALĪ* (SERPENTS REPRESENTING *MOHA* AND *SAṀSĀRA*)

Krishnamacharya was also familiar with the *Yogatārāvalī*. T.K.V. Desikachar and K. Desikachar attribute this *yoga* text to Ādiśaṅkara but Birch dates it to the *c.*12th-15th centuries CE.[220] Birch translates the first verse as follows:

> I pay homage to the gurus' lotus feet, which have revealed the knowledge of the bliss of one's own self. Unsurpassed, [these lotus-feet] act like toxicologists for curing the delusion that is the poison [known as] transmigration.[221]

Birch translates *jāṅgalika* as 'toxicologists'. He notes that the *Yogabhāvaprakāśikā* commentary glosses *jāṅgalika* as *viṣavaidya* (toxicologist), as does the *Amarakośa* thesaurus. These are valid points. He adds that *jāṅgalika* is usually spelled *jāṅgulika*, which is often translated as 'snake doctor', a doctor who deals in antidotes to snake venom. However, Monier-Williams translates both *jāṅgulika* and *jāṅgalika* as 'snake-charmer'.[222] Apte also translates *jāṅgalika* in the same way.[223] This opens up an alternative interpretation.

Another key phrase is *saṁsāra hālāhala moha*, which Birch accurately translates as 'the delusion that is the poison [known as] transmigration'. He adds that

> in the *Yogatārāvalī's* first verse, *jāṅgalika* is being used metaphorically to describe gurus who can cure a poison called Hālāhala. Rather than a snake poison, Hālāhala probably refers to either the mythological poison produced at the churning of the ocean and swallowed by Śiva ... or some plant-based poison. Therefore, it appears that the guru is being likened to a doctor who specializes in the general treatment of poisons (i.e. a toxicologist) rather than a snake doctor or charmer.[224]

---

219. Krishnamacharya (2011, p. 42).
220. Desikachar and Desikachar (2003); Birch (2015, p. 8).
221. Birch (2015, p. 4).
222. Monier-Williams (1899, p. 417).
223. Apte (1957, p. 732).
224. Birch (2015, p. 4 n.2).

I agree that *jāṅgalika* is metaphorical. However, I see no reference to the churning of the ocean or a plant-based poison in the *Yogatārāvalī* and Birch does not explain why he interprets the verse in that way. Verse 6 does, however, mention a female serpent (*uraga aṅganā*) which is awoken by the practice of *uḍyāṇa* (=*uḍḍīyāna*), *jālandhara* and *mūla bandha-s*. Verse 12 names that serpent *kuṇḍalī*. Given this explicit snake-based content and the widespread association of snakes with poison, it seems equally logical to interpret *jāṅgalika* in verse 1 more literally as 'snake charmer'. Reading this term as part of a snake metaphor, in line with other examples I present above, makes plausible the following commentary on verse 1 by T.K.V. Desikachar and K. Desikachar:

> The metaphor of a snake charmer (*Jāṅgalika*) used by *Śaṅkara* is very symbolic. He emphasizes that through the teacher (the snake charmer), the poison in us (our ignorance) which causes misery in our lives comes under control, much like the snake charmer controlling a venomous snake.[225]

If we accept this interpretation, my translation of verse 1 becomes the following:

> [I] praise the *guru-s*' lotus feet, by which happiness in knowledge of the *ātman* is certainly revealed. These snake charmers dispel a person's delusion, the deadly poison of rebirth (*saṁsāra hālāhala moha*), for the sake of peace.[226]

From this perspective, 'delusion, the deadly poison of rebirth' could refer to *kuṇḍalī* in verse 12 and the female snake in verse 6:

> When the female snake (*uraga aṅganā*) is awoken by [the practice of] *uḍyāṇa*, *jālandhara* and *mūla bandha-s*, the breath (*gandhavāha*) abandons its coming and going (inhalation and exhalation), entering into the interior of the mouth of *suṣumnā* (6).

---

225. Desikachar and Desikachar (2003, p. 11).

226.

> vande gurūṇāṁ caraṇāravinde sandarśitasvātmasukhāvabodhe |
> janasya ye jāṅgalikāyamāne saṁsārahālāhalamohaśāntyai || 1 ||

This is an unpublished version supplied by Jason Birch (2018), who is compiling a critical edition of the *Yogatārāvalī*. The Sanskrit differs slightly from an earlier version (Birch 2015, p. 4): *janasya ye* replaces *niḥśreyase* (unsurpassed), which Birch used in his above translation.

> When the awoken *kuṇḍalī* is restrained by *kevala kumbhaka* (stopping the breath), *prāṇa*, the remnant of what has been consumed, slowly slips away, turning inwards along the path *[suṣumnā]* to the middle of the *Viṣṇupāda* lotus (12).[227]

The poison in verse 1 can be interpreted as relating to *kuṇḍalī*, reflecting the association of snakes with poison.[228] Although Birch's interpretation of verse 1 is valid and logical, in light of the other examples in this chapter, the verse can also be read as another example of where snake metaphors are used to represent something to be overcome, such as *avidyā*, *ajñāna* or *māyā*. Here, the female snake, *kuṇḍalī*, could represent *moha*, the deadly poison of *saṁsāra*, just as snakes represent *saṁsāra* in *Śrīmadbhāgavatam* 12.13.21 (see above).[229]

5.14 A CAUTIONARY NOTE – *KUṆḌALINĪ* IN THE *ŚIVASAṀHITĀ*

Many *haṭhayoga* texts incorporate elements of *Advaita* doctrine. The *haṭha* text perhaps most 'profoundly influenced' by *Advaita* is the *Śivasaṁhitā*.[230] In its first chapter, which is overwhelmingly *Advaita* in stance, the snake-rope analogy is used in verses 1.38–44. As in the *Advaita* texts examined above, the snake represents the illusory perception that anything exists other than *Brahman*. In 4.46, *kuṇḍalinī* is described as *mahāmāyā* 'the great goddess of illusion',[231] in keeping with the above examples in

---

227. *Yogatārāvalī* – my translation of the unpublished Sanskrit supplied by Birch (2018):

> uḍyāṇajālandharamūlabandhair unnidritāyām uragāṅganāyām |
> pratyaṁmukhatvāt praviśan suṣumnāṁ gamāgamau muñcati gandhavāhaḥ || 6 ||
> pratyāhṛtaḥ kevalakumbhakena prabuddhakuṇḍalyupabhuktaśeṣaḥ |
> prāṇaḥ pratīcīnapathena mandaṁ vilīyate viṣṇupadāntarāle || 12 ||

228. *Kuṇḍalī* is, however, not explicitly described as blocking the *suṣumnā*, as in certain *Pāñcarātra* texts and the *Yogayājñavalkya*.

229. I have not seen the unpublished *Rājayogatarala* commentary on the *Yogatārāvalī* by Rāmasvāmīpaṇḍita/Parānandanātha. That commentary gives two to seven interpretations of each verse of the *Yogatārāvalī* and up to thirteen interpretations of individual words (Jayaraman 2018, pp. 66, 69). It would seem that the *Yogatārāvalī* lends itself to multiple interpretations. Birch seems to interpret *jāṅgalika* as a reference to something not stated in the text: 'the mythological poison produced at the churning of the ocean and swallowed by Śiva ... or some plant-based poison'. My alternative translation interprets *jāṅgalika* as a reference to something that is indeed in the text: the female snake, *kuṇḍalī*.

230. Kathirasan (2018, p. 5).

231. Translation – Mallinson (2007b, p. 84).

which snakes represent *māyā*. Verses 5.78–79 locate *kuṇḍalinī* in the *kanda*, between the anus and the penis, where she coils around all the *nāḍī-s* with her tail in her mouth.[232] Note the different location of the *kanda* compared to that given in the *Yogayājñavalkya*. *Kuṇḍalinī* is located in *mūlādhāra* rather than Krishnamacharya's specified location of *nābhi*. Otherwise the picture so far is consistent with Krishnamacharya's teaching that *kuṇḍalinī* is nothing more than a blockage to the *suṣumnā*.

However, *Śivasaṁhitā* 4.105 states that 'The wise yogi should thoroughly agitate Kundalini, who is asleep in the Adhara lotus, and force her upwards by raising the apana wind.' 4.107 adds that 'Shaking off sleep, the serpent rises up automatically'.[233] Later, in the context of a discussion on the *sahasrāra* lotus and a *yogi* who 'has perfected samadhi',[234] *kuṇḍalinī śakti* 'achieves absorption' (*laya*) at the *kula* lotus,[235] from which nectar drips.[236] The *kula* lotus seems to be somewhere in the head,[237] perhaps on the crown or in the palate. The overall picture is of a mobile *kuṇḍalinī*.

Even though the text uses the snake-rope metaphor and describes *kuṇḍalinī* as *mahāmāyā*, *kuṇḍalinī* still rises all the way to the head and is not a blockage only, as in the *Yogayājñavalkya*. The *Śivasaṁhitā* is part of the *Śaiva* tradition of *Śrīvidyā*, which was adopted by the *Śaiva* pontiffs of Kanchipuram and Śṛṅgeri.[238] This could explain the mixing of *Advaita* and tantric/haṭhayogic content in the *Śivasaṁhitā*. However, in the text's depiction of *kuṇḍalinī*, *Śaiva* doctrine seems to have been more important than the *Advaita*-based snake metaphors I described earlier in this chapter.

Hence, even when the writers of texts draw from the wide and substantial stream of thought in which snakes represent something to be overcome, they do not necessarily describe *kuṇḍalinī* as a blockage only. Contrasting or contradictory streams of thought may flow through the same tradition or even the same text.

---

232. Mallinson (2007b, p. 122).
233. Translation – Mallinson (2007b, pp. 101–102).
234. *Śivasaṁhitā* 5.191, 5.195 – Mallinson (2007b, pp. 150, 151).
235. *Śivasaṁhitā* 5.198 – Mallinson (2007b, p. 152).
236. *Śivasaṁhitā* 5.197 – Mallinson (2007b, p. 152).
237. Mallinson (2007b, p. 73) notes that in the *Śivasaṁhitā*, *kula* means the *ādhāra* lotus. In the immediate context of *Śivasaṁhitā* 4.2–8, *kula* clearly refers to *mūlādhāra* at the lower terminus of the *suṣumnā* between the anus and the penis. The same is true of 5.87–88. However, in 5.197–8, *kula* refers to a lotus from which nectar drips, so it is probably near the palate or elsewhere in the head, perhaps the crown.
238. Mallinson (2007b, pp. ix, xiv).

5.15 ARE SNAKES 'VERY EVIL'?

K. Desikachar claimed that in India, black snakes are considered 'very evil'. Several quotations in this chapter have described snakes using the word 'evil', apparently in agreement. There is, however, no exact equivalent to 'evil' in Sanskrit. One possibility is *pāpa*, which is usually translated as 'sin' as it is a violation of *dharma*.[239] *Adharma*, the opposite of *dharma*, is 'the place where evil and suffering make their appearance'.[240] However, according to the *Mahābhārata*, 'The nature of each individual is the source of that individual's *dharma*. And so it happens that snakes must bite, demons must cheat, gods must send gifts, for this lies in their nature and is their *dharma*'.[241] A biting snake is not, therefore, evil in the sense of *adharma* or *pāpa*.

The concept of evil is 'very culture-bound'.[242] At the root of the word's diverse usage in English are teachings from Christianity of a cosmic battle between good and evil. The purely-good Holy Trinity and purely-good angels oppose the purely-evil Satan and his purely-evil demons. This neat dichotomy does not apply in Hinduism. Demons (*asura-s*) and gods (*deva-s*) fight but this is not a struggle between good and evil: 'Each group has its own task; the one builds up, the other tears down', each following their own *dharma*.[243] Unlike in Christianity, 'evil' cannot be ultimately overcome. We have seen how Kṛṣṇa 'prefers to keep the forces of good and evil in balance' by checking Kāliya, not destroying him.[244] Hence, 'the English term "evil" is loaded with connotations that may not apply to Hindu traditions'.[245]

Problems also arise in *Vedānta*. Gächter claims that in *Vedānta*, 'Evil ... is equated with the lack of knowledge (*avidyā*) which is the blindness and delusion caused by God.'[246] Although this would seem to support K. Desikachar's case, Gächter's statement is almost self-refuting. Reflecting his *Śrīvaiṣṇava* tradition (see Chapter 6), M.A. Alwar told me that *māyā* cannot be called evil as it is the force of the Lord himself, who is not evil.[247]

239. Gächter (1998, p. 394).
240. Gächter (1998, p. 395).
241. *Mahābhārata* 14.26, 9–10, translation – Gächter (1998, p. 395).
242. Gächter (1998, p. 394).
243. Gächter (1998, p. 398).
244. Gächter (1998, pp. 400, 402).
245. Gupta (2013, p. 64).
246. Gächter (1998, p. 395).
247. Alwar (2018).

Balasubramanian concurred, adding that *māyā/avidyā* is just 'something which must be overcome'.[248]

When K. Desikachar claimed that the black snake is considered 'very evil' in India, he was speaking to a European audience in a church near Paris. Perhaps he used 'evil' as a shorthand term that he thought Westerners would understand. It was also a brief comment that he did not explain. However, because of the word's cultural specificity and its ambiguity in the South Asian context, it is best avoided.

5.16 SUMMARY

Part of K. Desikachar's claim was that the metaphor of a black snake that 'needs to be crushed' is 'constantly repeated' in Indian mythology and art. The evidence presented above for Viṣṇu, Garuḍa and Gaṇeśa, whom K. Desikachar mentioned, and Śiva, whom he did not, is mixed. Stories and iconographical features can be interpreted in different ways, and they are only sometimes consistent with K. Desikachar's case.

It should be remembered that the diverse texts I quote from are from various traditions that used the same terms in different ways and in different ontological frameworks. For example, *avidyā* in *Advaitavedānta* is not the same as *avidyā* in *Viśiṣṭādvaitavedānta* or *avidyā* in *Patañjali*. Saṅkarṣaṇa is interpreted differently in the *Śrīmadbhāgavatam* and *Pāñcarātra* texts. I am not claiming that the above quotations can be combined into a single grand system. A survey across traditions is valid nonetheless as K. Desikachar's claim was about 'Indian' thought in general rather than any single tradition.

Substantial textual evidence shows that snakes represent a variety of things that must be overcome: *māyā* (illusion/magic), *avidyā* (nescience), *ajñāna* (nescience), *ahaṁkāra* (ego),[249] *ahaṁmāna* (egotism), *abhimāna* (erroneous self-conception), *māna* (pride), and *moha* (delusion) – the deadly poison of *saṁsāra* (rebirth). K. Desikachar's claim that snakes represent *avidyā* is therefore true, at least in some contexts. I have found no evidence directly supporting K. Desikachar's claim that snakes represent *asmitā*

248. Balasubramanian (2018).

249. T.K.V. Desikachar stresses that *ahaṁkāra* (ego) is not mentioned in *Patañjali* and is therefore not something to be overcome (T.K.V. Desikachar in Kaminoff 2012, p. 22). Other texts and traditions, however, do advocate overcoming ego (*ahaṁkāra*), egotism (*ahaṁmāna*) or erroneous self-conception (*abhimāna*), which are all sometimes represented by snakes.

(*kleśa*), but I have presented evidence of a snake representing *abhimāna*, which seems comparable.

There is substantial evidence that snakes represent binding, confirming A.G. Mohan's claim. I have also presented evidence that snakes represent covering, which like binding must be overcome. The serpentine metaphors given above seem to illustrate in different but comparable ways a central theme in South Asian thought: how the self (*ātman, puruṣa, jīva*) is confined during embodiment and what must be overcome to achieve liberation. In some contexts, for the embodied *jīva* to be liberated, the serpentine bonds of *avidyā* must be cut. In other contexts, for the self to be realized, its serpentine covering must be removed.

The examples in this chapter also validate a final metaphor. For *prāṇa* to carry the *jīva* up to the crown of the head, exit the body and proceed to liberation, it must first overcome the covering/binding effect of *avidyā* in the form of the serpentine *kuṇḍalinī* blockage to the *suṣumnā*. It is noteworthy that one meaning of *kuṇḍala*, a term related to *kuṇḍalinī*, is 'a fetter, tie, collar',[250] which emphasizes the connection to binding.

When representing a blockage only, *kuṇḍalinī* is a clear example of the side of Cozad's framework on which snakes represent something negative. Many texts, however, describe *kuṇḍalinī* differently. They draw from other (primarily *Śaiva*) streams of thought in which *kuṇḍalinī* is not (just) a blockage but (also) a mobile energy that ascends all the way to *sahasrāra*. Perhaps those accounts represent the other side of Cozad's framework, on which snakes represent something positive:

> Just as the snake, an object of dread because of its poison, stands as a symbol of all evil forces, as long as she lies motionless within us, Kuṇḍalinī is related to our obscure, unconscious energies, both poisoned and poisonous. However, once they are awakened and under control, these same energies become effective and confer a true power. ... as the evil nature of her power is transformed, she proves to be a priceless treasure. ... this poison transforms itself into an all-pervading power.[251]

Abhinavagupta, an eminent teacher of Kashmir Śaivism, also compared a mobile *kuṇḍalinī* energy to a cobra with an odd number of heads, which is how *nāga-s* are described:

---

250. Apte (1957, p. 580). *Kuṇḍala* more commonly means an earring.
251. Silburn (1988, pp. 15, 27).

> This supreme energy blossoming into bliss is adorned like a five-hooded cobra as she rises from the inferior to the superior center.[252]

Nevertheless, the use of snake imagery in the *Sātvatasaṁhitā* to represent *māyā* may have influenced the writers of later *Pāñcarātra* texts including the *Pādmasaṁhitā* to represent *kuṇḍalī* as a blockage only. This *Pāñcarātra* teaching eventually filtered through into the *Yogayājñavalkya*, which influenced Krishnamacharya. However, Krishnamacharya was not a *Pāñcarātrin.* He was a member of the closely related tradition of Śrīvaiṣṇavism, to which we now turn.

252. *Tantrāloka* 29.248–251, translation – Silburn (1988, p. 97).

6
Kuṇḍalinī in Śrīvaiṣṇavism

6.1 EARLY ŚRĪVAIṢṆAVISM – NĀTHAMUNI AND YĀMUNA

Śrīvaiṣṇavism combines three main sources of tradition: first, the triad of the *Upaniṣad-s*, *Bhagavadgītā* and *Brahmasūtra*; second, the devotional poems of the Tamil *Āḻvār* saints;[1] and third, *Pāñcarātra*.[2] To these are added sources of law and folklore, including *Purāṇa-s* and *Itihāsa-s* (epics).[3]

These traditions were integrated in the 10th century CE by Nāthamuni, who is said to have received *Āḻvār* poems 'as a revelation'.[4] According to Vedāntadeśika (see below), Nāthamuni's authority stems from foremost *Āḻvār*, Nammāḻvār, who 'was manifest' to Nāthamuni when he was 'in a yogic state'.[5]

None of Nāthamuni's texts are extant.[6] He is said to have written the *Yogarahasya* (*yoga* secret). According to tradition, Nāthamuni arranged to teach the text to one of his disciples, Yāmuna (see below), who failed to keep his appointment. The *Yogarahasya* was therefore lost.[7] The Krishnamacharya Yoga Mandiram published a text of that name attributed to Nāthamuni with a hagiographical story in which Krishnamacharya is said to have received the text directly from Nāthamuni as a revelation.[8]

The authorship of this *Yogarahasya* is contested by three of Krishnamacharya's longest-standing students. First, T.K.V. Desikachar wrote 'I tend to think that the *Natnamuni's Yoga Rahasya* (sic) that he taught

1. See Chari (1997).
2. Narayanan (2011, p. 556); Oberhammer and Rastelli (2007).
3. Lipner (1986, p. 5); Narayanan (2011, p. 556).
4. Narayanan (2011, p. 556).
5. Clooney (2011, p. 210).
6. Narayanan (2011, p. 562).
7. Neevel (1977, p. 197).
8. T.K.V. Desikachar (1998).

us is quite likely to be a combination of his own commentary and the lessons he received though he would not accept it.'[9] Second, A.G. Mohan states that 'there is no doubt that the text known as the *Yoga Rahasya* was not compiled by Nathamuni, ... The text is an assorted collection of verses on yoga and related subjects written by Krishnamacharya.'[10] Third, according to Srivatsa Ramaswami, Krishnamacharya 'wanted to represent the Vaishnava Yoga, yoga based on vaishnavite philosophy, and also ... the therapeutic benefits of some of the procedures, like pranayama, etc. So he wrote that book. I don't know when he wrote that, because during the class he used to quote from Yoga Rahasya, he would say "this is what Yoga Rahasya says." ... But later on [T.K.V.] Desikachar was able to collect all of them and publish it as a book, I found that some of the shlokas he taught in the class are not there, and some of the shlokas the (sic) he did not teach were actually there.'[11] Despite this strong evidence, Kausthub Desikachar maintains that Krishnamacharya received the *Yogarahasya* by 'divine intervention'.[12] While the *Yogarahasya* illustrates how Krishnamacharya oriented *yoga* towards devotion,[13] it says nothing about *kuṇḍalinī*.

---

9. T.K.V. Desikachar (1991, p. 19).
10. Mohan and Mohan (2010, p. 137).
11. Ramaswami (no date), my addition in brackets.
12. K. Desikachar (2005, p. 35). In his foreword to the second edition of the *Yogarahasya*, Kausthub Desikachar wrote that 'Objections are likely to be raised against the attribution of the authorship of the *Yoga Rahasya* now published, to *Nāthamuni*, for the *Yoga Rahasya* is believed to have been irretrievable (sic) lost. However, as we go through the text of the *Yoga Rahasya* we find that there is no reason to entertain uncertainty about its authorship. If this work was not discussed earlier by anybody, it is nobody's fault. It is God's will (*saṁkalpa*) that a descendent of *Nāthamuni* alone should try and revive this work' (K. Desikachar in T.K.V. Desikachar 2003, p. 14). Connolly (2007, pp. 207–209) presents such objections, arguing that much of the content seems 'more compatible with the idea that Krishnamacharya himself was the author'. Furthermore, K.S. Balasubramanian, professor of Sanskrit at the Kuppuswami Sastri Research Institute, Chennai, told me that the text is definitely written in 20th century Sanskrit, not having the linguistic style that Nāthamuni would have used. Balasubramanian cited two scholars who held that view: Dr M. Narasimhachari and Dr A. Thiruvengadathan (Balasubramanian 2018). Curiously, the tale of Krishnamacharya receiving the *Yogarahasya* in a divine vision from Nāthamuni is predated by an alternative hagiographical story. T.K.V. Desikachar told Paul Harvey that Krishnamacharya had been given a manuscript of the *Yogarahasya* by a 'mysterious stranger' in Afghanistan, who said 'This is for you' (Singleton and Fraser 2014, pp. 97–98). Harvey's account is confirmed by François Lorin (2018), who noted during a 1968 lesson with T.K.V. Desikachar that the *Yogarahasya* had been 'given by a Muslem yogi in Afghanistan to Krishnamacharya in 1916'.
13. Stern (2005).

Another of Nāthamuni's lost texts is the *Nyāyatattva*, which provided justification for accepting *Pāñcarātra*.[14] After Nāthamuni died in *c*.920 CE,[15] further justification was provided by his grandson, Yāmuna (*c*.916 CE–1036/1038 CE).[16] After his studies, Yāmuna was taken to the Srirangam Temple and became its leader.[17] His *Āgamaprāmāṇyam* 'sets out to prove by scripture and logic that the texts of *Pāñcarātra Āgama* have an authority equal to that of the Vedas, because they are god's direct revelation'.[18] For Krishnamacharya, Yāmuna's seal of approval for *Pāñcarātra* could have been important. Consider an 1984 interview:

> Q: Many that (sic) the great yogi is one whose Kundalini has risen to higher levels and reached sahasrara after ascending susumna nadi ...
> A [Krishnamacharya]: If Kundalini is described in Vedas and if its nature is known from Vedic literature, then I will accept this. Kundalini is very simply physical. *If a person controls a nadi, he controls Kundalini.* This is not important. Kundalini yoga is not a yoga at all.[19]

Kuṇḍalinī-kuṇḍalī is not mentioned in Vedic literature proper, but it is mentioned in *Pāñcarātra Āgama-s*. Yāmuna's granting of equal authority to *Pāñcarātra* and the *Veda-s* could have enabled Krishnamacharya to justify his faith in texts such as the *Pādmasaṁhitā* and *Ahirbudhnyasaṁhitā*, which describe *kuṇḍalī* as a blockage.

---

14. Kumar (2012, p. 470).
15. van Buitenen (1971, p. 3).
16. Neevel (1977, p. 14).
17. Kumar (2012, p. 471).
18. van Buitenen (1971, p. 5). Yāmuna's main agenda seems to have been 'not only to establish the veracity of the ritual procedures [of *Pāñcarātra*] in line with the vedic rituals, but perhaps also more importantly to point out to his other Brahman counterparts that it is worthy of Brahmanical practice' (Kumar 2012, p. 470). The *haṭhayoga* content of *Pāñcarātra* texts, which is much less voluminous than the content on ritual, was not central to his project.
19. Krishnamacharya (1984). The interview then changes topic without explaining why Krishnamacharya dismisses *'kundalini yoga'*. In a later interview, T.K.V. Desikachar stated that 'The main goal in yoga is *vairāgya*, being detached and, *brahmacarya*, seeking truth. The practices that do not help in these goals are *vāmācāra*, practices worth condemning. He [Krishnamacharya] called *kuṇḍalini yoga, vāmācāra*. He has studied all the *śāstra-s* and yoga texts and even written his own articles on *kuṇḍalini* but never referred to anything called *kuṇḍalini yoga*. The pursuit of powers is contrary to the goal of *vairāgya* and therefore not classifiable as yoga' (T.K.V. Desikachar 1993, p. 11).

Yāmuna refers to *Patañjali's yoga* several times in another text, the *Ātmasiddhi*. However, Yāmuna may have been honouring earlier respected sages rather than reflecting contemporary practice.[20] There is more evidence of the influence of *Patañjali's yoga* on Yāmuna's nephew, Rāmānuja, the foremost *Śrīvaiṣṇava* theologian.[21]

6.2 RĀMĀNUJA

Rāmānuja was born near Chennai in *c.*1017 CE.[22] After becoming a renunciate, he moved to Srirangam and became pontiff.[23] After a period of exile near Mysore, he returned to Srirangam, where he died in *c.*1137 CE, supposedly aged 120.[24]

Rāmānuja developed a theology later called *Viśiṣṭādvaita Vedānta* (qualified non-dualism). The development of *Viśiṣṭādvaita* 'is variously marked by assimilations, identifications, equations and absorptions of many elements, each of which shows a surprising diversity in origin, amounting almost to mutual contradiction'.[25] However, Rāmānuja did not further Yāmuna's efforts to reconcile *Pāñcarātra* and *Vedānta*. Indeed, there was 'very little explicit identification between his views and those of Pañcarātra'.[26] Instead, Rāmānuja commented on the mainstream triad of the *Upaniṣad-s*, the *Bhagavadgītā* and the *Brahmasūtra*, citing predominantly Vedic sources. This may have been in an attempt to win mainstream Brahmanical acceptance of his doctrine, which could have been compromised if he had quoted from sources not universally recognised, such as *Pāñcarātra*.

Rāmānuja's opponents included *Sāṁkhya* and Śaṅkara's *Advaitavedānta*.[27] Rāmānuja challenged *Patañjali's Yoga* on the nature of *Īśvara*, but instead of rejecting the system completely, he reconstructed it 'strictly in terms

20. Neevel (1977, pp. 146, 147).
21. Narayanan (2011, p. 557).
22. Lipner (1986, p. 1).
23. Devanandan (1950, p. 119).
24. Narayanan (2011, p. 557).
25. Devanandan (1950, p. 114).
26. Lipner (1986, p. 5).
27. Lipner (1986, pp. 6, 7).

of his theistic doctrine'.[28] Rāmānuja kept what suited his purposes and ignored or radically reformulated the remainder.[29]

> ... the aim of the first four stages of Rāmānuja's Yoga is basically the same as that of the first four stages of Patañjali's Yoga, namely, the suppression of normal consciousness ... However, this aim is to be accomplished, not with a view to eventually suppressing *all* states of consciousness, but with a view to meditation – remembrance on the Supreme Person.[30]

In Rāmānuja's *dhāraṇā* and *dhyāna*, attention is focused on God.[31] This contrasts with *Patañjali* chapter 3, where none of the proposed objects of meditation is God. In Rāmānuja's system there is no *samādhi. Dhāraṇā* results in *ātma darśana*, a vision of the self in which the *jīvātman* is *śeṣa* (servant) to the *paramātman.* Furthermore, 'the *darśana* which follows from *dhyāna* is purely subjective; Yoga does not give knowledge of the Supreme Person, nor does it result directly in "union" with the Divine'.[32] Instead, *ātma darśana* intensifies devotion.[33]

Yoga in Śrīvaiṣṇavism is one of five daily ritual activities called *pañcakāla*, which were adopted into Śrīvaiṣṇavism from *Pāñcarātra.* They are *abhigamana* (approaching), *upādāna* (appropriating), *ijyā* (worship), *svādhyāya* (chanting and studying) and *yoga. Abhigamana* encompasses all morning rites and is considered a way of approaching God. *Upādāna* means collecting objects needed for ritual worship. *Ijyā* means daily *pūja. Svādhyāya* means reciting and studying sacred texts.[34]

Rāmānuja's *yoga* system hugely influenced Krishnamacharya's interpretation of *Patañjali.* For our purposes, it is sufficient to note Rāmānuja's emphasis on dependence on God for any spiritual progress,[35] a theme which will recur below when we examine the thought of Vedāntadeśika.

Before looking for *kuṇḍalinī* in Śrīvaiṣṇavism, I will first give some background on Rāmānuja's teaching on three topics that could have influenced

28. Lester (1976, p. 134).
29. Lester (1976, p. 141). Incorporating *Patañjali's yoga* into a Vedāntic framework would have posed ontological problems but further consideration of these is beyond the scope of this book.
30. Lester (1976, p. 107).
31. Lester (1976, p. 139–141).
32. Lester (1976, pp. 141, 125).
33. Lester (1976, p. 112, 113).
34. Rastelli (2018, pp. 225, 226).
35. Lester (1976, p. 128).

Śrīvaiṣṇavism's propensity to use the term *kuṇḍalinī:* first, *māyā* and *avidyā*; second, *tirodhāna* and related terms meaning covering; and third, the snake-rope metaphor.

First, *Advaitin-s* often use *māyā*, *avidyā* and *ajñāna* interchangeably, but *māyā* usually indicates a cosmic metaphysical principle whereas *avidyā* and *ajñāna* usually represent personal epistemological error.[36] Together they describe 'a cosmic veil of ignorance which deludes men into believing that the non-Ātman (all that which is not the Brahman) is real'.[37] *Advaita* teaches that when *avidyā* is removed, everything other than *Brahman* is seen to be metaphysically unreal. This doctrine 'left no room for the exercise of love and piety (bhakti)' and thereby 'laid the axe at the very root of Vaiṣṇavism'.[38] Rāmānuja therefore critiqued the *Advaita* doctrine of *māyā-avidyā*, interpreting differently the sources the *Advaitin-s* had used to create it, supplemented by quotations from *Purāṇa-s*.

Rāmānuja uses *māyā* to refer to 'things that have a wonderful nature, but not illusions', such as the weapons of *asura-s* (demons) and *rākṣasa-s* (monsters).[39] For example, Rāmānuja quotes from the *Viṣṇupurāṇa* on how *Viṣṇu* used his *sudarśana cakra* (discus) to nullify an opponent's thousand *māyā* weapons (*māyā sahasra*). Here *māyā* does not mean false or illusory.[40] Indeed, according to Narasimharāghavācāriyar of the Ahobilam Math (a major *Śrīvaiṣṇava* organization), *māyā sahasram* 'refers here to the cluster of weapons of wonderful power. ... Where is the need to dispatch Sudarśana to destroy something false!'[41]

In his *Śrībhāṣya* commentary on the *Brahmasūtra*, Rāmānuja notes that 'In the usual usage (*prayoga*) of the word '*māyā*' in the weapons etc. of *rākṣasa-s* and *asura-s*, it surely [does] not [designate] a false object (*mithyā-viṣaya*) everywhere (*sarvatra*).'[42]

---

36. Devanandan (1950, pp. 135, 136).
37. Devanandan (1950, p. 71).
38. Devanandan (1950, p. 118).
39. Devanandan (1950, pp. 131, 132).
40. *Rāmānujagītābhāṣya* 7.13, Ādidevānanda (no date, p. 253).
41. Narasimharāghavācāriyar (no date, p. 35).
42. *Śrībhāṣya* 1.1.1 – my translation of Śivaprasādadvivedī (2009, vol. 1 p.267):

    na hi sarvatra māyāśabdo mithyāviṣayaḥ āsurarākṣasāstrādiṣu satyeṣveva māyāśabdaprayogāt |

    Section 1.1.1 of the *Śrībhāṣya* discusses the nature of *Brahman* and concepts such as *māyā* and *karma*. Within that context, it gives a lengthy critique of *Advaitavedānta*.

Hence, Devanandan claims that Rāmānuja equates *māyā* with 'this wonderful world', which is 'so marvellous in many respects as to transcend the categories of human reason'.[43] While this is sometimes true, *māyā* has negative connotations elsewhere. Consider *Bhagavadgītā* 7.14:

> For this divine Māyā of Mine consisting of the three Guṇas (assumed for the purpose of sport) is hard to overcome. But those who take refuge in Me (Prapadyante) alone shall pass beyond the Māyā.[44]

Here, liberation involves transcending *māyā*. Elsewhere, Rāmānuja uses *avidyā* similarly. In the *Śrībhāṣya*, he defines *mokṣa* as 'the termination of *avidyā*'.[45] Rāmānuja's consideration of *māyā* and *avidyā* was based on his interpretation of Vedic sources, primarily the *Upaniṣad-s*, *Bhagavadgītā* and *Brahmasūtra*. He did not connect *māyā* and *avidyā* to *kuṇḍalinī-kuṇḍalī*, which has different origins. However, as termination of *avidyā* is the goal of Rāmānuja's system, his teaching would not be inconsistent with Krishnamacharya's representation of *avidyā* with *kuṇḍalinī*, which is to be destroyed.

The second topic that could have influenced Śrīvaiṣṇavism's propensity to use the term *kuṇḍalinī* is *tirodhāna* (covering). Rāmānuja's *Vedārthasaṁgraha*, which justifies his theology on the basis of the *Upaniṣad-s*, discusses *avidyā* and shows how it is connected to *tirodhāna:*

> Thus holds our [tradition]: *karma* causes real (*pāramārthika*) contraction (*saṁkoca*) and expansion (*vikāsa*) of one's innate consciousness (*caitanya*), [which is] a real inherent-quality of the self (*ātma dharma bhūtasya*). And [hence] all this said (in the *Advaita* counter argument, not given here) is refuted. [In] your [system of *Advaita*], however, consciousness (*prakāśa*) indeed *is* the self; consciousness [is] not [the self's] real inherent-quality (*dharma bhūta*). [Your system] admits neither contraction nor expansion of the consciousness. [In our system] *karma* etc., which produce obscuration (*tirodhāna*), prevent consciousness from expanding (*prakāśa prasāra an utpattim*). If *avidyā* [were merely] obscuration (*tirodhāna*), with the existence

43. Devanandan (1950, p. 132).
44. Translation – Ādidevānanda (no date, pp. 252–254).
45. *Śrībhāṣya* 1.1.1 – my translation of *avidyā-nivṛttiḥ-eva mokṣaḥ* from Śivaprasādadvivedī (2009, vol. 1 p.55). *Śrīvaiṣṇava* scholar M.A. Alwar (2010, p. 106) notes that *māyā, avidyā, prakṛti* and *tamas* 'are essentially synonyms'. He adds that *prakṛti* is known by the name *avidyā* 'since it veils the natural, blissful nature of the Individual Soul'. Note the aspect of covering.

> of this obscuration [would come] the destruction of consciousness (*prakāśa nāśa*), which is the real own-form (*svarūpa bhūta*) [of the self], as previously stated. However, [in] our [system], knowledge-consciousness (*jñāna prakāśa*), which is a real characteristic (*dharma bhūta*) of the eternal own-form (*nitya svarūpa*) [of the *ātman*], is contracted by *karma* in the form of *avidyā*. From this [contraction there is] confusion of the form of the self with the form of gods etc. (*deva ādi svarupa ātma abhimāna*). That is a distinction [between *Advaita* and *Viśiṣṭādvaita*].[46]

Rāmānuja does not reject *tirodhāna* (obscuration), which he uses in both the *Advaita* counter argument and his *Viśiṣṭādvaita* argument. Consciousness is obscured differently in the two systems. In *Advaita*, consciousness is simply veiled; in *Viśiṣṭādvaita*, it is enveloped and contracted by *avidyā/karma*.

Also in the *Vedārthasaṁgraha*, Rāmānuja summarizes:

> The heart of the entire *śāstra* [is] this here. The nature of the embodied selves (*jīvātman-s*) is essentially uncontracted (*asaṁkucita*), unlimited (*aparicchinna*) and untainted (*nirmala*) knowledge (*jñāna*). Those who have fallen, enveloped (*veṣṭitā*) by *avidyā* in the form of *karma*, [experience] contraction of knowledge, the form of which follows 'this and that' *karma*.[47]

Rāmānuja emphasizes that *karma/avidyā* contracts knowledge. More important for our purposes are the descriptions of enveloping. The word I translate as 'enveloped' is *veṣṭitā* from the root *veṣṭ*, as in Vṛtra, the snake demon in the *Ṛgveda* (see Chapter 5). *Veṣṭitā* can mean surrounded, enclosed, encircled, enveloped, wrapped up, stopped, blocked, impeded

---

46. My translation of the Sanskrit in van Buitenen (1956, p. 98):

> evamabhyupagacchatāmasmākamātmadharmabhūtasya caitanyasya svābhāvikasyāpi karmaṇā pāramārthikaṁ saṁkocaṁ vikāsaṁ ca bruvatāṁ sarvamidaṁ parihṛtam | bhavatastu prakāśa eva svarūpamiti prakāśo na dharmabhūtastasya saṁkocavikāsau vā nābhyupagamyete | prakāśaprasārānutpattimeva tirodhānabhūtāḥ karmādayaḥ kurvanti | avidyā cettirodhānaṁ tirodhānabhūtayā'vidyayāsvarūpabhūtaprakāśanāśaitipūrvamevoktaḥ|asmākaṁtvavidyārūpeṇa karmaṇā svarūpanityadharmabhūtaprakāśaḥ saṁkucitaḥ | tena devādisvarūpātmābhimāno bhavatīti viśeṣaḥ |

Rāmānuja immediately follows this passage with a quotation from the *Viṣṇupurāṇa* that equates *karma* and *avidyā*.

47. My translation of the Sanskrit in van Buitenen (1956, p. 116):

> atredaṁ sarvaśāstrahṛdayam – jīvātmānaḥ svayamasaṁkucitāparicchinnanirmalajñānasvarūpāḥ santaḥ karmarūpāvidyāveṣṭitāstattatkarmānurūpajñānasaṁkocamāpannāḥ |

or blockaded.[48] This enveloping is not very different from 'obscuration' (*tirodhāna*). It is also compatible with *Bhagavadgītā* 5.15, which states that knowledge is enveloped by nescience (*ajñānena āvṛtaṁ jñānaṁ*). *Āvṛta* (enveloped) comes from the root *vṛ* with the prefix *ā*, which together can mean covered, concealed, hidden, blocked up, obstructed or obscured.[49]

In summary, Rāmānuja's discussion of how the *ātman* is covered is rooted in his interpretation of the *Upaniṣad-s*, the *Brahmasūtra* and the *Bhagavadgītā*, not in his interpretation of *Pāñcarātra* or *haṭhayoga*. Nevertheless, *veṣṭitā*, *tirodhāna* and *āvṛta* (covering) in the above quotations all seem analogous with Krishnamacharya's conception of the role of *kuṇḍalinī* covering and blocking entry to the *suṣumnā*. This similarity left open the possibility of later *Śrīvaiṣṇava-s* using *kuṇḍalinī* in that way.

The third topic that could have influenced Śrīvaiṣṇavism's propensity to use the term *kuṇḍalinī* is Rāmānuja's treatment of the snake-rope metaphor (see Chapter 5). His *Śrībhāṣya* rejects Śaṅkara's use of the snake-rope metaphor:

> And [it is] not [the case that] in one who is afraid of an [apparent] serpent (*sarpa*), hearing the words 'the serpent [is] a rope' (*rajju*) immediately leads to the termination (*nivṛtti*) of the fear (*bhya*) of the perceived serpent. Here, the means to the firm conviction of the non-existence of the serpent also [lies] in the [determination that] 'this thing [is] motionless, poisonless, inanimate etc.'. The termination of fear [is found] in the truths from many observations (*bodha-s*) and logical deductions (*hetu-s*).[50]

Rāmānuja advocates two primary epistemological means: direct observation (*bodha*) of the motionless, lifeless state of the object, and logical deduction (*hetu*) that it must be a rope. Testimony that 'the snake is a rope' plays only a preliminary supportive role.

---

48. Apte (1957, p. 1499).
49. Macdonell (2001, p. 294).
50. *Śrībhāṣya* 1.1.1 – my translation of Śivaprasādadvivedī (2009, vol. 1 p.312):

> na ca sarpādbhītasya nāyaṁ sarpaḥ rajjureṣā iti ṣabdaśravaṇasamanantaraṁ bhyanivṛttidarśanena sarpābhāvabuddhihetutvaniścayaḥ atrāpi niśceṣṭam nirviṣam acetanamidaṁ vastvatyādyarthabodheṣu bahuṣu bhaya nivṛttihetuṣu satsu viśeṣaniścayāyogāt |

Verse 1.1.1 of the *Śrībhāṣya* discusses the nature of *Brahman* and concepts such as *māyā* and *karma*. Within that context, it gives a lengthy critique of *Advaitavedānta*.

Raju claimed that 'the school of Rāmānuja is not interested in giving any importance to Avidyā'.[51] That is an exaggeration. We have seen above that the destruction of *avidyā*, which binds and contracts embodied selves, is Rāmānuja's very definition of liberation. However, Rāmānuja's teaching that the world and even illusory objects (such as an imagined snake) are real gives *avidyā*, and especially *māyā*, a less prominent and less central role in his system than in *Advaita*. In particular, his rejection of the *Advaita* use of the snake-rope metaphor could potentially have made Rāmānuja and his followers disinclined to use the serpentine imagery of *kuṇḍalinī* to represent *māyā* or *avidyā*.

Whatever the reasons, *kuṇḍalinī*, and the *haṭhayoga* context in which it sits in *Pāñcarātra*, is absent in Rāmānuja's works. Nevertheless, I am not aware of anything in the writings or Yāmuna and Rāmānuja that contradicts or rules out Krishnamacharya's conception of *kuṇḍalinī* as a blockage. Indeed, there are three features that are quite compatible with it. First, Yāmuna ascribed the *Pāñcarātra* texts equal status to the *Veda-s*, leaving open the option of adopting the *Pādmasaṁhitā's* usage of *kuṇḍalī*. Second, Rāmānuja described *avidyā* as binding a man by enveloping his embodied self – an action which texts from various traditions represent with snake metaphors (see Chapter 5). Third, Rāmānuja defined liberation as the destruction of *avidyā*, which *kuṇḍalinī* represents in Krishnamacharya's system.

Hence, after Rāmānuja's death in *c.*1137 CE, it would have been possible for a skilled theologian to embellish Rāmānuja's Vedāntic framework with teachings on *kuṇḍalinī-kuṇḍalī* found in *Pāñcarātra* texts such as the *Pādmasaṁhitā*. It would seem quite feasible, therefore, that to support Krishnamacharya's position on *kuṇḍalinī*, T.K.V. Desikachar quoted from the renowned 13th century *Śrīvaiṣṇava* polymath Vedāntadeśika, to whom we now turn.

6.3 VEDĀNTADEŚIKA

6.3.1 The polymath and his work

Veṅkaṭanātha, or Veṅkaṭeśa, was born in Thoopal, Kanchipuram, in *c.*1268 CE.[52] Adjacent temples mark his birthplace – see Plates 4 and 5.

51. Raju (1985, p. 448).
52. Rengarajan (2004, p. 206); Hopkins (2012, p. 462).

Plate 4
Srimad Desikan's Avatara Sthanam (left) and Thoopal Vedanta Desikar Temple (right), Kanchipuram.

Photograph: Simon Atkinson

Veṅkaṭanātha was educated by Ātreya Rāmānuja, his uncle. After Ātreya Rāmānuja died (*c.*1290–1295 CE), Veṅkaṭanātha succeeded him as Kanchipuram's foremost *ācārya* before moving to Srirangam, where he died in *c.*1369 CE.[53]

Veṅkaṭanātha was later given the epithets Vedāntadeśika (preceptor of *Vedānta*),[54] Kavitārkikasiṁha (lion among poets and logicians), Vedāntācārya (teacher of *Vedānta*), and Sarvatantrasvatantra (master of all disciplines).[55] One commentator in the tradition interpreted Sarvatantrasvatantra as master of five systems of philosophy (*Nyāya*, *Vaiśeṣika*, *Mīmāṁsā*, *Sāṁkhya* and *Yoga*) plus *Śaiva* and *Vaiṣṇava* doctrines.[56]

53. Hopkins (2012, pp. 462, 463); Rengarajan (2004, p. 206).
54. Hopkins (2012, p. 462).
55. Rengarajan (2004, p. 206); Hopkins (2012, p. 464); Singh (2008, p. 3).
56. Hopkins (2012, p. 464).

Plate 5
Vedāntadeśika idol in Srimad Desikan's Avatara Sthanam, Kanchipuram.

Photograph: P.V. Satakopa Tatacharya

More generally, Sarvatantrasvatantra encompasses mastery of 'scriptures', 'doctrines', 'rules', 'scientific works' and *mantra-s*.[57] In hagiographical accounts, Deśika is said 'to have drawn magic circles on the ground to fight back an attack by supernatural snakes, and, with the help of the divine bird Garuḍa himself, called into form by a *mantra*, to have destroyed the most potent of the serpents sent to vanquish him'.[58] See Plate 6. This tale is compatible with a stream of thought in which snakes represent something to be overcome.

Deśika was a prolific writer of philosophy, theology and poetry. Table 3 lists 123 compositions ranging from short poems to voluminous treatises.[59] Around 16 are lost.[60] His works include poems, an allegorical drama and hymns in Sanskrit, Tamil and Maharashtri Prakrit. He also wrote commen-

57. Hopkins (2012, p. 464).
58. Hopkins (2012, p. 463).
59. Based on Singh (2008, pp. 39–96 especially pp.39–41) with added information.
60. Rengarajan (2004, p. 206); Singh (2008, p. 93).

Plate 6
Vedāntadeśika saved from an attacking serpent by Garuḍa – fresco in Thoopal Vedanta Desikar Temple, Kanchipuram.

Photograph: Simon Atkinson

taries and original treatises on theology, philosophy and logic in Sanskrit and Maṇipravāla (a mixture of Sanskrit and Tamil).[61] Vedāntadeśika is often said to have 'put Rāmānuja's doctrine on the firmest logical and philosophical ground'.[62]

Vedāntadeśika is often described as the founder of the conservative Sanskrit-emphasizing *Vaṭakalai* sect, in contrast to their more socially-liberal, Tamil-emphasizing *Teṇkalai* rivals. There are many practical and doctrinal differences between the two sects, including the role of God's grace in liberation.[63] *Vaṭakalai-s* believe that the individual must make some effort to win God's grace, like a monkey holds on to its mother. *Teṇkalai-s* believe that nothing the individual does has any soterial effect,

61. Hopkins (2012, p. 468).
62. Hopkins (2012, p. 464).
63. See Varadachari (1983, appendix 2 pp.vii-lviii); Alwar (2010, pp. 195–220).

Table 3

Vedāntadeśika's works. L = lost (no longer extant); italic type indicates a secondary source, roman type indicates a primary source or translation thereof. Language of original text: S = Sanskrit, T = Tamil, M = Maṇipravāla, P = Prakrit. SSAA = Srirangam Srimath Andavan Ashramam.

Name of text	Language of text	References
Manuals of Śrīvaiṣṇava religion and esotericism		
1. Nyāsa Daśakam	S	SSAA (2017, pp. 558–563); Raghavan et al. (2013, pp. 259–261)
2. Nyāsa Viṁśati	S	SSAA (2017, pp. 540–557); Aiyangar (1979); Raghavan et al. (2013, pp. 262–274)
3. Vairāgya Pañcakam	S	SSAA (2017, pp. 384–391); Raghavan et al. (2013, pp. 102–104)
4. Haridina Tilakam		
5. Yajñopavīta Pratiṣṭhā = Yagnopanta Prathishta		Saṁpatkumārācāryaḥ (1941, appendix p. A)
6. Vaiśvadeva Kārikā		Saṁpatkumārācāryaḥ (1941, appendix p. B)
7. Śrī Vaiṣṇava-Dinacaryā = Sri Vaishnava Dinasari	T	Sathakopan (no date q)
8. Artha Pañcakam = Aruttha Panchakam	T	Sathakopan (no date a)
9. Pannirunāmam = *Panniru Naaman*	T	Sathakopan (no date n)
10. Āhāra Niyamam = *Aahaara Niyamam*	T	Sathakopan (no date c)
11. Tirumantra-curukku = Thirumanthira Churukku	T	Sathakopan (no date h)
12. Dvaya-curukku = Dhvaya Churukku	T	Sathakopan (no date g)
13. Carama śloka-curukku = Charama Śloka Churukku	T	Sathakopan (no date f)
14. Tattva Navanītam = Tathva Navaneetham = Tatva Navaneetham	M	Rangachar (2009, pp. 10–16); Krishnaswami (2012a, pp. 64–78); Srinivasaraghavan (1993, pp. 27–33)
15. Rahasya Navanītam = Rahsya Navaneetha	M	Rangachar (2009, pp. 17–22); Krishnaswami (2012a, pp. 79–93); Srinivasaraghavan (1993, pp. 34–41)

Name of text	Language of text	References
16. Upakāra Saṅgraham	M	Sowmianarayanan (no date a, no date b, no date c, no date d)
17. Sāra Saṅgraham	T	
18. Munivāhanabhogam	M	
19. Madhurakavihṛdayam	M	L – *Singh (2008, p. 46)*; *Raghavan (1979, p. 41)*
20. Tattva Traya-Culukam =Tathvatraya Chuḷakam	M	Rangachar (2009, pp. 66–89); Krishnaswami (2013a, pp. 1–62); Srinivasaraghavan (1993, pp. 161–188)
21. Rahasya Traya-culukam = Rahasyatraya Chuḷakam = Sāra Saṁkṣepa	T	Rangachar (2009, pp. 90–110); Krishnaswami (2013a, pp. 63–119); Srinivasaraghavan (1993, pp. 189–208)
22. Sāradīpam = Rahasya Traya Sāradīpam	T	L – *Singh (2008, p. 46)*; *Raghavan (1979, p. 43)*
23. Nigama Parimalam		L – *Singh (2008, p. 46)*; *Raghavan (1979, p. 47)*
24. Stheyāvirodham		L – *Singh (2008, p. 46)*; *Raghavan (1979, p. 43)*
25. Guruparaṁparā Sāram	T	Rangacharya (2004, pp. 1–9)
26. Virodha Parihāram	M	*Raghavan (1979, pp. 42–43)*
27. Tattva Śikhāmaṇi		L – *Singh (2008, p. 46)*; *Raghavan (1979, p. 41)*
28. Mummani Kovai = Mummaṇikkōvai	T	Hopkins (2007, pp. 27–35); Sathakopan (no date m)
29. Navaratnamālai = Navamaṇimālai?	T	Hopkins (2007, pp. 37–45); Hopkins (2002, pp. 115–134)
30. Panduppā		L – *Singh (2008, p. 46)*; *Raghavan (1979, p. 45)*
31. Kazalpā		L – *Singh (2008, p. 46)*
32. Ammanepā = Ammānippa	T	L – *Singh (2008, p. 46)*; *Raghavan (1979, p. 44)*
33. Usalpā = Ūsāṛpa	T	L – *Singh (2008, p. 46)*; *Raghavan (1979, p. 45)*
34. Achalpā		L – *Singh (2008, p. 46)*
35. Adaikāḷa Pattu = Aṭaikkalappattu = Adaikkalapaththu	T	Sathakopan (no date i); Hopkins (2002, p. 87 – partial translation)
36. Tirucchinnamālai	T	Sathakopan (no date r)
37. Añjali Vaibhavam	T	*Raghavan (1979, pp. 39–40)*
38. Rahasya Sikhāmaṇi	M	*Raghavan (1979, p. 42)*
39. Abhaya Pradāna-Sāra	M	L – *Singh (2008, p. 47)*

Name of text	Language of text	References
40. Sārāsāra	T	
41. Pradhāna Śatakam	T	
42. Rahasya Ratnāvalī-Hṛdayam	T	Krishnaswami (2012b, pp. 58–224); Srinivasaraghavan (1993, pp. 87–160)
43. Rahasya Ratnāvalī	T	Krishnaswami (2012b, pp. 58–224); Srinivasaraghavan (1993, pp. 83–86)
44. Tattva Ratnāvalī-Pratipādya-Saṅgraham	T	Krishnaswami (2012b, pp. 52–57); Srinivasaraghavan (1993, pp. 81–82)
45. Tattva Ratnāvalī = Tathva Rathnavali	T	Krishnaswami (2012b, pp. 34–51); Srinivasaraghavan (1993, pp. 76–80)
46. Rahasya Sandeśa Vivaraṇam	M	Rangachar (2009, pp. 63–65); Krishnaswami (2012b, pp. 27–33); Srinivasaraghavan (1993, pp. 73–75)
47. Rahasya Sandeśa = Rahasya Sandesham	M	Rangachar (2009, pp. 59–62); Krishnaswami (2012b, pp. 18–26); Srinivasaraghavan (1993, pp. 69–72)
48. Tattva Sandeśa = Tatthva Sandesham	M	Rangachar (2009, pp. 50–58); Krishnaswami (2012b, pp. 1–17); Srinivasaraghavan (1993, pp. 62–68)
49. Rahasya Mātṛkā = Rahasya Māthrukaa	M	Rangachar (2009, pp. 41–49); Krishnaswami (2012a, pp. 137–156); Srinivasaraghavan (1993, pp. 56–61)
50. Tattva Mātṛkā = Tathva Mathrukaa	M	Rangachar (2009, pp. 23–40); Krishnaswami (2012a, pp. 94–136); Srinivasaraghavan (1993, pp. 42–55)
51. Rahasya Padavī = Rahasya Padhavee	M	Rangachar (2009, pp. 4–9); Krishnaswami (2012a, pp. 50–63); Srinivasaraghavan (1993, pp. 22–26)
52. Tattva Padavī = Tathva Padhavee	T	Rangachar (2009, pp. 1–3); Krishnaswami (2012a, pp. 42–49); Srinivasaraghavan (1993, pp. 19–20)
53. Saṁpradāya Pariśuddhi	M	Krishnaswami (2012a, pp. 1–41); Srinivasaraghavan (1993, pp. 3–18)
54. Ārādhana Kārikā	S	A work of 2 verses *(Singh 2008, p. 47)* that may not be by Vedāntadeśika *(Raghavan 1979, p. 89)*
55. Prabandhasāram = Prabhandha Saaram	T	Sathakopan (no date p)
56. Hastigiri-Māhātmyam	M	*Srinivasan (2004)*
57. Paramapada-Sopānam	M	Sathakopan (no date o)

Name of text	Language of text	References
Theses on *Śrīvaiṣṇava* theology and ritualism		
58. Nikṣepa Rakṣā	S	Saṁpatkumārācāryaḥ (1941, pp. 1–40); Sri Uttamur Viraraghavachariar Centenary Trust (2003)
59. Pañcarātra Rakṣā = Pāñcarātrarakṣā	S	Aiyangar and Venugopalacharya (1996); Saṁpatkumārācāryaḥ (1941, pp. 94–154); Sri Uttamur Viraraghavachariar Centenary Trust (2003)
60. Saccaritra Rakṣā	S	Saṁpatkumārācāryaḥ (1941, pp. 41–63); Sri Uttamur Viraraghavachariar Centenary Trust (2003)
61. Dramiḍopaniṣatsāra	S	Rangachari (1974); Sathakopan (no date b)
62. Dramiḍopaniṣattātparya-Ratnāvalī	S	Rangachari (1974)
63. Rahasya Traya Sāram	M	SSAA (2008); Sri Ahobila Math (2012); Raghunathan (2018); *Rangacharya (2004)*
64. Bhūgola Nirṇaya	S	Saṁpatkumārācāryaḥ (1941, appendix pp. B–E)
65. Śilpārtha Sāram		L – *Singh (2008, pp. 51–52); Raghavan (1979, p. 47)*
Devotional and didactic poetry		
66. Hayagrīva Stotra	S	SSAA (2017, pp. 2–21); Raghavan et al. (2013, pp. 11–22)
67. Daśāvatāra Stotra	S	SSAA (2017, pp. 460–469); Raghavan et al. (2013, pp. 23–28)
68. Bhagavaddhyāna Sopāna	S	SSAA (2017, pp. 392–401); Raghavan et al. (2013, pp. 29–34); Hopkins (2002, pp. 156–162)
69. Gopāla Viṁśati	S	SSAA (2017, pp. 170–185); Raghavan et al. (2013, pp. 208–214); Hopkins (2007, pp. 105–118)
70. Śrī Stuti	S	SSAA (2017, pp. 402–419); Raghavan et al. (2013, pp. 226–234)
71. Abhīti Stava = Abheethisthava	S	SSAA (2017, pp. 572–593); Raghavan et al. (2013, pp. 35–46); Krishnaswami (2007, pp. 15–87)
72. Varadarāja Pañcāśat	S	SSAA (2017, pp. 204–235); Raghavan et al. (2013, pp. 84–101); Hopkins (2002, pp. 172–198)
73. Vegāsetu Stotra	S	SSAA (2017, pp. 244–251); Raghavan et al. (2013, pp. 127–130)
74. Aṣṭabhujāṣṭaka	S	SSAA (2017, pp. 236–243); Raghavan et al. (2013, pp. 131–134)

Name of text	Language of text	References
75. Kāmāsikāṣṭaka	S	SSAA (2017, pp. 252–257); Raghavan et al. (2013, pp. 135–138)
76. Paramārtha Stuti	S	SSAA (2017, pp. 296–303); Raghavan et al. (2013, pp. 139–142)
77. Śaraṇāgati Dīpikā	S	SSAA (2017, pp. 258–295); Raghavan et al. (2013, pp. 105–126)
78. Devanāyaka Pañcāśat	S	SSAA (2017, pp. 58–89); Raghavan et al. (2013, pp. 143–160); Hopkins (2002, pp. 199–215)
79. Acyuta Śataka	P	Śrīvatsāṅkācārya (2013); Raghavan et al. (2013 pp.161–190); Hopkins (2007, pp. 73–103)
80. Dehalīśa Stuti	S	SSAA (2017, pp. 186–203); Raghavan et al. (2013, pp. 215–225); *Hardy (1979)*
81. Nyāsa Tilaka	S	SSAA (2017, pp. 516–539); Raghavan et al. (2013, pp. 275–289)
82. Raghuvīra Gadya = Mahāvīravaibhavam	S	SSAA (2017, pp. 138–169); Raghavan et al. (2013, pp. 191–207)
83. Bhū Stuti	S	SSAA (2006, pp. 313–366); SSAA (2017, pp. 420–441); Raghavan et al. (2013, pp. 235–246)
84. Ṣoḍaśāyudha Stotra	S	SSAA (2017, pp. 310–318); Raghavan et al. (2013, pp. 294–298)
85. Sudarśanāṣṭaka	S	SSAA (2017, pp. 304–309); Raghavan et al. (2013, pp. 290–293)
86. Garuḍa Daṇḍaka	S	SSAA (2006, pp. 539–569); SSAA (2017, pp. 564–570); Raghavan et al. (2013, pp. 299–302)
87. Garuḍa Pañcāśat	S	SSAA (2006, pp. 571–731); SSAA (2017, pp. 22–57); Raghavan et al. (2013, pp. 303–325)
88. Yatirāja Saptati	S	SSAA (2017, pp. 470–515); Raghavan et al. (2013, pp. 326–351)
89. Dhāṭī Pañcaka	S	Venkatesan (2007)
90. Divya Deśa Mañgalāśāsana-Pañcaka		Included in the *Rahasyatrayasāram* and sometimes not considered an independent work *(Singh 2008, pp. 63–64)*
91. Pādukā Sahasra	S	Vedantadesikan (1999); Krishnaswami (2005, book 1, pp. 3–54)
92. Subhāṣita Nīvī	S	Nagarajan (1972); Iyer (1907)
Literary works		
93. Yādavābhyudaya	S	Thathachariar (1976); Balasubramanyam (1907, 1909); Krishnaswami (2005, book 1 pp. 57–107)

Name of text	Language of text	References
94. Saṅkalpa Sūryodaya	S	V. Krishnamacharya (1948a, 1948b); Iyengar (1977); Iyengar (1979); Viraraghavacharya (2017); *Laxmi (2008)*
95. Haṁsa Sandeśa	S	Chariar and Ayengar (1973); Bronner and Schulman (2009); Hopkins (2016)
96. Dayā Śataka	S	SSAA (2017, pp. 320–383); Ayyangar (1960); Raghavan et al. (2013, pp. 47–83); Bronner and Schulman (2009)
97. Godā Stuti = Godha Stuti	S	SSAA (2017, pp. 442–459); Raghavan et al. (2013, pp. 247–258); Narasimhan (2009)
98. Yamaka Ratnākara		L? – *Singh (2008, p. 72)*
99. Samasyā Sahasra = Samayasahasri		L – *Singh (2008, pp. 72–73)*
Original philosophical treatises		
100. Nyāya Pariśuddhi	S	Śrīvatsāṅkācārya (2007); *Narayanan (2008)*; Saṁpatkumārācāryaḥ (1940)
101. Nyāya Siddhāñjana = Tarka Sidhānjana	S	Annangaracharyar (1941, pp. 210–238); Śāstri (1901); Saṁpatkumārācāryaḥ (1940); *Rangachar (2000)*
102. Tattva Muktā-Kalāpa	S	Śrīkṛṣṇatātācārya (1990); Narasimhachar (1940); Srinivāsagopālāchārya (1954, 1956); Srinivasachar and Narasimhachar (1933); Dvivedī (1983); *Chari (2004)*
103. Sarvārtha Siddhi	S	Srinivasachar and Narasimhachar (1933); Narasimhachar (1940); Srinivāsagopālāchārya (1954, 1956); Śrīkṛṣṇatātācārya (1990); Dvivedī (1983); *Chari (2004)*
104. Śata Dūṣaṇī	S	Dvivedī (1986); *Chari (1961)*
105. Seśvara Mīmāṁsā	S	Saṁpatkumārācāryaḥ (1940)
106. Mīmāṁsā Pādukā	S	Saṁpatkumārācāryaḥ (1940)
107. Adhikaraṇa Sārāvalī	S	Lakṣmīnṛsiṁhācārya (1940); *Chari (2008)*
108. Paramata-Bhaṅga	M	Nārāyaṇācārya (1979, 1982); *Chari (2011)*
109. Adhikaraṇa Darpaṇa		L – *Singh (2008, p. 88)*; *Raghavan (1979, p. 28)*
110. Vāditraya Khaṇḍana	S	Probably written by Vedāntadeśika's son, Kumāra Vedāntācārya *(Raghavan 1979, p. 51)*
111. Cakāra Samarthana		L – *Singh (2008, p. 88)*; *Raghavan (1979, p. 47)*

Name of text	Language of text	References
Commentaries		
112. Tattva Tīkā	S	Viraraghavacharya (1974); Śrīraṅgaśaṭhakopayatīndramahādeśika (1938); Saṁpatkumārācāryaḥ (1941, pp. 1–192)
113. Tātparya Candrikā	S	Shastri (2014)
114. Gītārtha Saṅgraha Rakṣā = Rahasya Rakṣā on Yāmuna's Bhagavadgītā Arthasaṅgraha	S	Sri Uttamur Viraraghavachariar Centenary Trust (2003); Shastri (2014); Kṛṣṇāprapannācārya and Govindācārya (2000)
115. Gītārtha Saṅgraha Pattu	T	Sathakopan (no date l)
116. Catuśślokī Bhāṣya = Rahasyarakṣā on Yāmunacharya's Catuśślokī	S	Śrīvatsāṅkācārya (no date)
117. Stotra Ratna Bhāṣya	S	Śrīvatsāṅkācārya (no date)
118. Gadya Traya Bhāṣya = Rahasyarakṣā	S	Śrīvatsāṅkācārya (no date)
119. Īśopaniṣad-Bhāṣya = Īśāvāsyopaniṣad Bhāṣya	S	Varadachari and Thathacharya (1975)
Other works The works below are attributed to Vedāntadeśika but not listed in *Singh (2008)*		
120. Amrita Ranjani = Amruta Ranjani	T	Sathakopan (no date e)
121. Adhikāra Sangraham	T	Sathakopan (no date d)
122. Amritāswādhini = Amruta Svādhini	T	Sathakopan (no date j)
123. Mei Virata Mānmiyam = Meyviratamāṉmiyam	T	Hopkins (2002, pp. 84–114)

The first entry for the names of texts 1 to 119 is written as by Singh. Further entries use variations in spelling and diacritics given in other sources.

Adapted from Singh (2008, pp. 39–96, especially pp. 39–41)

so he should be passive, like a kitten carried by its mother.[64] Vedāntadeśika, however, almost entirely eliminates the role of individual effort, emphasizing the devotee's helplessness when surrendering to God. This position resembles that of the *Teṉkalai*.[65]

64. Hopkins (2012, p. 465).
65. Hopkins (2012, p. 466).

Plate 7
The Parakāla Math, Mysore, 2018.

Photograph: Simon Atkinson

Vaṭakalai-s are usually associated with one of four main institutions: the Śrī Brahmatantra Svatantra Parakāla Math, the Ahobilam Math, the Srirangam Srimad Andavan Ashramam and the Poundarikapuram Srimad Andavan Ashramam. Krishnamacharya studied at the Śrī Brahmatantra Svatantra Parakāla Math in Mysore - see Plate 7. The Math is said to have been founded by Vedāntadeśika but Narayanan dates it to *c.*1378 CE - about nine years after Vedāntadeśika is said to have died.[66] The Ahobilam Math is located in the hills of Andra Pradesh. Various dates are given for its formation: 1320 CE, 1398 CE and the 15th century CE.[67] The Srirangam Srimad Andavan Ashramam (founded in the 18th century)

66. Narayanan (2011, p. 558). Vedāntadeśika is said to have died in 1369 - Hopkins (2012, p. 462).

67. Seshadri (1998, p. 80); Raghavan (2017–2018, p. 525); and Narayanan (2011, p. 558) respectively.

and the Poundarikapuram Srimad Andavan Ashramam are both based in Srirangam.[68]

In the next part of this chapter, I will first explore Vedāntadeśika's teachings on obscuration. Second, I will show how Vedāntadeśika incorporated some aspects of the stream of thought described in the previous chapter, in which snake metaphors are used to represent something to be overcome. Vedāntadeśika used snakes to represent both confusion over *dharma*, and *māyā*. Third, I will present two quotations on *kuṇḍalinī* that T.K.V. Desikachar attributed to Vedāntadeśika before searching for them in textual passages that deal with a related topic: the ascent of the self along the *suṣumnā* at the time of death. I will then scrutinize three passages where Vedāntadeśika used *kuṇḍalī* or related terms.

6.3.2 Vedāntadeśika on *tirodhāna*

The *Śatadūṣaṇī*, a major treatise, aims to refute *Advaita* positions and thereby establish *Viśiṣṭādvaita* doctrines.[69] It contains substantial information on *avidyā*, developing Rāmānuja's attempted refutation of *Advaita*. Vedāntadeśika's position on *tirodhāna* in the *Śatadūṣaṇī* could have influenced his propensity to use *kuṇḍalinī* to represent covering or a blockage. Recall from Chapter 5 that the *Vivekacūḍāmaṇi* and *Aṣṭāvakragītā* (both *Advaita* texts) use snake metaphors to describe the covering of the *ātman*. Recall also from Chapter 3 that in the *Ahirbudhnyasaṁhitā* (a *Pāñcarātra* text), one of *śakti's* five actions is *tirodhāna* (concealment), which I argued is compatible with that text's conception of *kuṇḍalinī* as a blockage. Hence, even though Śrīvaiṣṇavism's treatment of *tirodhāna* is based on Vedic sources, the position that it takes could have influenced whether the tradition used *kuṇḍalinī* similarly.

Vedāntadeśika proposes eight alternative explanations of how *tirodhāna* (obscuration) could operate along *Advaita* lines.[70] He rejects them all and concludes by offering a rebuttal of the *Advaita* position:

> Not on any account (*na kathañcit*) is good or clever speech possible (*ghaṭate*) [about] the obscuration (*tirodhāna*) of a really existing thing (*vastu*) [which is] indistinct (*nirviśeṣa*), eternal (*nitya*), self-illuminating (*svayamprakāśa*),

68. Seshadri (1998, p. 82); Chari (1994, p. 30); Narayanan (2011, p. 558).
69. Chari (1961, p. 5).
70. Chari (1961, pp. 142, 143).

> and whose eternal consciousness (*jñāna antara*) is imperceptible via the senses (*agocara*) either to itself or to another.[71]

Vedāntadeśika criticizes only the way *tirodhāna* works in *Advaita*. He does not reject the term *tirodhāna*, using it himself in his own system. For example, according to Vedāntadeśika's *Gītārthasaṅgraharakṣā*, chapter 7 of the *Bhagavadgītā* discusses the concealment (*tirodhāna*) of the own form (*svarūpa*) of the supreme person (*paramapuruṣa*) by *prakṛti*.[72] A few words later, Vedāntadeśika quotes *mama māyā duratyayā* from *Bhagavadgītā* 7.14, which means 'my illusion, difficult to go beyond'. He thereby links *tirodhāna* to *māyā*, which conceals God's nature. Similarly, in the *Varadarājapañcāśat*, Vedāntadeśika describes Lord Varadarāja as being 'concealed by *māyā*' (*māyā nigūḍam*).[73]

Hence, despite rebutting *Advaitins*' usage of *tirodhāna*, Vedāntadeśika used the term, and synonyms of it, himself. This leaves open the possibility that Vedāntadeśika could have described how *kuṇḍalinī* blocks the entry of the *jīvātman* into the *suṣumnā*, just as *nigrahaśakti* obscures the *jīva* in the *Ahirbudhnyasaṁhitā* (see Chapter 3).

6.3.3 The snake and the rope in Vedāntadeśika's works

Vedāntadeśika supported Rāmānuja's rebuttal of the *Advaita* snake-rope analogy, in which the snake represents *avidyā* and the unreality of the phenomenal world. In the *Śatadūṣaṇī*, Vedāntadeśika argues that an unreal snake cannot cause fear. For Rāmānuja and Deśika, that which is not real cannot reveal what is real. The snake is not completely non-real (*sarvathā mithyā*) 'because it exists in some other place and at some other

71. My translation of the end of *Vāda* 35 of the *Śatadūṣaṇī* from the Sanskrit in Chari (1961, p. 143) and Dvivedī (1986, vol. 3 pp.69, 70):

> na kathañcidapi nirviśeṣanityasvayamprakāśe, svasya parasya vā jñānāntarāgocare vastuni tirodhānavācoyuktirghaṭate iti ||

72. *Gītārthasaṅgraharakṣā*, Section 11 – my summary translation of Kṛṣṇāprapannācārya and Govindācārya (2000, p. 17):

> tāvadupāsyabhūtaparamapuruṣasvarūpayāthātmyam, prakṛtyā tattirodhānam

Vedāntadeśika's *Gītārthasaṅgraharakṣā* is a gloss on Yāmuna's *Gītārthasaṅgraha*, which is a commentary on the *Bhagavadgītā*.

73. *Varadarājapañcāśat* 28, translation – Raghavan et al. (2013, p. 94). The text describes Lord Varadarāja, the presiding deity at the main *Vaiṣṇava* temple in Kanchipuram.

time'.[74] Given this position, one might have expected Vedāntadeśika to be disinclined to use a snake metaphor to represent something to be overcome such as *avidyā* and, by extension, *kuṇḍalinī*. Vedāntadeśika does, however, use snake metaphors extensively in other texts, including the *Gītārthasaṅgraharakṣā* and *Garuḍapañcāśat*.

First, in his commentary on verse 5 of Yāmuna's *Gītārthasaṅgraḥ*, Vedāntadeśika compares Arjuna's confusion between *dharma* and *adharma* in the *Bhagavadgītā* to the confusion between seeing a snake and a rope.[75] This edges Vedāntadeśika closer to using the snake-rope metaphor to represent *avidyā* or *māyā*. Second, the *Garuḍapañcāśat* mentions a 'serpent of illusion':

> Garuḍa, standing tall in front of Murāri (Viṣṇu) like a mirror of gems to be his sole object of vision, [is] an antidote to the fear (*bhaya*) from drinking the poison (*viṣa*) [of the] serpent of illusion (*māyā bhujaṅgī*).[76]

Even though Vedāntadeśika supported Rāmānuja's critique of the use of the snake-rope metaphor in *Advaita*, he used similar snake metaphors himself to represent *māyā* and confusion between *dharma* and *adharma*, both of which must be overcome. Hence, it would not have been a huge leap for Vedāntadeśika to have used a snake metaphor to represent something else to be overcome: the *kuṇḍalinī-avidyā* blockage to the *suṣumnā*. It would seem quite feasible therefore that, according to T.K.V. Desikachar, Vedāntadeśika used the term *kuṇḍalinī* in this way.

6.3.4 Vedāntadeśika quotations on *kuṇḍalinī*

T.K.V. Desikachar gave two specific quotations from Vedāntadeśika on *kuṇḍalinī:*

---

74. Chari (1961, p. 22).

75. Kṛṣṇāprapannācārya and Govindācārya (2000, p. 11): dharmādharmabhayaṁ rajjusarpabhayamitivat |

76. My translation of the Sanskrit in Raghavan et al. (2013, p. 307):

> agre tiṣṭan udagro maṇimukura ivānanyadṛṣṭermurāreḥ
> pāyānmāyābhujaṅgī viṣamaviṣabhayād gāḍhamasmān garutmān | 8a

The *Garuḍapañcāśat* praises Garuḍa, the eagle vehicle of Viṣṇu. In 8a, the female snake (*bhujaṅgī*) is portrayed negatively as *vyālī* (commentary in SSAA 2006, p. 612), which can mean wicked, vicious, villainous, cruel or fierce (Apte 1957, p. 1519). See later this chapter for details of how the same text portrays snakes more positively in another verse.

1 'According to *Vedāntadeśika*, the *brahmanaḍi* is the location of *Kuṇḍalini*. It is called the 101st Naḍi.'[77]
2 'According to *Vedāntadeśika*, the grace of the Lord is a must for the *prāṇa* to enter *suṣūmna* after the *kuṇḍalini* is reduced.'[78]

T.K.V. Desikachar did not indicate which of Vedāntadeśika's many works these quotations come from. They are, however, reminiscent of a section of the *Brahmasūtra* and Rāmānuja's *Śrībhāṣya* commentary thereon. Recall from Chapter 1 that the *Kaṭha Upaniṣad* describes one hundred and one *nāḍī-s* of the heart, one of which rises to the crown of the head. *Brahmasūtra* 4.2.16 reflects this to describe how the *jīva* (the self) exits the body at the moment of death. The *sūtra* includes an element of grace:

> Due to yogic remembrance (*anusmṛti yoga* = meditation) on the passage for those who are allowed to escape and due to the efficacy of knowledge, [the *jīva*] is favoured with kindness, that abode shines from the top, and that doorway (*dvāra*) is illuminated, [so the *jīva* exits] through [the *nāḍī*] 'beyond 100' (*śata adhikayā* - the 101st *nāḍī*).[79]

This verse, based on early *Upaniṣad-s*, predates any use of '101st *nāḍī*' by Vedāntadeśika. There is no hint of *Pāñcarātra* influence and no mention of *kuṇḍalinī*.[80]

Rāmānuja's *Śrībhāṣya* elaborates:

> The wise one departs [the body] via the 101st *nāḍī* at the crown of the head. The wise one does not make the wrong decision [and enter another *nāḍī*]. The wise one, as a consequence of knowledge, which is dear to the supreme person (*parama puruṣa*) [and] fit for his propitiation, and due to the yogic remembrance (*anusmaraṇa yoga*) of the passage (*gati*) to the *ātman's* escape, by the affectionate grace (*prasannena hārdena*) of the supreme person, the wise one is favoured. And therefore that abode of the *jīva*, the heart place,

---

77. T.K.V. Desikachar (2000, p. 49), commenting on *Yogayājñavalkya* 4.24. The *Brahmanāḍī* is synonymous with the *suṣumnā* (T.K.V. Desikachar 2000, p. 49).

78. T.K.V. Desikachar (2000, p. 50), commenting on *Yogayājñavalkya* 4.25.

79. My translation of Śivaprasādadvivedī (2009, vol. 4 p.248): tadoko 'grajjvalaṁ tatprakāśitadvāro vidyāsāmarthyāt taccheṣagatyanusmṛtiyogācca hārdānugṛhītaḥ śatādhikayā ||

80. Vireswarananda (2007, pp. 21, 22) examines *Brahmasūtra* 2.2.42–45 and concludes that 'we cannot but see the refutation of the Pāñcarātra system in these Sūtras'. There is no such refutation in 4.2.16, where *Pāñcarātra* terminology is simply not used.

> is illuminated 'flaming at the top'. Due to the favour of the supreme person, the doorway is illuminated, the wise one identifies that *nāḍī*, and by it he goes into the passage (*gati*).[81]

This extract shows no *Pāñcarātra* influence. Unsurprisingly, it does not mention *kuṇḍalinī* and it describes the *ātman* rising from the heart, not *prāṇa* and the *ātman* rising from *nābhi*, as in the *Yogayājñavalkya*. Nevertheless, with some creative exegesis it would have been possible for a skilled theologian such as Vedāntadeśika to write a gloss on the *Śrībhāṣya* integrating *kuṇḍalinī* as a blockage to the 101st *nāḍī*, thereby mixing *Vedāntic* and *Pāñcarātra* teachings. Therefore, Vedāntadeśika's texts commentating on *Brahmasūtra* 4.2.16 and the *Śrībhāṣya* thereon seem a promising place to search for the quotations that T.K.V. Desikachar presents.

Vedāntadeśika's main gloss on the *Śrībhāṣya*, the *Tattvaṭīkā*, is now incomplete and does not cover the above verse.[82] However, at least eleven other Vedāntadeśika texts discuss the *jīvātman* entering the *suṣumnā*, some commenting directly on the *Brahmasūtra* and *Śrībhāṣya*. Whereas the *Yogayājñavalkya* describes a meditative visualization of the ascent of the *jīva* while the practitioner is alive, those eleven texts describe what happens after death. I will review the eleven texts in the following order:

- *Rahasyatrayasāram*
- *Adhikārasangraham*
- *Nyāyasiddhāñjana*
- *Adhikaraṇasārāvalī*
- *Śaraṇāgatidīpikā*
- *Acyutaśatakaṁ*
- *Meyviratamāṉmiyam*
- *Pādukāsahasraṁ*
- *Paramapadasopāna*
- *Upakārasaṅgraham*
- *Hastigirimāhātmyam*

---

81. My translation of Śivaprasādadvivedī (2009, vol. 4 p.249):

> evaṁ prāpte pracakṣmahe – śatādhikayeti | vidvān śatādhikayā mūrdhanyayaiva nāḍyotkrāmati | na cāsyā viduṣo durvivecatvam; vidvān hi paramapuruṣārādhanabhūtātyarthapriyavidyāsāmarthyāt vidyāśeṣabhūtatayā' 'tmano 'tyarthapriyagatyanusmaraṇayogācca prasannena hārdena paramapuruṣeṇānugṛhīto bhavati; tatśca tadokaḥ tasya jīvasya sthānaṁ hṛdayaṁ, agrajvalanaṁ bhavati – agre jvalanaṁ prakāśanaṁ yasya tadadimagrajvalanaṁ | paramapuruṣaprasādāt prakāśitadvāro vidvan tāṁ nāḍīṁ vijānātīti tayā viduṣo gatirupapadyate || 4.2.16 ||

82. Saṁpatkumārācāryaḥ (1941, pp. 1–192).

6.3.5 *Rahasyatrayasāram*

The *Rahasyatrayasāram* is Vedāntadeśika's *magnum opus.*[83] Krishnamacharya was taught it by Śrī Kṛṣṇa Brahmatantra Swatantra Parakāla Swāmi in Mysore sometime between 1909 and 1914.[84] Although it is written in Maṇipravāla, Krishnamacharya 'could explain all the verses as if he was familiar with the language'.[85]

The *Rahasyatrayasāram* primarily discusses three important *mantra-s* but it also includes substantial *Viśiṣṭādvaita* doctrine. The 20th chapter describes how the *ātman* exits the body at the time of death:

> The Lord combines the ten external sensory organs with the mind. The Lord unites the organs of action and knowledge and the mind with life breath. The Lord connects the life breath along with the eleven sensory organs with *jīva.* The lord combines the *jīva* who is already connected with the organs and the life breath, with the five subtle elements extracted after churning the triple twined central bone in the middle of the back of the gross body. The Lord who is naturally compassionate, rests this *jīva*, which is combined with sensory organs, life breath and subtle elements by keeping it close to himself in the form He has assumed in the heart.[86]

So far, the process is identical for those destined for heaven and those destined for rebirth.[87] Then Viṣṇu leads the *jīva-s* through different *nāḍī-s* to different destinations:[88]

> In the heart, the *jīva* shines like a bright lamp. It has innumerable rays which are the veins. These are in many colours like white, black, purple, blue, golden yellow, and red. Among these there is one vein which is looking upward. The *jīva* which passes through this vein pierces the orbit of the Sun and crossing the world of Brahmā reaches a higher state. There are hundred (sic) veins going upward. The *jīva* which passes through these obtain (sic) the body of gods and reaches the world of gods. There is a type of veins which look downward. These are dim in luminosity. Those who pass through these veins lose themselves, and are reborn in this world to experience the fruits of *karma.* The Lord ensures that the *jīva* of the *prapanna* avoids those specific

83. Rangacharya (2004, p. xv); Singh (2008, p. 51).
84. Srivatsan (1995, pp. 33, 34); Srivatsan (1997, pp. 17, 18).
85. Srivatsan (1997, p. 91).
86. Raghunathan (2018, pp. 379, 380).
87. Raghunathan (2018, p. 380).
88. Raghunathan (2018, p. 367).

> veins which are entrances to heaven and hell and which are similar to the routes followed by thieves and as such are meant for the thieves of the soul. The Lord makes the *jīva* of the *prapanna* take the *brahma-nāḍī* which is over and above the hundred veins (going upward) and which is the entrance to the route of the shining path called *arcirādi* and move forward with the help of the rays of the Sun.[89]

> The Supreme Omnipotent Lord is like the father who jumps into a huge well full of mud to rescue his child who has fallen into the well. At the time of departure, the same Lord standing in the subtle sky which is located in the lotus of the heart, makes us enter the hundred and first vein in order to commence us on our journey to Śrī Vaikuṇṭha.[90]

The *ātman* continues along the 'shining path' (*arcirādi mārga*) and *mokṣa* is achieved in heaven (*vaikuṇṭha*).[91] The 21st chapter states that

> The loving *Hārda* [God] takes the *mumukṣu* [seeker of liberation] who has entered the *mūrdhanya* vein [at the top of the palate], from the gross body called *brahmapura*, through the *brahmā* vein which is the main exit, ... passing through an extremely small hole in the dead centre of the orb of the Sun ... [92]

The *mumukṣu* then passes various deities before Viṣṇu appears.[93]

In support of his account, Vedāntadeśika quotes from a plethora of texts. These include some *Pāñcarātra Saṁhitā-s*, including the *Ahirbudhnyasaṁhitā* and *Pādmasaṁhitā*, but he includes no quotations from the *haṭhayoga* sections of those texts.

Note that entry into the *suṣumnā* is due to the Lord's compassion, making the *Rahasyatrayasāram* compatible in principle with the second quotation that T.K.V. Desikachar attributes to Vedāntadeśika. There is, however, no mention of *kuṇḍalinī* in the *Rahasyatrayasāram*.

---

89. Raghunathan (2018, p. 381). A *prapanna* is a devotee dedicated to *prapatti*, surrender to God.
90. Raghunathan (2018, pp. 386, 387).
91. Raghunathan (2018, pp. 367, 368).
92. Raghunathan (2018, p. 389), my insertions in brackets.
93. Raghunathan (2018, pp. 388–400).

6.3.6 *Adhikārasangraham*

The Tamil *Adhikārasangraham* has thirty-two sections, each summarizing a chapter of the *Rahasyatrayasāram*. Section 27 discusses the exit of the devotee from the body:

> In the ChEthanam's heart, 101 naadis (nerve pathways) originate. There is one special naadi in the middle of the 100 naadis. It is called Brahma naadi or Moordhanya naadi or Sushumnai. The jeevans that travel by any one of the 100 naadis --other than the Brahma naadi- reach lOkAs other than SrI Vaikuntam. Prapanna Jeevan alone is assisted by the Lord to travel by Brahma naadi and archirAdhi mArgam (the path of light) and reach SrI Vaikuntam.[94]

Kuṇḍalinī is not mentioned.

6.3.7 *Nyāyasiddhāñjana*

The Sanskrit *Nyāyasiddhāñjana* discusses *prameya* (that which is knowable), one of the categories of the *Nyāya* philosophical system, and attempts to show that it is in line with *Viśiṣṭādvaita* teachings. One topic is how the *jīva* exits the body via the *suṣumnā:*

> For one wanting to leave (*uccikramiṣata*) [the body], first the faculty of speech and the rest [of the senses] become undivided (*avibhāga*) from the mind. That combination (*saṁyukta*) of all *indriya-s* and the mind [becomes undivided] from *prāṇa*. And that *prāṇa*, combined (*saṁyukta*) with eleven *indriya-s*, [becomes undivided] from the *jīva*. And that, combined with *indriya-s* and *prāṇa*, [becomes undivided] from the five elements. And these *indriya-s*, combined with *prāṇa* and the *jīva*, [become undivided] from the *paramātman*. The account so far is common to the wise and the unwise; and the case of the unwise was told earlier. But the wise one pleasantly exits the body via the *mūrdhanya/brahmanāḍī*.[95]

---

94. Translation – Sathakopan (no date d, p. 40), verbatim.

95. My translation of *Nyāyasiddhāñjana* from Annangaracharyar (1941, p. 220) and Śāstri (1901, p. 76):

> uccikramiṣataḥ sarvasya pūrvaṁ vāgindriyaṁ tadanu ca śoṣāṇi navendriyāṇi manasā sahāvibhāgaṁ gacchanti | tacca sarvendriyasaṁyuktaṁ manaḥ prāṇena | sa caikādaśendriyasaṁyukto jīvena | sa cendriyaprāṅasaṁyuktaḥ pañcabhūtaiḥ | tāni cendriyaprāṇajīvasaṁyuktāni paramātmanā | etāvacca vidvadaviduṣoḥ sādhāraṇam | aviduṣastu viśeṣaḥ prāgevoktaḥ | vidvāṁstu sarvo 'pi mūrdhanyayā brahmanāḍyā sukhena śarīrāt niṣkrāman |

This passage closely resembles the *Rahasyatrayasāram*. The *Nyāyasiddhāñjana* continues, describing the progress of the *jīva* and subtle body along the *arcirādi mārga* towards Viṣṇu in heaven (*vaikuṇṭha*). *Kuṇḍalinī* is absent.

6.3.8 *Adhikaraṇasārāvalī*

The Sanskrit *Adhikaraṇasārāvalī* is both a 'poetic synopsis' of the *Tattvaṭīkā* and an exposition of themes from the *Brahmasūtra*.[96] One theme is *utkrānti* - the exit of the *jīvātman* from the body.

According to the *Adhikaraṇasārāvalī*, the *jīva*, *indriya-s*, *manas* and *prāṇa* exit the body together through the *mūrdhanya nāḍī* (*suṣumnā*). First, all *indriya-s* merge with *manas*. *Manas* then merges with *prāṇa*, which merges with *tejas*.[97] *Tejas* here represents 'all other elements' of the physical body.[98] This makes the *Adhikaraṇasārāvalī* compatible with the *Rahasyatrayasāram*. The *Adhikaraṇasārāvalī* then discusses how the *jīva* and subtle body find the best exit from the physical body with Viṣṇu's grace:

> In a very subtle web (*jāla*) of *nāḍī-s*, it is not easy to discern the way of the liberation *nāḍī* (*mukti nāḍī/mūrdhanya nāḍī*) by the effort (*niyamata*) of the one being released (*mucyamānasya puṁsaḥ*). ... Pleased with the knowledge [of the seeker of liberation], with great grace and kindness (*hārda prasadana mahasā*) [Viṣṇu deems him] fit to enter the *nāḍī* (492).
>
> Together with and possessing another, [who is] perfect in herself (Lakṣmī), the all-knowing one (Viṣṇu), purifier of seven worlds, dwelling concealed (*sthagita*) in the centre of the heart lotus, having opened (*bhittvā*) the *nāḍī* called *suṣumnā*, which supports the whole form (*rupa*) from *nābhi* to the top of the head, and having thrown up (*ut-kṣipya*) that middle road the one desiring liberation like an arrow that has been shot, [Viṣṇu] will lead [him] (493).[99]

Rāmānuja describes the coming together of the components as a process of 'combination, connection or union but not of merger' (Raghunathan 2018, p. 379 n.34). Hence, *yuktaṁ* here could mean 'joined', 'yoked', 'connected with' (Apte 1957, pp. 1312, 1313) or 'combined' (Monier-Williams 1899, p. 853), while *saṁ* usually means 'together' or 'completely'. I therefore translate *saṁyukta* as 'combination' or 'combined'.

96. Singh (2008, p. 87).

97. Chari (2008, pp. 262–265).

98. Chari (2008, p. 265).

99. *Adhikaraṇasārāvalī* 492–493 – my translation of Lakṣmīnṛsiṁhācārya (1940, pp. 741–742):

> nāḍījāle 'tisūkṣme na bhavati suśakā muktināḍī vivektuṁ
> tasmānmūrdhanyanāḍīgatiraniyamato mucyamānasya puṁsaḥ |

There are four noteworthy aspects. First, the *suṣumnā* is opened by Viṣṇu, not by the aspirant, as in *haṭhayoga.* Second, according to T.K.V. Desikachar, 'We have to visualise *kuṇḍalini* as the place of the Lord and *jīva*.'[100] We saw in Chapter 2 how T.K.V. Desikachar inconsistently locates *kuṇḍalinī* at both *nābhi* (as in the *Yogayājñavalkya*) and at *mūlādhāra* (contrary to the *Yogayājñavalkya*). Vedāntadeśika follows the major *Upaniṣad-s*, the *Brahmasūtra* and Rāmānuja's *Śrībhāṣya* thereon in locating the Lord in the heart. This is inconsistent with Desikachar's statement.

Third, in certain major *Upaniṣad-s*, the *Brahmasūtra* and the *Śrībhāṣya*, the *suṣumnā* stretches from the heart to the crown. Here, however, Vedāntadeśika extends its lower terminus down to *nābhi.* This edges his account closer to those of the *Yogayājñavalkya*, *Pādmasaṁhitā* and *Ahirbudhnyasaṁhitā*, hinting at *Pāñcarātra* influence. Nevertheless, *kuṇḍalinī* is mentioned in neither the *Adhikaraṇasārāvalī* nor two commentaries.[101]

Fourth, after discussing the entry of the *jīva* and its entourage into the *suṣumnā*, Vedāntadeśika describes their progression along the *arcirādi mārga.* This path is named after the deity *arcis* (light or fire), the realm into which the *jīva* passes 'through the rays of the sun' after exiting the body.[102] According to Vedāntadeśika, 'The total eradication of *avidyā*, which is the cause of bondage requires the exit of the *jīva* from the body and also its movement through the *arcirādi mārga* to the higher abode'.[103] Only then, after the *jīva* sheds its subtle body (*sūkṣma śarīra*), does it achieve *mokṣa.*[104] Hence, for Vedāntadeśika, entry into the *suṣumnā* does not imply eradication of *avidyā.*

The *Adhikaraṇasārāvalī* is a formal theological text supporting Rāmānuja's position with Vedāntic sources. Other than the extension of *suṣumnā* down to *nābhi*, I can see no sign of *Pāñcarātra* influence. If Vedāntadeśika wanted to use the term *kuṇḍalinī*, he would have had more artistic license to do so in less formal genres, to which we now turn.

... vidyāsamprītahārdaprasadanamahasā svārhanāḍīpraveśāt || 492 ||
svādhīno hārdasaṁjñassvayamavikalayā sampadā sākamekaḥ
sthitvā hṛtpadmamadhye sthagitanijatanussaptalokagṛihasthaḥ |
nāḍīcakre suṣumnāṁ nikhiladhṛtikarīṁ nābhimūrdhāntarūpāṁ
bhittvā tanmadhyarandhraprahitamiṣumivotkṣipya netā mumukṣum || 493 ||

100. T.K.V. Desikachar (2000, p. 50 n.3).
101. Both commentaries are in Lakṣmīnṛsiṁhācārya (1940, pp. 741, 742).
102. Chari (2008, p. 273).
103. Chari (2008, p. 268).
104. Chari (2008, p. 267).

6.3.9 *Śaraṇāgatidīpikā*

The Sanskrit poem *Śaraṇāgatidīpikā* outlines liberation through *prapatti* (surrender to God). Verse 38 describes the *jīva's* entry into the *suṣumnā:*

> [When their] pre-determined life[span] suddenly ends, [whether] in the day or night, or [whether] the sun is north or south [of the equator], O Lord, you, dwelling in the heart, single-handedly cause devotees (*prapanna-s*) to enter the 101st *nāḍī* (*śata ādhikāṁ nāḍīm*).[105]

Kuṇḍalinī is absent.

6.3.10 *Acyutaśatakaṁ*

The Prakrit poem *Acyutaśatakaṁ* is addressed to the deity Acyuta. Verse 84 discusses exiting the body through the *brahmanāḍī:*

> O Acyuta, when will you see me, like [your] dear child, resting in you in [my] heart? When will I be going along the *brahmanāḍī* (*brahma dhamanī mārga*), delivered (*datta*) [by] the first ray [of] the sun?[106]

Neither the verse nor the Sanskrit commentary mention *kuṇḍalinī.*

---

105. My translation of SSAA (2017, p. 272):

> savyānyayorayanayorniśi vāsare vā saṅkalpitāyuravadhīn sapadi prapannān |
> hārdaḥ svayaṁ nijapade viniveśayiṣyan nāḍīṁ praveśayasi nātha śatādhikāṁ tvam || 38 ||

106. My translation of the Sanskritized text in Śrīvatsāṅkācārya (2013, p. 75), informed by the Sanskrit commentary therein:

> hārde tvayi kadā viśrāntaṁ brahmadhamanīmārgagamiṣyantaṁ |
> dinakaradattāgrakaramacyuta drakṣyasi dayitaḍimbhamiva mām || 84 ||

Agrakaram could be translated as 'finger' (Monier-Williams 1899, p. 6), which may have prompted Raghavan et al. (2013, p. 185) to use 'offered a helping hand by the Sun' in their translation. I translate *agrakaram* as 'first ray' of the sun (Monier-Williams 1899, p. 6) because in the *Rahasyatrayasāram*, 'The Lord makes the *jīva* of the *prapanna* take the *brahma-nāḍī* ... and move forward with the help of the rays of the Sun' (Raghunathan 2018, p. 381). The Sanskrit commentary in Śrīvatsāṅkācārya (2013, p. 75) confirms that (the plural form of) *agrakara* is shorthand for *kiraṇān-calāni*, which are moving or transitory rays of light (Apte 1957, pp. 573, 701).

6.3.11 *Meyviratamāṉmiyam*

The Tamil *Meyviratamāṉmiyam* covers similar ground, describing Lord Varadarāja as follows:

> He has the power to sever the ties of all karmas linked to the pure and impure; the strength to guide worthy souls, at the time of their death, up the narrow inscrutable channel of Brahmā.[107]

The Tamil for 'the narrow inscrutable channel of Brahmā' is *tamaṉi neṟi*, which Hopkins equates with the 'Brahmā nāṭī', i.e. 'the Brahmā vein at the top of the skull'.[108] *Kuṇḍalinī* is not mentioned.

6.3.12 *Pādukāsahasraṁ*

The *Pādukāsahasraṁ* is a devotional Sanskrit work about the jewel-covered sandals (*pādukā-s*) of Lord Rāma, Viṣṇu's *avatār.* It describes the *jīva* entering the *suṣumnā:*

> O sandals of Viṣṇu, in the final moment of an old person abiding there [in the heart], may he find the entrance (*gati*) of the middle *nāḍī* (=*suṣumnā*), from where he can go forth, due to unsurpassed brilliance from you (520).
>
> O sandals, for a seeker of liberation coming out via the middle *nāḍī*, *mūrdhanya*, these jewels create a collection of ropes hanging down from *Brahmaloka* (483).[109]

The implication is that the seeker of liberation can use the ropes to climb to heaven (*Brahmaloka*). Vedāntadeśika uses considerable artistic licence as neither *Brahmasūtra* 4.2.16 nor the *Śrībhāṣya* thereon mention Viṣṇu's sandals. Nevertheless, the *Pādukāsahasraṁ* does not mention *kuṇḍalinī.*

---

107. Translation – Hopkins (2002, p. 105).
108. Hopkins (2002, p. 279 n.150).
109. My translation of the Sanskrit in Vedantadesikan (1999, pp. 340, 318)

> bhavatyante tvāṁ praṇatasya jantoḥ tadoko 'grajvalanaṁ tvatprakāśaiḥ |
> mato nāḍyā madhyamayā viniryan gatiṁ vindet keśavapādarakṣe || 520 ||
> mukundapādāvani madhyanāḍyā mūrdhanyayā niṣpatato mumukṣoḥ |
> ābrahmalokādavalambanārthaṁ ratnāni te raśmigaṇaṁ sṛjanti || 483 ||

6.3.13 *Paramapadasopāna*

The *Paramapadasopāna* is mainly in Tamil with some Sanskrit verses. It aims to establish *prapatti* as the sole means of liberation. The text describes how the *jīva* ascends seven steps on the ladder (*sopāna*) towards liberation and leaves the body via the *suṣumnā*. When that *jīva* adopts *bhakti* or *prapatti*, Viṣṇu 'stands by with this noble intention to exit that jeevan from its bodily prison and lead it to His Supreme Abode'.[110] Sathakopan translates Tamil and Sanskrit passages together:

> At the time of death, our Lord unites the jnAna Indhriyams (Ear, faculty of speech, eyes, nose and body) as well as the Karma Indhriyams (Mouth, hands, legs, mala dhvAram and Jala dhvAram) of the Prapanna Jeevan with the mind; thereafter, our Lord unites the Mind with PrANa Vaayu ... Next, the PrANa Vaayu is united with the JeevAthmA. This jeevan combined with Mukhya PrANan gets united with the pancha bhUthams. At this stage, our most merciful Lord removes the fatigue experienced by the Jeevan from all these exertions by embracing it closely. Finally, our Lord exits the Jeevan from its bodily cage with the eleven holes (two Eye holes, two ear orifices, two nostrils, mouth, mala dhvAram, Jala dhvAram, nAbhi dhvAram and Ucchi dhvAram or Brahma randhram). Our most compassionate Lord exits the Prapanna Jeevan through the primary door of Brahma Randhram or Brahma Naadi dhvAram, which is the first stage of travel via archirAdhi Maargam (the path of Light).[111]

Mala dvāram, *jala dvāram* and *nābhi dvāram* are the anus, urethra and navel, respectively. *Ucchi* is from the Sanskrit root *ucchid*, to dispel.[112] *Ucchi dvāram* indicates the opening through which Viṣṇu dispels the *jīva* from the body. *Kuṇḍalinī* is absent.

6.3.14 *Upakārasaṅgraham*

The Tamil *Upakārasaṅgraham* discusses favours the Lord bestows on *jīva-s*, including when they leave the body. At the time of death, devotees receive a 'gracious look' from Viṣṇu:

---

110. Sathakopan (no date o, p. 24).

111. *Paramapadasopāna* 6, translation – Sathakopan (no date o, pp. 25–26), verbatim.

112. Apte (1957, p. 399).

> This look of the Lord removes in a fraction of a second all the bonds that had held the jIva bound to the material world. The bonds included virtuous acts by which he had good benefits; just like fetters made of gold. There were bonds of sinful acts by which he had suffered, like a prisoner in a jail bound by iron fetters. All these are broken just by the gracious look of the Lord.[113]

It would have been possible for Vedāntadeśika to describe such bonds in terms of a *kuṇḍalinī* blockage obstructing entry into the *suṣumnā*. He did not. Instead, Vedāntadeśika states that at the time of leaving the body, the *jīva* is graced by the Lord ensuring that a *prapanna* enters the mouth (*mukha*) of the special *nāḍī* (*nāḍī viśeṣa*) known as the *brahmanāḍī*. The Lord prevents his entry into other *nāḍī-s* leading to heaven, hell or rebirth.[114]

On exiting the body,

> The jIvAtma is accompanied by his senses, mind and elements, in the subtle state. The Lord lifts the jIva with his subtle body from the gross body and proceeds. This looks like a father picking up his child who has fallen in to the muddy soil and gets it out to the shore.[115]

This confirms that the aggregation of *jīva*, senses, mind and elements detailed in the *Rahasyatrayasāram* and *Nyāyasiddhāñjana* above is the subtle body (*sūkṣma śarīra*). *Kuṇḍalinī* is absent.

6.3.15 *Hastigirimāhātmyam*

This Tamil dance-drama summarizes topics from the *Śrībhāṣya*. It states that *Brahman's* grace helps the *jīva* to locate the *madhyanāḍī*, which is 'concealed in its subtleness' and 'otherwise could not be cognised'.[116] The *nāḍī* is not blocked by *kuṇḍalinī*, which is absent.

To summarize the evidence so far, I have presented eleven texts describing the *jīva's* entry into the *suṣumnā*. They range from formal treatises to informal poems and are written in Sanskrit, Tamil, Prakrit and Maṇipravāla. This variety of genres and languages gave Vedāntadeśika ample space, artistic licence and linguistic freedom to describe *kuṇḍalinī* blocking the *suṣumnā*. He did not. Vedāntadeśika's eleven accounts seem

113. Sowmianarayanan (no date c, p. 123), verbatim.
114. Sowmianarayanan (no date c, p. 127).
115. Translation - Sowmianarayanan (no date c, p. 136), verbatim.
116. *ceruku viraginār*, translation - Srinivasan (2004, pp. 237, 238).

to be based almost entirely on the *Upaniṣad-s*, *Brahmasūtra* and *Śrībhāṣya*, none of which mention *kuṇḍalinī-kuṇḍalī*. Nevertheless, Vedāntadeśika did use the term *kuṇḍalī* elsewhere.

6.3.16 *Pāñcarātrarakṣā*

Another promising place to search for *kuṇḍalinī/kuṇḍalī* is Vedāntadeśika's lengthy text devoted to the defence of *Pāñcarātra* – the *Pāñcarātrarakṣā*. Indeed, T.K.V. Desikachar claimed that this text is an 'important reference book' on *kuṇḍalinī*.[117] This claim would seem plausible given that certain *Pāñcarātra* texts include teachings on *kuṇḍalī* in line with Krishnamacharya's position (see Chapter 3).

The *Pāñcarātrarakṣā* shows how the teachings of *Pāñcarātra* support the doctrine of *prapatti*. It emphasizes the worship of Vāsudeva (Viṣṇu) and the daily ritual routine of devotees, including *yoga*.[118]

A lengthy introductory verse includes both *kuṇḍalī* and *dvijihva* ('two tongued'), which is a synonym for *kuṇḍalinī* in *Yogayājñavalkya* 12.17 (see section 2.6). Both terms are, however, used differently here:

> May the eloquent teachings – their words set in place long ago, in the early years of the Age of Perfection – overwhelm the opponents of those who adhere to a position of men such as myself, we who have seen the outlines of the faultless path of reason, as the rays from the crest-jewels of serpents, toyed with by eagles who dine upon their fork-tongued kind and shake their head in astonishment at those who see into the essence of the entire Veda, provide waving lamps to accompany their recitation.[119]

Here *kuṇḍalī* simply means a serpent. *Dvijihva-aśana*, literally 'whose food is the fork-tongue[d] one', is 'the totemic Vaiṣṇava bird' Garuḍa (and his relatives).[120] The snakes represent 'the opponents of Veṅkaṭanāth's views',

117. T.K.V. Desikachar (2000, p. 51).

118. Singh (2008, pp. 49, 50).

119. Translation – Cox (2017, pp. 93–94) of *Pāñcarātrarakṣā* verse 3, apparently based on the text in Aiyangar and Venugopalacharya (1996, p. 1):

> ārohantvanavadyatarkapadavīsīmādṛśāṁ mādṛśāṁ
> pakṣe kārtayuge niveśitapadāḥ pakṣe patadbhyaḥ parān |
> sarvānuśravasāradarśisaśiraḥ kampadvijihvāśana-
> krīḍākuṇḍalimauliratnaghṛṇibhiḥ sārātrikāḥ sūktayaḥ ||

120. Cox (2017, p. 95). I added the brackets.

the term 'fork-tongued' having similar connotations in Sanskrit and English.[121] Snakes again represent something to be overcome but neither *kuṇḍalī* nor *dvijihva* mean *kuṇḍalinī śakti* here.

The *Pāñcarātrarakṣā* contains no other mention of *kuṇḍalinī* or *kuṇḍalī*. I also searched for thirty synonyms: *phaṇī, nāgī, cakrī, vakrī, sarasvatī, lalanā, rasanā, kṣatrī, lalāṭī, śaktiḥ, śaṅkhinī, rajvī, bhujaṅgī, śeṣā, sarpiṇī, maṇiḥ, ādhāraśaktiḥ, kuṭilā, karālī, prāṇavāhinī, aṣṭavakrā, ṣaḍādhārā, vyāpinī, kalanādharā, kurītī,*[122] *kuṭilāṅgī, īśvarī, arundhatī, parameśvarī,*[123] and *kuṇḍalikā*.[124] None of these terms are used to mean *kuṇḍalinī* in the *Pāñcarātrarakṣā. Śakti* is used for an ability to do something. *Kuṇḍale*, the locative singular of *kuṇḍala*, is used to mean an earring in a description of the clothing and possessions of a *Vaiṣṇavī*, a female *Vaiṣṇava*.[125] *Kuṇḍalinī* is absent.

Where *yoga* is mentioned, it is as the last of the *pañcakāla* – the five daily duties of a devotee. *Yoga* in the *Pāñcarātra Saṁhitā-s* includes thinking of God until one falls asleep but can also involve *prāṇāyāma* and mental dissolution of the *tattva-s*.[126] However, Rastelli writes that Vedāntadeśika's conception of *yoga* was heavily dependent on the *Vaikuṇṭhagadya* - a text traditionally attributed to Rāmānuja discussing how to perform *prapatti*. The *Pāñcarātrarakṣā's* coverage of *yoga* is 'a kind of commentary on this text'.[127] *Yoga* in the *Pāñcarātrarakṣā* therefore 'starts with the devotee's taking refuge in God'. Nārāyaṇa should be remembered daily and visualized in heaven with his consort, Śrī. The devotee then 'intensifies his wish to obtain God' and receives a *mantra*. Visualizing the feet of God then removes all *kleśa-s*.[128] The text largely ignores aspects of *Pāñcarātra* that Vedāntadeśika does not see as directly related to *prapatti*, such as *haṭhayoga*.

The *Pāñcarātrarakṣā* quotes a verse from a text it calls the *Yogayājñavalkya*.[129] However, it is not the text discussed in Chapter 2 (the

121. Cox (2017, pp. 96, 97).
122. *Haṭharatnāvalī* 2.125–127 – Gharote, Devnath and Jha (2002, pp. 84, 85).
123. *Haṭhapradīpikā* 3.104, 106.
124. Brunner, Oberhammer and Padoux (2004, p. 110).
125. Apte (1957, p. 580); Aiyanger and Venugopalacharya (1996, p. 83). Vaiṣṇavī is also the name of a goddess. She is said to have been produced by the combined powers of Sarasvatī, Lakṣmī, and Kālī, which represent *sattva*, *rajas* and *tamas*, respectively (Gupta and Gupta no date).
126. Rastelli (2018, pp. 236–245).
127. Rastelli (2018, pp. 248, 249).
128. Rastelli (2018, pp. 249–252).
129. Aiyanger and Venugopalacharya (1996, p. 66).

Yogayājñavalkya Saṁhitā). It is verse 7.98 from the text often called the *Bṛhadyogiyājñavalkyasmṛti*,[130] with which the *Yogayājñavalkya Saṁhitā* is often confused.[131] Other prominent writers over several centuries have also referred to the *Bṛhadyogiyājñavalkyasmṛti* as the *Yogayājñavalkya*.[132]

In conclusion, T.K.V. Desikachar's claim that the *Pāñcarātrarakṣā* is an 'important reference book' on *kuṇḍalinī* is incorrect. The text is silent on *kuṇḍalinī*. However, two other texts by Vedāntadeśika do use the term *kuṇḍalī* - the *Garuḍapañcāśat* and *Saṅkalpasūryodaya*.

6.3.17 *Garuḍapañcāśat*

The *Garuḍapañcāśat* is a Sanskrit poem in praise of Garuḍa, Viṣṇu's avian vehicle (see section 5.10). It describes Garuḍa as having a snake earring, using both *kuṇḍala* and *kuṇḍalī*. Verse 36 describes how Garuḍa is decorated with snakes, which form a bracelet on his left hand, his sacred thread, belt and garland. Other serpents adorn his crown, right hand and each ear.[133] Verse 40 describes the serpent adorning Garuḍa's ear, as in Plate 3, as *kuṇḍalī*:

> In shame [from] the existence of the splendour of [Garuḍa's] long beautiful ear, having contracted (*saṁkṣipya*) [its] own body (*svabhoga*), eating air, [with] head slightly bowed down, and breathing very slowly, *[kuṇḍalī]* desires to enter somewhere concealed due to the wish to be reflected in [Garuḍa's] clear cheek. May [this] serpent lord (*kuṇḍalī-indra*) [forming] Garuḍa's earring (*kuṇḍala*) quickly cast off our faults (*doṣa-s*).[134]

---

130. Kuvalayananda and Kokaje (2010, p. 75); Gharote and Bedekar (2010, p. 45).
131. Wujastyk (2017).
132. Digambaji, Jha and Sahay (2005, p. 31).
133. Raghavan et al. (2013, pp. 318, 319).
134. My translation of SSAA (2006, p. 697), informed by the Sanskrit commentary therein:

> drāghīyaḥ karṇa pāśadyuti paribhavana vrīlayeva svabhogaṁ
> saṁkṣipyāśnan samīraṁ daravinatamukho niśvasan mandamandam |
> āsīdatgaṇḍabhitti prati phalana miṣāt kvāpi gūḍhaṁ vivikṣuḥ
> kṣipraṁ doṣān kṣipennaḥ khagapatikuhanākuṇḍalaḥ kuṇḍalīndraḥ || 40 ||

It is unclear why the snake earring would want to enter (*vivikṣuḥ*) somewhere (*kva-api*) concealed (*gūḍhaṁ*) if it wished to be reflected (*prati-phalana*). Furthermore, *svabogaṁ saṁkṣipya* could mean 'having restricted [its] own enjoyment', perhaps in an intentional double meaning with 'having contracted [its] own body'.

In this verse, *kuṇḍalī* is described with a term that could mean either 'destroyed' or 'reduced', which would be in line with the quotations T.K.V. Desikachar presented. *Saṁkṣipya* can mean having compressed, curtailed, diminished, destroyed, contracted, or condensed.[135] In the context, however, 'destroyed' is nonsensical and the snake is contracting itself rather than destroying itself. Moreover, the snakes in verses 36–45 are benevolent and asked to grant boons such as auspiciousness (verse 38) or to destroy sins (verse 43). There is no sense of *kuṇḍalī* or the other snakes covering the *ātman* or obstructing entry to the *suṣumnā*. Indeed, in verse 45 the snake on Garuḍa's hip is asked to free us from such an obstruction: the 'confinement of *karma* bondage' (*karma bandhaṁ nirundhyāt*). The Sanskrit commentary from the Srirangam Srimath Andavan Ashramam on verse 40 states that *kuṇḍalī-indra*, serpent lord, is synonymous with *phaṇipatiḥ*,[136] which is an epithet of Śeṣa, Vāsuki or Patañjali.[137] Here, *kuṇḍalī* does not represent *kuṇḍalinī śakti.*

6.3.18 *Saṅkalpasūryodaya*

I have found only one text in which Vedāntadeśika uses *kuṇḍalī* in connection with *nāḍī-s* and *prāṇa* – a ten-act allegorical drama called the *Saṅkalpasūryodaya*, the 'Dawn of Divine will'.[138] I have examined two respected commentaries:[139] the *Prabhāvalī* by Nṛsiṁharāja and the *Prabhāvilāsa* by 'Ahobala of Ātreya family'.[140]

Nṛsiṁharāja is also called Nṛsiṁhadeva.[141] Both Chari and Raghavan date him to the 17th–18th centuries CE while Phillips and Potter give his birth date as 1740 CE, and Rengarajan estimates that he lived in the 16th century.[142] Nṛsiṁharāja/Nṛsiṁhadeva wrote commentaries on

135. Macdonell (2001, p. 78).
136. SSAA (2006, p. 697).
137. Apte (1957, p. 1144).
138. Laxmi (2008, p. 51).
139. Laxmi (2008, p. 40); V. Krishnamacharya (1948a, p. xxi); V. Krishnamacharya (1948b, p. viii).
140. V. Krishnamacharya (1948a, 1948b).
141. Raghavan (1979, p. 59); Phillips and Potter (2017, p. 450); Śrīkṛṣṇatātācārya (1990).
142. Chari (1994, p. 30); Raghavan (1979, p. 59); Phillips and Potter (2017, p. 450); Rengarajan (2004, p. 211).

three major Vedāntadeśika texts: the *Śatadūṣaṇī*,[143] *Tattvamuktākalāpa*,[144] and *Nikṣeparakṣā*.[145] Hence, he would have been highly familiar with Vedāntadeśika's theology.

Less information is available about 'Ahobala of Ātreya family', i.e. 'Ahobalācarya'.[146] 'Ātreya family' means the Ātreya *gotra* - the clan of Vedāntadeśika's uncle and preceptor, Ātreya Rāmānuja.[147] The only 'Ahobala' I have found is Ahobala Sūri, who lived around 1565 CE and wrote several texts.[148] However, Srivastava cites an 'Ahobala Suri' who wrote poetry about the life of Rāmānuja in the late 14th century CE.[149] Schrader wrote the name of the commentator to the *Saṅkalpasūryodaya* as 'Atreyāhobala-sudhī'.[150] This spelling could be a variant of Ātreya Ahobala Sūri. Although Ahobala's details are more sketchy than those of Nṛsiṁharāja, he also seems to have written from a *Śrīvaiṣṇava* perspective rather than that of a non-sectarian literary critic or *haṭhayoga* commentator.

The *Saṅkalpasūryodaya's* characters personify *Viśiṣṭādvaita* concepts. The hero is *Viveka* (discernment/discrimination). Assisted by positive characters including *Sattva* and *Saṁvṛtti Satya* (relative truth), he leads *Puruṣa* towards *mokṣa*. *Viveka* is resisted by *Mahāmoha* (great delusion), accompanied by other villains including *Kāma* (desire), *Rāga* (desire),[151] *Dveṣa* (aversion), *Abhiniveṣa* (fear of death) and *Krodha* (anger). The adversaries come to blows, *Mahāmoha* is felled by *Viveka*, and *Kāma* is killed. *Puruṣa* then approaches *mokṣa*. Finally, *Viṣṇubhakti* (devotion to Viṣṇu) appears in 10.3, making a declaration:

> What is the use of having restrained (*nirudhya*) by [mental] strength the assemblage of *prāṇa-s* and sense organs, having meditated (*vicintya*) on the *kuṇḍalī [nāḍī]*, having counted (*vigaṇayya*) the *nāḍī-s*, *dhātu-s*, *marma* points

143. Raghavan (1979, p. 59); Rengarajan (2004, pp. 105, 211); Phillips and Potter (2017, p. 450).
144. Rengarajan (2004, p. 105); Śrīkṛṣṇatātācārya (1990); Phillips and Potter (2017, p. 450).
145. Raghavan (1979, p. 59); Phillips and Potter (2017, p. 450).
146. V. Krishnamacharya (1948a, p. xxii); V. Krishnamacharya (1948b, p. viii).
147. Rengarajan (2004, p. 19); Dasgupta (1975, p. 118).
148. Phillips and Potter (2017, pp. 397, 398).
149. Srivastava (no date, p. 293).
150. Schrader (1911, p. viii).
151. According to A.G. Mohan (2018a), *rāga* is the desire to repeat a pleasant experience, in line with the definition in *Patañjali* 2.7, whereas *kāma* is the desire for something one has not yet experienced.

etc. [or] being established (*sthitimatā*) in the three *Veda-s* (*nigama-traya*)? Only if absorbed (*ava-sthitā*) in steady application to me (*mayi-sthitiḥ*) is he said to be released (*mucyate*).[152]

At first sight, a key phrase would seem to be *marut karaṇa maṇḍalīṁ kuṇḍalīṁ*. *Marut* means wind or *prāṇa*, *karaṇa* usually means the instrument by which something is done, and *maṇḍalīṁ* usually means coiled or a snake.[153] This suggests '*kuṇḍalī*, the coiled *prāṇa* mover', which makes little sense.

The verse can only be understood if we view the syntax differently. There are three *-ya* 'gerunds' (*nirudhya*, *vicintya* and *vigaṇayya*), each referring to a different object. Although *maṇḍalīṁ* and *kuṇḍalīṁ* are adjacent feminine accusative-singular nouns, they are not part of the same phrase, being referred to by different *-ya* 'gerunds'. *Kuṇḍalī* is the object of *vicintya*, not *nirudhya*.

My translation follows Nṛsiṁharāja's commentary, which states that *kuṇḍalī* is a *nāḍī* called *kuṇḍala* (*kuṇḍala-ākhya-nāḍīm*), i.e. a coiled, serpentine or sinuous *nāḍī*. Ahobala's commentary adds that *kuṇḍalī* is *suṣumnā nāḍī*. My translation also agrees with that of Abhinava Desika Uttamur T. Viraraghavacharya (1897–1983) – a respected *Śrīvaiṣṇava* contemporary of T. Krishnamacharya. Viraraghavacharya states that *kuṇḍalī* is 'a special *nāḍī* near to *nābhi*' (*nābhi samīpe nāḍī viśeṣaṁ*).[154] This reflects *Śrībhāṣya* 4.2.7, which states that the *jīva* exits the body 'via a special *nāḍī*' (*nāḍī viśeṣeṇa*), i.e. *suṣumnā*. However, the *Śrībhāṣya* does not describe that special *nāḍī* as coiled or serpentine.

Marut means *prāṇa* or *prāṇa-s*. Nṛsiṁha and Ahobala state in virtually identical words that *karaṇa* is the name of sense organs (*karaṇānām-indriyāṇām*). The commentators also agree that *maṇḍalīm* means *samūham* – a collection, multitude, assemblage or aggregate.[155] Hence, *marut karaṇa maṇḍalīṁ*

---

152. *Saṅkalpasūryodaya* 10.3 – my translation of Krishnamacharya V. (1948b, p. 797):

nirudhya tarasā marutkaraṇamaṇḍalīṁ kuṇḍalīṁ
vicintya vigaṇayya vā dhamanidhātumarmādikam |
kimatra nigamatrayasthitimatāpi lālabhyate
mayi sthitiravasthitā yadi kimucyate mucyate || 10.3 ||

153. Apte (1957, pp. 1223, 1224).

154. Viraraghavacharya (2017, p. 479).

155. Apte (1957, p. 1643). Definitions of *maṇḍalin*, a related term, include 'forming a circle or ring, surrounding, enclosing' (Monier-Williams 1899, p. 776), hinting at something being collected or contained.

means 'the assemblage of *prāṇa-s* and sense organs'. Viraraghavacharya agrees that it is '*prāṇa*, *apāna* etc. airs and sense organs' (*prāṇāpānādivāyūn indriyāṇi ca*).[156] Another commentary in Kannada by the Sri Brahmatantra Svatantra Parakāla Math agrees that *marut karaṇa mandalīṁ* includes *karma indriya-s* and *jñāna indriya-s*, together with the five *prāṇa-s*.[157] My translation is also very similar to that of M.R.R. Iyengar and broadly in line with that of Laxmi.[158]

No translation or commentary explains why five *prāṇa-s* and ten *indriya-s* form an 'assemblage' (*maṇḍalīm* = *samūham*). Recall the process forming the subtle body described in the *Rahasyatrayasāram* and *Nyāyasiddhāñjana*. Prior to entering the *suṣumnā*, the ten *indriya-s* first unite with the mind and then with *prāṇa*. Hence, Vedāntadeśika probably referred to the subtle body as *maṇḍalīṁ*.

Overall, neither the *Saṅkalpasūryodaya* nor any of the commentaries paint a picture of *kuṇḍalinī/kuṇḍalī* consistent with Krishnamacharya's usual teaching that it is a blockage to *prāṇa*. Krishnamacharya did, however, once describe *kuṇḍalinī* as a *nāḍī*. A.G. Mohan quotes Krishnamacharya as saying that 'In haṭha-yoga practice, kuṇḍalinī is a nāḍī to be controlled.'[159] Mohan told me that here Krishnamacharya used *kuṇḍalinī* as a synonym for *suṣumnā*.[160] In doing so, he was reflecting established *Śrīvaiṣṇava* teaching. I am not aware of Krishnamacharya describing *kuṇḍalinī* in this way elsewhere. The idea that *kuṇḍalī-kuṇḍalinī* is a *nāḍī* has, however, been influential. In his critical edition of the *Yogayājñavalkya*, Divanji defined *kuṇḍalinī* as a 'serpent-like artery', despite the lack of evidence for this in the text.[161]

In summary, Vedāntadeśika only mentions *kuṇḍalī* in passing in the *Saṅkalpasūryodaya*. The verse does not support Krishnamacharya's usual description of *kuṇḍalinī-kuṇḍalī* as a blockage. Indeed, Deśika is dismissive of *haṭhayoga*, downplaying the importance of *kuṇḍalī* compared to devotion to Viṣṇu.

---

156. Viraraghavacharya (2017, p. 479).
157. Iyengar (1979, pp. 418, 419) – as summarized to me by R.K. Narayan of The Academy of Sanskrit Research, Melkote.
158. Iyengar (1977, p. 332); Laxmi (2008, pp. 123, 124).
159. Mohan and Mohan (2017, p. 91).
160. Mohan (2018b).
161. Divanji (1954, p. 122).

6.3.19 Vedāntadeśika quotations on *kuṇḍalinī* reconsidered

This chapter has shown that *kuṇḍalinī* is in neither *Brahmasūtra* 4.2.16 nor in Rāmānuja's *Śrībhāṣya* thereon, which are based on certain *Upaniṣad-s* and not *Pāñcarātra*. The chapter has further shown that *kuṇḍalinī* is not used in some eleven texts by Vedāntadeśika that discuss the topic of that *sūtra: Rahasyatrayasāram, Adhikārasangraham, Nyāyasiddhāñjana, Adhikaraṇasārāvalī, Śaraṇāgatidīpikā, Acyutaśatakaṁ, Meyviratamāṉmiyam, Pādukāsahasraṁ, Paramapadasopāna, Upakārasaṅgraham* and *Hastigirimāhātmyam.*

T.K.V. Desikachar's claim that the *Pāñcarātrarakṣā* is an 'important reference book' on *kuṇḍalinī* is false. Vedāntadeśika uses *kuṇḍalī* in the *Garuḍapañcāśat* but not to mean a blockage or *kuṇḍalinī śakti.* In the *Saṅkalpasūryodaya, kuṇḍalī* is a synonym of the *suṣumnā*, not a blockage to it.

Reconsider the two quotations that T.K.V. Desikachar claimed to come from Vedāntadeśika:

1 'According to *Vedāntadeśika*, the *brahmanaḍi* is the location of *Kuṇḍalini.* It is called the 101st Naḍi.'[162]

Vedāntadeśika does not teach that the *brahmanāḍī/suṣumnā* is the location of *kuṇḍalinī/kuṇḍalī.* In the *Saṅkalpasūryodaya*, the *suṣumnā* is *kuṇḍalī.* This is very different.

2 'According to *Vedāntadeśika*, the grace of the Lord is a must for the *prāṇa* to enter *suṣūmna* after the *kuṇḍalini* is reduced.'[163]

If we were to delete 'after the *kuṇḍalini* is reduced', the quotation would be correct. Vedāntadeśika does emphasize that God's grace is essential for the subtle body (including *prāṇa*) to enter the *suṣumnā.* However, by adding 'after the *kuṇḍalini* is reduced', T.K.V. Desikachar misrepresents Vedāntadeśika, who did not present *kuṇḍalinī* as a blockage to the *suṣumnā* that can be reduced.

I present considerable evidence above to support these conclusions. Nevertheless, it could be argued that the evidence does not constitute

162. T.K.V. Desikachar (2000, p. 49).
163. T.K.V. Desikachar (2000, p. 50).

definite proof that Vedāntadeśika did not use the terms *kuṇḍalinī* or *kuṇḍalī* in line with Krishnamacharya's teachings. I surveyed over ninety of Vedāntadeśika's works, some in greater detail than others – see Table 3. However, Vedāntadeśika wrote so many texts that teachings about *kuṇḍalinī* as a blockage to the *suṣumnā* could be hiding in an obscure text I have not examined. I therefore sought guidance from the pontiff of one of the four main *Vaṭakalai* organizations: the Srirangam Srimath Andavan Ashramam.

6.3.20 Audiences with the 12th Swāmi of the Andavan Ashramam

I was granted two audiences with the 12th Swāmi of the Andavan Ashramam: Śrīmat Śrī Varāha Mahādeśika Swāmi. He was known as Dr Shri Srimushnam Vangipuram Yamunachariar before he took up his post. We met on 12 and 14 December 2018 at the Srirangam Srimath Andavan Ashramam in Srirangam. See Plate 8.

The Andavan Swāmi told me that Vedāntadeśika uses *kuṇḍala* in the *Pāñcarātrarakṣā* to mean an earring but *kuṇḍalinī* is not mentioned. He said that when the *Pāñcarātrarakṣā* discusses *yoga*, it means only remembering

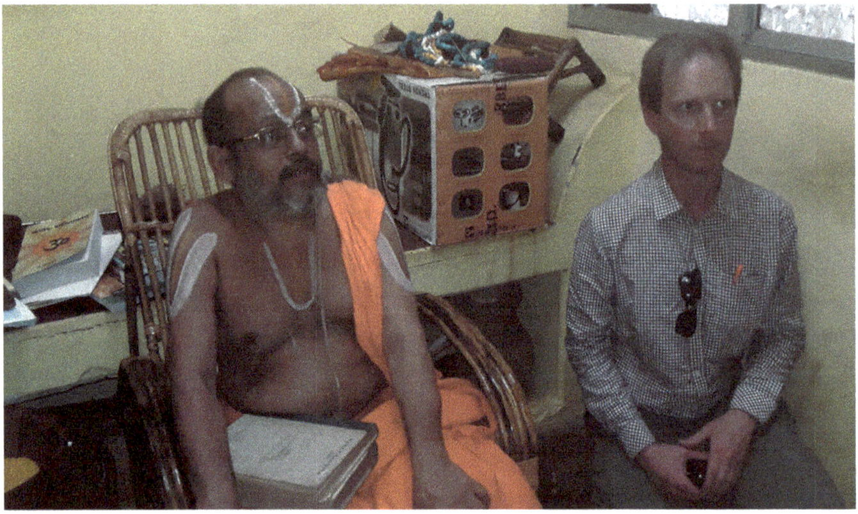

Plate 8
The 12th Swāmi of the Srirangam Srimath Andavan Ashramam, Śrīmat Śrī Varāha Mahādeśika Swāmi, with Simon Atkinson.

Photograph: R. Thirunarayanan

God before going to sleep, which is one of the five daily *pañcakāla* observances of a *Śrīvaiṣṇava* devotee; the text does not discuss *haṭhayoga.*

The Swāmi added that the *Garuḍapañcāśat* uses the term *kuṇḍalī* to describe a snake on Garuḍa's ear but it does not represent a blockage to the *suṣumnā.* Furthermore, the *Saṅkalpasūryodaya* uses *kuṇḍalī* to mean a special *nāḍī*, i.e. *suṣumnā.* This is the teaching of Śrīvaiṣṇavism, he confirmed. The Swāmi concluded that *kuṇḍalinī* is not mentioned in the sense of a blockage to the *suṣumnā* in any of Vedāntadeśika's texts or indeed in any other *Śrīvaiṣṇava* text. That idea is therefore 'unacceptable', he stated.

6.3.21 Reflections on T.K.V. Desikachar

Vedāntadeśika's *Pāñcarātrarakṣā* is one of seven 'important reference books on *kuṇḍalini*' that T.K.V. Desikachar lists: '*Prapancasāra* of *Śankarācārya, Mantra Mahodadhi, Mantra Ratnākara, Brahmayamila, Manu Nārāyaniyam, Rudrayamila, Pāñcarātra rakṣa* of Vedānta Deśika.'[164] In addition to the *Pāñcarātrarakṣā*, I have examined the first two books on this list.

First, the *Prapañcasāra* is attributed to Ādiśaṅkara but its authorship is questioned.[165] It is a non-sectarian compilation of highly tantric forms of worship of many deities. The text locates *kuṇḍalinī* at *mūlādhāra*,[166] contradicting Krishnamacharya's teaching that *kuṇḍalinī* is located at *nābhi.* It describes numerous 'aspects' of *kuṇḍalinī* based on *Śaiva, Śākta, Vaiṣṇava, Saura* (sun-worshipping) and *Gānapatya* (Gaṇeśa-worshipping) traditions.[167] In her threefold aspect, *kuṇḍalinī* is known *inter alia* as *agni*, Paramātmā, the tantric goddess Tāra, and the three *guṇa-s.*[168] In her fivefold aspect, she is represented by the five *vāyu-s* (*prāṇa, apāna, vyāna, udāna* and *samāna*), which contradicts Krishnamacharya's teaching that *kuṇḍalinī* is not a form of *prāṇa.* Notably, in her eightfold form she is the eight *prakṛti-s.*[169] This is the teaching of the *Pādmasaṁhitā, Ahirbudhnyasaṁhitā* and the *Yogayājñavalkya.* It might be possible to extract further *Vaiṣṇava* teachings from the *Prapañcasāra* consistent with Krishnamacharya's position, but to do so one would have to be very selective. In the *Prapañcasāra*,

164. T.K.V. Desikachar (2000, p. 51).
165. Avalon (1989, pp. 1–4); Feuerstein (1998, p. 464).
166. Avalon (1989, p. 17).
167. Avalon (1989, pp. 17–19, 68).
168. Avalon (1989, p. 17, 18).
169. Avalon (1989, p. 19).

there is little, if anything, that relates to what is actually taught by students of T.K.V. Desikachar, as far as I know.

The second text on T.K.V. Desikachar's list is the *Mantramahodadhi.* It is an encyclopaedic compilation of tantric *mantra-s* from various traditions to invoke an array of gods and goddesses, replete with instructions on *nyāsa*, *yantra* and *maṇḍala. Kuṇḍalinī* is seldom mentioned and not described in terms that support Krishnamacharya's position:

> With concentration he shall meditate on the Supreme Kundalini power that is situated in the Muladhara Cakra ... He shall awaken the Kundalini from its Mūlādhara resort and transport it to the Anahata Cakra, stationed in the Heart ... through the Suṣumna. The Jīva or individual soul shall be contemplated in the form of a flame of a lamp and though (sic) of as having reached the Brahma Randhra (the Aperture in the Crown of the Head) where the Brahman (Supreme Soul) is reputed to be stationed. The aspirant shall repeat the Hansa Mantra and unite the Jīva along with the Kundalini with the Brahman.[170]

> The intelligent devotee then performs Antaryāga (Internal Sacrifice) in the pedestal in the form of his own body. ... He shall worship the deity of his choice in the Heart. Then he raises the Kuṇḍalinī and takes it to the greatest absolute stationed in the Cerebral Aperture.[171]

The *Mantramahodadhi* is not an 'important reference book' on *kuṇḍalinī*, as T.K.V. Desikachar claims. Desikachar taught Bernard Bouanchaud *mantra* according to the text.[172] However, the *Mantramahodadhi* bears virtually no relation to anything else taught in the tradition, as far as I am aware. Rather than shedding light on Krishnamacharya's teaching on *kuṇḍalinī*, the *Mantramahodadhi* contradicts it.

It would seem then that T.K.V. Desikachar was influenced on the topic of *kuṇḍalinī* not only by Krishnamacharya, but also by a range of sources, not all of which are compatible with his father's position. The rest of T.K.V. Desikachar's list of 'important reference books' on *kuṇḍalinī* are not easily accessible so I leave it to other scholars to research them. Given that the *Prapañcasāra*, *Mantramahodadhi* and *Pāñcarātrarakṣā* say so little about the origins of Krishnamacharya's position on *kuṇḍalinī*, I would be surprised

170. Board of Scholars (2014, p. 2).
171. Board of Scholars (2014, p. 510).
172. Bouanchaud (2019, p. 44).

if the other books revealed much more. The addition of Vedāntadeśika's *Pāñcarātrarakṣā* to the end of his list looks like a tokenistic attempt to acknowledge Śrīvaiṣṇavism. But why did T.K.V. Desikachar incorrectly cite Vedāntadeśika in particular? I would like to suggest a possible explanation.

T.K.V. Desikachar's writings contain many references to God, perhaps in an attempt to represent his father's beliefs. For example, 'faith in God is absolutely necessary for any healing'.[173] 'If happiness is our goal, there can be only one direction for the mind and that is toward God.'[174] 'Living great masters can aid only to the extent that they can help us to understand the greatness of God. They are the intermediaries. But the first and final aim must be this infinite force, God.'[175] 'The main concern is the development of a sustained and deep relationship with God; this should always be the primary interest.'[176]

Despite such statements, T.K.V. Desikachar did not subscribe to Śrīvaiṣṇavism, as two interviews show. Firstly, in a 1992 interview with Leslie Kaminoff, T.K.V. Desikachar reflected on his father:

> While I respect him, I don't live like him ... So many things that he expressed through his life are not possible for me. Many things that he did are irrelevant to me. He spoke in Sanskrit and I speak in English. ... he would always have his mark on his forehead, he had a tuft, he would wear a shirt only when it was very cold. I don't have a forehead mark. It doesn't make any sense to me – I don't have a tuft because I never had one and I'm 90% Westerner compared to my father. I wear Western clothes, I speak English ... though I have a lot of respect for the tradition, the details of tradition have lost their meaning.[177]

A 2008 interview with Leanne Wong goes further:

> Q. [Wong] *Do you believe in God?*
> A. [T.K.V. Desikachar] People ask me, do you believe in God? I say no, I don't believe in God because I have not seen God.
>
> I don't mind chanting for God, but I don't have any belief in God. My belief is in my teacher called Krishnamacharya. This is my God. I have seen him, I have interacted with him, I have seen his qualities, I have seen his ability,

173. T.K.V. Desikachar (1982, p. 20).
174. T.K.V. Desikachar and Cravens (1998, p. 201).
175. T.K.V. Desikachar (1982, p. 47).
176. T.K.V. Desikachar (1982, p. 58).
177. T.K.V. Desikachar in Kaminoff (2012, p. 24).

> and I am amazed that he has done wonders for people. He lived for 100 years, and he healed a lot of people. With all respect, I don't have any faith in God, and many people are angry at me.
>
> I learned all the meditation practices from my father. He taught me about Shiva, Vishnu, and I'll teach whoever has faith. If someone believes in Lakshmi, Jesus, prophet Mohammad, or Jewish God, I never tell in public that I don't agree, or forget about Lakshmi, Jesus, prophet Mohammad, or Jewish God. What they like is what we must honor. We should not impose on what we don't accept. That is what is very important.
>
> Every day, I go for a walk, my wife goes to a Ganesha temple, and then afterward, she goes to a Krishna temple. I always follow her so she is happy. I will not say I am not interested. I just go with her. So, this is what I honor.[178]

Further information comes from T.K.V. Desikachar's students. Desikachar regarded his father as his God, inspired by the description in *Patañjali* 1.26 of *Īśvara* as a *guru*.[179] This differs from the stance of Śrīvaiṣṇavism, which criticized *Patañjali's* description of *Īśvara*. Johar notes that when T.K.V. Desikachar started to study with Krishnamacharya, it was on the condition he would learn '*yoga* without God'. Nevertheless, T.K.V. Desikachar greatly respected people,

> And this same respect then reflects in the way he respected his teacher. I mean, that is admirable ... the steadfast respect for his teacher, who he respects, and yet he also knows that he will not be like him. You see, that makes the person doubly respectful, that I respect the man knowing very well that I cannot or I will not be like him.
>
> He used to say that, you know, 'how can I follow tradition, which is like thousands of years old, when I can't even be like my father, which is just one generation removed? If I can't just follow and emulate the generation before me, how can I make tall claims about these thousands of years of tradition?'[180]

Yet T.K.V. Desikachar did make 'tall claims' about Vedāntadeśika. According to S. Sridharan, from the Krishnamacharya Yoga Mandiram, we would not have obtained a '360-degree view' of Krishnamacharya without T.K.V. Desikachar.[181] However, the scope and depth of Krishnamacharya's learn-

178. Wong (2008, p. 9).
179. Sridharan (2017).
180. Johar (2017).
181. Sridharan (2017).

Plate 9
Vedāntadeśika's parents have dreams foretelling his birth – fresco in Thoopal Vedanta Desikar Temple, Kanchipuram.

Photograph: Simon Atkinson

ing was so great that it would have been impossible for any one person, even his son, to accurately reflect all aspects.

I can suggest a reason why T.K.V. Desikachar felt impelled to quote Vedāntadeśika. Vedāntadeśika's parents had dreams foretelling his birth. His mother dreamed of swallowing a bell.[182] See Plate 9. Similarly, the names of Krishnamacharya's six children are said to have come to him in dreams.[183] Before T.K.V. Desikachar's birth, Krishnamacharya dreamed of Vedāntadeśika, after whom he named his son.[184] 'Clearly, in Krishnamacharya's mind, the destiny of his child was linked to his

182. Hopkins (2012, p. 462); Singh (2008, p. 4).

183. T.K.V. Desikachar and Cravens (1998, pp. 94, 95).

184. Krishnamacharya Yoga Mandiram (2006, p. 7). T.K.V. Desikachar's full name was Tirumalai Krishnamacharya Venkata Desikachar. Venkata comes from Veṅkateśvara, the deity of the Tirumalai region (Krishnamacharya Yoga Mandiram 2006, p. 9), after whom Vedāntadeśika was himself named Veṅkaṭanātha (Hopkins 2012, p. 462).

dream of the great acarya.'[185] Mindful of this weight of expectation, T.K.V. Desikachar may have felt obliged to cite Vedāntadeśika, despite not following his tradition.

Having given a detailed critique of T.K.V. Desikachar's writings on *kuṇḍalinī*, I want to put my comments into a wider context. Desikachar was greatly respected by his students and 'did not take one Paisa' for his teaching at the Krishnamacharya Yoga Mandiram.[186] He regarded it as his *guru dakṣiṇā*.[187] He also keenly observed his students.[188] 'He would often see things in people that they had not seen in themselves as yet' and was 'able to convert ordinary human beings into extraordinary human beings'.[189]

T.K.V. Desikachar 'was truly brilliant, and an excellent teacher'.[190] He had both a 'remarkable sense of analysis' and an 'extraordinary ability to instantly understand what ails a person and what would be a good solution'.[191] Desikachar's qualities included 'curiosity', 'openness',[192] 'humility' and 'integrity'.[193] He was also 'lively and witty' and 'very humane'.[194]

Overall, T.K.V. Desikachar is regarded by his students as having communicated Krishnamacharya's teachings very well but he also added to them. 'He had the habit of saying that he was only passing down his father's teaching, but those who worked with him know that it is actually Desikachar's teaching that we were taught and must preserve.'[195] But we should not preserve his mistakes. If we truly respect T.K.V. Desikachar, we should correct his mistakes to the best of our ability.

6.4 AṢṬĀṄGAYOGANIRŪPAṆAM

The *Aṣṭāṅgayoganirūpaṇam* is the only purportedly *Śrīvaiṣṇava* text I am awareof dedicated to *yoga*. Evidence that it is *Śrīvaiṣṇava* includes repeated references to Nārāyaṇa. There is an explicit mention in verses 28–9 of

185. Krishnamacharya Yoga Mandiram (2006, p. 7).
186. Sridharan (2017). There used to be a hundred paisas in one Indian rupee.
187. Sathish (2017).
188. Sathish (2017).
189. Ananthanarayanan (2016); Chandrasekhar (2017) respectively.
190. Maréchal (2019, p. 23).
191. Daouk (2019, p. 41); Sriram (2019, p. 30) respectively.
192. Krusche (2019, p. 63).
193. Lorin (2019, p. 52).
194. Margherita (2019, p. 81).
195. Nicolas (2019, p. 201).

the *pañcakāla* (the five daily activities of *Pāñcarātra* and Śrīvaiṣṇavism), including the practice of *yoga* in the evening. In a foreword to the Krishnamacharya Yoga Mandiram translation, Sridharan comments that the text 'links the Aṣṭāṅgayoga to Pāñcarātra āgama and thus supports śrīvaiṣṇavism'.[196] Jayaraman (the translator) adds that the initial verses of the *Aṣṭāṅgayoganirūpaṇam* resemble those in the *Lakṣmīsahasranāma*, a *Vaiṣṇava* text, so 'the author might be a Vaisṇavaite'.[197]

The core of the text is *Patañjali's aṣṭāṅgayoga*, interwoven with *Vedānta*. Added to this framework are various *haṭhayoga* concepts and practices, including verses which describe both *kuṇḍalī* and *prāṇa* as entering the *suṣumnā:*

> Having awoken the sleeping *kuṇḍalī*, [one] should make [it] enter the *suṣumnā* (32a).
> [The wise one] should inhale air (*vāyu*) through the *iḍā* and should make [it] enter the *suṣumnā* (36b).[198]

These two verses display the same inconsistency which we explored above. One could, of course, play the same 'get out of jail free card' as K. Desikachar did, arguing that *kuṇḍalinī* rises only as far as *agni* in the abdomen, where it is incinerated, leaving the *suṣumnā* open for *prāṇa* to ascend to the top of the head. Indeed, verse 33 describes 'the *yogi*' (i.e. the *jīva*, not *kuṇḍalī*) as emerging from the *brahmarandhra:*

> The *yogi* should utter *oṁ*, remembering Viṣṇu. Coming out of the *Brahmarandhra*, [he] should enter the ray of sunlight (33).
> Having entered the highest place through the path of light (*arcirādika mārga*), [and] having obtained communion (*sāyujya*) with the Supreme Lord, [the *yogi*] will experience joy for a long time (34).[199]

---

196. S. Sridharan in Jayaraman (2013, p. 6).
197. Jayaraman (2013, p. 11).
198. My translation of the Sanskrit in Jayaraman (2013, pp. 30, 31):

> udbodhya kuṇḍalīṁ suptāṁ suṣumnāyāṁ praveśayet | 32a |
> iḍayā vāyumākṛṣya suṣumnāyāṁ praveśayet || 36b ||

In 36b, the subject is *vicakṣaṇaḥ*, the wise, learned, clear-sighted or far-seeing one (Apte 1957, p. 1430) from the previous line, 36a.

199. My translation of the Sanskrit in Jayaraman (2013, pp. 30, 31):

> omityuccārayedyogī ramānāthamanusmaran |
> brahmarandhrādvinirgacchan praviśedarcirākṛtim || 33 ||

Unlike in *Brahmasūtra* 4.2.16, Rāmānuja's *Śrībhāṣya* thereon and the quotations from Vedāntadeśika discussing that passage, the communion with the Supreme Lord in the *Aṣṭāṅgayoganirūpaṇam* is not permanent:

> After descending the *suṣumnā* path very slowly, *prāṇa* etc. should be restored to [their] various original locations (41).[200]

Jayaraman interprets *prāṇa-ādīn* (*prāṇa* etc.) as 'vital airs like prāṇa', presumably meaning *prāṇa, apāna, vyāna, samāna* and *udāna*.[201] It could also refer to the subtle body (*sūkṣma śarīra*) – see the sections on the *Rahasyatrayasāram*, *Nyāyasiddhāñjana* and *Saṅkalpasūryodaya* above.

The *Aṣṭāṅgayoganirūpaṇam* only explicitly refers to three *cakra-s*/lotuses/places: the heart lotus (*hṛdaya ambujam* in 37), the *ājñā* place (*ājñā sthāna* in 38) and the place of the central thousand-petalled lotus (*sahasra patra kamala madhya sthaṁ* in 39).

Curiously, 37a states that

> [The *yogi*] should enter the heart lotus with the ray of light from the abdominal fire (*koṣṭha-agni*).[202]

Jayaraman comments that 'the rays of the abdominal fire ... seems to be unheard of outside this text'.[203] Nevertheless, the concept is reminiscent of *Brahmasūtra* 4.2.16, in which the base of the *suṣumnā* in the heart is illuminated from above, enabling the favoured *jīva* to enter the correct *nāḍī* leading to liberation (see above). Here, the heart lotus is illuminated from below. The *Brahmasūtra* account, however, locates the lower terminus of the *suṣumnā* at the heart, whereas the *Aṣṭāṅgayoganirūpaṇam* locates it at an undisclosed location below the heart. Jayaraman states that the location

---

Arcir-ākṛtim is literally '[that which has] the form of a ray (of sunlight)'.

arcirādikamārgeṇa praviśya paramaṁ padam |
sāyujyaṁ parameśasya labdhvānandī bhavecciram || 34 ||

200. My translation of the Sanskrit in Jayaraman (2013, p. 33):

suṣumnāyāstathā mārgādavaruhya śanaiḥ śanaiḥ |
prāṇādīn sthāpayedvāyau tattatsthāneṣu pūrvavat || 41 ||

201. Jayaraman (2013, p. 33).
202. My translation of the Sanskrit in Jayaraman (2013, p. 32):

arciṣā saha koṣṭhāgneḥ praviśet hṛdayāṁbujam | 37a |

203. Jayaraman (2013, p. 32).

of the abdominal fire 'corresponds to the place of maṇipūraka cakra'[204] (=*nābhi*). This contrasts with *Pāñcarātra* texts such as the *Pādmasaṁhitā*, which locate fire in the perineum.

The original location of *kuṇḍalī* is not specified in the *Aṣṭāṅgayoganirūpaṇam* and this apparently *Śrīvaiṣṇava* text does not use *kuṇḍalī* as a synonym for *suṣumnā*, as in Vedāntadeśika's *Saṅkalpasūryodaya*, raising questions about whether the *Aṣṭāṅgayoganirūpaṇam* really is an orthodox *Śrīvaiṣṇava* work. Moreover, the text describes *kuṇḍalī* entering the *suṣumnā* and does not even mention its role as a blockage to *prāṇa*. That makes it inconsistent with the *Pādmasaṁhitā*, the *Ahirbudhnyasaṁhitā* and Krishnamacharya's position, which is based on the *Yogayājñavalkya*.

---

204. Jayaraman (2013, p. 32).

7

Discussion and conclusion

Chapter 2 showed that the *Yogayājñavalkya* account of *kuṇḍalinī* is on the surface quite clear. *Kuṇḍalinī* is located at *nābhi*, the navel, in the centre of the *kanda*. It blocks the entry of *prāṇa* into the *suṣumnā* and other *nāḍī-s*. When burned by *agni* (fire) and fanned by *prāṇa*, *kuṇḍalinī* awakens and straightens, allowing *prāṇa* and *agni* to enter the *suṣumnā* and ascend. The main difference with some other texts is the apparent absence of statements that *kuṇḍalinī* ascends the *suṣumnā*. This perspective formed the textual foundation of Krishnamacharya's position.

One verse in the critical edition of the *Yogayājñavalkya*, however, undermines Krishnamacharya's position by describing *kuṇḍalinī* rising to the *sahasrāra* at the crown of the head. A.G. Mohan could only overcome this inconvenience by being very selective over which manuscripts he accepted for a particular word, and then critically editing the critical edition accordingly. T.K.V. Desikachar significantly mistranslated the *Yogayājñavalkya*, introducing great ambiguity about the location of *kuṇḍalinī*. My respect for T.K.V. Desikachar as a *yoga* teacher remains intact and I still consider myself part of this broad tradition. However, I approach Desikachar's Sanskrit translations with great caution. I also respect A.G. Mohan as a *yoga* teacher and I have more confidence in his translations of the Sanskrit he presents. In future, however, I will check the original Sanskrit.

Most scholars agree that the *Yogayājñavalkya* is not one of the oldest texts on *yoga*, as A.G. Mohan and T.K.V. Desikachar claim. Chapter 3 showed that some verses on *kuṇḍalinī* in the *Yogayājñavalkya* were probably borrowed from the *Vasiṣṭhasaṁhitā* but originate in *Pāñcarātra*. The teachings they contain are also found in a *Vaikhānasa* text. By following *Pāñcarātra* teachings, Krishnamacharya revived the buried textual roots of his own *Śrīvaiṣṇava* tradition. However, the number of texts supporting Krishnamacharya's position is small and there are *Śaiva* and *Śākta* texts describing *kuṇḍalinī* in other terms, including as an energy that rises. Defenders of Krishnamacharya's position therefore need to be very selective in which texts they cite as valid testimony.

Chapter 3 also showed how one *Pāñcarātra* text, the *Ahirbudhnyasaṁhitā*, mainly describes *kuṇḍalinī* as a blockage at *nābhi*. The text also describes the goddess as having five powers. One of these, the power to cover/obscure, roughly corresponds to the *kuṇḍalinī* blockage to the *suṣumnā*, but any such connection seems implicit rather than explicit. Moreover, the *Ahirbudhnyasaṁhitā* is internally inconsistent. A separate chapter describes *kuṇḍalinī* rising from *mūlādhāra* to the throat. Defenders of Krishnamacharya's position therefore need to be very selective about not only which texts to cite, but also about which parts of those texts to reject. Another grey area traceable to *Pāñcarātra* is a description of *kuṇḍalinī* rising to the heart. K. Desikachar attempted to maintain the coherence of Krishnamacharya's position by employing elaborate but unconvincing exegesis to paper over cracks like this. A more convincing explanation is that such inconsistencies and grey areas in *Pāñcarātra* texts are probably due to remnants of *Śaiva* teachings incompletely and incoherently reworked into a *Pāñcarātra Vaiṣṇava* framework.

Chapter 4 showed how Krishnamacharya forged connections between *haṭhayoga* and *Patañjali* using the *Haṭhapradīpikā's* equation of the *kuṇḍalinī* blockage with *avidyā*. This equation enabled Krishnamacharya to give a corporeal location to *avidyā* at *nābhi*, which is in the *kanda*. However, Krishnamacharya showed some creative ambiguity in where he located the *kanda*. In one quote, he equated it with *mūlādhāra*, apparently in an attempt to bridge the gap between inconsistent texts. There was also conceptual drift in where *kuṇḍalinī* was located by his students. Srivatsa Ramaswami located *kuṇḍalinī* at *nābhi* and *agni* in the perineum, as in the *Yogayājñavalkya*, and explained the effect of inverted postures in that context. In contrast, T.K.V. Desikachar's justification of inversions required those positions of *kuṇḍalinī* and *agni* to be reversed, relocating *kuṇḍalinī* to *mūlādhāra*. This could partially explain why T.K.V. Desikachar mistranslated the *Yogayājñavalkya* by including *mūlādhāra* and locating *kuṇḍalinī* there. A complementary explanation could be that Desikachar was attempting to bridge the gap between inconsistent texts, some of which locate *kuṇḍalinī* at *nābhi* and some of which locate it at *mūlādhāra.*

Chapter 5 showed that representing a blockage to *prāṇa* with *kuṇḍalinī* is consistent with a stream of South Asian thought running through diverse texts and traditions. In different contexts, snakes represent something to be overcome, including *māyā*, *avidyā*, *ajñāna*, *moha*, ego(tism), pride, *saṁsāra*, covering/obscuring, and binding. This stream of thought may have influenced the writers of the *Vaiṣṇava Saṁhitā-s* to redefine the originally *Śaiva* concept of *kuṇḍalinī* as a blockage only. However, even if writers used serpent metaphors to represent something to be overcome, it does not necessarily follow that they also used *kuṇḍalinī* to represent a blockage.

Chapter 6 showed that T.K.V. Desikachar significantly misrepresented Vedāntadeśika, the *Śrīvaiṣṇava* polymath after whom he was named. T.K.V. Desikachar's quotations from Vedāntadeśika on *kuṇḍalinī* are inaccurate. Furthermore, Deśika's *Pāñcarātrarakṣā* is not an 'important reference book' on *kuṇḍalinī*, as T.K.V. Desikachar claimed. I found three places where Vedāntadeśika used the term *kuṇḍalī* but none were in the sense of *kuṇḍalinī śakti* as a blockage. According to the highly authoritative Andavan Swāmi, an expert on Vedāntadeśika, *kuṇḍalinī-kuṇḍalī* is not used in that sense anywhere in Vedāntadeśika's writings, or in any other *Śrīvaiṣṇava* text. Although Krishnamacharya revived the buried roots of his tradition in following certain *Pāñcarātra* teachings, he also went against established *Śrīvaiṣṇava* doctrine, which for centuries has sidelined *haṭhayoga* and equated *kuṇḍalī* with the *suṣumnā*, the special *nāḍī* which is coiled or serpentine (*kuṇḍala*). Hence, Krishnamacharya was indeed both a traditionalist and a very radical reformer.

The chapter also showed that despite not using *kuṇḍalinī-kuṇḍalī* to represent a blockage, Vedāntadeśika did use serpent metaphors to represent something to be overcome. This reinforces a conclusion from Chapter 5: even when writers used serpent metaphors to represent something to be overcome, they did not necessarily use *kuṇḍalinī-kuṇḍalī* to represent a blockage.

Further research is required on conceptions of *kuṇḍalī-kuṇḍalinī* across various *Vaiṣṇava* sects.[1] There seems to be some diversity. For example, *Vaiṣṇava* Rāmānandī Tyāgī-s are perhaps the largest sect of renunciates in

1. Including the traditions of Caitanya, Mādhava, Nimbārka, Rādhāvallabha and Vallabha.

North India.[2] A minority of Tyāgī-s practise *haṭhayoga* but they have long forgotten the *Śaiva* tantric origins of some of the techniques.[3] They therefore use the term *kuṇḍalinī* in much the same way as *Śaiva-s* do to represent an energy that rises. From fieldwork, Mallinson observes that

> Tyāgīs, who would never let themselves be called *tāntrikas*, are happy to discuss the raising of Kuṇḍalinī through the *cakras*, and the attainment of *siddhis* such as the power of flight and the ability to drink *amṛta*, all of whose origins can be traced in tantric texts.[4]

In contrast, in the Bengali Sahajiyā *Vaiṣṇava* tradition, *kuṇḍalinī* 'functioned more on a structural level', particularly as *baṅka nāḍī* or the 'crooked river'.[5] This *bāṅkānadī* flows 'upward against the current' and is based on 'the yogically reversed ascent of sexual fluids'.[6] It closely resembles *kuṇḍalī* - the coiled or serpentine *nāḍī* (*kuṇḍala ākhya nāḍī*) from the *Saṅkalpasūryodaya*, which *Śrīvaiṣṇava-s* equate with the *suṣumnā*.

It is not surprising that when *Vaiṣṇava* traditions co-opted the originally *Śaiva* terms *kuṇḍalī* and *kuṇḍalinī*, they sometimes redefined and remoulded them to fit with their own theology. In Śaivism, various accounts of *kuṇḍalinī* are based on its equation with the goddess and her need to reunite with her spouse, Śiva, by rising up the *suṣumnā*. This differs from *Vaiṣṇava* traditions, where the relation between Viṣṇu and his consort Śrī-Lakṣmī is different.[7]

Although Krishnamacharya was aware of the *Śrīvaiṣṇava* teaching on *kuṇḍalinī*, using it once, his main position was that *kuṇḍalinī* is a blockage to the *suṣumnā* and nothing more. Was he correct and were others wrong? Before coming to a conclusion, I shall take a step back to outline some other text-based systems of *cakra-s* and *kuṇḍalinī*.

Hindu accounts of *cakra-s* gradually emerged during the second half of the first millennium CE.[8] *Śaiva Siddhānta* sources usually list five centres

---

2. Lamb (2011, p. 478); Mallinson (2005, p. 107).
3. Mallinson (2005, p. 113).
4. Mallinson (2005, p. 113).
5. Czyżykowski (2018).
6. Hayes (2003, p. 165); Hayes (2011, p. 510). Note the difference between *bāṅkānadī* in Hayes (2003, 2011) and *baṅka nāḍī* in Czyżykowski (2018).
7. See Foulston and Abbott (2012); Kinsley (1986, pp. 19–34); Kumar (1997); Pattanaik (2002); and Rhodes (2012).
8. White (2003, p. 145).

at the heart, throat, palate, between the eyebrows and the crown.[9] In the 7th century *Śaiva Siddhānta* text *Sārdhatriśatikālottara*, 'Kuṇḍalinī is visualized in the region of the heart, after being summoned there from her home in the crown of the head, where she dwells eternally with Śiva.'[10] As Wallis comments,

> in none of the Tantrik sources is *kuṇḍalinī-śakti* described as lying dormant at the base of the spine. This idea, found in *haṭha-yoga* sources, would have been absurd to the Tāntrikas, for if *kuṇḍalinī* was dormant, you would be in a coma. Rather, in the Tantrik sources, *kuṇḍalinī* dwells in the crown of the head, for the Goddess is eternally inseparable from her other half. In Tantrik yoga-sādhanā, she is invited to descend to the relevant *cakra* (often the heart, sometimes the *kanda*), creating a rubber-band like tension that then can be used to catapult the soul (individual consciousness) up to the highest center.[11]

The first list of the 'standard' *cakra* names was in the 9th–10th century CE *Kubjikāmata*, but they were not called *cakra-s* or associated with the elements.[12] Also, in *Kubjikāmata* 5.84, '*śakti* dwells in the form of a sleeping serpent in both the cranial vault and the navel'.[13] Abhinavagupta (10th–11th centuries CE) then described upper and lower *kuṇḍalinī-s* as 'two phases of the same energy, in expansion and contraction'.[14] Some texts, including the *Siddhasiddhāntapaddhati*, have three *kuṇḍalinī-s*, lower, middle and higher.[15] 'In the most common formulations', a single *kuṇḍalinī* ascends through the *cakra-s* and unites with Śiva at the crown.[16] The seven *cakra* system (six plus one) has only dominated since around the 15th century CE.[17]

Given this variety, 'there is no "standard" system of the *cakras*. Every school, sometimes every teacher within each school, has had their own

---

9. White (2003, p. 146).
10. Wallis (2013, p. 221).
11. Wallis (2013, p. 478 n.165).
12. White (2003, pp. 146–150).
13. White (2003, p. 152).
14. White (2003, p. 152).
15. Mallinson and Singleton (2017, p. 179).
16. Mallinson and Singleton (2017, p. 179).
17. Wallis (2016).

cakra system.'[18] Similarly, there is no 'standard' account of *kuṇḍalinī*. Its position and nature vary between schools and texts.

Wallis concurs:

> there's a huge variety in the chakra systems we find in the original literature. One is not more 'right' than another, *except relative to a specific practice.* For example, if you're doing a five-element practice, you use a five-chakra system ... If you're internalizing the energy of six different deities, you use a six-chakra system. ... English sources tend to present the chakra system as an existential fact, using descriptive language ... But in most of the original Sanskrit sources, we are not being taught about the way things are, we are being given a specific yoga practice ... *for a specific purpose* ... The texts are prescriptive – they tell you what you ought to do to achieve a specific goal by mystical means.[19]

If we were to extend Wallis's argument from *cakra-s* to *kuṇḍalinī*, it would imply that *kuṇḍalinī* could be located at *nābhi* for some practices, such as the merging of *prāṇa* and *apāna* in the abdomen in directional breathing, while *kuṇḍalinī* could be located at *mūlādhāra* for other practices, such as burning the *kuṇḍalinī* blockage in inverted postures. However, this is not taught in the tradition following Krishnamacharya. In my experience of teachers trained by T.K.V. Desikachar and his students, the *kuṇḍalinī* blockage and the six-plus-one *cakra* system tend to be taught as existential facts (things that have objective existence) rather than as just one possibility of what could be visualized, practised or experienced. I will challenge that presentation below.

Whether consciously or otherwise, T.K.V. Desikachar seems to have selectively cherry-picked parts of his description of *kuṇḍalinī* from contradictory texts and creatively combined them. From the *Yogayājñavalkya*,

---

18. White (2003, p. 144). Krishnamacharya taught that in addition to the usual six-plus-one *cakra-s* there are three more: *sūrya cakra* 'just above the navel', *manas cakra* near the stomach, and *Brahmaguha/lalāta cakra* 'above the forehead'. According to T.K.V. Desikachar (1994b, pp. 5–6), Krishnamacharya 'must have received this teaching from his *guru* Rama Mohana Brahmacari'. In my experience, however, this teaching is not stressed in the contemporary broad tradition following Krishnamacharya.

19. Wallis (2016). Flood (2006, p. 162) broadly agrees:

> Visualising the body as being mapped with these subtle centres is clearly an entextualisation of the body, a mapping of the cosmos and journey of the self to its transcendent source in ways specified within the tradition. Indeed, to seek to understand the *cakras* outside of this context as if they are intended as extra-textual, ontological structures is incoherent.

based on *Pāñcarātra/Vaikhānasa* accounts, he maintained that *kuṇḍalinī* is a blockage only. However, he effectively rejected Krishnamacharya's written statement that *kuṇḍalinī* 'is found above and below Nābhicakra'.[20] Instead, he drew from texts that locate *kuṇḍalinī* at *mūlādhāra*, which are usually comparatively recent.[21] Writing with Kausthub Desikachar, T.K.V. Desikachar claimed that

> All texts confirm that it is the *Prāṇa* that indeed moves into the *Suṣūmnā* (beginning at the *Mūlādhāra Cakra* and terminating at the *Sahasrāra Cakra*), and not the *Kuṇḍalini*.[22]

That is not true. Even the *Yogayājñavalkya*, Krishnamacharya's main source text on *kuṇḍalinī*, describes *prāṇa* as rising from *nābhi* (which is the lower terminus of *suṣumnā*) not *mūlādhāra*. One verse of the critical edition of the *Yogayājñavalkya* describes *kuṇḍalinī* as causing the *sahasrāra* to open at the crown of the head (see Chapter 2). *Kuṇḍalinī* also ascends to *sahasrāra* in the *Yogakuṇḍalī Upaniṣad:*

> Having pierced the *rudra granthi* (the 'knot' between the eyebrows), *śakti* (*kuṇḍalinī*) pierces [the last of the] six lotuses and rejoices in the company of Śiva in the thousand [-petalled] lotus.[23]

---

20. Jayaraman (2015, p. 217).
21. Mallinson and Singleton (2017, p. 178); Hatley (2013, pp. 285, 286).
22. Desikachar and Desikachar (2003, p. 19). This claim is presented in a footnote to some commentary on verse 3 of the *Yogatārāvalī*. In that commentary, Desikachar and Desikachar (2003, p. 17) state that 'it is widely believed that *Prāṇāyāma* is one of the most effective tools with which to cleanse the *nāḍī-s*, especially in the process of bringing the *prāṇa* into the *Suṣūmṇā* (the primary *nāḍī* at the center of the body), by destroying the impurity known as *Kuṇḍalini*'. In the footnote, Desikachar and Desikachar (2003, p. 19) cite *Yogayājñavalkya* 12.11 and *Haṭhapradīpikā* 3.118, both of which are consistent with their claim. However, Desikachar and Desikachar give no caveat to qualify or limit their wide-ranging claim about what 'All texts confirm'.
23. *Yogakuṇḍalī Upaniṣad* 1.86 – my translation of Sastri (1920, p. 321):

> rudragranthiṁ ca bhittvaiva kamalāni bhinatti ṣaṭ |
> sahasrakamale śaktiḥ śivena saha modate ||

Verse 1.82 makes it clear that *śakti* is indeed *kuṇḍalinī*.

Krishnamacharya (2011, p. 42) cites the *Dyhānabindu*, *Śāṇḍilya*, *Yogaśika*, *Yogakuṇḍalī*, *Nādabindu*, *Amṛtabindu* and *Garba Upaniṣad-s* among the books that 'served as authority in compiling' his *Yogamakaranda*. However, they are not cited specifically for *kuṇḍalinī*

Other such *Śaiva*-influenced texts describe *kuṇḍalinī* as not just a blockage but (also) as a mobile energy rising to the head. For example, section 5.14 showed that the *Śivasaṁhitā* describes *kuṇḍalinī śakti* as rising to either the palate or the *Sahasrāra*. Furthermore, section 6.3.21 showed that the *Mantramahodadhi*, which T.K.V. Desikachar calls an 'important reference book' on *kuṇḍalinī*, describes *kuṇḍalinī* as rising to the cerebral aperture, where it unites with *Brahman*. All texts certainly do not say the same thing.

A.G. Mohan is more circumspect. He acknowledges a variety of conceptions of *kuṇḍalinī*, including systems where *kuṇḍalinī* rises to *sahasrāra* and where *kuṇḍalinī* represents *śakti*.[24] Krishnamacharya taught Mohan that in the *Gheraṇḍasaṁhitā*, due to the practice of *śakticālana*, 'the serpent kuṇḍalinī, feeling suffocated, awakes and rises upwards to the brahmarandhra'.[25] Krishnamacharya added that 'the goal in haṭha-yoga is to burn the kuṇḍalinī; in śākta traditions, it is to awaken the kuṇḍalinī. ... In the śākta tradition, kuṇḍalinī is considered the deity of prāṇa. The approach there is different.'[26] Nevertheless, the tone and emphasis of Mohan's teaching shows that he accepts Krishnamacharya's teaching that *kuṇḍalinī* is a blockage only.[27]

Another of Krishnamacharya's long-term students is more ambivalent. In a 2014 lecture, Srivatsa Ramaswami told *yoga* students that Krishnamacharya taught two accounts of *kuṇḍalinī* - the one in the

---

references. *Śāṇḍilya Upaniṣad* 7.36.3 also clearly states that *kuṇḍalinī* can exist high up the *suṣumnā:*

> If that *kuṇḍalinī* sleeps in the part (of the body/*suṣumnā*) above the throat (*kaṇṭha*), [it] is for liberation. [If it sleeps] below [the throat, it is] for the bondage of the confused. (My translation of Sastri 1920, p. 542):
>
> sā kuṇḍalinī kaṇṭhordhvabhāge suptā cedyogināṁ muktaye bhavati |
> bandhanāyādho mūḍhānām || 1.36.3 ||

The Amṛtabindu, *Nādabindu* and *Garba Upaniṣad-s* say nothing about *kuṇḍalinī*. The other texts in the *Yogamakaranda* list are not easily accessible: *Rājayoga-ratnākara*, *Yogasāra-mārga*, *Yogaphala-pradīpikā*, *Rāvaṇa-nāḍī*, *Bhairava-kalpa*, *Śrī-tattva-nidhi*, *Yogaratna-kāṇḍa*, *Mano-nārāyaṇīya*, *Rudra-yāmala*, *Brahma-yāmala*, *Atharvaṇa-rahasya*, *Kapila-sūtra* and *Sūta-saṁhitā* (Krishnamacharya 2011, p. 42). I therefore leave it to other scholars to investigate them. I suspect that these texts may give varying descriptions of *kuṇḍalinī*, like the texts on the list that I have examined.

24. Mohan (no date b, pp. 14–17).
25. Mohan and Mohan (2017, p. 100).
26. Mohan and Mohan (2017, pp. 58, 91).
27. Mohan (2014, 2015, 2018a).

Yogayājñavalkya and one in which *kuṇḍalinī* rises through the *suṣumnā* to the top of the head to reach 'the abode of Śiva'. Although Krishnamacharya did not dismiss the latter account, he much preferred the teaching that *kuṇḍalinī* is a blockage only, Ramaswami said. This teaching links with the Vedāntic idea that *śakti* is equivalent to *māyā-avidyā*, which is to be eliminated, he added. Ramaswami, however, usually describes *kuṇḍalinī* as rising to avoid offending practitioners of '*Kuṇḍalinī Yoga*', who object to *kuṇḍalinī* being defined as a blockage.[28]

In a handout from a teacher training course in California, Ramaswami outlined three alternative accounts of *kuṇḍalinī*. First, he related *kuṇḍalinī* to *avidyā* in *Vedānta*, in which one should 'overcome illusion'. Second, he stated that in *tantra*, 'sakti rises to siva in the sahasraha' (sic), which implies the equation of *śakti* and *kuṇḍalinī*. Third, in Krishnamacharya's interpretation of *haṭhayoga*, the agenda is to 'destroy *kuṇḍalinī*', which represents *avidyā*. Ramaswami concluded by advising trainees to 'decide which approach is palatable to you and practise that'.[29] Given Ramaswami's more open perspective, what can we conclude? If the texts present a variety of different accounts, perhaps we need to look to other sources of information.

In the introduction, I introduced the concept of *pramāṇa-s*, valid sources of knowledge. I outlined how *Sāṁkhya*, *Patañjali* and *Viśiṣṭādvaita* emphasize personal experience over inference and testimony from reliable people or sacred texts. I also asked readers to consider when reading Chapters 2 to 6 whether the sources of information I presented represent

1 the *testimony of Krishnamacharya based on his own experience* and communicated in his own writings, transcriptions of interviews with him or in the writings of his students;
2 the *inference of Krishnamacharya* communicated in his own writings, transcriptions of interviews with him or in the writings of his students;
3 the original *testimony of a follower of Krishnamacharya based on his or her own experience*;
4 the original *inference of a follower of Krishnamacharya*; or
5 *testimony* based on traditional *texts*.

28. Ramaswami (2014).

29. Ramaswami (2008). I did not attend the teacher training course myself but I have seen this course handout.

The vast majority of the information I have presented supporting Krishnamacharya's position is based on testimony from traditional texts. That may be partly explained by my research focus on finding the textual roots of Krishnamacharya's teaching but there are very few statements of Krishnamacharya's personal experience to cite (see below). Furthermore, Krishnamacharya certainly emphasized textual justification of his beliefs, as have his followers. Srivatsan wrote of Krishnamacharya that

> Every person who met him could not but be amazed and even awed by the range and depth of his knowledge. The fluency of his discourse and the multitude of illustrations and quotations he could use from the ancient texts to make his point was astounding.[30]

Furthermore,

> When Śrī Krishnamacharya was teaching, his explanations were always closely linked to the old texts. There was scarcely one explanation that did not contain a reference to an appropriate quotation from one of the writings of the sages of old.[31]

I am not aware of any teacher following Krishnamacharya whose teachings on *kuṇḍalinī* are openly based on accounts of their own personal experience. Individual teachers may have had experiences that they privately conceptualize in terms of *kuṇḍalinī* and that they wish to keep secret. However, all teachers that I have heard teaching about *kuṇḍalinī* in workshops, retreats, one-to-one lessons or informal conversations have cited only ideas from traditional texts or more recent statements from within the tradition. As I have shown, however, textual justification for Krishnamacharya's position requires selectivity in which texts to choose and which parts of those chosen texts to reject. It also requires standardization or simplification of the diversity of textual accounts.

Some of the examples I have presented also show considerable evidence of inference, sometimes extended to elaborate exegesis. Speaking in Glasgow in 2015, A.G. Mohan also asked the question: 'Why is it that

---

30. Srivatsan (1997, p. 11).

31. T.K.V. Desikachar (1995, p. 225). This statement formed part of a question posed to T.K.V. Desikachar in a book authored by him. Desikachar answered without challenging the basis of the question so he did not disagree with the statement.

the only area of our lives where we do not use critical analysis is *yoga*?'[32] However, the critical analysis that Mohan himself displays in his writings and workshops related to *kuṇḍalinī* is based mainly on analysis of and inference from textual sources and Krishnamacharya's statements rather than his personal experience, as far as I can tell. The same seems to be true for the writings of T.K.V. Desikachar.

It would seem that the overall emphasis of the broad tradition's teachings on this topic effectively reverses *Patañjali's* hierarchy of 1. direct perception from personal experience, 2. inference and 3. valid testimony. The tradition has in effect created a different pecking order, at least in relation to *kuṇḍalinī* – 1. testimony (from texts and revered teachers within the tradition); 2. inference and exegesis (based mainly on texts); and 3. personal experience.

Mohan and Mohan caution against relying on personal experience that contradicts textual sources:

> If knowledge or practices arise from roots that are well researched and widespread, they are likely to be more useful and sound. Similarly, if the origin of an idea is well supported in ancient texts, that fact tells us that the idea may have greater validity. If the origin of an idea is the experience of a single individual, or only my own experience, I should probably view that idea with more care.[33]

The thrust of Mohans' statement is clear: we should evaluate personal experience according to the extent to which it is 'well supported in ancient texts'. If there is a discrepancy between our personal experience and what the texts say, then the implication is that the differences are due to imperfections in ourselves, our experiences or how we interpret those experiences rather than imperfections in the texts. I will challenge that view below.

One way to view our own experience with care, as Mohan and Mohan advocate, is to consider whether it is a general experience common to many, or a specific experience particular to one's self. Recall from the introduction that according to Vyāsa's commentary on *Patañjali* 1.7, inference and testimony (whether from a person or a text) can only give information on general or generic (*sāmānya*) qualities of an object or experience whereas direct perception is mainly concerned with individual, specific

32. Mohan (2015).
33. Mohan and Mohan (2015, p. 50).

or particular (*viśeṣa*) qualities.[34] Just because specific information is not contained in a text and is not told to someone by a trustworthy person does not make it invalid – far from it. It is clearly fraught with danger to generalize from our personal experience. But I would argue that it could be equally unwise to use a simplified general account based on textual sources to dismiss, invalidate, downgrade or reclassify a personal experience that may have specific as well as general qualities.

The tradition's emphasis on the testimony of textual sources is not absolute. T.K.V. Desikachar seems to have placed more emphasis on personal experience in his general teaching. This does not seem to have been due to Krishnamacharya's influence. T.K.V. Desikachar taught *yoga* to the spiritual teacher J. Krishnamurti. According to Lorin, Krishnamurti had a 'profound' influence on Desikachar, who copied Krishnamurti's 'way of returning the question to the questioner, to encourage her or him to find the answer by her or himself'.[35] T.K.V. Desikachar was very reluctant to feed Leslie Kaminoff with information during 'the few precious times' when they had one-to-one lessons. When Kaminoff asked a question, Desikachar used to reply by asking 'What does your experience tell you about your answer to that question?'[36] This clearly emphasizes personal experience but what if the experience of the questioner contradicts T.K.V. Desikachar's own teaching? Consider T.K.V. Desikachar's response to a question:

> Question: I have read that when kuṇḍalinī is released, it is like a powerful electric shock going through a wire. If the wire isn't heavy enough to carry the current, it burns out. So they are saying it is dangerous and we must be prepared.

---

34. For example, I find *paścimatānāsana* (a symmetrical seated forward-bend) a difficult posture. After practising it, I often experience a spasm in the muscles of my lower back, which I have to address with a counter pose. This direct experience is not common to everyone. I once met a *yoga* student who told me that she finds the posture so easy that she can even go to sleep in *paścimatānāsana*. If I had concluded that a general (*sāmānya*) feature of *paścimatānāsana* were that it causes muscular spasms in people's backs, I would have been gravely mistaken. I would argue though that my experience does indeed give valuable information about the specific (*viśeṣa*) qualities and effects of *paścimatānāsana* as I experience it in my body.

35. Lorin (2019, p. 55).

36. Kaminoff (2017).

> Response: What is the danger? ... There is no shock here. When a person sees the truth the only shock is that he sees he was a fool before! There is no question of 440 volts or anything like that.[37]

This response effectively equates *kuṇḍalinī* with *avidyā*, emphasizing mental rather than bodily experience. T.K.V. Desikachar states that this explanation is based on the *Yogayājñavalkya* - i.e. textual testimony rather than personal experience. He presents the absence of an experience like an electric shock as a general feature of an experience involving *kuṇḍalinī*. I have heard this passage quoted by followers of T.K.V. Desikachar as an insightful statement that shows how other schools of *yoga* have misinterpreted teachings about *kuṇḍalinī*. In effect, the quotation has become a tradition-specific statement of doctrine that is revered like an ancient text. The implication is that any individual who experiences something like an electric shock is not having an experience involving *kuṇḍalinī*. There is indeed 'no question of 440 volts or anything like that'. Therefore, an experience like an electric shock could be better explained in other terms, perhaps involving the menopause, stress or neurological conditions. There is clearly a danger that using *yoga* terminology could prevent diagnosis of a serious medical condition. Feuerstein reports a case in which a student with a brain tumour was told by a *yoga* teacher that she 'was simply experiencing a *kundalinī* awakening'.[38] But what about someone without an identifiable medical condition who has been having experiences very much like an electric shock? How should they interpret T.K.V. Desikachar's statement? And how should they interpret other greatly contrasting accounts of *kuṇḍalinī* that imply the opposite: bodily experiences resembling electric shocks are actually characteristic of *kuṇḍalinī* awakening? Consider a statement by Swāmi Sivananda, another highly influential 20th century *yoga* teacher:

> When you feel vibrations of Prana in different parts inside your body, when you experience jerks like the shocks of electricity, know that Kundalini has become active.[39]

Lee Sannella, a medical doctor who cofounded the Kundalini Clinic in San Francisco, also uses the analogy of electricity.[40] Based on the testimony

37. T.K.V. Desikachar (1980, p. 247).
38. Feuerstein (2007, p. 140).
39. Sivananda (1994, p. xviii).
40. Sannella (1992, p. 32).

of his patients, he acknowledges that some experiences connected with *kuṇḍalinī* are determined by personal factors. However, he lists 'such physical sensations as itching, fluttering, tingling, intense heat and cold' as some of the '"archetypal" features' of an experience involving *kuṇḍalinī*.[41] I would argue that descriptions involving *kuṇḍalinī* are more likely to have useful explanatory power for those experiencing sensations like electrical discharges than for those who experience only the shock of what a fool they were before.

Sannella goes further, challenging the usefulness of traditional theoretical accounts of *kuṇḍalinī* based on texts:

> The yogin who applies himself to the age-old techniques of kundalini arousal inevitably does so on the basis of the classical model of the kundalini. He fully expects the kundalini energy to awaken in the basal center and to travel upward to the crown center, where it generates untold bliss. It is therefore very likely that he would ignore any phenomena that do not fit the prescription ... By the same token, it seems highly likely that those who undergo spontaneous kundalini awakenings, without preconditioned notions about this process, are the better observers. They would notice phenomena that, from the classical viewpoint, have no significance or do not even exist. They do not hold in their heads the yogin's elaborate metaphysical framework, which acts as a reality filter. Hence they are more sensitive to the unique manifestations of the kundalini experience, certainly on the somatic level.[42]

I would argue that T.K.V. Desikachar's statement, in presenting the absence of sensations like electric shocks as a general defining feature of an experience involving *kuṇḍalinī* rather than a feature specific to some people, could act as a 'reality filter' very similar to the one that Sannella describes. Desikachar's statement could be regarded as useful and insightful for those who only experience the shock of what a fool they were before. But someone experiencing sensations resembling electricity passing through their body would have to critically analyse Desikachar's statement to determine whether descriptions involving *kuṇḍalinī* could shed light on their

41. Sannella (1992, p. 24).

42. Sannella (1992, pp. 33, 34) As we have seen, there is no single 'classical model of the kundalini': there are many. If we substitute that phrase with 'a certain textual model of *kuṇḍalinī*', and change 'the classical viewpoint' to 'a classical viewpoint', then the rest of the quotation stands.

own experience. This critical analysis should take into account their own experience and the testimony of those outside the tradition who have had similar experiences. It should also take into account that T.K.V. Desikachar relied entirely on texts to understand *kuṇḍalinī*, admitting that he had not experienced it himself (see Chapter 2).

Krishnamacharya gave a different description of *kuṇḍalinī* awakening that does involve a bodily experience: 'Like a muscle releasing, the blockage of kuṇḍalinī perishes.' Furthermore, 'Internally, the feeling of kuṇḍalinī arousal is like a muscle dissolving and mind becoming totally focused.'[43] These two sentences are the only evidence I have come across that Krishnamacharya's conception of *kuṇḍalinī* may have been partly based on his own direct experience.

It seems that there are a variety of similar but different experiences that can be described using the term *kuṇḍalinī*. Not all of them exactly follow the various descriptions in *haṭha* texts. Can we really say that only one very narrowly defined personal experience can be described using the term *kuṇḍalinī*? Can we say that one text is correct and that others contradicting it are wrong? Can we gauge progress in our practice by how well our experience matches the textual accounts of *kuṇḍalinī* and *cakra-s*?

After reviewing a number of inconsistent textual descriptions of *cakra-s* and *nāḍī-s*, Connolly concludes that

> These differences between textual descriptions of the cakras and nāḍīs and of their ontological status inevitably raise questions about their use as indicators of [what Ken Wilber calls] 'progressive and permanent milestones along the evolutionary path of your own unfolding', and, indeed, about treating any of these levels/stages schemes as accurate models of human development and progress.[44]

Connolly's statement, which I interpret as extendable to *kuṇḍalinī*, may well be correct. It does not follow, however, that the various accounts of *cakra-s*, *nāḍī-s* and *kuṇḍalinī* are useless (as Connolly acknowledges[45]).

According to Wallis, *cakra-s* in tantric traditions are something to be visualized in meditation but are 'phenomenologically based', reflecting

43. Mohan and Mohan (2017, pp. 81, 96).
44. Connolly (2019, p. 81). By 'progressive and permanent milestones along the evolutionary path of your own unfolding', Connolly is quoting Ken Wilber, whose ideas he had examined in the previous four pages.
45. Connolly (2019, p. 6).

either 'emotional and/or spiritual energy' or 'visionary experiences had by meditators'.[46] The same seems true for *kuṇḍalinī.* Krishnamacharya's equation of *kuṇḍalinī* with *avidyā*, and the accompanying *kleśa-s* of *asmitā*, *rāga*, *dveṣa* and *abhiniveśa*, places these emotions (or psychological drives) centre stage in his system. Krishnamacharya's system also gives these *kleśa-s* a bodily location via *kuṇḍalinī.* Perhaps we should not be surprised if there is debate over where that bodily location should be. As Wallis continues:

> The chakras aren't like organs in the physical body; they aren't fixed facts that we can study like doctors study neural ganglia ... The energy body (*sūkshma-sharīra*) is an extraordinarily fluid reality, as we should expect of anything nonphysical and supersensuous. The energy body can present, experientially speaking, with any number of energy centers, depending on the person and the yogic practice they're performing.[47]

T.K.V. Desikachar's first western student, François Lorin, attended a talk in which Krishnamacharya said that some people experience *cakra-s* in different places. By extension, Lorin told me that *kuṇḍalinī* is 'a symbolic approach to something that cannot be located. It may not be felt in the same way in the same place for everyone'.[48] This could help explain why *kuṇḍalinī* is described in various texts at the heart, navel and at the base of the spine, or in the perineum. So what can we conclude?

Writing about *cakra-s*, Wallis calls for 'some humility':

> This is still mostly uncharted territory. So when it comes to the chakras, don't claim you know. Tell your yoga students that every book on the chakras presents only one possible model ... Let's admit we don't fully understand these ancient yoga practices yet; and instead of seeking to be an authority on some oversimplified version of them, you can invite yourself and your students to look more clearly, more honestly, more carefully, and more non-judgementally at their own inner experience.[49]

I would argue the same about *kuṇḍalinī.* Some within the tradition argue that all other *yoga* traditions interpret *kuṇḍalinī* incorrectly and only

46. Wallis (2016).
47. Wallis (2016).
48. Lorin (2018).
49. Wallis (2016).

Krishnamacharya's position is correct. That is not convincing. It is possible to be so entrenched in a tradition that we cannot see the hole we have dug ourselves into. Krishnamacharya's conception of *kuṇḍalinī* seems to have been partly inspired by his personal experience and it does have a valid textual basis but it is only one of several textually-valid conceptions. I have identified just a handful of *Vaiṣṇava* texts describing *kuṇḍalinī* as a blockage only but there are also *Śaiva* texts describing it as a mobile energy. Does that mean that Krishnamacharya's view has no value? I would argue not.

I would like to quote T.K.V. Desikachar one last time:

> *Question* – If we burn up kuṇḍalinī bit by bit, does more prāṇa gradually enter the suṣumṇā?
> *Answer* – We must be careful that we do not go too far in using images to describe certain experiences. We should never forget that they are images and not the experience itself. Nevertheless, we could imagine it just exactly as you do.[50]

In other words, Krishnamacharya's teaching about *kuṇḍalinī* is a model. Although it seems to have been derived more from texts than from experience, I would argue that it should be regarded not as an ontological model, but as an experiential model. It does not describe how something is: it describes how something feels – physically, mentally and emotionally.

The received wisdom, articulated above by A.G. Mohan, is that we should evaluate personal experience according to how well it conforms with accounts in ancient texts. I propose to turn that idea on its head. I would advocate evaluating ancient texts, or simplified, standardized and distorted theoretical models based on them,[51] according to how well they shed light upon real people's real experiences. I am reminded of the words of George Box: 'all models are wrong but some are useful'.[52] Perhaps the usefulness of Krishnamacharya's model depends less on the extent to which it derives from respected texts and more on the extent to which it describes experience and guides practice.

50. T.K.V. Desikachar (1995, p. 139).
51. According to Bandler and Grinder, who founded the psychological system of Neuro Linguistic Programming, creating models involves three processes: deletion (of detail), generalization (narrowing of scope) and distortion – Connolly (2020).
52. Box (1979, p. 202). Box was an economist, but he made the statement 'all models are wrong but some are useful' in the context of models in physical or biological sciences.

APPENDIX

Dating the *Yogayājñavalkya* and related texts

T.K.V. Desikachar regards the *Yogayājñavalkya* as 'one of the oldest texts on Yoga', dating it to 'the period between the second and the end of the third centuries' (apparently CE).[1] A.G. Mohan dates it to between the 2nd century BCE and the 4th centuries CE, claiming that 'Its very age lends credibility to the authenticity of the views on yoga expounded therein.'[2] T.K.V. Desikachar cites no evidence for his claim, but Mohan seems to rely upon the arguments of Divanji,[3] summarizing them in an appendix to his translation.[4]

Divanji argues that the *Yogayājñavalkya* dates from the 2nd century BCE to the 4th century CE.[5] His primary argument is that the *Yājñavalkyasmṛti*, which he dates from 200 BCE to 300 CE, must have been written by the same author as the *Yogayājñavalkya*. This is highly questionable. Divanji himself concedes that the *Yājñavalkya* of the *Bṛhadāraṇyaka Upaniṣad* 'must be deemed to be another sage of the same name'.[6] There is no reason why that argument cannot be extended to the authorship of the *Yājñavalkyasmṛti*, removing the main reason for dating the *Yogayājñavalkya* so early.

A secondary argument from Divanji is that the commentary on the *Śvetāśvatara Upaniṣad* attributed to *Śaṅkara* seems to contain several quotations 'from a work of Yājñavalkya', which Divanji traces to Chapters 4 to 7 of the *Yogayājñavalkya*.[7] Balasubramanian agrees, concluding that 'we can safely assume that *Yogayājñavalkya* is prior to Śaṅkara and therefore earlier to (sic) 8th Cent. AD'.[8] Śaṅkara is traditionally dated as 788–822 CE but the authenticity of that

---

1. T.K.V. Desikachar (2000, p. xix); T.K.V. Desikachar (1995, p. 230). Although at first sight his statement seems to indicate between the second and fourth centuries *CE*, T.K.V. Desikachar does not specify whether the dates are BC/BCE or AD/CE. Desikachar may have inaccurately reported the estimate given by Divanji (1954, p. 105) of between the 2nd century *BCE* and the 4th century *CE* although I have no evidence to support that interpretation.
2. Mohan (no date, p. 19).
3. Divanji (1954, pp. 103–105).
4. Mohan (no date, pp. 135–139).
5. Divanji (1954, p. 105).
6. Divanji (1954, p. 105). This does not prevent T.K.V. Desikachar (2000, pp. XIII–XVII) from equating the various Yājñavalkya figures.
7. Divanji (1954, p. 104).
8. Balasubramanian (2017, p. 35).

commentary on the *Śvetāśvatara Upaniṣad* is highly questionable,[9] as is the use of it to date the *Yogayājñavalkya* so early.

Less controversially, Balasubramanian also cites texts by Mādhava that quote the *Yogayājñavalkya*, which would date the *Yogayājñavalkya* to the 14th century or before.[10] There are also quotations from the *Yogayājñavalkya* in the *Yoga Upaniṣad-s*, which Balasubramanian dates to 12th–15th centuries CE, leading him to give a 'later terminus' of the 12th or 13th centuries CE.[11] This is closer to other scholars' estimates. According to Buoy, the *Yogayājñavalkya* is from between about the 10th century and the end of the 14th century CE.[12] Buoy's estimate overlaps with those of Larson and Bhattacharya, and Feuerstein, who date the *Yogayājñavalkya* to the 13th–14th centuries CE.[13] These estimates mean that the *Yogayājñavalkya* may still predate the *Haṭhapradīpikā*, which is generally dated to the 14th–15th centuries CE.[14] According to Mohan and Mohan, Krishnamacharya also believed that many later texts borrow from the *Yogayājñavalkya*.[15] The texts that Mohan and Mohan cite as evidence are some of the examples given by Divanji: the *Haṭhapradīpikā*, *Yogakuṇḍalī Upaniṣad* and *Yogatattva Upaniṣad*.[16] Connolly, however, dismisses such arguments as 'wishful thinking', arguing that instead of these texts borrowing from the *Yogayājñavalkya*, 'the opposite is equally likely to be true: the *Yogayajñavalkya* has borrowed from them'. Connolly adds that the *Yogayājñavalkya* must be later than the most recent of the texts from which it borrowed, probably the *Haṭhapradīpikā*.[17] However, it seems just as likely that the *Haṭhapradīpikā* took verses directly from earlier texts from which the *Yogayājñavalkya* had also borrowed. For example, Mallinson's analysis of the *Haṭhapradīpikā* identifies no verses coming from the *Yogayājñavalkya* but does identify 15.5 verses on *āsana-s* and *prāṇāyāma* from the *Vasiṣṭhasaṁhitā* that are also in the *Yogayājñavalkya*.[18] See Chapter 3.

Connolly further argues that the *Yogayājñavalkya* 'shows many signs of lateness' such as the use of the term *śakti* to refer to *kuṇḍalinī* and the inclusion of ten *yama-s*, ten *niyama-s*, fourteen *nāḍī-s* and ten *vāyu-s*, all of which suggest connections with post-*Siddha Śāktiism* and the *Yoga Upaniṣad-s*.[19] However, an

9. Feuerstein (1998, p. 562).
10. Balasubramanian (2017, pp. 28, 29, 33).
11. Balasubramanian (2017, p. 34).
12. Buoy (1994, pp. 84, 117).
13. Larson and Bhattacharya (2008, p. 476); Feuerstein (1997, p. 350).
14. Larson and Bhattacharya (2008, p. 11); Feuerstein (1997, p. 121); Buoy (1994, pp. 5, 119); Mallinson (2011, p. 772).
15. Mohan and Mohan (2013, p. iii).
16. Mohan and Mohan (2013, p. v); Divanji (1954, p. 104).
17. Connolly (2007, pp. 250–251 n.29).
18. Mallinson (2014, p. 235).
19. Connolly (2007, p. 251).

intermediate position is also possible: the *Yogayājñavalkya* could have borrowed from some earlier texts and yet still predate some later texts that either borrowed from it or took verses directly from the earlier sources.

Buoy dates the *Yogayājñavalkya* to the 10th to 14th centuries CE, stating that it is without doubt later than the *Vasiṣṭhasaṁhitā*, which he dates to before *c.*1250 CE.[20] Digambaji, Jha and Sahay also date the *Vasiṣṭhasaṁhitā* to *c.*1250 CE, arguing that the *Yogayājñavalkya* borrowed over half of its 496 verses from it.[21]

Balasubramanian, however, stresses that this direction of borrowing has not been proven. He believes that the *Vasiṣṭhasaṁhitā* postdates the *Yogayājñavalkya*, from which it borrowed verses.[22] Balasubramanian also notes that many verses of the *Ahirbudhnyasaṁhitā* are 'strikingly similar' to equivalents in the *Yogayājñavalkya*, but he mentions no other *Pāñcarātra Saṁhitā*.[23] Whatever the direction of borrowing between the *Yogayājñavalkya* and the *Vasiṣṭhasaṁhitā*, I have shown in Chapter 3 that some verses on *kuṇḍalinī* common to those two texts originate in the *Pādmasaṁhitā*, which Mallinson and Singleton date to *c.*10th century CE but which Schwarz-Linder dates to the early 12th to late 13th centuries CE.[24]

In summary, although there is not complete consensus on the dating of these texts or the directions of borrowing, the weight of scholarly opinion suggests that the *Yogayājñavalkya* was written towards the end of the period between the 10th and 14th centuries CE. Most scholars believe it borrowed more than half its verses from the *Vasiṣṭhasaṁhitā*, which was written around the 13th century CE. The *Vasiṣṭhasaṁhitā* in turn took some verses on *kuṇḍalinī* from the *Pādmasaṁhitā*, which is *c.*10th–13th centuries CE.

---

20. Buoy (1994, pp. 84 n.360, 118).
21. Digambaji, Jha and Sahay (2005, pp. 31, 32).
22. Balasubramanian (2017, pp. 119, 120).
23. Balasubramanian (2017, p. 121).
24. Mallinson and Singleton (2017, p. 179); Schwarz-Linder (2014, pp. 30, 31).

Table 4
Summary of dating estimates for six texts.

Text	Dating estimates
Vimānārcanākalpasaṁhitā	• Colas (2010, pp. 158): early in the period between the 9th and 14th centuries CE • Mallinson (2014, p. 227): *c.*9th century CE (citing Colas) • Mallinson (2011, p. 772): *c.*10th century CE
Ahirbudhnyasaṁhitā	• Schrader (1916, pp. 19, 97–99): 300–800 CE • Larson and Bhattacharya (2008, p. 142): 300–800 CE (citing Schrader) • Colas (2010, p. 157): 'a later Saṃhitā' (no date given) • Sanderson (2001, p. 35): after *c.*1000–1050 CE • Schwarz-Linder (2014, p. 30): after 1050 CE
Pādmasaṁhitā	• Mallinson and Singleton (2017, p. 179): *c.*10th century CE • Schwarz-Linder (2014, p. 31): early 12th to late 13th centuries CE
Vasiṣṭhasaṁhitā	• Digambaji, Jha and Sahay (2005, pp. 31–32): *c.*1250 CE • Buoy (1994, p. 118): before *c.*1250 CE • Mallinson (2014, p. 227): *c.*13th–14th centuries CE
Yogayājñavalkya	• Divanji (1954, p. 105): 2nd century BCE to 4th century CE • Balasubramanian (2017, p. 35): before 8th century CE • Buoy (1994, pp. 84, 117): 10th to early 14th centuries CE • Larson and Bhattacharya (2008, p. 476): *c.*13th or 14th centuries CE • Feuerstein (1997, p. 350): *c.*13th or 14th centuries CE
Haṭhapradīpikā	• Larson and Bhattacharya (2008, p. 11): *c.*1350–1400 CE • Feuerstein (1997, p. 121): mid 14th century CE • Buoy (1994, p. 119): 15th century CE • Mallinson (2011, p. 772): 15th century CE (citing Buoy)

GLOSSARY

This glossary is only for terms not translated or explained in the immediate context or in notes. The terms are listed in English alphabetical order as though there were no diacritics. Sanskrit words often have multiple meanings. In most cases, I give here only the meanings relevant to how the terms are used in this book. The definitions and explanations are deliberately simplistic.

abhimāna	Erroneous self-conception.
ācārya	A spiritual teacher or preceptor.
adharma	Literally, 'that which does not support'. The opposite of *dharma*.
Advaita	A nondualist branch of the Hindu school of philosophy known as *Vedānta*.
Advaitin	A follower of *Advaita*.
āgama	Certain Hindu religious traditions of ritual and mysticism, such as *Pāñcarātra* and *Vaikhānasa*, or the texts of such traditions.
agni	Fire. *Agni* is sometimes called *jāṭharāgni* when in the abdomen, but the *Yogayājñavalkya* and several other texts locate it in the perineum.
ahaṁkāra	Ego.
ahi	Snake.
Ahobilam Math/Mutt	One of the four main *Vaṭakalai Śrīvaiṣṇava* organizations.
ajñāna	Nescience, spiritual ignorance. *Ajñāna* is effectively synonymous with *avidyā* in *Advaita* (but not in *Patañjali's Yogasūtra*).
ajñatva	Nescience – apparently a synonym for *ajñāna/avidyā* in the *Ahirbudhnyasaṁhitā*.
amṛta	Nectar.
Ananta	Literally 'infinite' – one of the names of the *nāga* Śeṣa/Saṅkarṣaṇa.
aṅgula	A unit of measurement equal to the width of a finger.
antaḥ kumbhaka = *antarkumbhaka*	The pause after the inhale in *prāṇāyāma*. It is often abbreviated to AK by followers of Krishnamacharya.
apāna (*vāyu*)	One of the five forms of *prāṇa* (breath or vital energy). It is usually located in the abdomen.
Āraṇyaka	A group of Vedic texts interpreting the rituals detailed in Vedic *Saṁhitā-s* and stipulating other forms of worship.

arcirādi mārga — The path that a *jīva* takes towards heaven at the time of death after passing through the *suṣumnā* and emerging from the crown of the head.

āsana — A *yoga* posture or sitting position.

asita/Asita — A black snake (in general)/the name of a specific black snake.

asmitā — Literally 'am-ness'. According to T.K.V. Desikachar, when a *kleśa*, *asmitā* leads to 'false identity': the *buddhi* is mistaken for the true self, the *ātman*.

asmitva — Literally 'am-ness'. A near synonym of *asmitā* in the *Ahirbudhnyasaṁhitā*.

aṣṭāṅgayoga — The eight 'limbs' of *yoga* found in the Yogasūtra of *Patañjali: yama, niyama, āsana, prāṇāyāma, pratyāhāra, dhāraṇā, dhyāna* and *samādhi*.

ātman — The true innermost self, according to many Hindu traditions.

avatār — An incarnation of the divine on earth, especially in Vaiṣṇavism.

avidyā — Nescience, spiritual ignorance. It is defined differently in various traditions.

bāhya kumbhaka — The pause after the exhale in *prāṇāyāma*. It is often abbreviated to BK by followers of Krishnamacharya.

bandha — A bind or lock. It can refer to the physical bodily seals of *haṭhayoga: uḍḍīyāna bandha, jālandhara bandha, mūla bandha* or *jihvā bandha*. It can also refer to various types of binding or bondage.

Bhāgavata — An ancient religious tradition of worshipping Viṣṇu which combined with other elements to form Vaiṣṇavism.

bhakti — The devotional worship of a deity.

Brahmā — The creator god of Hinduism. He should not be confused with *Brahman*, *brahmin* or *Brāhmaṇa*.

Brahman — The highest principle in *Vedānta*. In *Advaita*, *Brahman* is the single non-personal consciousness. In *Viśiṣṭādvaita*, it is the supreme personal God, Viṣṇu. *Brahman* should not be confused with *brahmin*, *Brāhmaṇa* or Brahmā.

Brāhmaṇa — A group of Vedic texts explaining the rituals detailed in Vedic *Saṁhitā-s*.

brahmanāḍī — Usually a synonym of the *suṣumnā*. In some texts it is a central channel within the *suṣumnā*.

brahmarandhra — The entrance to the *suṣumnā nāḍī* at its base, or the exit from the *suṣumnā* at its top.

brahmarudra — A synonym for the *suṣumnā nāḍī*.

Brahmasūtra — A text synthesizing teachings from early *Upaniṣad-s* into a single doctrine of Vedānta.

brahmin	A member of the priestly class of the Hindu caste system.
buddhi	The mental faculty of wisdom, discrimination and discernment in *Sāṁkhya* and *Vedānta.*
cakra	Literally wheels or circles, *cakra-s* are said to be located at the junctions between *nāḍī-s.*
candra	The moon.
cinmudrā	A hand gesture in which the thumb and index finger are brought together.
dehamadhya	The centre of the body, which is located between the anus and penis according to the *Yogayājñavalkya* and certain other texts.
dhāraṇā	Concentration.
dharma	Duty or righteousness – literally 'that which supports'.
dhātu	One of seven bodily tissues of *Āyurveda* – plasma, blood, muscle, fat, bone, nerve tissue/bone marrow and reproductive tissue.
dhyāna	Meditation.
dṛṣṭi	That which sees = the *ātman*
dṛśya	That which is seen = *prakṛti*
dvijihva	A snake: literally, 'the two-tongued one'. The English equivalent is 'the fork-tongued one'.
Gārgī	The wife of the sage Yājñavalkya. In the *Yogayājñavalkya*, she is taught *yoga* by her husband, who addresses his speech to her.
Garuḍa	A celestial bird of prey that is said to feed on snakes and to act as the vehicle of Viṣṇu.
Gṛhyasūtra-s	Texts describing Vedic domestic rituals, including those of births and marriages.
guṇa	The most common use of *guṇa* relates to three qualities or constituents of *prakṛti* – *rajas* (activity, passion), *tamas* (darkness, inertia, binding, obscuration) and *sattva* (clarity, lucidity, purity). See also *saguṇa dhyāna.*
guru dakṣiṇā	The payment made by a student to a teacher in exchange for instruction.
Hanūmān	A powerful monkey warrior said to have served Rāma in the *Rāmāyaṇa.*
haṭhayoga	A type of *yoga* which places great emphasis on manipulating *prāṇa* by means of *āsana*, *mudrā*, *bandha* and especially *prāṇāyāma.*
hṛdaya	The heart. Rather than referring to the physical blood-pumping organ, *hṛdaya* frequently denotes a *cakra* or lotus near the physical heart.

iḍā — One of the three principal *nāḍī-s*. It is usually described as being on the left of the *suṣumnā* and terminating at the left nostril.

Indra/*indra* — In early Vedic texts, Indra is the king of heaven. In other contexts, *indra* can more generally mean 'lord' or 'the best'.

indriya — A sense organ. Eleven sense organs are described in many Hindu texts: five organs of sensory reception, five organs of action, and the mind.

Īśvara — Literally, the Lord. In the *Yoga Sūtra* of *Patañjali*, *Īśvara* is described as a *guru* and a special self, untouched by the effects of *prakṛti*. In Vedānta, *Īśvara* usually means the supreme God.

jālandhara bandha — A physical *haṭhayoga* technique involving contraction of the throat by lowering the chin onto the chest. It is said to prevent the *amṛta* (nectar) from dripping down from the head.

jāṭharāgni — The digestive fire said to be in the abdomen.

jihvā bandha — A physical *haṭhayoga* technique involving the tongue. It is said to stop the upward movement of *prāṇa* through all the *nāḍī-s* except *suṣumnā*.

jīva/jīvātman — The individual self, in contrast to the *paramātman*.

Jyotsnā — The commentary on the *Haṭhapradīpikā* by Brahmānanda.

kāma — Desire for something not yet experienced.

Kanchipuram — An important ancient temple town in Tamil Nadu. The birthplace of Vedāntadeśika.

kanda — The lower terminus and junction of the three principal *nāḍī-s*. Various texts locate the *kanda* in different places.

karma — Action and the psychological results of that action on the actor.

Kashmir Śaivism — A highly tantric Śiva-worshipping tradition that developed in Kashmir in the middle ages.

kleśa-s — Causes of psychological affliction. According to *Patañjali*, *avidyā* (nescience) is the root affliction. From it develop *asmitā* ('am-ness'), *rāga* (desire), *dveṣa* (aversion) and *abhiniveśa* (fear of death).

kriyāśakti — The active part of *śakti* in the *Ahirbudhnyasaṁhitā*. Also called *sudarśana*.

kuṇḍala — Literally 'coiled'. It is usually an earring, a bracelet, the coil of a rope, a fetter, tie or collar.

kuṇḍalī — In texts describing *haṭhayoga*, *kuṇḍalī* is usually a synonym of *kuṇḍalinī*. In other places, it simply means 'coiled'.

kuṇḍalinī — According to Krishnamacharya, *kuṇḍalinī* is a blockage to the *suṣumnā nāḍī* that prevents *prāṇa* from entering it. He equated *kuṇḍalinī* with *avidyā*. More commonly, *kuṇḍalinī* is

	described as a type of energy that enters the *suṣumnā* and rises.
Lakṣmī	Also known as Śrī, Lakṣmī is the consort of Viṣṇu. She is generally regarded as a benevolent goddess of wealth and prosperity.
layayoga	A tantric tradition of meditative absorption. Related to *haṭhayoga* and *rājayoga.*
mahāmudrā	Literally, the 'great seal'. It is a physical technique of *haṭhayoga* that followers of Krishnamacharya regard as a tool to burn the *kuṇḍalinī* blockage to the *suṣumnā.*
māna	Pride.
maṇḍala	A mystical geometric diagram of tantric origins. Similar to a *yantra.*
maṇipūra = *maṇipūraka* = *maṇipūrāka*	A *cakra* said to be at or close to the navel. It can be regarded as equivalent to *nābhi cakra.*
mantra	A sacred sound, word or phrase that is recited as a spiritual practice.
marma points	Pressure points on the surface of the body, according to *Āyurveda.*
math/muṭṭ/maṭha	A monastery, seminary, college or temple.
māyā	An illusion, apparition, magic, trick, sorcery. It is often related to *śakti*, *prakṛti* and *avidyā.*
Mīmāṁsā	One of the six orthodox schools of South Asian philosophy. Primarily concerned with Vedic ritual.
moha	Delusion.
mokṣa	Spiritual liberation.
mudrā	In *haṭhayoga*, *mudrā-s* are physical techniques that usually involve restricting and redirecting the flow of *prāṇa* around the body, often with the aim of awakening *kuṇḍalinī.* In traditions such as *Pāñcarātra*, *mudrā-s* are gestures used in ritual.
mūla bandha	This physical *haṭhayoga* technique is described variously in different texts. Most descriptions involve a contraction of the perineum or anus. It is said to force *apāna* upwards or to arouse *kuṇḍalinī.*
mūlacakra	Literally, 'root *cakra*'. It is not necessarily equivalent to *mūlādhāra cakra.* In the *Yogayājñavalkya*, *nābhi cakra* is the *mūlacakra.*
mūlādhāra	In some *haṭhayoga* texts, *mūlādhāra* is the lowermost *cakra*, located at the base of the spine or in the perineum.
mūrdhanya nāḍī	A synonym for the *suṣumnā nāḍī.*

nābhi	Literally, 'the navel'. In some *haṭhayoga* texts, such as the *Yogayājñavalkya*, *nābhi* is a place that seems equivalent to *maṇipūra cakra* in other texts.
nāda	The unstruck internal sound described in some *haṭhayoga* texts.
nāḍī	A channel in the human body through which *prāṇa* is said to move. It includes nerves, arteries and veins, with which it is sometimes equated by commentators.
nāḍīśuddhi = *nāḍīśodhana*	A breathing practice through which *nāḍī-s* are purified. Some texts include it as a type of *prāṇāyāma*. Other texts describe it separately.
nāga	Powerful semi-divine serpents. They are portrayed negatively or positively in different texts.
nāgadoṣa	'Snake blemish': an astrological problem that is said to cause inauspicious planetary alignments in one's horoscope, leading to late marriage and infertility.
Nāgaloka	A subterranean realm said to be inhabited by *nāga-s*.
Nārāyaṇa	One of the names of Viṣṇu.
nigrahaśakti	One of the five functions of *kriyāśakti* in the *Ahirbudhnyasaṁhitā*. *Nigrahaśakti* is said to be responsible for covering one's consciousness, binding and obscuring the real nature of the self.
nyāsa	A tantric technique in which the hands are placed at bodily locations where *mantra-s* are 'installed'. In Śrīvaiṣṇavism, it is also used as a synonym for *prapatti*.
Nyāya	One of the six orthodox schools of South Asian philosophy. It is primarily concerned with logic and epistemology (the study of what can be known and how it can be known).
ontological	Related to ontology: a branch of metaphysics. Ontology addresses the nature of being, i.e. how things really are according to a particular philosophical or theological system.
Pāñcarātra (= *Pañcarātra*)	An ancient sect of *Vaiṣṇava* temple priests and their texts. Similar to *Vaikhānasa*.
Pāñcarātrin	A person following the tradition of *Pāñcarātra*.
Parakāla Math	One of the four main religious organizations of the *Vaṭakalai* branch of Śrīvaiṣṇavism. Krishnamacharya studied there as a young man.
Paramātman	The supreme Self, in contrast to the *jīvātman*. The *Paramātman* is said to be equivalent to *Brahman*. In Vaiṣṇavism, it is equivalent to Viṣṇu.
pāśa	A noose – a type of weapon of various gods. When made of a snake, it is a *nāgapāśa*.

Patañjali's Yogasūtra-s/Patañjali Yogadarśana A *yoga* text of four chapters from around 200 CE. It is arguably the oldest text devoted to *yoga* alone and it is the foundational text for the school of philosophy known as *yoga*. It is sometimes referred to as just *Patañjali*, the traditional name of the author, and sometimes just as the *Yoga Sūtra*. Krishnamacharya equated it with *rājayoga*.

phaṇi A snake.

piṅgalā One of the three principal *nāḍī-s*. It is usually described as being on the right of the *suṣumnā* and terminating at the right nostril.

prakṛti Created nature. It is defined differently by different systems of South Asian philosophy. In the dualistic system of *Sāṁkhya*, *prakṛti* is everything that is not the *puruṣa* (self). In *Advaitavedānta*, *prakṛti* is equivalent to *māyā* (illusion).

prāṇa The vitalistic principle, energy or life force, which is said to permeate the bodies of all living organisms. It is usually equated to air and breath. There are five main categories of *Prāṇa: prāṇa, apāna, vyāna, udāna* and *samāna*.

praṇava The *mantra* '*oṁ*'.

prāṇāyāma The control of *prāṇa* inside the body by regulating, restraining and directing the physical breath.

prapanna A person practising *prapatti*.

prapatti Devotional surrender to God in Śrīvaiṣṇavism.

pratyāhāra The action of withdrawing the senses from their objects.

pūja Worship.

Purāṇa A type of Hindu text, mainly produced in the common era, that often includes elaborate mythological accounts of the creation of the world and the genealogy of deities.

puruṣa The individual self. In the dualistic system of *Sāṁkhya*, it is the counterpart of *prakṛti*. In both *Sāṁkhya* and *Patañjali*, discerning the difference between *puruṣa* and *prakṛti* is a key aim. The meaning of *puruṣa* in the *Pādmasaṁhitā* seems similar. In parts of the *Ahirbudhnyasaṁhitā*, *puruṣa* means the aggregate of all selves rather than an individual self.

rāga The desire to repeat pleasant experiences.

rajas Representing activity and passion, *rajas* is said to be one of the three *guṇa-s* (components/strands/qualities) of *prakṛti*, alongside *tamas* and *sattva*.

rākṣasa A type of mythical monster.

saguṇa dhyāna Meditation with qualities or attributes – e.g. meditation upon an image of Viṣṇu.

sahasrāra	Said to be located on the crown of the head, the *sahasrāra* is often described as the highest spiritual centre to which *prāṇa*, or in some texts *kuṇḍalinī*, ascends.
Saiddhāntika	Relating to the tradition of *Śaiva Siddhānta.*
Śaiva	Related to the god Śiva – especially traditions that worship Śiva as the principal deity.
Śaiva Siddhānta	One of the main tantric *Śaiva* traditions.
Śākta	Relating to the goddess *Śakti* – especially traditions that worship *Śakti* as the principal deity.
śakti/Śakti	Capacity, ability, power, the Goddess. In some systems, *śakti* is synonymous with *kuṇḍalinī.*
śakticālana	The *haṭhayoga* process of awakening the *kuṇḍalinī* by physical means, including the action of *paridhāra* – moving the abdominal muscles from left to right and from right to left.
samādhi	In *Patañjali's Yoga Sūtra*, *samādhi* is the final stage of *aṣṭāṅga yoga.* It is the deep ecstatic absorption of the meditator with the subject of meditation.
Sāṁkhya	One of the six orthodox schools of South Asian philosophy. This dualistic system is primarily concerned with the distinction between the self (*puruṣa*) and non-self (*prakṛti*). *Sāṁkhya* hugely influenced both *Pāñcarātra* and the *Yoga Sūtra* of *Patañjali.*
Sāṁkhyakārikā	The main surviving text of *Sāṁkhya.*
saṁsāra	The cycle of mundane existence, including transmigration and rebirth.
Saṅkarṣaṇa	Another name for the *nāga* called Śeṣa or Ananta.
sarpa	Snake.
Sattva	Representing clarity, lucidity and purity, *sattva* is one of the three *guṇa-s* (components/strands/qualities) of *prakṛti*, alongside *rajas and tamas.*
Sāttvic	Relating to *sattva.*
Śeṣa	Another name for the *nāga* called Saṅkarṣaṇa or Ananta.
siddhi	An accomplishment or attainment, either in the sense of achieving success in one's practice or in the sense of achieving supernatural powers.
Śiva	One of the principal Hindu gods. According to *Śaiva* schools, he is the Supreme Godhead.
Śrī	Also known as Lakṣmī, Śrī is the consort of Viṣṇu. She is generally regarded as a benevolent goddess of wealth and prosperity. In other contexts, Śrī is an honourific term used before a name of a person, text or organization.
Śrībhāṣya	*Rāmānuja's* commentary on the *Brahmasūtra.*

Srirangam — An important temple town in Tamil Nadu and one of the main centres of Śrīvaiṣṇavism. The location of the headquarters of the Srirangam Srimad Andavan Ashramam.

Srirangam Srimad Andavan Ashramam — One of the four main organizations of the *Vaṭakalai* branch of Śrīvaiṣṇavism. Founded in the 18th century.

Śrīvaiṣṇava — Relating to Śrīvaiṣṇavism or a follower of Śrīvaiṣṇavism.

Śrīvaiṣṇavism — A branch of Vaiṣṇavism mainly followed in South India in which the goddess Śrī-Lakṣmī is worshipped alongside Viṣṇu.

sṛṣṭi — Creation. In different parts of the *Ahirbudhnyasaṁhitā*, *sṛṣṭi* means one of the five manifestations of *kriyāśakti* and the pronunciation of sounds.

śruti — That which is heard. The *Veda*-s are called *śruti* because they are considered to be revealed teachings that are 'heard' by the sages that wrote them.

sthiti — As one of the five manifestations of *kriyāśakti* in the *Ahirbudhnyasaṁhitā*, *sthiti* means steadying or preservation. More generally, it can mean being established in something, such as the teachings of a tradition, devotion to a deity or one's *yoga* practice.

sudarśana — Viṣṇu's discus weapon. Also a synonym for *kriyāśakti* in the *Ahirbudhnyasaṁhitā*.

suṣumnā (= *suṣumṇā* in the *Yogayājñavalkya*) — Described as the most important *nāḍī*, the *suṣumnā* is said to be a duct along which the *jīva*, *prāṇa* and *agni* can rise to the crown of the head. Its lower terminus is located in different places in different texts: *hṛdaya* (the heart), *nābhi* (the navel) or *mūlādhāra*. Synonyms of *suṣumnā* include *brahmarudra*, *mūrdhanya-nāḍī*, *brahma-nāḍī* and *nāḍī viśeṣa*. Notably, the *Saṅkalpasūryodaya* equates the *suṣumnā* with *kuṇḍalī*.

Takṣaka — The name of a *nāga*.

tamas (= *tamoguṇa*) — Representing darkness, inertia, binding and obscuration, *tamas* is said to be one of the three *guṇa*-s (components/strands/qualities) of *prakṛti*, alongside *sattva* and *tamas*.

tāmasic — Relating to *tamas*.

tantra — A group of esoteric spiritual traditions and their texts. *Tantra* provides practices for developing a power in individuals that usually remains latent. It often features elaborate rituals, mystic diagrams, *nyāsa* and *mantra*. Teachings about *kuṇḍalinī* originated in *Śaiva tantra*.

tantric — Related to *tantra*.

Teṇkalai One of the two branches of Śrīvaiṣṇavism, the other being *Vaṭakalai.*

tirodhāna The covering, concealing, veiling or obscuring of the true nature of the *ātman.*

uḍḍīyāna bandha (= *uḍyāṇa* in the *Yogatārāvalī*) A physical *haṭhayoga* technique in which the abdomen is drawn inwards towards the spine. It is said to encourage *prāṇa* to ascend the *suṣumnā.*

Vaikhānasa An ancient sect of *Vaiṣṇava* temple priests and their texts. Similar to *Pāñcarātra.*

vaikuṇṭha Heaven.

Vaiṣṇava Relating to Viṣṇu or traditions of Vaiṣṇavism, which worship him.

Vaiṣṇavism One of the main divisions of Hinduism. In Vaiṣṇavism, *Viṣṇu* is worshipped as the principal deity.

Varāha The name of Viṣṇu's boar *avatār.*

vāsana A subtle impression: a trace of an action that is left in one's mind after an experience.

Vāsudeva A manifestation of God. In Śrīvaiṣṇavism, Vāsudeva is the first of four manifestations (*vyūha-s*) of *Viṣṇu.*

Vāsuki The name of a *nāga.*

Vaṭakalai One of the two branches of Śrīvaiṣṇavism, the other being *Teṇkalai.*

vāyu Air, wind or breath. Often synonymous with *prāṇa.*

Vedānta One of the six orthodox schools of South Asian philosophy. Primarily concerned with the teachings of the *Upaniṣad-s*, *Bhagavadgītā* and the *Brahmasūtra*. Its main divisions are *Advaita* (non-dualist), *Viśiṣṭādvaita* (qualified non-dualist) and *Dvaita* (dualist).

Vedāntic Relating to *Vedānta.*

Veda-s Often 'the *Veda-s*' refers to the four *Saṁhitā-s* ('collections') of the *Ṛgveda*, *Yajurveda*, *Sāmaveda* and *Atharvaveda*, which are among the oldest Hindu texts. Technically, 'the *Veda-s*' also includes three later groups of texts which sprang from the *Saṁhitā-s: Brāhmaṇa-s*, *Āraṇyaka-s* and *Upaniṣad-s.*

Vedic Related to the *Veda-s.*

vīṇā A South-Asian stringed musical instrument.

Viśiṣṭādvaitavedānta The interpretation of *Vedānta* developed by Rāmānuja and his followers. It is often called 'qualified non-dualism'.

Viṣṇu One of the principal *Hindu* gods. According to Vaiṣṇavism, he is the Supreme Godhead.

Vṛtra The name of a snake demon in the *Ṛgveda.*

Vyāsa	The traditional name of the author of the first commentary on the *Yogasūtra* of *Patañjali*. Some scholars now believe that the *Yogasūtra* and that commentary were written by the same author(s).
vyūha	*Pāñcarātra* and Śrīvaiṣṇavism teach that Viṣṇu emanates in four *vyūha-s* or manifestations.

BIBLIOGRAPHY

Authors are listed in English alphabetical order of their surname (or organizational name), as though there were no diacritical marks.

Ādidevānanda, S. (trans.) (no date) *Śrī Rāmānuja Gītā Bhāṣya*, Madras: Sri Ramakrishna Math

Adishakti.org (no date) *Kundalini*, available at www.adishakti.org/kundalini.htm (Accessed: 12 July 2018)

Adyar Library and Research Centre (trans.) (1972) *The Haṭhayogapradīpikā of Svātmārāma With the Commentary Jyotsnā of Brahmānanda and English Translation*, Chennai: Adyar Library and Research Centre

Aiyangar, C.D. (1933) *Hinduism in the Light of Visishtadvaitism*, Chittoor: D.T. Printing Works

Aiyangar, D.R. (trans.) (1979) *Nyaasa Vimsati of Vedanta Desika*, Madras: Visishtadvaitha Pracharini Sabha

Aiyangar, M.D. and Venugopalacharya, T. (eds) (1996) *Śrī Pāñcarātrarakṣā of Śrī Vedānta Deśika*, 3rd edition, Madras: Adyar Library and Research Centre

Aiyangar, S.K. (1940) *A History of Tirupati*, vol. 1, Madras: Tirumalai-Tirupati Devastanam Committee

Allocco, A.L. (2013) 'Fear, Reverence and Ambivalence: Divine Snakes in Contemporary South India', *Religions of South Asia*, vol. 7, pp. 230–248

Allocco, A.L. (2014) 'The Blemish of "Modern Times": Snakes, Planets, and the Kaliyugam', *Nidān*, vol. 26, no. 1, pp. 1–21

Alwar, M.A. (2010) *Essentials of Viśiṣṭādvaita*, Bangalore: Shri Kashi Sesha Sastri Religious Trust

Alwar, M.A. (2018) Pers. Com. (Meeting in Mysore), 08 December

Ananthanarayanan, R. (2016) *A Memorial Lecture Series in honour of Sri TKV Desikachar | Speaker Raghu Ananthanarayanan | Part 4*, Chennai: Krishnamacharya Yoga Mandiram, available at www.youtube.com/watch?v=bo4DcPEIZuI (Accessed: 08 August 2018)

Annangaracharyar, K.P.B. (ed.) (1941) 'Nyāyasiddhāñjanam', in *Śrīmadvedāntadeśikagranthamālā*, book no.3, pp. 210–238, Conjeevaram: Granthamala Office

Apte, P.P. (trans.) (2005) *Sātvata-Saṁhitā (With English Translation)*, Melkote: Academy of Sanskrit Research

Apte, V.S. (1957) *The Practical Sanskrit-English Dictionary*, 2nd edition, Pune: Prasad Prakashan

Atmashraddhananda, S. (ed.) (2016) *Understanding Pratika: Symbols in the Indian Tradition*, Chennai: Sri Ramakrishna Math

Avalon, A. (ed.) (1989) *Prapañcasāra Tantra of Śaṅkarācārya*, Delhi: Motilal Banarsidass

Avalon, A. (trans.) (1974) *The Serpent Power*, 7th edition, New York: Dover Publications

Ayyangar, D.R. (trans.) (1960) *Daya Satakam of Vedanta Desika*, Tirupati: T.T Devasthanams

Balasubramanian, A.V., Desikachar, T.K.V., Prabhakar R. and Sriram, R. (eds) (2001) *Pātañjalayogadarśanam: Text with Chant-Notation in Sanskrit and Roman Script and Ādiśeṣāṣṭakam of Sri. T. Krishnamacharya*, 4th edition, Chennai: Krishnamacharya Yoga Mandiram

Balasubramanian, K.S. (2017) *Yogayājñavalkya: A Critical Study*, Dharwad: Karnataka Historical Research Society

Balasubramanian, K.S. (2018) Pers. Com. (Meeting at Kuppuswami Sastri Research Institute, Chennai), 06 December

Balasubramanyam, T.K. (ed.) (1907) *Yadavabhyudaya by Sriman Vedanta Desika*, vol. 1, Srirangam: Sri Vani Vilas Press

Balasubramanyam, T.K. (ed.) (1909) *Yadavabhyudaya by Sriman Vedanta Desika*, vol. 2, Srirangam: Sri Vani Vilas Press

Bartley, C.J. (2002) *The Theology of Rāmānuja*, London: Routledge Curzon

Bäumer, B.S. (trans.) (2018) 'The Yoga of the *Netra Tantra:* A Translation of Chapters VII and VIII with Introduction', in B.S. Bäumer and H. Stainton (eds), *Tantrapuṣpāñjali: Tantric Traditions and Philosophy of Kashmir*, New Delhi: Indira Gandhi National Centre for the Arts and Aryan Books International, pp. 3–33

Begley, W.E. (1973) *Viṣṇu's Flaming Wheel: The Iconography of the Sudarśana-Cakra*, New York: New York University Press

Bhandarkar, R.G. (1965) *Vaiṣṇavism Śaivism and Minor Religious Systems*, Varanasi: Indological Book House

Bhaṭṭācārya, V.R. and Mādhavācārya, S. (eds) (1926) *Śrīvimānārcanākalpaḥ*, Chennai (Madras): Veṅkaṭeśvara Mudraṇālaya

Bhaṭṭācārya, R. and Mādhavācārya, S. (eds) (1998) *Vimānārcana Kalpa (Sage Marichi Samhita)*, Tirupati: Tirumala-Tirupati Devasthanams

Birch, J. (2011) 'The Meaning of *haṭha* in Early Haṭhayoga', *Journal of the American Oriental Society*, vol. 131, no. 4, pp. 527–554

Birch, J. (2014) 'Rājayoga: The Reincarnations of the King of All Yogas', *International Journal of Hindu Studies*, vol. 17, no. 3, pp. 399–442

Birch, J. (2015) 'The Yogatārāvalī and the Hidden History of Yoga', *Nāmarūpa*, no. 20, pp. 4–13

Birch, J. (2018) Pers. Com.

Bist, U.S. (2008) *Gītārthasaṅgraha: Explanation and Discussions*, New Delhi: Satyam Publishing House

Board of Scholars (trans.) (2014) *The Mantramahodadhi of Mahidhara*, 4th edition, Delhi: Sri Satguru

Bouanchaud, B. (1997) *The Essence of Yoga: Reflections on the Yoga Sūtras of Patañjali*, Portland: Rudra Press

Bouanchaud, B. (2019) 'Bernard Bouanchaud', in S. Oubrier and B. Viard (eds), *T.K.V. Desikachar: A Question of Transmission*, Sainte Cécile les Vignes: Les Cahiers de Présence d'Espirit, pp. 43–48

Box, G.E.P. (1979) 'Robustness in the Strategy of Scientific Model Building', in R.L. Launer and G.N. Wilkinson (eds), *Robustness in Statistics*, Cambridge: Academic Press, pp. 201–236

Brahmānandatripāṭhī (ed.) (1993) *Śrīmadbhāgavatamahāpurāṇam*, vol. 2, Delhi: Caukhambā Saṁskṛta Pratiṣṭhāna

Bronner, Y. and Schulman, D. (trans.) (2009) *Self-Surrender, Peace, Compassion and the Mission of the Goose: Poems and Prayers from South India by Appayya Dīksita, Nīlakantha Dīksita, Vedānta Deśika*, New York: New York University Press and JJC Foundation

Brunner, H., Oberhammer, G. and Padoux, A. (eds) (2004) *Tāntrikābhidhānakośa 2*, Vienna: Österreichischen Akademie der Wissenschaften

Brzezinski, J.K. (trans.) (2015) *Yoga-Taraṅgiṇī: A Rare Commentary on Gorakṣa-śataka*, Delhi: Motilal Banarsidass

Bühnemann, G. (2008) *Tantric Forms of Gaṇeśa According to the Vidyārṇavatantra*, New Delhi: D.K. Printworld

Bühnemann, G. (2018) '*Nāga, Siddha* and Sage: Visions of Patañjali as an Authority on Yoga', in K. Baier, P.A. Maas and K. Preisendanz (eds), *Yoga in Transformation: Historical and Contemporary Perspectives*, Göttingen: Vienna University Press, pp. 575–622

Buoy, C. (1994) *Les Nātha-Yogin et les Upaniṣads*, Paris: Diffusion de Boccard

Chandramohan, P. (2008) *Garuḍa in Medieval Art and Mythology*, Delhi: Sharada Publishing House

Chandrasekhar, V. (2017) *A Memorial Lecture Series in honour of Sri TKV Desikachar | V Chandrasekhar | P12*, Chennai: Krishnamacharya Yoga Mandiram, available at www.youtube.com/watch?v=4Zohe7RKiAA (Accessed: 07 August 2018)

Chapple, C. and Kelly, E.P. (trans.) (1990) *The Yoga Sūtras of Patañjali*, Delhi: Sri Satguru

Chari, S.M.S. (1961) *Advaita and Viśiṣṭādvaita: A Study Based on Vedānta Deśika's Śatadūṣaṇī*, London: Asia Publishing House

Chari, S.M.S. (1994) *Vaiṣṇavism: Its Philosophy, Theology and Religious Discipline*, Delhi: Motilal Banarsidass

Chari, S.M.S. (1997) *Philosophy and Theistic Mysticism of the Āḷvārs*, Delhi: Motilal Banarsidass

Chari, S.M.S. (2004) *Fundamentals of Viśiṣṭādvaita Vedānta: A Study based on Vedānta Deśika's Tattva-muktā-Kalāpa*, 2nd edition, Delhi: Motilal Banarsidass

Chari, S.M.S. (2008) *The Philosophy of Viśiṣṭādvaita Vedānta: A Study Based on Vedānta Deśika's Adhikaraṇa-Sārāvalī*, Delhi: Motilal Banarsidass

Chari, S.M.S. (2011) *Indian Philosophical Systems: A Critical Review Based on Vedānta Deśika's Paramata-bhaṅga*, New Delhi: Munshiram Manoharlal

Chariar N.V.D. and Ayengar K.R. (trans.) (1973) *Hamsasandesa of Vedanta Desika*, Madras: Vedanta Desika Research Society

Charlton, D. (2016) 'The Guna in Practice', unpublished handout given to participants at Roy, R. *Support, Direction and Space in Prāṇāyāma*, St David's: St Non's Retreat Centre, 19–21 February

Chinmayananda, S. (trans.) (1970) *Talks on Sankara's Vivekachoodamani*, Mumbai: Central Chinmaya Mission Trust

Chinmayānanda, S. (trans.) (2001) *Discourses on Aṣṭāvakra Gītā*, Mumbai: Central Chinmaya Mission Trust

Choudary, D.K.K. (2014) *Śiva in Indian Art*, Delhi: Agam Kala Prakashan

Clooney, F.X. (2011) 'From Person to Person: A Study of Tradition in the Guruparaṃparāsāra of Vedānta Deśika's Śrīmat Rahasyatrayasāra', in F. Squarcini (ed.), *Boundaries, Dynamics and Construction of Traditions in South Asia*, London: Anthem Press, pp. 203–224

Clooney, F.X. and Nicholson, H. (2001) 'Vedānta Deśika's Īśvarapariccheda (Definition of the Lord) and the Hindu Argument about Ultimate Reality', in R.C. Neville (ed.), *Ultimate Realities*, Albany: State University of New York Press, pp. 95–124

Colas, G. (2010) 'Vaiṣṇava Saṃhitās', in K.A. Jacobsen (ed.), *Brill's Encyclopedia of Hinduism, vol. 2: Sacred Texts and Languages, Ritual Traditions, Arts, Concepts*, Leiden: Brill, pp. 153–167

Colas, G. (2011) 'Vaikhānasa', in K.A. Jacobsen (ed.), *Brill's Encyclopedia of Hinduism, vol. 3: Society, Religious Specialists, Religious Traditions, Philosophy*, Leiden: Brill, pp. 589–605

Connolly, P. (1992) *Vitalistic Thought in India*, Delhi: Sri Satguru

Connolly, P. (2007) *A Student's Guide to the History and Philosophy of Yoga*, London: Equinox

Connolly, P. (2019) *Understanding Religious Experience*, Sheffield: Equinox

Connolly, P. (2020) Pers. Com.

Coomaraswamy, A.K. (1942) 'Sarpabandha', *Journal of the American Oriental Society*, vol. 62, no. 4, pp. 341–342

Courtright, P.B. (1985) *Gaṇeśa: Lord of Obstacles, Lord of Beginnings*, Oxford: Oxford University Press

Cox, W. (2017) *Modes of Philology in Medieval South India*, Leiden: Brill

Cozad, L. (2004) *Sacred Snakes: Orthodox Images of Indian Snake Worship*, Aurora: Davies Group

Czyżykowski, R. (2018) 'The Problem of *Kuṇḍalinī* in the Context of Yogic Aspects of the Bengali Tantric Vaiṣṇava (Sahajiyā) Tradition', *Religions of South Asia*, vol. 12, no. 2, pp. 185–206

Daouk, M. (2019) 'Malek Daouk', in S. Oubrier and B. Viard (eds), *T.K.V. Desikachar:*

A Question of Transmission, Sainte Cécile les Vignes: Les Cahiers de Présence d'Espirit, pp. 35–42

Das, B. (trans.) (2005) *Śrī Nārada Pañcarātra of Śrī Kṛṣṇa Dvaipāyana Vyāsa*, Vrindaban: Rasbihari Lal & Sons

Dasa, A.G. (no date) *Thiru Urakam, Kanchipuram, Tamilnadu, India*, Available at www.facebook.com/media/set/?set=a.1386810768061115.1073741846.100001966163587&type=3) (Accessed: 07 March 2019)

Dasgupta, S. (1975) *Indian Philosophy Volume III: Principal Dualistic and Pluralistic Systems*, Delhi: Motilal Banarsidass

Datta, M. (2012) *Mythology and Iconography of Gaṇeśa (With Special Reference to the Purāṇas)*, Kolkata: Ramakrishna Mission Institute of Culture

De Michelis, E. (2004) *A History of Modern Yoga*, London: Continuum

Desikachar, K. (2005) *The Yoga of the Yogi: The Legacy of T Krishnamacharya*, Chennai: Krishnamacharya Yoga Mandiram

Desikachar, K. (2010) *Du feu dans le ventre, de la lumière dans le coeur: Étude des nadi-s, cakra-s et du langue secret du yoga*, Neuilly sur Seine: 167 bd Bineau, 29–31 Janvier

Desikachar, K. (2012) *Sun and Moon: The Path of Hatha Yoga*, Crawley: Crawley Town Football Club, 19–20 May

Desikachar, K. (trans.) (2016) *The Haṭhayogapradīpikā Jyotsnāyutā*, Chennai: Media Garuda

Desikachar, M. (2011) *La Respiration Qui Soigne: Le pranayama et ses applications dans le domaine de la santé. Un stage intensif avec Menaka Desikachar*, Neuilly sur Seine: 167 bd Bineau, 04-06 Mars

Desikachar, T.K.V. (1980) *Religiousness in Yoga: Lectures on Theory and Practice*, Lanham: University Press of America

Desikachar, T.K.V. (1982) *The Yoga of T. Krishnamacharya*, Madras: Krishnamacharya Yoga Mandiram

Desikachar, T.K.V. (1991) 'The Study of Yoga Rahasya: An Interview with T.K.V. Desikachar', *KYM Darśanam*, vol. 1, no. 1, Madras: Krishnamacharya Yoga Mandiram, pp. 16–19

Desikachar, T.K.V. (1993) 'Questions on T. Krishnamacharya Answered by T.K.V. Desikachar', *KYM Darśanam*, vol. 2, no. 3, Madras: Krishnamacharya Yoga Mandiram, pp. 8–12

Desikachar, T.K.V. (1994a) 'Śīrṣāsana as a Viparīta Karaṇī Mudrā', *KYM Darśanam*, February, Madras: Krishnamacharya Yoga Mandiram, pp. 7–14

Desikachar, T.K.V. (1994b) 'Yoga Makaranda', *KYM Darśanam*, February, Madras: Krishnamacharya Yoga Mandiram, pp. 3–6

Desikachar, T.K.V. (1995) *The Heart of Yoga*, Rochester: Inner Traditions International

Desikachar, T.K.V. (trans.) (1998) *Śrī Nāthamuni's Yogarahasya*, 1st edition, Chennai: Krishnamacharya Yoga Mandiram

Desikachar, T.K.V. (trans.) (2000) *Yogayājñavalkya Samhitā*, Chennai: Krishnamacharya Yoga Mandiram

Desikachar, T.K.V. (trans.) (2003) *Śrī Nāthamuni's Yoga Rahasya*, 2nd edition, Chennai: Krishnamacharya Yoga Mandiram

Desikachar, T.K.V. and Cravens, R.H. (1998) *Health, Healing and Beyond: Yoga and the Living Tradition of Krishnamacharya*, New York: Aperture Foundation

Desikachar, T.K.V. and Desikachar, K. (trans.) (2003) *Ādi Śaṅkara's Yoga Tārāvali*, Chennai: Krishnamacharya Yoga Mandiram

Devanandan, P.D. (1950) *The Concept of Māyā*, London: Lutterworth Press

Digambaji, S., Jha, P. and Sahay, G.S. (trans.) (2005) *Vasiṣṭha Saṃhitā (Yoga Kāṇḍa)*, 2nd edition, Lonavla: Kaivalyadhama

Divanji, P.C. (ed.) (1954) *Yoga-Yājñavalkya, BBRA Society Monograph No.3*, Bombay: Bombay Branch of the Royal Asiatic Society

Doniger-O'Flaherty, W. (1976) *The Origins of Evil in Hindu Mythology*, Berkeley: University of California Press

Dunsmuir, C.V. (2015) *The Technology of Breathing/Prāṇāyāma*, Cobham: Yoga Sp8ce, 07 June

Dvivedī, Ś. (ed.) (1983) *Tattvamuktākalāpa*, Ayodhya: Tattvamuktākalāpasaṅgha

Dvivedī, Ś. (ed.) (1986) *Śatadūṣaṇī*, vol. 3, Ayodhya: Tattvamuktākalāpasaṅgha

Dwivedī, Ā.V. (ed.) (2001) *Sātvata-Saṁhitā with Commentary by Alaśiṅga Bhaṭṭa*, Varanasi: Sampurnanand Sanskrit University

Emeneau, M.B. (1960) 'Nāgapaśa, Nāgabandha, Sarpabandha, and Related Words', *Bulletin of the Deccan College Research Institute*, vol. 20, no. 1/4, pp. 291–300

Ferguson, J. (1868) *Tree and Serpent Worship*, London: W.H. Allen and Co.

Feuerstein, G. (trans.) (1989) *The Yoga-Sūtra of Patañjali*, Rochester: Inner Traditions International

Feuerstein, G. (1997) *The Shambhala Encyclopedia of Yoga*, Boston: Shambhala

Feuerstein, G. (1998) *The Yoga Tradition*, Prescott: Hohm Press

Feuerstein, G. (2007) *Yoga Morality*, Prescott: Hohm Press

Flood, G. (2006) *The Tantric Body*, London: I.B. Tauris

Foulston, L. and Abbott, S. (2012) *Hindu Goddesses: Beliefs and Practices*, Eastbourne: Sussex Academic Press

Frazier, J. (2013) 'Colors', in K.A. Jacobsen (ed.), *Brill's Encyclopedia of Hinduism, vol. 5: Religious Symbols, Hinduism and Migration, Contemporary Communities Outside South Asia, Some Modern Groups and Teachers*, Leiden: Brill, pp. 7–13

Gächter, O. (1998) 'Evil and Suffering in Hinduism', *Anthropos*, vol. 93, pp. 393–403

Gambhīrānanda, S. (trans.) (1958) *Eight Upaniṣads*, vol. 2, 1st edition, Kolkata: Advaita Ashrama

Gambhīrānanda, S. (trans.) (1989) *Eight Upaniṣads*, vol. 1, 2nd edition, Kolkata: Advaita Ashrama

Gangadharan, N. (1972) *Garuḍa Purāṇa: A Study*, Varanasi: All India Kashiraj Trust

Gharote, M.L. and Bedekar, V.A. (trans.) (2010) *Bṛhadyogiyājñavalkyasmṛti (English Translation)*, 2nd edition, Lonavla: Kaivalyadhama S.M.Y.M Samiti

Gharote, M.L., Devnath, P. and Jha, V.K. (trans.) (2002) *Haṭharatnāvalī (A Treatise on*

Haṭhayoga) of Śrīnivāsayogī, Pune: Kaivalyadama S.M.Y.M. Samiti

Goldman, R.P. and Sutherland-Goldman, S.J. (2011) *Devavāṇīpraveśikā*, Delhi: Motilal Banarsidass

Gonda, J. (1977) *Medieval Religious Literature in Sanskrit: A History of Indian Literature* vol. 2, fasc. 1, Wiesbaden: Harrassowitz

Goodall, D. (2004) '*Kuṇḍalinī, kuṇḍalī, kuṇḍalikā* (ou *kuṭilā*)', in H. Brunner, G. Oberhammer and A. Padoux (eds), *Tāntrikābhidhānakośa 2*, Vienna: Österreichischen Akademie der Wissenschaften, p. 110

Govindācārya (ed.) (1953) *Śrī Pārameśvara Saṁhitā*, Srirangam: Kodaṇḍarāmasannidhi

Griffith, R.T.H. (trans.) (1897) *The Hymns of the Rigveda*, vol. 2, 2nd edition, Benares: E.J. Lazarus

Grimes, J. (trans.) (2004) *The Vivekacūḍāmaṇi of Śaṅkarācārya Bhagavatpāda*, Aldershot: Ashgate

Gupta, G.K. (2013) 'May Calamities Befall Us at Every Step: the Bhāgavata's Response to the Problem of Evil', in R.M. Gupta and K.R. Valpey (eds), *The Bhāgavata Purāṇa: Sacred Text and Living Tradition*, New York: Columbia University Press, pp. 63–75

Gupta, M.D. and Gupta, P. (no date) *Mother Vaishnavi*, New Delhi: Dreamland

Gupta, S. (trans.) (2000) *Lakṣmī Tantra: A Pāñcarātra Text*, Delhi: Motilal Banarsidass

Handa, O.C. (1992) *Śiva in Art: A Study of Śaiva Iconography and Miniatures*, New Delhi: Indus

Hardy, F. (1979) 'The Philosopher as Poet: A Study of Vedāntadeśika's 'Dehalīśastuti', *Journal of Indian Philosophy*, vol. 7, no. 3, pp. 277–325

Hariharānanda Āraṇya, S. (trans.) (1983) *Yoga Philosophy of Patañjali*, Albany: State University of New York Press

Harvey, P. (2011) *Introductory Haṭha Study Course*, Bristol: Yogāñjali Centre, 10–11 December

Harvey, P. (2013) *Introductory Study Course on the Bhagavad Gītā*, Bristol: Yogāñjali Centre, 12–13 April

Harvey, P. (2015a) *These five Kleśa surround the heart of every individual*, Available at www.yogastudies.org/category/cys-journal/sampradaya-posts/krishnamacharya-quotations/krishnamacharya-quotes-sutra/page/4 (Accessed: 21 August 2019)

Harvey, P. (2015b) *Haṭha Energetics Workshop*, Module 2, Weekend 2, Nailsworth, 04-05 July

Harvey, P. (2016) *Upaniṣad Mysticism Workshop*, Module 1, Nailsworth, 02-03 July

Harvey, P. (2017) Pers. Com. at Bhagavad Gītā: Yoga in Action, Gloucester: Churchdown Community College, 15 October

Harvey, P. (2018) *Sūtra Psychology Workshop: The Yoga Sūtra of Patañjali Chapter Two Sādhana Pādaḥ*, Module 2, Nailsworth, 10–11 March and 7–8 July

Harvey, P. (2020) Pers. Com.

Harvey, P. (no date) *Prāṇāyāma within Rāja Yoga and Haṭha Yoga*, available at https://

yogastudies.org/wp-content/uploads/Pr%C4%81%E1%B9%87%C4%81y%C4%81ma_within_R%C4%81ja_Yoga_and_Ha%E1%B9%ADha_Yoga.pdf (Accessed: 26 November 2020)

Hatley, S. (2013) 'Nābhi', in D. Goodall and M. Rastelli (eds), *Tāntrikābhidhānakośa 3*, Vienna: Österreichischen Akademie der Wissenschaften, pp. 283–285

Hatley, S. (forthcoming) 'Kuṇḍalinī', in *Encyclopedia of Indian Religions*, New York: Springer

Haughton-Woods, J. (trans.) (1914) *The Yoga-System of Patañjali*, Delhi: Motilal Banarsidass

Hayes, G.A. (2003) 'Metaphoric Worlds and Yoga in the Vaiṣṇava Sahajiyā Tantric Traditions of Medieval Bengal', in I. Whicher and D. Carpenter (eds), *Yoga: The Indian Tradition*, London: Routledge, pp. 162–184

Hayes, G.A. (2011) 'Sahajiyās', in K.A. Jacobsen (ed.), *Brill's Encyclopedia of Hinduism vol. 3: Society, Religious Specialists, Religious Traditions, Philosophy*, Leiden: Brill, pp. 507–513

Hersnack, P. (2018) *The Living Breath: An Art of Yoga*, Montpellier: Art of Yoga

Hersnack, P. (2019) 'Peter Hersnack (interviewed by Colette Ecuer)', in S. Oubrier and B. Viard (eds), *T.K.V. Desikachar: A Question of Transmission*, Sainte Cécile les Vignes: Les Cahiers de Présence d'Espirit, pp. 89–95

Hopkins, S.P. (2002) *Singing the Body of God: The Hymns of Vedāntadeśika in Their South Indian Tradition*, Oxford: Oxford University Press

Hopkins, S.P. (2007) *An Ornament for Jewels: Love Poems for the Lord of Gods by Vedāntadeśika*, Oxford: Oxford University Press

Hopkins, S.P. (2012) 'Vedāntadeśika', in K.A. Jacobsen (ed.), *Brill's Encyclopedia of Hinduism, vol. 4: Historical Perspectives, Poets, Teachers and Saints, Relation to other Religions and Traditions, Hinduism and Contemporary Issues*, Leiden: Brill, pp. 462–469

Hopkins, S.P. (trans.) (2016) *The Flight of Love: A Messenger Poem of Medieval South India by Veṅkaṭanātha*, Oxford: Oxford University Press

Hume, R.E. (trans.) (1931) *The Thirteen Principal Upanishads*, 2nd edition, New Delhi: Oxford University Press

Iyengar, D.K. (trans.) (1979) *Saṅkalpasūryodaya*, Mysore: Sri Brahmatantra Svatantra Parakala Mutt

Iyengar, M.R.R. (trans.) (1977) *Sankalpa Suryodayam: A Sanskrit Allegorical Drama in Ten Acts by Vedanta Desika*, Madras: Vedanta Desika Research Society

Iyer, L.V.R. (ed.) (1907) *The Subhasita Nivi of Srimad Vedanta Desikar with the Commentaries of Sreenivasa Suri and Narakesari*, Madras: The Oriental Press

Iyer, N.C. (ed.) (1987) *The Bṛhat Saṁhitā of Varāha Mihira*, 2nd edition, Delhi: Sri Satguru

Jackson, W.J. (2011) 'Smārta', in K.A. Jacobsen (ed.), *Brill's Encyclopedia of Hinduism vol. 3: Society, Religious Specialists, Religious Traditions, Philosophy*, Leiden: Brill, pp. 546–555

Jacobsen, K.A. (2011) 'Patañjala Yoga', in K.A. Jacobsen (ed.), *Brill's Encyclopedia of Hinduism, vol. 3: Society, Religious Specialists, Religious Traditions, Philosophy*, Leiden: Brill, pp. 745–759

Jagannathan, S. and Krishna, N. (1992) *Ganesha: The Auspicious ... The Beginning*, Bombay: Vakils, Feffer & Simons

Jayaraman, M. (trans.) (2013) *Aṣṭāṅga-Yoga-Nirūpaṇam & Nādānusandhāna-Pañcakam*, Chennai: Krishnamacharya Yoga Mandiram

Jayaraman, M. (trans.) (2015) *Yoga-Yājñavalkya-Saṁhitā: The Yoga Treatise of Yājñavalkya*, 2nd edition, Chennai: Krishnamacharya Yoga Mandiram

Jayaraman, M. (2018) 'Unique Insights from Rājayogatarala of Rāmasvāmipaṇḍita: An Unpublished Commentary on Yogatārāvalī Ascribed to Śaṅkarācārya', *International Journal of Yoga Philosophy, Psychology and Parapsychology* (Official Publication of the Swami Vivekananda Yoga Anusandhana Samsthana University), vol. 6, no. 2, pp. 66–73, July-December

Johar, N. (2017) *A Memorial Lecture Series in Honour of Sri TKV Desikachar | Speaker Shri Navtej Johar | P8*, Chennai: Krishnamacharya Yoga Mandiram, available at www.youtube.com/watch?v=SOavUkZ6GnY (Accessed: 08 August 2018)

Joshi, K.L. (ed.) (2007) *Matsya Mahāpurāṇa*, vol. 1, Delhi: Parimal Publications

Kaminoff, L. (2012) 'Leslie Kaminoff Interviews T.K.V. Desikachar in Madras, October 1992', *Nāmarūpa*, no. 15, pp. 20–28

Kaminoff, L. (2016) *Breath-Centered Practice in the Tradition of Krishnamacharya: Demystifying the Bandhas*, Cambridge: Camyoga, 16 September

Kaminoff, L. (2017) *The History and Tradition of Krishnamacharya and Desikachar and Demystifying the bandhas*, Cambridge: Camyoga, 02 December

Kathirasan, K. (2018) *The Advaita Vedānta of Śiva Saṁhitā: First Ever Vedāntic Exposition*, Delhi: Motilal Banarsidass

Kern, H. (ed.) (1865) *The Bṛhat Sañhita' of Vara'ha-Mihira*, Calcutta: Asiatic Society of Bengal

Keshavadas, S.S. (1988) *Lord Ganesha*, Oakland: Vishwa Dharma Publications

Khecaranatha, S. (2017) *The Three Phases of Sadhana*, available at embodiedphilosophy.courses/blog/three-phases-of-sadhana (Accessed: 12 July 2018)

Kinsley, D.R. (1986) *Hindu Goddesses: Visions of the Divine Feminine in the Hindu Religious Tradition*, Berkeley: University of California Press

Kochhar, R. (2010) 'Rāhu and Ketu in Mythological and Astronomological Contexts', *Indian Journal of History of Science*, vol. 45, no. 2, pp. 287–297

Krishna, N. (1980) *The Art and Iconography of Vishnu-Narayana*, Bombay: D.B Taraporevala Sons & Co.

Krishnamacharya Healing and Yoga Foundation (no date) *The Tradition*, Available at http://khyf.net/the-tradition (Accessed: 20 February 2020)

Krishnamacharya, T. (1984) 'Yoga of Sri Krishnamacharya', *Yoga Review (Quarterly Journal of the Indian Academy of Yoga, Varanasi)*, vol. 4, nos.3&4, p. 75

Krishnamacharya, T. (2001) *Yogāñjalisāram*, 4th edition, Chennai: Krishnamacharya

Yoga Mandiram
Krishnamacharya, T. (2011) *Yoga-Makaranda, The Nectar of Yoga, Part One*, 2nd edition, Chennai: Media Garuda
Krishnamacharya, V. (ed.) (1948a) *Saṁkalpasūryodaya of S'rī Veṅkaṭanātha with the commentaries Prabhāvilāsa of Ahobala and Prabhāvalī of Nṛsiṁharāja, Part 1, Acts 1-5*, Madras: The Adyar Library
Krishnamacharya, V. (ed.) (1948b) *Saṁkalpasūryodaya of S'rī Veṅkaṭanātha with the commentaries Prabhāvilāsa of Ahobala and Prabhāvalī of Nṛsiṁharāja, Part 2, Acts 6-10*, Madras: The Adyar Library
Krishnamacharya Yoga Mandiram (2006) *TKV Desikachar: A Tribute*, Chennai: Krishnamacharya Yoga Mandiram
Krishnamacharya Yoga Mandiram (ed.) (2007) *Mantra Mālā*, Chennai: Krishnamacharya Yoga Mandiram
Krishnan, Y. (1999) *Gaṇeśa: Unravelling an Enigma*, Delhi: Motilal Banarsidass
Krishnaswami, K.R. (trans.) (2005) *Three Great Epic Creations of Sri Vedantha Desika*, Bangalore: A&K Prakashana
Krishnaswami, K.R. (2007) *Sathyāgāla: Abeethisthava*, Bangalore: A&K Prakashana
Krishnaswami, K.R. (trans.) (2012a) *Sri Vedantha Desikar's Chillarei Rahasyangal*, vol. 1, Bangalore: A&K Prakashana
Krishnaswami, K.R. (trans.) (2012b) *Sri Vedantha Desikar's Chillarei Rahasyangal*, vol. 2, Bangalore: A&K Prakashana
Krishnaswami, K.R. (trans.) (2013a) *Sri Vedantha Desikar's Chillarei Rahasyangal*, vol. 3, Bangalore: A&K Prakashana
Krishnaswami, K.R. (2013b) *The Unique Power of Sudharshana-Naarasimha*, Bangalore: A&K Prakashana
Kṛṣṇāprapannācārya and Govindācārya (eds) (2000) *Śrīmadgītārthasaṅgraḥ Śrīvedāntadeśikānugṛhītaḥ Gītārthasaṅgraharakṣāsaṁvalitaḥ*, Delhi: Yatirājaprakāśanam Śrīmuktinātha Pīṭha Veda Vidyāśramaḥ
Krusche, H. (2019) 'Hellfried Krusche', in S. Oubrier and B. Viard (eds), *T.K.V. Desikachar: A Question of Transmission*, Sainte Cécile les Vignes: Les Cahiers de Présence d'Espirit, pp. 59–67
Kumar, P.P. (1997) *The Goddess Lakṣmī: The Divine Consort in South Indian Vaiṣṇava Tradition*, Atlanta: Scholars Press
Kumar, P.P. (2005) 'The Sāṃkhya-Yoga Influence on Śrīvaiṣṇava Philosophy with Special Reference to the Pāñcarātra System', in K.A. Jacobsen (ed.), *Theory and Practice of Yoga: Essays in Honour of Gerald James Larson*, Leiden: Brill, pp. 129–142
Kumar, P.P. (2012) 'Yāmunācārya', in K.A. Jacobsen (ed.), *Brill's Encyclopedia of Hinduism, vol. 4: Historical Perspectives, Poets, Teachers and Saints, Relation to other Religions and Traditions, Hinduism and Contemporary Issues*, Leiden: Brill, pp. 470–475
Kundalini Research Project (no date) *History of Kundalini*, available at www.kundaliniresearchproject.net/resources/kundalini/history (Accessed: 21

August 2019)
Kuvalayananda, S. and Kokaje, R. (eds) (2010) *The Bṛhadyogiyājñavalkyasmṛti*, 3rd edition, Poona: Kaivalyadhama S.M.Y.M. Samiti
Kuvalayānanda, S. and Shukla, S.A. (trans.) (2006) *Gorakṣaśatakam*, Lonavla: Kaivalyadhama S.M.Y.M. Samiti
Lad, V.D. (2002) *Textbook of Ayurveda, Volume One: Fundamental Principles of Ayurveda*, Albuquerque: The Ayurvedic Press
Lahiri, A.K. (1984) *Vedic Vṛtra*, Delhi: Motilal Banarsidass
Lakshmithathachar, M.A. and Varadachari, V. (trans.) (2009) *Īśvarasaṁhitā: Critically Edited and Translated in Five Volumes*, New Delhi and Delhi: Indira Gandhi National Centre for the Arts and Motilal Banarsidass
Lakshmithathachar, M.A. (2018) Pers. Com. (Meeting in Melkote), 05 December
Lakṣmīnṛsiṁhācārya, K. (ed.) (1940) *Adhikaraṇasārāvaliḥ*, Srirangam: Sri Ahobila Mutt
Lal, L. (1991) *Ganesha Beyond the Form*, Bombay: IBH Publishers
Lamb, R. (2011) 'Rāmānandīs', in K.A. Jacobsen (ed.), *Brill's Encyclopedia of Hinduism, vol. 3: Society, Religious Specialists, Religious Traditions, Philosophy*, Leiden: Brill, pp. 478–488
Larson, G.J. and Bhattacharya, R.S. (2008) *Encyclopedia of Indian Philosophies, vol. XII, Yoga: India's Philosophy of Meditation*, Delhi: Motilal Banarsidass
Laxmi, R. (2008) *Saṅkalpasūryodaya: A Literary Analysis*, Delhi: Sharada Publishing House
Lester, R.C. (1976) *Rāmānuja on the Yoga*, Madras: Adyar Library and Research Centre
Lipner, J.J. (1986) *The Face of Truth*, Albany: State University of New York Press
Lorin, F. (2018) Pers. Com.
Lorin, F. (2019) 'François Lorin', in S. Oubrier and B. Viard (eds), *T.K.V. Desikachar: A Question of Transmission*, Sainte Cécile les Vignes: Les Cahiers de Présence d'Espirit, pp. 49–58
Macdonell, A.A. (2001) *A Practical Sanskrit Dictionary*, Delhi: Winsome Books India
Maheshananda, S. and Sharma, B.R. (2012) *A Critical Edition of Jyotsnā (Brahmānanda's Commentary on Haṭhapradīpikā)*, Lonavla: Kaivalyadhama S.M.Y.M Samiti
Mallinson, J. (trans.) (2004) *The Gheranda Samhita: The Original Sanskrit and An English Translation*, Woodstock: YogaVidya.com
Mallinson, J. (2005) 'Rāmānandī Tyāgīs and Haṭha Yoga', *Journal of Vaishnava Studies*, vol. 14, no. 1, pp. 107–121
Mallinson, J. (trans.) (2007a) *The Khecarīvidyā of Ādinātha: A Critical Edition and Annotated Translation of an Early Text of Haṭhayoga*, London: Routledge
Mallinson, J. (trans.) (2007b) *The Shiva Samhita: A Critical Edition and An English Translation*, Woodstock: YogaVidya.com
Mallinson, J. (2011) '*Haṭha Yoga*', in K.A. Jacobsen (ed.), *Brill's Encyclopedia of Hinduism, vol. 3: Society, Religious Specialists, Religious Traditions, Philosophy*,

Leiden: Brill, pp. 770–781
Mallinson, J. (2014) '*Haṭhayoga's* Philosophy: A Fortuitous Union of Non-Dualities', *Journal of Indian Philosophy*, vol. 42, pp. 225–247
Mallinson, J. (2020) 'The *Amṛtasiddhi: Haṭhayoga's* Tantric Buddhist Source Text', in D. Goodall, S. Hatley, H. Isaacson and S.Raman (eds), *Śaivism and the Tantric Traditions: Essays in Honour of Alexis G.J.S. Sanderson*, Leiden: Brill, pp. 409–425
Mallinson, J. and Singleton, M. (2017) *Roots of Yoga*, UK: Penguin
Maréchal, C. (1989) 'Enseignments', *Viniyoga*, Decembre, no. 24, pp. 40–51
Maréchal, C. (2019) 'Claude Marechal', in S. Oubrier and B. Viard (eds), *T.K.V. Desikachar: A Question of Transmission*, Sainte Cécile les Vignes: Les Cahiers de Présence d'Espirit, pp. 17–26
Maréchal, C. (no date) *Teachings*, available at http://yogaanatomy.org/wp-content/uploads/2015/03/Claude-Marechal-Teachings.pdf (Accessed: 03 October 2017)
Margherita, M. (2019) 'Marina Margherita', in S. Oubrier and B. Viard (eds), *T.K.V. Desikachar: A Question of Transmission*, Sainte Cécile les Vignes: Les Cahiers de Présence d'Espirit, pp. 69–81
Markel, S. (1990) 'The Imagery and Iconographic Development of the Indian Planetary Deities Rāhu and Ketu', *South Asian Studies*, vol. 6, no. 1, pp. 9–26
Martin-Dubost, P. (1997) *Gaṇeśa: The Enchanter of the Three Worlds*, Mumbai: Franco-Indian Research
Matchett, F. (1986) 'The Taming of Kāliya: A Comparison of the Harivaṃśa, Viṣṇu-Purāṇa and Bhāgavata-Purāṇa Versions', *Religion*, vol. 16, pp. 115–133
Matsubara, M. (1994) *Pāñcarātra Saṃhitās & Early Vaiṣṇava Theology*, Delhi: Motilal Banarsidass
Mehta, G. (2006) *Eternal Ganesha from Birth to Rebirth*, London: Thames & Hudson
Mohan, A.G. (1993) *Yoga for Body, Breath, and Mind*, Portland and Los Angeles: Rudra Press and International Association of Yoga Therapists
Mohan, A.G. (2014) *The Legacy and the Teachings of Sri T. Krishnamacharya: Lecture and Q&A*, Birmingham: Singing Tree Conference Centre, 04 June
Mohan, A.G. (2015) *A.G. Mohan and Indra Mohan: Yogic Mindfulness Weekend*, Glasgow: Kinning Park Centre, 12–13 September
Mohan, A.G. (2018a) *A.G. Mohan and Indra Mohan: Svastha Yoga in Glasgow*, Glasgow: Kinning Park Centre, 25–26 August
Mohan, A.G. (2018b) Pers. Com., Glasgow: Kinning Park Centre, 25 August
Mohan, A.G. (no date a) *Spirituality in Sexuality: Is this Krishnamacharya's Teaching?* Available at https://www.youtube.com/watch?v=F1HLVVK468E (Accessed: 07 July 2015)
Mohan, A.G. (trans.) (no date b) *Yoga Yajnavalkya*, 1st edition, Madras: Ganesh & Co.
Mohan, A.G. and Mohan, G. (2010) *Krishnamacharya: His Life and Teachings*, Boston: Shambhala

Mohan, A.G. and Mohan, G. (trans.) (2013) *Yoga Yājñavalkya*, 2nd edition, Chennai: Svastha Yoga

Mohan, A.G. and Mohan, G. (2015) *Yoga Reminder*, Chennai: Svastha Yoga

Mohan, A.G. and Mohan, G. (trans.) (2017) *Haṭha Yoga Pradīpikā: Translation with Notes from Krishnamacharya*, Chennai: Svastha Yoga

Mohan, A.G. and Mohan, I. (2004) *Yoga Therapy: A Guide to the Therapeutic Use of Yoga and Ayurveda for Health and Fitness*, Boston: Shambhala

Mohan, A.G., Mohan, I. and Mohan, G. (2006) *Yoga and Ayurveda for Health and Healing*, London: The Special Yoga Centre, 29–30 July

Mohanty, A., Vaishnavi, P., Jana, P., Majumdar, A., Ahmed, A., Goswami, T. and Sahay, R.R. (2016) 'Nrityabodha: Towards Understanding Indian Classical Dance Using a Deep Learning Approach', *Signal Processing: Image Communication*, vol. 47, pp. 529–548

Monier-Williams, M. (1899) *A Sanskrit English Dictionary*, Delhi: Motilal Banarsidass

Mookerjee, A. (1986) *Kundalini: The Arousal of the Inner Energy*, 3rd edition, Rochester: Destiny Books

Moors, F. (trans.) (2012) *Liberating Isolation: The Yogasūtra of Patañjali*, Chennai: Media Garuda

Motilal Banarsidass (eds) (1951) *The Linga-Purāṇa: Part 1*, Delhi: Motilal Banarsidass

Nagar, S.L. (1992) *Garuda: The Celestial Bird*, Delhi: Book India Publishing

Nagar, S.L. (1994) *Śiva in Art, Literature and Thought*, New Delhi: Indus Publishing

Nagarajan, K.S. (trans.) (1972) *Vedanta Desika's Subhashithanivi*, Madras: Vedanta Desika Research Society

Narasimhachar, S. (ed.) (1940) *Tattvamuktākalāpa and Sarvārthasiddhi with the commentaries of Ānandadāyinī and Bhāvaprakāśa*, vol. 2, Mysore: University of Mysore Oriental Library Publications

Narasimhan, U. (trans.) (2009) *Godha Stuti of Swami Vedanta Desika: Word to Word Meaning and Notes in English*, Bangalore: published by the author

Narasimharāghavācāriyar, U.V.V.S.T. (ed.) (no date) *Śrīmad Bhagavad-Gītā: Gītā Sāram, Part 2, Chapter 7–12*, Chennai: TCN Trust

Nārāyaṇācārya, V. (ed.) (1979) *Paramatabhaṅgaḥ, Part I, with Deśikāśaya Prakāśa (Commentary)*, Madras: Elango Achukoodam

Nārāyaṇācārya, V. (ed.) (1982) *Sri Nigamānta Mahādesika's Paramata-Bhaṅgam, Part II, with Desikāsaya Prakāsa (Commentary)*, Madras: Elango Achukoodam

Narayanan, V. (2008) *The Epistemology of Viśiṣṭādvaita: A Study Based on the Nyāyapariśuddhi of Vedānta Deśika*, New Delhi: Munshiram Manoharlal

Narayanan, V. (2011) 'Śrīvaiṣṇavism', in K.A. Jacobsen (ed.), *Brill's Encyclopedia of Hinduism, vol. 3: Society, Religious Specialists, Religious Traditions, Philosophy*, Leiden: Brill, pp. 556–573

Neevel, W.G. (1977) *Yāmuna's Vedānta and Pāñcarātra: Integrating the Classical and the Popular*, Missoula: Scholars Press

Nevrin, K. (2005) 'Krishnamacharya's Viniyoga: On Modern Yoga and Sri

Vaishnavism', *Journal of Vaishnava Studies*, vol. 14, no. 1, pp. 65–93

Nicolas, M. (2019) 'Michel Nicolas', in S. Oubrier and B. Viard (eds), *T.K.V. Desikachar: A Question of Transmission*, Sainte Cécile les Vignes: Les Cahiers de Présence d'Espirit, pp. 197–201

Niranjanananda Saraswati, S. (1994) *Prana Pranayama Prana Vidya*, Munger: Bihar School of Yoga

Oberhammer, G. (1977–1978) 'An Unknown Source in Śaṅkara's Refutation of the Pāñcarātra', *Annals of the Bhandarkar Oriental Research Institute*, vol. 58/59, pp. 221–233

Oberhammer, G. and Rastelli, M. (eds) (2007) *On the Mutual Influences and Relationship of Viśiṣṭādvaita Vedānta and Pāñcarātra*, Vienna: Österreichischen Akademie der Wissenschaften

Oldham, C.F. (1905) *The Sun and the Serpent: A Contribution to the History of Serpent-Worship*, London: Archibald Constable & Co

Padmanabhan, S. and Sampath, R.N. (eds) (1974) *Padma Samhita*, Part 1, Madras: Pancaratra Parisodhana Parisad

Padoux, A. (1990) *Vāc: The Concept of the Word in Selected Hindu Tantras*, Delhi: Sri Satguru

Pandurang, S. (ed.) (1989) *Atharvaveda Samhita with the Commentary of Sayanacharya*, vol. 2, Varanasi: Krishnadas Academy

Pandurangi, K.T. (ed.) (1998) *Śrīmad Bhāgavatam*, vol. 2, Bangalore: Dvaita Vedanta Studies and Research Foundation

Pandurangi, K.T. (ed.) (2000) *Śrīmad Bhāgavatam*, vol. 4, Bangalore: Dvaita Vedanta Studies and Research Foundation

Parakāla Math (no date a) *Acharya Lineage*, available at www.parakalamatham.org/Sri-Matham/Acharya-Lineage (Accessed: 10 July 2019)

Parakāla Math (no date b) *130th Thirunakshatra Celebrations of Srimadh Abhinava Ranganatha Brahmatantra Parakala Swami*, available at www.parakalamatham.org/Events/130th-Thirunakshatra-Celebrations-of-Srimadh-Abhinava-Ranganatha-Brahmatantra-Parakala-Swami (Accessed: 06 February 2019)

Parthasarathy, A. (1983) 'Subramanya: Karthikeya', in S. Nityanand (ed.), *Symbolism in Hinduism*, Mumbai: Central Chinmaya Mission Trust, pp. 148–151

Parthasarathy, V. (2014) *Garuḍa Past and Present: A Bird's Eye View of South Indian Traditions*, Bangalore: Navbharath Enterprises

Pattanaik, D. (1997) *Shiva: An Introduction*, Mumbai: Vakils, Feffer and Simons

Pattanaik, D. (2002) *Lakshmi: The Goddess of Wealth and Fortune*, Mumbai: Vakils, Feffer and Simons

Pattanaik, D. (2011) *7 Secrets of Shiva*, Chennai: Westland

Phillips, S.H. and Potter K.H. (2017) *Encyclopedia of Indian Philosophies, vol. XX, Viśiṣṭādvaita Vedānta*, Delhi: Motilal Banarsidass

Prabhupāda, A.C.B.S. (trans.) (1982a) *Śrīmad Bhāgavatam Third Canto 'The Status*

Quo', Part Four: Chapters 25–33, Manila: Bhaktivedanta Book Trust

Prabhupāda, A.C.B.S. (trans.) (1982b) *Śrīmad Bhāgavatam Fifth Canto 'The Creative Impetus', Part Two: Chapters 14–26*, Manila: Bhaktivedanta Book Trust

Prakash-Sarasvati, S.S. and Vidyalankar, S. (trans.) (1984) *Ṛgveda Samhitā*, vol. 12, New Delhi: Veda Pratishthana

Raghavan, S.S., Lakshmi-Kumari, M.S. and Narasimhachary, M. (trans.) (2013) *Śrī Vedānta Deśika's Stotras (With English Translation)*, 3rd edition, Madras: Sripad Trust

Raghavan, V.K.S.N. (1979) *History of Viśiṣṭādvaita Literature*, Delhi: Ajanta Publications

Raghavan, V.K.S.N. (2017–2018) 'Contribution of Śrī Ahobila Math for the Propagation of Rāmānuja's Philosophy', in T. Boyd and T. Narayanan-Kutty (eds), *Śrī Rāmānuja's Sahasrābdi Volume (Brahmavidyā), vols.81–82, The Adyar Library Bulletin*, Chennai: Adyar Library and Research Society, pp. 519–552

Raghunathan, N. (trans.) (2018) *Śrīmad Rahasyatrayasāram of Śrī Vedānta Deśika*, Madras: The Samskrta Academy

Raju, P.T. (1985) *Structural Depths of Indian Thought*, New Delhi: South Asian Publishers

Rāmānujācārya, M.D. (ed.) (1916) *Ahirbudhnya Saṃhitā of the Pāncarātra Āgama*, Madras: Adyar Library

Ramanuja.org (no date) *Sribhashya Class: About the Instructor*, available at https://ramanuja.org/sri/SribhashyaClass/Teacher (Accessed: 23 July 2019)

Ramaswami, S. (2007) 'My studies with Śrī Krishnamacharya', *Nāmarūpa*, no. 6, pp. 13–23

Ramaswami, S. (2008) '*M6.5 Nadis*', unpublished handout on a teacher training course with Srivatsa Ramaswami, Los Angeles: Loyola Marymount University

Ramaswami, S. (2014) *My overview of Krishnamacharya's Yoga: Workshop with Ramaswami*, London: Jivamukti Yoga, Saturday 31 May

Ramaswami, S. (2020) *Yogayājñavalkya*, detailed notes taken by Dr Karin Horowitz when attending an online course, Loyola Marymount University, 30 July to 07 August

Ramaswami, S. (no date) *Huge Variety of Krishnamacharya's Teachings: Interview with Srivatsa Ramaswami*, available at wildyogi.info/en/issue/huge-variety-krishnamacharyas-teachings-interview-srivatsa-ramaswami (Accessed: 11 July 2018)

Ram-Prasad, C. (2010) 'Avidyā', in K.A. Jacobsen (ed.), *Brill's Encyclopedia of Hinduism, vol. 2: Sacred Texts and Languages, Ritual Traditions, Arts, Concepts*, Leiden: Brill, pp. 706–709

Rangachar, M.E. (2000) *The Philosophy of Viśiṣṭādvaita: As Expounded by Śrī Vedānta Deśika in the Nyāya-siddhāñjana*, Bangalore: Sri Nithyananda Printers

Rangachar, N.S.A. (trans.) (2009) *English Rendering of Eleven Rahasya Granthas of Sri Vedanta Desika*, Bangalore: Published by the author

Rangachari, R. (ed.) (1974) *Vedanta Desika's Dramidopanishad Tatparya Ratnavali and Sara*, Madras: Vedanta Desika Research Society

Rangacharya, N.S.A. (2004) *Essence of Srimad Rahasyatraya Saram of Sri Nigamanta Maha Desikar*, Bangalore: Published by the author

Rao, P.V.L.N. (2008) *Kanchipuram: Land of Legends, Saints and Temples*, New Delhi: Readworthy

Rao, S.K.R. (2005a) *The Āgama Encyclopaedia, vol. 3: Vaikhānasa Āgamas*, 2nd edition, Delhi: Sri Satguru

Rao, S.K.R. (2005b) *The Compendium on Gaṇeśa*, 2nd edition, Delhi: Sri Satguru

Rastelli, M. (2011) 'Pāñcarātra', in K.A. Jacobsen (ed.), *Brill's Encyclopedia of Hinduism, vol. 3: Society, Religious Specialists, Religious Traditions, Philosophy*, Leiden: Brill, pp. 444–457

Rastelli, M. (2018) 'Yoga in the Daily Routine of the Pāñcarātrins', in K. Baier, P.A. Maas and K. Preisendanz (eds), *Yoga in Transformation: Historical and Contemporary Perspectives*, Göttingen: Vienna University Press, pp. 223–257

Rastelli, M. (forthcoming) 'Nādīs, Prāṇās and Prāṇāyāma: a Yogic Text Crossing the Boundaries of Tradition', in P.S. Fillozat and D. Goodall (eds), *Mélangues à la mémoire de N. Ramachandra Bhatt*

Rengarajan, T. (2004) *Dictionary of Vaiṣṇavism*, Delhi: Eastern Book Linkers

Rhodes, C. (2012) *Invoking Lakshmi: The Goddess of Wealth in Song and Ceremony*, New Delhi: Dev Publishers & Distributors

Rodrigues, H.P. (2009) 'Asuras and Daityas', in K.A. Jacobsen (ed.), *Brill's Encyclopedia of Hinduism*, vol. 1, Leiden: Brill, pp. 473–478

Roy, R. (2013) *Taittiriya Upanisad Study Retreat*, Hampshire: Park Place Pastoral Centre, 08–10 March

Roy, R. (2016) *St Nons Retreat, Feb 2016: Support, Direction and Space in Pranayama*, St David's: St Non's Retreat Centre, 19–21 February

Roy, R. and Charlton, D. (2019) *Embodying the Yoga Sūtra: Support, Direction, Space*, London: Pinter & Martin

Rukmani, T.S. (trans.) (1999) *Yogavārttika of Vijñānabhikṣu, vol. 4: Kaivalyapāda*, New Delhi: Munshiram Manoharlal

Rukmani, T.S. (trans.) (2001) *Yogasūtrabhāṣyavivaraṇa of Śaṅkara, vol. 2: Vibhūtipādaḥ and Kaivalyapādaḥ*, New Delhi: Munshiram Manoharlal

Ryan, S. (2004) *Association for Yoga Studies Stage Two Foundation Course*, London: Kagyu Samye Dzong

Sahi, J. (1980) *The Child and the Serpent: Reflections on Popular Indian Symbols*, London: Penguin

Saṁpatkumārācāryaḥ, A. (ed.) (1940) *Śrīmadvedāntadeśikagranthamālāyāṁ: Mīmāṁsāpādukā, Seśvaramīmāṁsā, Nyāyapariśuddhḥi, Nyāyasiddhāñjanaṁ ca*, Kañjīvaram: Granthamālākāryālayaḥ

Saṁpatkumārācāryaḥ, A. (ed.) (1941) *Śrīmadvedāntadeśikagranthamālāyāṁ - Tattvaṭīkā - Nikṣeparakṣā - Saccaritrarakṣā - Śrīpāñcarātrarakṣā - Savyākhyāna*

Bhūgolanirṇayādikam, Kañjīvaram: Granthamālākāryālayaḥ

Sanderson, A. (2001) 'History Through Textual Criticism in the Study of Śaivism, the Pāñcarātra and the Buddhist Yoginītantras', in F. Grimal (ed.), *Les Sources et Le Temps, Sources and Time, A colloquium 11–13 January 1997*, Pondicherry: Institut Français de Pondichéry, pp. 1–47

Sanderson, A. (2009) 'The Śaiva Age: The Rise and Dominance of Śaivism During the Early Medieval Period', in S. Einoo (ed.), *Genesis and Development of Tantrism*, Tokyo: University of Tokyo Institute of Oriental Culture, pp. 41–350

Sannella, L. (1992) *The Kundalini Experience*, 2nd edition, Lower Lake: Integral Publishing

Sargeant, W. (ed.) (1994) *The Bhagavad Gītā*, Albany: State University of New York Press

Sastri, A.M. (ed.) (1920) *The Yoga Upaniṣad-s with the Commentary of Śrī Upaniṣad-Brahmayogin*, Madras: Adyar Library and Research Centre

Śāstri, K.S. (ed.) (1938) *The Yogayājñavalkya*, Trivandrum: Government Press

Śāstri, S.S.A.S.T.S.P.S.M.M.R.M. (ed.) (1901) *Nyāyasiddhāñjanam by Venkaṭanātha Deśika*, Benares: Sanskrit College

Sathakopan, O.K.S.V. (trans.) (no date a) *Aruttha Panchakam*, available at www.sadagopan.org/pdfuploads/Arutha Panchakam.pdf (Accessed: 07 August 2018)

Sathakopan, O.K.S.V. (trans.) (no date b) *SvAmi DeSikan's dramiDopanishat sAraH*, available at www.sadagopan.org/pdfuploads/Dramidopanishat Saram.pdf (Accessed: 07 August 2018)

Sathakopan, O.K.S.V. (trans.) (no date c) *Swami Desikan's Aahaara Niyamam*, available at www.sadagopan.org/pdfuploads/Ahara Niyamam.pdf (Accessed: 07 August 2018)

Sathakopan, O.K.S.V. (trans.) (no date d) *Swami Desikan's Adhikara Sangraham*, available at www.sadagopan.org/pdfuploads/Adhikara Sangraham.pdf (Accessed: 07 August 2018)

Sathakopan, O.K.S.V. (trans.) (no date e) *Swami Desikan's Amruta Ranjani*, available at www.sadagopan.org/pdfuploads/Amruta Ranjani.pdf (Accessed: 07 August 2018)

Sathakopan, O.K.S.V. (trans.) (no date f) *Swami Desikan's Charama Śloka Churukku*, available at www.sadagopan.org/pdfuploads/Charamasloka Churukku.pdf (Accessed: 07 August 2018)

Sathakopan, O.K.S.V. (trans.) (no date g) *Swami Desikan's Dhvaya Churukku*, available at www.sadagopan.org/pdfuploads/Dvaya Churukku.pdf (Accessed: 07 August 2018)

Sathakopan, O.K.S.V. (trans.) (no date h) *Swami Desikan's Thirumanthira Churukku*, available at www.sadagopan.org/pdfuploads/Thirumantra Churukku.pdf (Accessed: 07 August 2018)

Sathakopan, O.K.S.V. (trans.) (no date i) *Swamy Desikan's Adaikkalapaththu*, available at www.sadagopan.org/pdfuploads/Adaikalapathu.pdf (Accessed: 07 August

2018)

Sathakopan, O.K.S.V. (trans.) (no date j) *Swamy Desikan's Amruta SvAdhini*, available at www.sadagopan.org/pdfuploads/Amruta Svadhini.pdf (Accessed: 07 August 2018)

Sathakopan, O.K.S.V. (trans.) (no date k) *Swamy Desikan's abhayapradAna SAram*, available at www.sadagopan.org/pdfuploads/Abhaya Pradhana Saram - ASR.pdf (Accessed: 07 August 2018)

Sathakopan, O.K.S.V. (trans.) (no date l) *Swamy Desikan's Geethaarta Sangraham*, available at www.sadagopan.org/pdfuploads/Gitartha Sangraham.pdf (Accessed: 07 August 2018)

Sathakopan, O.K.S.V. (trans.) (no date m) *Swamy Desikan's Mummanikkovai*, available at www.sadagopan.org/pdfuploads/Mummanikovai.pdf (Accessed: 07 August 2018)

Sathakopan, O.K.S.V. (trans.) (no date n) *Swamy Desikan's Panniru Naaman*, available at www.sadagopan.org/pdfuploads/Panniru Namam.pdf (Accessed: 07 August 2018)

Sathakopan, O.K.S.V. (trans.) (no date o) *Swamy Desikan's Paramapada Sopanam*, available at www.sadagopan.org/pdfuploads/Paramapada Sopanam.pdf (Accessed: 07 August 2018)

Sathakopan, O.K.S.V. (trans.) (no date p) *Swamy Desikan's Prabhandha Saaram*, available at www.sadagopan.org/pdfuploads/Prabhanda Saram.pdf (Accessed: 07 August 2018)

Sathakopan, O.K.S.V. (trans.) (no date q) *Swamy Desikan's Sri Vaishnava Dinasari*, available at www.sadagopan.org/pdfuploads/Vaishnava Dinasari.pdf (Accessed: 07 August 2018)

Sathakopan, O.K.S.V. (trans.) (no date r) *Swamy Desikan's Thiruchinnamaalai*, available at www.sadagopan.org/pdfuploads/Thiruchinnamalai.pdf (Accessed: 07 August 2018)

Sathish, L. (2004) Pers. Com. - One-to-One Lessons on the Haṭhapradīpikā (Haṭhayogapradīpikā), Chennai: Krishnamacharya Yoga Mandiram, 20–31 December

Sathish, L. (2017) *A Memorial Lecture Series in Honour of Sri TKV Desikachar | Mala Srivatsan & Latha Sathish | P10*, Chennai: Krishnamacharya Yoga Mandiram, available at www.youtube.com/watch?v=by8mHmo5C-g (Accessed: 07 August 2018)

Schrader, F.O. (1911) 'Presents to the Adyar Library', in *Supplement to The Theosophist*, Madras: Theosophical Society, May

Schrader, F.O. (1916) *Introduction to the Pāñcarātra and the Ahirbudhnya Saṃhitā*, Madras: Adyar Library

Schreiner, P. (2011) 'Rāja Yoga', in K.A. Jacobsen (ed.), *Brill's Encyclopedia of Hinduism, vol. 3: Society, Religious Specialists, Religious Traditions, Philosophy*, Leiden: Brill, pp. 760–769

Schwarz-Linder, S. (2014) *The Philosophical and Theological Teachings of the Pādmasaṃhitā*, Vienna: Österreichischen Akademie der Wissenschaften

Seshadri, K. (1998) *Srivaishnavism and Social Change*, Calcutta: K.P. Bagchi & Company

Sharma, A. (1986) 'The Significance of Viṣṇu Reclining on the Serpent', *Religion*, vol. 16, pp. 101–114

Sharma, A. (1997) *The Rope and the Snake: A Metaphorical Exploration of Advaita Vedānta*, New Delhi: Manohar

Sharma, D.B.S. (2013) *The Philosophy of Sādhanā: With Special Reference to the Trika Philosophy of Kashmir*, Delhi: Divine Books

Sharvani, Z.A.K. and Sattar, S.A. (2016) 'Visishtādvaita and Wahdatul-Wujūd: Points of Comparison and Departure', *Tattva: Journal of Philosophy*, vol. 8, no. 1, pp. 1–18

Shastri, G.S.S. (ed.) (2014) *The Bhagavad-Gītā with Eleven Commentaries*, Delhi: Parimal Publications

Shastrī, M.N.D. (ed.) (1968) *The Garuḍa-Purāṇam*, 2nd edition, Varanasi: Chowkhamba Sanskrit Series Office

Silburn, L. (1988) *Kuṇḍalinī: The Energy of the Depths*, Albany: State University of New York Press

Singer, M.G. (2004) 'The Concept of Evil', *Philosophy*, vol. 79, no. 2, pp. 185–214

Singh, S. (2008) *Vedānta Deśika: His Life, Works and Philosophy, A Study*, 2nd edition, Varanasi: Chaukhamba Amarabharati Prakashan

Singleton, M. (2010) *Yoga Body: The Origins of Modern Postural Practice*, Oxford: Oxford University Press

Singleton, M. (2011) 'Modern Yoga', in K.A. Jacobsen (ed.), *Brill's Encyclopedia of Hinduism, vol. 3: Society, Religious Specialists, Religious Traditions, Philosophy*, Leiden: Brill, pp. 782–788

Singleton, M. (2012) '*Yoga Makaranda* of T. Krishnamacharya', in D.G. White (ed.), *Yoga in Practice*, Princeton: Princeton University Press, pp. 337–352

Singleton, M. and Fraser, T. (2014) 'T. Krishnamacharya, Father of Modern Yoga', in Singleton M. and Goldberg, E. *Gurus of Modern India*, Oxford: Oxford University Press, pp. 83–106

Sivananda, S. (1994) *Kundalini Yoga*, 10th edition, Shivanandanagar: Divine Life Society

Śivaprasādadvivedī (ed.) (2009) *Śrībhāṣyam*, Vārāṇasī: Caukhambā Vidhyābhavan

Sjoman, N.E. (1999) *The Yoga Tradition of the Mysore Palace*, 2nd edition, New Delhi: Abhinav Publications

Smith, F. (2013) 'Krishnamacharya', in K.A. Jacobsen (ed.), *Brill's Encyclopedia of Hinduism, vol. 5: Religious Symbols, Hinduism and Migration, Contemporary Communities outside South Asia, Some Modern Groups and Teachers*, Leiden: Brill, pp. 498–501

Smith, H.D. (1963) *Pāñcarātraprāsādaprasādhanam: Chapters 1–10 of the 'kriyāpāda',*

Pādmasaṃhitā, A Pañcarātra Text on Temple Building, Madras: published by the author

Sowmianarayanan, A.S.S. (trans.) (no date a) *Swamy Desikan's Chillarai RahasyangaL SrI UpakAra Sangraham, part 1, vol. 1*, available at www.sadagopan.org/pdfuploads/Upakara Sangraham Part 1-v1.pdf (Accessed: 07 August 2018)

Sowmianarayanan, A.S.S. (trans.) (no date b) *Swamy Desikan's Chillarai RahasyangaL SrI UpakAra Sangraham, part 1, vol. 2*, available at www.sadagopan.org/pdfuploads/Upakara Sangraham Part 1-v2.pdf (Accessed: 07 August 2018)

Sowmianarayanan, A.S.S. (trans.) (no date c) *Swamy Desikan's Chillarai RahasyangaL SrI UpakAra Sangraham, part 2*, available at www.sadagopan.org/pdfuploads/Upakara Sangraham Part 2.pdf (Accessed: 07 August 2018)

Sowmianarayanan, A.S.S. (trans.) (no date d) *Swamy Desikan's Chillarai RahasyangaL SrI UpakAra Sangraham, part 3*, available at www.sadagopan.org/pdfuploads/Upakara Sangraham Part 3.pdf (Accessed: 07 August 2018)

Sri Ahobila Math (eds) (2012) *Śrīmadrahasyatrayasārāḥ with the commentary Śrī Sārabodhinī*, Chennai: Sri Ahobila Math

Sridhar, D. (2018) *Vedānta deśika: The Peerless Poet-Preceptor*, Coimbatore: Jagathguru Sri Jayendra Saraswathi Trust

Sridharan, S. (2017) *A Memorial Lecture Series in honour of Sri TKV Desikachar | Speaker S Sridharan (Trustee) | Part.5*, Chennai: Krishnamacharya Yoga Mandiram, available at www.youtube.com/watch?v=wIi05PqTy9Y (Accessed: 08 August 2018)

Śrīkṛṣṇatātācārya, N.R. (ed.) (1990) *Tattvamuktākalāpa [Part-1] of Śrīmadveṅkaṭanātha Mahādeśika, With Three Commentaries Sarvārthasiddhi by Śrīmadveṅkaṭanātha, Ānandadāyinī by Nṛsiṁhadeva, & Akṣarātha by Devanāthatātācārya*, Varanasi: Sampurnanand Sanskrit University

Srinivasachar, D. and Narasimhachar, S. (eds) (1933) *Tattvamuktākalāpa and Sarvārthasiddhi with the Ānandadāyinī and the Bhāvaprakāśa*, vol. 1, Mysore: University of Mysore Oriental Library Publications

Srinivāsagopālāchārya, T.T. (ed.) (1954) *Tattvamuktākalāpa and Sarvārthasiddhi of Sri Vedāntāchārya with the Commentaries Ānandadāyinī and Bhāvaprakāśa*, vol. 3, Mysore: University of Mysore Oriental Research Institute Publications

Srinivāsagopālāchārya, T.T. (ed.) (1956) *Tattvamuktākalāpa and Sarvārthasiddhi of Sri Vedāntāchārya with the Commentary Ānandadāyinī of Sri Nṛsimharāja*, vol. 4, Mysore: University of Mysore Oriental Research Institute Publications

Srinivasan, G.R. (trans.) (2004) *The Hastigiri Māhātmyam of Vedāntadeśika*, Chennai: Śrī Vedāntadeśika Vidhya Trust

Srinivasaraghavan, A. (trans.) (1993) *The Minor Rahasyas of Sri Vedanta Desika (Amrtaranjani Rahasyas)*, Madras: Sri Visishtadvaita Pracharini Sabha

Sriram (2019) 'Sriram', in S. Oubrier and B. Viard (eds), *T.K.V. Desikachar: A Question of Transmission*, Sainte Cécile les Vignes: Les Cahiers de Présence d'Espirit, pp. 27–34

Śrīraṅgaśaṭhakopayatīndramahādeśika (ed.) (1938) *Tattvaṭīkā*, Madras: Śrīvaiṣṇavasiddhānta Pracāra Sabhādhyakṣa, available at https://archive.org/details/tattvatika015532mbp/page/n1/mode/2up (Accessed: 26 November 2020)

Sri Uttamur Viraraghavachariar Centenary Trust (eds) (2003) *Rakṣāgranthāḥ: Nikṣeparakṣā, Saccaritrarakṣā, Śrībhagavadrāmānujīya Nityagrantha Sahitā, Śrīpāñcarātrarakṣā, Gītārtha Saṁgraharakṣā Ca*, 2nd edition, Chennai: Sri Uttamur Viraraghavachariar Centenary Trust

Srivastava, V.B. (no date) *Dictionary of Indology*, New Delhi: V&S Publishers

Srivatsan, M. (1995) 'Guru Paramparā', *KYM Darśanam*, Krishnamacharya Yoga Mandiram, vol. 4, no. 2, pp. 33–36

Srivatsan, M. (1997) *Śrī Krishnamacharya the Pūrnācārya*, Chennai: Krishnamacharya Yoga Mandiram

Śrīvatsāṅkācārya, C.V. (ed.) (2007) *Śrīmadveṅkaṭanāthasya Nyāyapariśuddhiḥ*, 2 vols., Tirupati: Rashtriya Sanskrit Vidyapeetha

Śrīvatsāṅkācārya, C.V. (ed.) (2013) *Acyutaśatakaṁ with the Jyotsnā Commentary of T.A.T. Kumāratātācārya*, Chennai: Srirangam Srimath Andavan Ashramam

Śrīvatsāṅkācārya, C.V. (ed.) (no date) *Srimad Vedanta Desika's Chatusslokibhashyam, Sthothraratnabhashyam and Gadyatrayabhashyam*, Madras: Sri Vedantha Desika Seventh Centenary Trust

SSAA (eds) (2006) *Śrīmannigamāntamahādeśikastotrāṇi*, vol. 4, Chennai: Srirangam Srimath Andavan Ashramam

SSAA (eds) (2008) *Śrīmadrahasyatrayasāraḥ*, Chennai: Srirangam Srimath Andavan Ashramam

SSAA (eds) (2017) *Śrī Deśika Strotrāṇi*, 4th edition, Chennai: Srirangam Srimath Andavan Ashramam

Stern, E. (2005) 'Nathamuni's Secret of Devotion and the Yoga of Krishnamacharya', *Journal of Vaishnava Studies*, vol. 14, no. 1, pp. 95–106

Stern, E. (2010) Foreword to Jois, K. P. *Yoga Mala*, New York: North Point Press, pp. xv–xix

Thathachariar, K.S.K. (trans.) (1976) *Yadavabhyudayam: A Kavya on the Life of Lord Krishna by Vedanta Desika*, Madras: Vedanta Desika Research Society

Tilak Mahārāshtra University (eds) (1941) *Rgveda-Samhitā with the Commentary of Sāyaṇāchārya*, vol. 3, Poona: Tilak Mahārāshtra University Vaidika Saṁshodhana Maṇḍala

Tokunaga, M. and Smith, J. (eds) (2013) *Mahābhārata: Karṇa Parva, Critical Edition Prepared by Scholars at Bhandarkar Oriental Research Institute BORI*, available at https://sanskritdocuments.org/mirrors/mahabharata/mahabharata-bori.html (Accessed: 21 October 2019)

van Buitenen, J.A.B. (trans.) (1956) *Rāmānuja's Vedārthasaṃgraha: Introduction, Critical Edition and Annotated Translation*, Poona: Decan College

van Buitenen, J.A.B. (1971) *Yāmuna's Āgama Prāmāṇyam or Treatise on the Validity of*

Pāñcarātra, Madras: Rāmānuja Research Society

Varadachari, K.C. and Thathacharya, D.T. (trans.) (1975) *Isavasyopanishad Bhashya by Sri Vedanta Desika, Critically Edited with Introduction, Translation and Notes*, Madras: Vedanta Desika Research Society

Varadachari, V. (1982) *Agamas and South Indian Vaisnavism*, Madras: Prof. M. Rangacharya Memorial Trust

Varadachari, V. (1983) *Two Great Acharyas: Vedanta Desika and Manavala Mamuni*, Madras: Prof. M. Rangacharya Memorial Trust

Veda Bharati, S. (trans.) (1986) *Yoga-Sūtras of Patañjali with the Exposition of Vyāsa: A Translation and Commentary, vol. 1: Samādhi-pāda*, Honesdale: The Himalayan International Institute of Yoga Science and Philosophy of the U.S.A.

Vedantadesikan, V.N. (trans.) (1999) *Sri Paadukasahasram (of Sri Vedanta Desika)*, Chennai: Lifco

Venkatesan, T.C.A. (ed.) (2007) *Dhati Panchakam Vyakhyana Saram*, Unknown Publisher, available from https://archive.org/details/DhatiPanchakamVyakhyanaSaramEnglish (Accessed: 26 November 2020)

Vijnananand, S. (trans.) (2011) *Nārada-Pañcarātram (English Translation with Sanskrit Text)*, Delhi: Parimal Publications

Viraraghavacharya, T.U. (ed.) (2017) *Sri Vedanta Desika's Sankalpa Suryodaya Drama with Sanskrit Commentary and Tamil Translation*, 2nd edition, Chennai: Sri Uttamur Viraraghavachariar Centenary Trust

Viraraghavacharya, U. (ed.) (1974) *Tattwateeka (a Commentary on Sribhashya) by Srimad Vedāntadeśika*, Madras?: Unknown Publisher

Vireswarananda, S. (trans.) (2007) *Brahma-Sūtras*, 2nd edition, Delhi: Bharatiya Kala Prakashan

Vireswarananda, S. and Adidevananda, S. (trans.) (2008) *Brahma-Sūtras Śrī-Bhaṣya*, Kolkata: Advaita Ashrama

Virupakshananda, S. (trans.) (1995) *Sāṁkhya Kārikā of Īśvara Kṛṣṇa with the Tattva Kaumudī of Śrī Vācaspati Miśra*, Madras: Sri Ramakrishna Math

Vogel, J. (1926) *Indian Serpent-Lore or The Nāgas in Hindu Legend and Art*, London: Arthur Probsthain

Vyas, R.T. (ed.) (1992) *Vālmīki Rāmāyaṇa: Text as Constituted in its Critical Edition*, Vadodara: Oriental Institute

Wallis, C.D. (2013) *Tantra Illuminated*, 2nd edition, Boulder: Mattamayūra Press

Wallis, C.D. (2016) *The Real Story on the Chakras: The Six Most Important Things You Never Knew about the Chakras*, available at https://hareesh.org/blog/2016/2/5/the-real-story-on-the-chakras (Accessed: 15 July 2019)

Wallis, C.D. (2018) *What is Kuṇḍalinī?* Available at ww.youtube.com/watch?v=Zwzt9XtSq5Q (Accessed: 02 April 2020)

Wessels-Mevissen, C. (2013) 'Divine Attributes and Emblems', in K.A. Jacobsen (ed.), *Brill's Encyclopedia of Hinduism, vol. 5: Religious Symbols, Hinduism and Migration, Contemporary Communities outside South Asia, Some Modern Groups and*

Teachers, Leiden: Brill, pp. 28–35

Whicher, I. (1998) *The Integrity of the Yoga Darśana: A Reconsideration of Classical Yoga*, Albany: State University of New York Press

White, D.G. (2003) 'Yoga in Early Hindu Tantra', in I. Whicher and D. Carpenter (eds), *Yoga: The Indian Tradition*, London: Routledge, pp. 143–161

White, D.G. (2014) *The Yoga Sutra of Patanjali: a Biography*, Princeton: Princeton University Press

Whitney, W.D. and Lanman, C.R (trans.) (1905) *Atharva-Veda Saṁhitā*, vol. 1, Cambridge: Harvard University

Wilson, H.H. (trans.) (1888) *Ṛig-Veda Sanhitā*, London: Trübner & Co

Wong, L. (2008) 'Independent Spirit: A 0 with TKV Desikachar', *Fit Yoga*, April, pp. 8, 9, 92, available at www.yogastudies.org/wp-content/uploads/April2008FitYogaDesikachar.pdf (Accessed: 28 January 2016)

Wujastyk, D. (2017) 'The Yoga Texts Attributed to Yājñavalkya and their Remarks on Posture', *Asian Literature and Translation*, vol. 4, no. 1, pp. 159–186

Yadav, N. (1997) *Ganeśa in Indian Art and Literature*, Jaipur: Publication Scheme

Zimmer, H. (1962) *Myths and Symbols in Indian Art and Civilization*, New York: Harper & Brothers

INDEX

Entries are in English alphabetical order, as though diacritical marks did not exist. Plain numbers indicate page numbers. Notes are indicated by 'n.' so '46n.62' means page 46, note 62.

abhigamana (approaching) 133
abhimāna (erroneous self-conception) 92, 99, 126–127, 136
Abhinavagupta 127, 186
see also Kashmir Śaivism
abhiniveśa (fear of death) see *kleśa*
Acyutaśatakaṁ 146, 160, 171
adharma 125, 152
Adhikaraṇasārāvalī 147, 158–159, 171
Adhikārasangraham 148, 157, 171
adhomukha śvānāsana 77
Ādiparvan of the *Mahābhārata* see *Mahābhārata*
Ādiśeṣāṣṭakam 113
Advaita (vedānta) 6, 46n.62, 95–98, 123–124, 134–138, 150–152
āgama 6, 7, 45, 131, 179
see also *Pāñcarātra, Vaikhānasa*
Āgamaprāmāṇyam 131
agni (fire) 7, 12, 14–19, 24–30, 37–40, 42, 49, 60–61, 63n.26, 65–74, 84n.1, 117, 159, 173, 179–183
see also *jāṭharāgni*, flame
Agnipurāṇa 109
ahaṁkāra (ego) 34–35, 44, 91, 95–96, 113, 126
ahaṁmāna (egotism) 96–99, 126
ahaṅkṛiti (ego) 44
ahi (snake) 97, 99, 116
Ahirbudhnyasaṁhitā 41–51, 56, 68, 71, 73, 120, 131, 150–151, 173, 183, 201–202
Ahobala 167–169
Ahobilam Math/Mutt 134, 149
ājñā see *cakra*
ajñāna (nescience) 95–97, 126, 134, 184
ajñatva (nescience) 45
Alwar, M.A. 38n.32, 86n.13, 101–104, 112, 125, 135n.45
āma (toxin) 73
amṛta (nectar) 70n.52, 109, 185
Amṛtabindu Upaniṣad 188–189n.23
Amṛtasiddhi 27, 70n.52
anāhata see *cakra*
Ananta 89, 91
see also Saṅkarṣaṇa, Śeṣa
antaḥ kumbhaka (holding the breath in) 72, 77, 79, 80
see also *bāhya kumbhaka, prāṇāyāma*
antakāreṇa (destruction) 44, 50
anugraha (favouring) 44, 50
anumāna (inference) 6
apāna (breath in abdomen) 37, 39, 50n.74, 58–59, 65–74, 124, 170, 173, 180, 187
see also *antaḥ kumbhaka, bāhya kumbhaka, prāṇa, prāṇāyāma*
āptavacana (testimony) 6, 137, 183, 190–198
arcirādi marga (shining path) 156–159, 162, 179
āsana (posture) 2, 4, 65–66, 71–72, 74, 77–78, 81–83, 98
adhomukha śvānāsana 77
bhujaṅgāsana 72n.58
dvipādapītham 72n.58
jānuśīrṣāsana 77
mayūrāsana 52n.88, 56

paścimatānāsana 74, 193n.34
sarvāṅgāsana 71
śīrṣāsana 71, 72, 77
upaviṣṭakoṇāsana 74
ūrdhvamukha śvānāsana 77
asita (black snake) 88, 94
asmitā (am-ness) see *kleśa*
asmitva (egotism) 45, 46n.63
see also *kleśa*
aṣṭāṅgayoga (eight-limbed *yoga*) 113, 179
Aṣṭāṅgayoganirūpaṇam 178–181
aṣṭaprakṛti see *prakṛti*
Aṣṭāvakragītā 96–99, 150
asura (demon) 94, 125, 134
Atharvaveda 88, 94, 108
ātman (essence/self) 17, 45–46, 48, 53, 76, 82, 91, 95–97, 100, 103n.103, 122, 127, 134–137, 150, 154–156,
see also *jīva, jīvātman, paramātman, puruṣa*
Ātmasiddhi 132
avidyā (nescience) see *kleśa*

bāhya kumbhaka (holding the breath out) 72, 79, 80
see also *antaḥ kumbhaka*
Balasubramanian, K.S. 19, 22, 29n.100, 33, 126, 130n.12, 199–202
bandha (bind/lock/belt) 18, 37, 45, 60n.11, 66, 69, 107, 112, 117–120, 167
see also binding
jālandhara bandha 40n.38, 65, 122
jihvā bandha 65
mūla bandha 18, 58, 65, 69, 72, 122
uḍḍīyāna bandha 58, 65, 69, 72, 122
baṅka nāḍī (crooked river) see *nāḍī*
Bhagavadgītā 35, 66n.41, 82, 95, 129, 132, 135, 137, 151–152
see also *Mahābhārata*
bhakti (devotion) 134, 162, 168
see also *prapatti*
bhujaga (snake) 92, 97, 118n.196
bhujaṅga (snake) 52n.85, 115, 117
bhujaṅgāsana 72n.58
see also *āsana*
bhūtiśakti (material cause of the world) see *śakti.*
bīja mantra (seed syllable) 2, 54
binding 44–45, 50, 60, 76, 107, 112, 114–120, 127, 138, 159, 167, 184, 189n.23
see also *bandha*
bindu (semen) 5, 47
Birch, Jason 11, 59n.5, 121–123
black serpent/snake 84, 88, 94, 97, 99–101, 105, 108, 111, 120, 125–126
Bouanchaud, Bernard 7, 8, 174
Brahmā (creator god) 34, 36, 89, 105, 108, 155, 156, 161
Brahman 5, 17, 35, 43, 45–46, 60, 95–96, 99, 119, 123, 134, 174, 189
see also *paramātman*
brahmanāḍī (nerve of *Brahman*/ Brahmā) see *nāḍī*
Brahmānanda 58, 61, 62, 64, 70
brahmarandhra (*suṣumnā's* entrance/ exit) 16–18, 23–24, 26, 35, 37–42, 76, 179, 189
brahmarudra (nerve of *Brahman*/ Brahmā) see *nāḍī*
Brahmasūtra 91, 97, 129, 132, 134–135, 153–154, 158–159, 161, 164, 171
brahmin (one of priestly caste) 87–89, 99, 131n.18
breath/breathing see *apāna, prāṇa, prāṇāyāma*
Bṛhadyogiyājñavalkyasmṛti 166
see also *Yājñavalkyasmṛti, Yogayājñavalkya*
Bṛhatsaṁhitā 92, 99
buddhi (wisdom faculty) 34, 35, 44, 81

cakra (junction of *nāḍī-s*, wheel) 14, 18, 21, 40n.38, 84, 98, 108, 180, 185–188, 196, 197
ājñā 180
anāhata/hṛd/hṛdaya/hṛdabja/heart 5, 16, 21, 25–28, 34, 37–39, 40–41, 45, 47–49, 51–52, 56, 95–96, 113, 153–161, 174, 180, 183, 186, 197
see also *hṛd granthi*
maṇipūra 15, 181
see also *nābhi*
mūlacakra 14
mūlādhāra 13–22, 47–51, 60–63, 70–73, 76, 84n.1, 108, 124, 159, 173–174, 183–184, 187–188
nābhi 7, 12–16, 19–25, 29, 34, 36–38, 41–42, 47–48, 53, 60–63, 67, 69–71, 76, 96, 124, 158–159, 162, 169, 173, 181, 182–184, 188
see also *maṇipūra*
sahasrāra 6, 18–19, 25–27, 35, 59, 61, 72, 74, 124, 127, 131, 182, 188–190
sudarśana cakra see *sudarśana*
svādhiṣṭhāna 14
candra (moon) 27, 28, 43, 48, 70n.52, 81, 99, 100
Chāndogya Upaniṣad 5, 96n.61, 100
Chandraśekarabhāratī, H.H. 98
Charlton, David 79–81, 97n.64
cinmudrā (hand gesture) 65
Connolly, Peter 1n.8, 33n.8, 130n.12, 196, 200
covering 23, 34, 41–46, 50, 53, 76, 87, 94–97, 100n.95, 101, 103n.103, 116, 118, 120, 127, 134–137, 150, 183–184
Cozad, Laurie 86–89, 110, 127
Daouk, Malek 178n.191
Dattātreyayogaśāstra 5
dehamadhya (centre of the body) 12, 13, 19, 38, 53, 68–71
see also *vahnimaṇḍala*
Desikachar, Kausthub xiii, 2, 20–22, 40, 61–64, 71, 84–85, 88, 92, 94, 101, 103–105, 107–114, 117, 121–122, 125–126, 130, 183, 188
Desikachar, Menaka x, xiii, 50n.74
Desikachar, T.K.V. xiii, 1–2, 6, 10–22, 26, 30, 34–35, 37–40, 49–50, 58, 63–65, 69–75, 121–122, 126n.249, 129–130, 131n.19, 152–153, 159, 164, 166, 171–178, 182–189, 192–199
dhāraṇā (concentration) 7, 24, 65, 76–77, 82, 133
see also *dhyāna, samādhi*
dharma (duty/essential nature) 52n.85, 89, 125, 135–136, 152
dhyāna (meditation) 7, 15, 16, 76–77, 82, 133
see also *dhāraṇā, samādhi*
dṛṣṭa (direct perception) 6
dṛṣṭi (seeing) 47n.64, 48
dṛśya (the seen) 47n.64, 48, 92
Dunsmuir, Colin 64–65
dveṣa (aversion) see *kleśa*
dvijihva (snake) 25–29, 164–165
dvipādapītham (two-foot support) 72n.58

earth (element) 21, 106
ego see *ahaṁkāra*
egotism see *ahaṁmāna*
elements 2, 21, 35, 44, 155, 157–158, 163, 187
epistemology 6–9, 190–198
evil 84, 88, 91–92, 94, 100, 104, 106–107, 110, 114, 118, 119, 125–127

fire see *agni*
flame 12, 15, 16, 18, 24, 25, 28, 68, 70–73, 174
see also *agni*, *dehamadhya*, *jāṭharāgni*, *vahnimaṇḍala*

Gaṇeśa 84, 105–108, 119, 126, 173, 176
Gaṇeśapurāṇa 107, 108
Garuḍa 84, 86, 89, 108–111, 118–119, 126, 140–141, 152, 164, 166–167, 171, 173
see also Suparṇa, Garutmān
Garuḍapañcāśat 152, 166, 171, 173
Garuḍapurāṇa 93, 109, 115
Gāruḍa Upaniṣad 110
Garutmān 108, 109, 152n.76
see also Garuḍa, Suparṇa
Gheraṇḍasaṁhitā 4, 13, 23, 80, 189
Gītārthasaṅgraḥ 152, 152
Gītārthasaṅgraharakṣā 151, 152
Gorakṣapaddhati 28, 68, 69n.50, 72
Gorakṣaśataka 68, 69n.50, 71
granthi (knot) 5, 45, 188
Gṛhyasūtra 88, 106
guṇa (constituent, quality) 23n.72, 36, 42, 44, 95, 120, 135, 173
rajas (activity) 23n.72, 44, 95, 165n.125
sattva (lucidity) 23n.72, 44, 95, 102, 165n.125, 168
tamas (darkness, obscuration) 23n.72, 44–45, 72, 91, 95, 97, 99, 100n.95, 102, 135n.45, 165n.125

Harivaṁśa 89, 101–104
Harvey, Paul 40n.38, 64–65, 74, 77–79, 83, 130n.12
Hastigirimāhātmyam 144, 163, 171
Haṭhapradīpikā (Haṭhayogapradīpikā) 4, 28, 31n.2, 58–66, 70, 74, 76–79, 119n.205, 165n.123, 183, 200–202
haṭhayoga 2, 4–6, 31, 35, 40, 49, 58–97, 123–124, 127–128, 131, 137–138, 156, 159, 165, 170, 173, 178–181, 183–190
Hatley, Shaman 5n.28, 14, 21n.60, 188n.21
Heart see *hṛdaya*, *hṛdayākāśa*, *hṛd granthi*, *hṛdi*
Hersnack, Peter 55n.98, 72n.58, 81
Hiraṇyākṣa 105
hitā (nerve) see *nāḍī*
Hopkins, Steven P. 161
hṛdabja (water heart) 47, 48
see also *cakra*
hṛdaya (heart) 5, 16, 21, 25–28, 34, 37–41, 45, 47–49, 51, 52n.85, 56, 95–96, 153–161, 174, 180, 183, 186, 197
see also *cakra*
hṛdayākāśa (space of the heart) 37, 39
see also *cakra*
hṛd granthi (knot of the heart) 45
see also *cakra*
hṛdi (heart) 25, 28
see also *cakra*
hundred and first *nāḍī* see *nāḍī*

iḍā (nerve on the left) see *nāḍī*
Indra/*indra* (god of heaven/lord/the best) 28, 87–89, 109, 118, 166–167
indriya (sense organ) 82, 157, 158, 169–170
inversion (inverted *āsana*/*mudrā*) 68–73
Īśvara (god/lord) 15, 17, 105, 132, 176
Īśvarasaṁhitā 52, 110, 120
Iyengar, B.K.S. xii, 1

jālandhara bandha 40n.38, 65, 122
jānuśīrṣāsana 77
jāṭharāgni (abdominal fire) 37–40, 49, 61, 70, 180

see also *agni, dehamadhya,* flame, *vahnimaṇḍala*
jaṭharaparivṛtti 74
Jayākhyasaṁhitā 33n.9
Jayaraman, M. 22, 26–28, 71n.56, 179–180
jihvā bandha (tongue lock) 65
jīva (individual self) 5, 14, 35–36, 42–45, 53, 91–92, 114, 127, 151, 153–163, 169, 174, 179–180
see also *ātman, jīvātman, paramātman, puruṣa*
jīvātman (individual self) 43, 46, 82–83n.110, 115n.185, 133, 136, 154, 158, 163
see also *ātman, jīva, paramātman, puruṣa*
Johar, N. 176
Jois, Pattabhi xii, 1
Jyotsnā 28, 58–62, 64, 70, 71n.56

Kālī 119–120, 165n.125
Kāliya 101–104, 125
kāma (desire) 5, 52n.85, 168
Kaminoff, Leslie 65n.41, 66–67, 70–71, 193
Kānchi Kāmakoṭi Piṭha 98
kanda (egg/bulb) 12–14, 20, 23–25, 30, 34, 41, 53, 60–63, 76, 123–124, 182–183, 186
karma (action) 45, 82, 106–107, 120, 135–136, 155, 161, 162, 167
karma indriya (organ of action) 162, 170
Kashmir Śaivism 50, 127
Kaṭha Upaniṣad 5, 153
Kaulajñānanirṇaya 21
Ketu 99, 100, 115
khecarī (tongue *mudrā*) 2, 4
Khecarīvidyā 28
kleśa (affliction) 45, 46n.63, 64–66, 78, 82, 95, 114, 127, 165, 197
abhiniveśa (fear of death) 64, 66, 168, 197
asmitā (am-ness) 64, 84, 92, 114, 126, 197
see also *asmitva*
avidyā (nescience) 43, 45, 48, 64, 66, 75, 78, 81–83, 84–85, 99, 104, 114, 125–127, 134–138, 150–152, 159, 183–184, 190, 194, 197
dveṣa (aversion) 64, 168, 197
rāga (desire) 45, 46n.63, 64, 119, 168, 197
Krishnamacharya
background 1–5
critical attitude 2–6
quotations 6, 19–20, 25, 35, 37, 49, 59, 61, 63, 75–77, 82, 113, 131, 170, 189, 196
Krishnamacharya Yoga Mandiram (KYM) 2, 11, 22, 114, 129, 143, 176, 178, 179
kriyāśakti (instrumental cause of the world) see *śakti*
Kṛṣṇa 73n.63, 84, 89–91, 95, 96, 98, 100–104, 116, 117, 125, 176
see also Rāma, Varāha, Vāsudeva, Viṣṇu
Kubjikāmata 186
kumbhaka (breath retention) 72, 79, 80, 123
kuṇḍala (earring, fetter, coiled) 112, 127, 165, 166, 169, 172, 184–185
kuṇḍalā (obstructing blockage) 51
kuṇḍala-ākhya-nāḍī (sinuous nerve) see *nāḍī*
kuṇḍalī 13n.26, 21, 34, 39, 41–42, 46–51, 53, 59–60, 76n.80, 120, 123, 128, 164–173, 179, 181, 184–185
kuṇḍalī-indra (serpent-lord) 166–167
kuṇḍalī nāḍī (sinuous nerve) 167–170
see also *nāḍī*

kuṇḍalinī
= *āma* 73
= *avidyā/māyā* 35–36, 64–65, 75–76, 82, 135, 183, 197
awakening of 24–25, 34, 37–40, 42, 59, 63, 69–71, 81–82, 174, 182, 189, 195
= blockage 6, 13, 20–21, 23–24, 30, 34, 37, 41–42, 53, 60, 100, 101, 127, 137, 182, 184, 189
= *dvijihva* 25–29, 164–165
and elements 21–22
= *kleśa-s* 64–65, 197
Krishnamacharya's experience of 196
location of 13–23, 47–49, 51, 53, 60–63, 69–72, 182, 186–188, 197
= *nigrahaśakti* 44–47, 73, 151
= *prakṛti* see *prakṛti*
= *prāṇa* 49–50, 107–108, 112–114, 173, 183, 188–189
rising 34, 37–41, 47–49, 59–60, 124, 127–128, 174, 182–183, 188–190
= *saṁskāra* 76, 114
= *suṣumnā* 167–173

Lakshmithathachar, M.A. 52n.85, 91, 120n.212
Lakṣmī 119, 158, 165n.125, 176, 185
see also Śrī
Lakṣmīsahasranāma 179
Lakṣmītantra 91
layayoga (yoga of meditative absorption) 5, 74
Liṅgapurāṇa 109
Lorin, François 130n.12, 178n.193, 193, 197

madhya nāḍī (central nerve) see *nāḍī*
Mahābhārata 88–89, 108–109, 116–118, 125
see also *Bhagavadgītā*
mahāmāyā (great illusion) 123–124
see also *māyā*
mahāmudrā (great seal) 64–65, 74, 77
Maitri Upaniṣad 5, 83n.110
mala (impurity) 45, 73, 74, 84n.1, 162
Mallinson, James 5, 27n.89, 28n.91, 31n.2, 34, 39, 51n.82, 52n.88, 56, 62–63, 70n.52, 185, 202
māna (pride) 98–99, 126
see also *abhimāna, ahaṁmāna*
māna-ahi (serpent of pride) 99
Mānavagṛhyasūtra 106
maṇḍala (geometric diagram) 50, 54, 70, 174
Māṇḍūkyakārikā 97
maṇipūra see *cakra*
mantra 2, 14–15, 23n.72, 33, 47–49, 54, 67, 74, 109, 140, 155, 165, 174
Mantramahodadhi 174, 189
mantrayoga 74
Maréchal, Claude 4n.21, 66, 73
Matsyapurāṇa 115–116
māyā (illusion) 35–36, 42–43, 45, 60–61n.11, 94–95, 105, 118–119, 120, 123–126, 128, 134–135, 138, 151–152, 184, 190
māyā bhujaṅgī (serpent of illusion) 152
māyāvinaṁ (wicked sorcerer)105
mayūrāsana 56
Meyviratamāṉmiyam 148, 161, 171
Moha (delusion) 45, 119, 121–123, 126, 168, 184
Mohan, A.G. 1–4, 10–12, 18, 20, 22–23, 27–29, 35, 38–39, 48, 49, 59, 63, 73–78, 79n.93, 81–82, 114, 130, 170, 182, 189, 191–192, 199–200
mokṣa (liberation) 52n.85, 118, 135, 156, 159, 168
moon 27–28, 43, 48, 70n.52, 81, 99–100
Moors, Frans 8
mudrā (seal) 2, 4, 5, 40n.38, 64–65, 67, 78

cinmudrā (hand seal) 65
khecarī mudrā (tongue seal) 2, 4
mahāmudrā (great seal) 64–65, 74, 77
vajrolī mudrā (sexual seal) 2, 4
viparītakaraṇī mudrā (inversion) 71–72
mukti nāḍī see *nāḍī*
mūla bandha 18, 58, 65, 69, 72, 122
mūlacakra see *cakra*
mūlādhāra see *cakra*
mūrdhanya nāḍī see *nāḍī*

nābhi see *cakra*
nāda (mystical sound) 17–20, 48
Nādabindu Upaniṣad 188–189n.23
nāḍī (nerve) 5, 13, 15–16, 21, 23–24, 30, 41, 47–48, 53–54, 58–59, 63, 65, 76, 87, 124, 131, 153–163, 167–173, 180, 182–185, 196
see also *vaiṣṇavī*
baṅka nāḍī (crooked river) 185
brahmanāḍī (nerve of *Brahman*/ Brahmā) 20, 58–59, 153, 156–157, 160, 163, 171
brahmarudra (nerve of *Brahman*/ Brahmā) 53–54
hundred and first *nāḍī* 153–156, 160, 171
iḍā (nerve on the left) 48, 84n.1, 179
kuṇḍala-ākhya-nāḍī (sinuous nerve) 169, 184
kuṇḍalī nāḍī (sinuous nerve) 169, 184
madhyanāḍī (central nerve) 163
mukti nāḍī (nerve of liberation) 158
mūrdhanya nāḍī 156–159
nāḍīśuddhi/nāḍīśodhana (purification of nerves) 78, 80
nāḍī viśeṣa (special nerve) 163, 169, 173
piṅgalā (nerve on the right) 48, 84n.1
suṣumnā (central nerve) 5–6, 13–14, 18–20, 23–26, 34–42, 45, 49, 53–54, 58–61, 70–78, 92, 96, 122–124, 127, 131, 150–163, 169–174, 179–181, 182–185, 188–190, 198
nāga (sacred snake) 38–39, 85–128
see also snake
nāgabandha (snake bind) 120
nāgadoṣa (snake blemish) 85, 100
nāgakkal/nāga stone 86
Nāgaloka (snake-realm) 88, 91
nāgam astra (snake arrow) 117
nāgapāśa (snake noose) 107, 119–120
nāgaśakti (snake power) 114
nāga udarabandha (snake belt) 84, 107–108, 166
nāga yajñopavīta (serpentine sacred-thread) 107, 110, 112, 122, 166
Nāradapāñcarātrasaṁhitā 52
Narasimha Bharati Swamigalavaroo 98
Narayan, R.K. x, xi, 170n.157
Nārāyaṇa 89, 165, 178
see also *Brahman*, Kṛṣṇa, Rāma, Viṣṇu
Nāthamuni 129–131
nauli (a cleansing action) 4
neti (a physical cleansing action) 4
Netratantra 51
nigrahaśakti (binding/covering power) 44–50, 73, 151
nirodha (restriction) 14n.35, 77
nityasūri (resident of heaven) 110
noose see *pāśa*
Nṛsiṁharāja/Nṛsiṁhadeva 167–169
nyāsa (hand placement) 33, 50, 54, 65, 67, 174
Nyāya (system of logic) 139, 157
Nyāyasiddhāñjana 157–158, 163, 170–171, 180
Nyāyatattva 131

pādabandha (foot bind) 117
Pādmasaṁhitā 32–41, 54, 56, 67, 68n.50, 71, 120, 128, 131, 138, 156, 159, 201–202
Pādukāsahasraṁ 161, 171
pañcakāla (five daily acts) 133, 165, 173, 179
Pāñcarātra 33–51, 56, 89, 91–92, 110, 120–121, 126, 128, 129, 131–133, 137–138, 153–156, 159, 164–166, 171, 181, 182–184
Pāñcarātrarakṣā 145, 164–166, 171–175, 184
Pañcatantra 93
Pāñcaviṁśa Brāhmaṇa 88
pannaga (snake hood) 93
pāpa (sin) 53, 100n.95, 125
Parakāla Math, Mysore see Śrī Brahmatantra Svatantra Parakāla Math, Mysore
Paramapadasopāna 144, 162, 171
Paramasaṁhitā 37
paramātman (supreme essence) 16–17, 35, 43, 75n.71, 91, 133, 157, 174
  see also *Brahman, jīvātman*
Pārameśvarasaṁhitā 52n.85
Paripāṭal 110
pāśa (noose) 119–120
  kālapāśa (noose of time) 119
  karmapāśa (noose of action) 120
  nāgapāśa (snake noose) 107, 119–120
paścimatānāsana 74, 193n.34
Patañjali/Yogasūtra of *Patañjali/Patañjali Yogadarśana* 4, 6–8, 47–48, 64–66, 73–83, 92, 95, 113, 126n.249, 132–133, 167, 176
  see also *rājayoga*
phaṇi/phaṇī (snake) 120, 165
phaṇipatiḥ (snake lord) 167
piṅgalā (nerve on the right) see *nāḍī*
poison 101–104, 108–111, 119, 121–123, 126–127, 137, 152
Poundarikapuram Srimad Andavan Ashramam 149–150
Prabhāvalī 167
Prabhāvilāsa 167
prakṛti (created nature) 35–36, 42–44, 76, 78, 80–82, 95, 135n.45, 151
  see also *māyā*
  aṣṭaprakṛti (eight constituents of nature) 23–24, 34–35, 41, 53–54, 173
pramāṇa (valid knowledge source) 6–9, 190–198
prāṇa (breath, vital force) 5–7, 14–19, 23–25, 30, 34, 37–42, 49–51, 53–54, 58–63, 65–78, 113, 123, 127, 153–158, 162, 167–173, 179–180, 184–189, 194, 198
  see also *antaḥ kumbhaka, apāna, bāhya kumbhaka, prāṇāyāma, vāyu*
praṇava 16, 17
prāṇāyāma (breath control) 2, 4, 15–16, 37, 42, 65–66, 74, 77–83, 165
  see also *antaḥ kumbhaka, apāna, bāhya kumbhaka, prāṇa, vāyu*
Prapañcasāra 173–174
prapanna (devotee) 155–157, 160, 162–163
prapatti (surrender to God) 160, 162, 164–165
  see also *bhakti*
pratyāhāra (sense control) 77
pratyakṣa (direct perception/experience) 6–7, 190–198
pṛthivī (earth element) 21, 106
Purāṇa-s 105, 108–109, 112, 129, 134
  Agnipurāṇa 109
  Gaṇeśapurāṇa 107–108
  Garuḍapurāṇa 85, 93, 109, 114–115
  Harivaṁśa 89, 101–104
  Liṅgapurāṇa 109
  Matsyapurāṇa 115–116

Śrīmadbhāgavatam 91–92, 98–99, 104–105, 123, 126
Viṣṇudharmottarapurāṇa 99
Viṣṇupurāṇa 102–105, 134, 136n.46
puruṣa (the self) 35, 44, 75, 80–82, 127, 168
see also *ātman, jīva, jīvātman*

rāga (desire) see *kleśa*
Rahasyatrayasāram 145, 155–158, 160n.106, 163, 170, 180
Rāhu 99–100, 103
rajas (activity) see *guṇa*
rājayoga (royal *yoga*) 62, 65, 74–79
see also *Patañjali*
Rājayogatarala 123n.229
Rāma 118–119, 161
see also Kṛṣṇa, Varāha, Vāsudeva, Viṣṇu
Rāmānandī Tyāgī-s 184–185
Rāmānuja 91n.42, 132–138, 151, 157–158n.95, 165
Ramaswami, Srivatsa 1, 26, 69–72, 75n.70, 98, 130, 183, 189–190
Rāmāyaṇa 118–120
Rastelli, Marion 51n.84, 56n.112, 133n.34, 165
Ṛddhimant 109
Ṛgveda 87–88, 93, 105, 108, 114–116, 136
Roy, Ranju 79–81
rudra granthi (knot of Rudra) 188

śabda (testimony) 6–9, 137, 190–198
saguṇa dhyāna (meditation with form) 15–16, 120
Śaiva Siddhānta 21, 185–186
Saivism 4, 48, 50–51, 60n.11, 62, 112, 124, 127, 139, 173, 183–186, 189, 198
Śākta (relating to Śakti) 63, 173, 183, 189
śakti/Śakti (force/power/godess) 6, 14, 36, 42–50, 53, 59–61, 76n.80, 82, 94, 112, 114, 124, 165, 171, 186, 188–190, 200
bhūtiśakti (material cause of the world) 43–44, 46n.63
kriyāśakti (instrumental cause of the world) 43–50
nāgaśakti (snake power) 114
nigrahaśakti (concealing power) 45–49, 73, 151
śakticālana (moving *kuṇḍalinī* forcefully) 59, 189
samādhi (meditative absorption) 7, 75n.71, 76, 124, 133
see also *dhāraṇā, dhyāna, saṁyama*
sāmānya (general/generic) 7, 192, 193n.34
Sāmaveda 88
Sāmavidhāna Brāhmaṇa 88
Sāṁkhya 6, 33, 44, 77, 80, 132, 139
Sāṁkhyakārikā 6, 8
saṁsāra (transmigration/rebirth) 99, 104, 121–123, 126, 184
saṁskāra (subliminal tendency) 47, 65, 76, 114
saṁyama (dhāraṇā+dhyāna+samādhi) 7, 76
saṁyoga (confusion) 81, 92n.43
Saṅkalpasūryodaya 147, 167–171, 173, 185
Śaṅkara (Ādiśaṅkara) 46n.62, 78, 91, 95–98, 121–122, 137, 173, 199–200
Saṅkarṣaṇa 89–92, 113–114, 126
see also Ananta, Śeṣa, *vyūha*
śara bandha (arrow bind) 118
Śaraṇāgatidīpikā 146, 160, 171
Sārdhatriśatikālottara 21, 186
sarga (exhaling) 47
Śārṅgadharapaddhati 27
sarpa (serpent) 54n.91, 95n.57, 97, 99, 112, 137, 152n.75

sarpa jaṭābandha (serpentine hair band) 112
sarvāṅgāsana (shoulderstand) 71
Śatadūṣaṇī 147, 150–151, 168
Śatapathabrāhmaṇa 88
Ṣaṭcakranirūpaṇa 13, 23, 108
Sathish, Latha 67n.48, 178n.187–188
sattva (lucidity) see *guṇa*
Sātvatasaṁhitā 119–121, 128
sauparṇa (a weapon) 117
  see also Suparṇa
Schwarz-Linder, Silvia 34–41, 56, 201–202
serpent see snake
Śeṣa 83n.110, 86, 89–92, 107, 110–111, 113–115, 119, 133, 167
  see also Ananta, Saṅkarṣaṇa
Śeṣin (controller) 83n.110, 91
Siddhasiddhāntapaddhati 186
siddhi (accomplishment/attainment) 16, 101, 185
sin 53, 100n.95, 125
Singleton, Mark 4n.23, 34, 39, 56, 201–202
Śīrṣāsana 71–72
Śiva 27, 96, 107, 112–114, 121, 126, 176, 185–186, 188, 190
Sivananda, Swami 23n.72, 194
Śivasaṁhitā 4, 13, 23, 85, 123–124, 189
snake 24–27, 34–35, 37–40, 42n.43, 42n.45, 52n.85, 53–54, 59, 84–128, 137, 140–141, 151–152, 164–167, 169–170, 173, 184–186
  see also *nāga*
  snake and rope 97–98, 115–116, 123–124, 137–138, 151–152
  snakebite 88, 95, 97, 99, 125
  snake charmer 121–123
  snake jewel/pearl/gem 53–54, 86, 92–93, 103, 115, 164
Śrī (the goddess) 165, 185
  see also Lakṣmī
Śrībhāṣya 134–135, 137, 153–154, 159, 161, 163–164, 169, 171, 180
Śrī Brahmatantra Svatantra Parakāla Math, Mysore 102, 149, 170
Sridharan, S. 176–179
Śrīmadbhāgavatam 91–92, 98–99, 104–105, 126
Śrīmat Śrī Varāha Mahādeśika Swāmi 172–173, 184
Srirangam Srimad Andavan Ashramam 142, 149, 167, 172–173
Śrīvaiṣṇavism 1–4, 33, 55, 91–92, 101, 110, 114, 129–181, 183–185
Śrīvidyā 124
Śṛṅgeri (Muṭṭ) 98, 124
sṛṣṭi (creation) 44–50
śruti (valid testimony) 7–9, 137, 183, 190–198
sthiti (steadying/preservation) 44, 50, 168–169
sudarśana (Viṣṇu's discus) 44, 50, 105, 114, 134
  see also *kriyāśakti* under *śakti*
sun 17, 48, 70n.52, 99–100, 103, 117, 155–156, 159–160, 173
Suparṇa/*suparṇa* 108, 117–118
  see also Garuḍa, Garutmān, *sauparṇa*
suṣumnā (central nerve) see *nāḍī*
svādhiṣṭhāna see *cakra*
svādhyāya (chanting/studying texts) 1, 2, 55n.98, 65, 67, 133, 175
Svātmārāma 58–63
Śvetāśvatara Upaniṣad 35, 95, 199–200

Taittirīya Āraṇyaka 53, 55n.98
Taittirīya Brāhmaṇa 53, 55n.98
Taittirīya branch of the Black *Yajurveda* 55
Taittirīya Upaniṣad 55n.98
Takṣaka 93
tamas (darkness, obscuration) see *guṇa*

tantra 5, 21, 33, 48, 53–54, 60–61n.11, 65, 67, 70n.52, 173–174, 185–186, 190, 196
Tantrāloka 128n.252
tattva (ontological category) 33, 43–44, 81, 165
Tattvaṭīkā 148, 154, 158
Teṇkalai (a sect) 141, 148
  see also *Vaṭakalai*
tirobhāva (concealment) 45
  see also covering, *nigrahaśakti*
tirodhāna (concealment) 44–46, 135–137, 150–151
  see also covering, *nigrahaśakti*
tirohita (concealed) 45
  see also covering, *nigrahaśakti*

uḍḍīyāna bandha 58, 65, 69, 72, 122
Ulagalanda Perumāl Temple, Kanchipuram 86
upādāna (appropriating) 133
Upakārasaṅgraham 162–163, 171
Upaniṣad-s 4, 5, 96, 130, 132, 135, 137, 153, 159, 164, 171
  Amṛtabindu 188–189n.23
  Bṛhadāraṇyaka 96n.61, 199
  Chāndogya 5, 96n.61, 100
  Dyhānabindu 188n.23
  Garba 188–189n.23
  Gāruḍa 110
  Kaṭha 5, 153
  Maitri 5, 83n.110
  Māṇḍūkya 97
  Nādabindu 188–189n.23
  Śāṇḍilya 188–189n.23
  Śvetāśvatara 35, 95, 199–200
  Taittirīya 55n.98
  Yogakuṇḍalī 188, 200
  Yogaśika 188n.23
  Yogatattva 200
  Yoga Upaniṣad-s 200
upaviṣṭakoṇāsana 74

uraga aṅganā (female snake) 122
Urakathan 86
ūrdhvamukha śvānāsana 77

vahnimaṇḍala (place of fire) 70
  see also *dehamadhya, Vaiṣvānara*
Vaikhānasa 52–56, 114n.183, 182–183, 188, 202
  see also *Pāñcarātra*
Vaikhānasasmārtasūtra 54
Vaikuṇṭha (heaven) 110, 155–158, 161, 163, 165
Vaikuṇṭhagadya 165
Vaiṣṇavism 31–57, 62, 98–99, 108–111, 129–181, 183–185
  see also *Pāñcarātra*, Śrīvaiṣṇavism, *Vaikhānasa*
vaiṣṇavī 41, 42n.43, 45–46, 48, 165
  see also *nāḍī*
Vaiṣvānara (fire) 15–16
  see also *dehamadhya*, fire, *vahnimaṇḍala*
vajrolī mudrā (sexual seal) 2, 4
Varadarājapañcāśat 145, 151
Varāha (*avatar* of Viṣṇu) 104–105
  see also Kṛṣṇa, Rāma, Viṣṇu
vāsana (subtle impression) 45, 65, 82
Vasiṣṭhasaṁhitā 31–33, 37, 39, 41, 52n.88, 56, 62, 67, 68n.50, 71, 182, 200–202
Vāsudeva 35, 89, 164
  see also Saṅkarṣaṇa, *vyūha*
Vāsuki 93, 107, 115, 167
Vaṭakalai (a sect) 141, 149, 172
  see also *Teṇkalai*
vāyu (air, breath) 6, 13, 17, 24–28, 37, 39, 66, 69, 73, 170, 173, 179, 200
  see also *prāṇa*
Vedānta (in general) 4, 33, 73n.63, 98, 125, 139, 179, 190
  see also *Advaita* and *Viśiṣṭādvaitavedānta*

Vedāntadeśika 6, 8, 55, 103–104, 129, 138–173, 176–178, 181, 184
Vedārthasaṁgraha 83n.110, 135–137
Veṅkaṭanātha see Vedāntadeśika
Veṅkaṭeśa see Vedāntadeśika
vighna (obstacle) 106
Vimānārcanākalpasaṁhitā 52–56, 92, 202
Vināyaka 106–107
viparītakaraṇī mudrā 71–72
Viraraghavacharya, Abhinava Desika Uttamur T. 169–170
visarga (aspiration) 47
visarjana (discharging) 47
viśeṣa (special, particular) 7, 192–193
  see also *nāḍī viśeṣa* under *nāḍī*
Viśiṣṭādvaitavedānta 6, 82–83n.110, 126, 129–181, 190
  see also Śrīvaiṣṇavism
Viṣṇu 42, 44–47, 50, 86, 89–90, 101–105, 108–111, 114, 115, 119–120, 134, 155–159, 161–164, 168, 170, 179, 185
  see also Kṛṣṇa, Rāma, Varāha, Vāsudeva
Viṣṇudharmottarapurāṇa 99
Viṣṇupurāṇa 102, 104, 134, 136n.46
Visvaksenasaṁhitā 91
Vivekacūḍāmaṇi 95–98, 100n.95, 101
Vṛtra 87, 118, 136
Vyāsa 7–8, 76, 78, 192–193
vyūha (emanation) 89–91
  see also Saṅkarṣaṇa, Vāsudeva

Wallis, Christopher 186–187, 196–197
Wujastyk, Dominik 11, 52

Yādavābhyudaya 103–104, 146
Yājñavalkyasmṛti 106, 199
  see also *Bṛhadyogiyājñavalkyasmṛti, Yogayājñavalkya*
Yajurveda 55, 85, 88, 116
Yāmuna 129, 131–132, 138, 151–152
Yamunachariar, Dr Shri Srimushnam Vangipuram172–173, 184
Yogāñjalisāram 1
Yogakuṇḍalī Upaniṣad 188, 200
Yogamakaranda 2, 4, 10, 20, 79n.93, 113, 121, 189n.23
Yogarahasya 129–130
Yogāsanagalu 4
Yogasūtra see *Patañjali*
Yogatārāvalī 98, 121–123
Yogatattva Upaniṣad 200
Yogayājñavalkya 10–30, 31–34, 37–42, 54, 56, 60–61, 63, 65–67, 68–74, 76, 96, 124, 128, 154, 159, 164–166, 170, 182, 187–188, 194, 199–202
  see also *Bṛhadyogiyājñavalkyasmṛti, Yājñavalkyasmṛti*

Zimmer, Heinrich 94, 102–105, 110

www.ingramcontent.com/pod-product-compliance
Lightning Source LLC
Chambersburg PA
CBHW050924240426
43668CB00020B/2428